Genograms

Assessment and Treatment

A Norton Professional Book

Genograms

Assessment and Treatment

FOURTH EDITION

Monica McGoldrick,
Randy Gerson,
Sueli Petry

W. W. NORTON & COMPANY
Independent Publishers Since 1923

Copyright © 2020, 2008 by Monica McGoldrick, Sylvia Shellenberger, and Sueli S. Petry
Copyright © 1999 by Monica McGoldrick and Sylvia Shellenberger
Copyright © 1985 by Monica McGoldrick and Randy Gerson

First edition published as GENOGRAMS IN FAMILY ASSESSMENT
All rights reserved
Printed in the United States of America

For information about permission to reproduce selections from this book, write to
Permissions, W. W. Norton & Company, Inc., 500 Fifth Avenue, New York, NY 10110

For information about special discounts for bulk purchases, please contact W. W. Norton
Special Sales at specialsales@wwnorton.com or 800-233-4830

Manufacturing by Versa Press
Book design by Joe Lops
Illustrator: Chris Ufer, Graphic World
Production manager: Katelyn MacKenzie

Library of Congress Cataloging-in-Publication Data

Names: McGoldrick, Monica, author. | Gerson, Randy, author. | Petry, Sueli S., author.
Title: Genograms : assessment and treatment / Monica McGoldrick, Randy Gerson, Sueli Petry.
Description: Fourth edition. | New York : W.W. Norton & Company, [2020] | Includes bibliographical
    references and index.
Identifiers: LCCN 2019034317 | ISBN 9780393714043 (paperback) | ISBN 9780393714050 (epub)
Subjects: LCSH: Genograms.
Classification: LCC RC488.5 .M395 2020 | DDC 616.89/156—dc23
LC record available at https://lccn.loc.gov/2019034317

W. W. Norton & Company, Inc., 500 Fifth Avenue, New York, N.Y. 10110
www.wwnorton.com

W. W. Norton & Company Ltd., 15 Carlisle Street, London W1D 3BS

1 2 3 4 5 6 7 8 9 0

To our families, from whom we have received our strengths and to whom we leave the legacy of all our endeavors.

Contents

Expanded Contents

Chapter 3: The Genogram Interview   71

Chapter 4: Tracking Family Patterns with Genograms   95

List of Illustrations

	Fig No.	Page No.

Acknowledgments

I am grateful to many people for their help in the development of this project. I owe special thanks to Randy Gerson, for the formative efforts he made to describe genogram patterns and to make them universally accessible through his creativity in computer applications and for the concerted efforts he made and we made together toward the computerizing of genograms- even though we never accomplished our goals. I thank my friend and colleague of many years, Michael Rohrbaugh, who persuaded me to write about genograms in the first place, and then challenged my assumptions and helped me clarify my thinking about genograms and their potential as a research and clinical tool.

My sisters, Morna and Neale, and my nephews and niece-in-law, Guy and Hugh Livingston and Maria Sperling, helped me develop the genograms in between their life adventures. My friends and life-mates have also been of immeasurable support to me in thinking about genograms and their implications for understanding families: Betty Carter, Froma Walsh, Carol Anderson, Nydia Garcia Preto, Paulette Moore Hines, Barbara Petkov, Roberto Font, Ken Hardy, Charlee Sutton, Jayne Mahboubi, Eliana Gil, Nollaig Byrne, Imelda Colgan McCarthy, Nancy Boyd Franklin, Elaine Pinderhughes, Celia Falicov, Liz Nicolai, Evelyn Lee, Miguel Hernandez, Marlene Watson, John Folwarski, Vanessa Mahmoud, Vanessa Jackson, Roxana Llerena Quinn, Carolyn Moynihan Bradt, Joanne Gilles-Donovan, Doug Schoeninger, Jim Bitter, Ron Arons, and David McGill. My refound friend and soulmate, Fernando Colon, provided inspiration, help, and affirmation particularly regarding the importance of non-biological kin networks. I thank my friend Robert Jay Green for challenging my unquestioning belief in the relevance of genograms, helping me to clarify for myself the deepest meanings of family and of "home." Michael Crouch, who is one of the most creative people in the medical field on the subject of genograms was a great re-connection for this edition. We are extremely fortunate not only for the chapter he has contributed, but for his strong editing and superior writing skills in reviewing the entire manuscript.

We are also extremely grateful to Dan Morin, creator of www.genopro.com, for his friendship and ongoing support for our work over many years and to his colleague Arturo Alvarado for the many, many hours he spent helping us with the creation of the genograms for this book. I am also ever grateful to our computer consultant, Ben Forest, who for so many years has helped me through numerous computer crashes and nightmares to keep writing and creating genograms.

And most of all I am grateful to Sueli Petry for her dedication to genograms and specifically to the hard work which is finally bringing this fourth edition to fruition. She came first as a student with a strong interest in genograms and grew into a friend and colleague and a steadfast support in thinking through the issues of genograms.

My deepest thanks go to the closest members of my own genogram, Sophocles Orfanidis, my husband of 50 years, and John Daniel Orfanidis, my son, whose birth coincided with the first edition of this book, and whose launching into adulthood coincided with the third, has now become a husband and father for the fourth. So our own genogram has had a wonderful expansion through my daughter-in-law Anna De Palma, her parents Renee and Bill De Palma, and my grandson Owen. I hope one day Owen along with my beloved grand nephew, Renzo Livingston, will come to share my enthusiasm for genograms and our genogram in particular. I look forward to how my own genogram will continue as the next generations expand our family. Of course, there would have been no book without the underlying support of my parents and all my other family who have gone before me—whether connected through biology, legal ties, or spiritual affinity, who are a part of my genogram. I stand on the shoulders of many supportive, creative, and generous kin, without whom I would not be writing this. With their support, I write for all those who will come after—whether connected through biology or through other intellectual, emotional, or spiritual ties. I feel the positive support of my parents, my aunt Mamie, my sisters, and nephews in everything I do. Those who are available have often been generous enough to read passages and give me feedback for this work.

But for this book—which was especially difficult to conceptualize organizationally—I want to appreciate in particular those who have helped me keep things organized throughout my life; the caretakers, housekeepers, and arrangers whose efforts allowed me to concentrate on my work, but who also taught me so much about the value of working hard to put things in order: Margaret Bush, who taught me everything about organic ordering of one's life on a daily basis; Ann Dunston, who helped every member of our family when they moved for almost 40 years—from 1956 until she died in 1993! I thank also the housekeepers and caretakers who helped us raise our son: Alexandra Doroshenko, Andrea Lauritzen, Angela McInerney, Karen Welsh, Meg Tischio, and Patricia Proano. I also thank those who ran my life and our offices since 1972: Myra Wayton, Jeaninne Stone, Rene Campbell, Fran Snyder, and in most recent years, Georgann Sorensen—all of whose love and good nature kept our office going. Without them I would never have been able to concentrate on this work.

I thank also Deborah Malmud, by far the most creative and supportive editor I have ever worked with. I always know she has my back.

—Monica McGoldrick

Working with Monica on this book has been an amazing journey. I am grateful for her mentorship from the first days when I joined her class as her student, and for her collegiality and friendship for the last twenty years. With her intellect, her stamina, and her serious work ethic, she challenged me to think ever more deeply about the families we treat, and about how to track relationships, legacies, and the many family patterns that all come together to form current family stories. It has been an incredible experience for me to be a part of this process. I first became interested in genograms and family patterns when I was in the first year of a master's graduate program in psychology and I saw Monica's videotape on the *Legacy of Loss*. I was moved by the family in that video and by Monica who made their genogram come to life. That experience was so powerful that I knew I wanted to know more about family systems. Monica is my mentor and my friend and I am ever grateful for her friendship, her energy, her joy of life and her love and respect for the work.

I am also grateful for the privilege of working with my dear friend and mentor Nydia Garcia-Preto, who challenged me to do better genograms and to include the context of the families' experiences of immigration, race, culture, and ethnicity as essential for family therapy. I am grateful for her friendship, as well for my friends and colleagues Barbara Petkov, Paulette Hines, Charlee Sutton, Roberto Font, Angelina Belli and the many others who have been part of the extended network of the Multicultural Family Institute, where we have collaborated on genograms and family therapy.

I would also like to thank my parents. My mother, Catarina Separovich de Carvalho changed her name to Catherine when she became an American citizen. She always lived as an outsider, first as a child of immigrants from Yugoslavia in Brazil, then as an adult immigrant from Brazil in the United States. She and my father, Aristides Berilo Carvalho, faced oppression daily, yet they transmitted the family patterns of hard work, love and the belief that life is essentially good, which certainly were values they inherited from the previous generations on my genogram. I am grateful for my many other family members and friends; all of whom are part of my genogram. Finally, I am grateful for my husband and life-companion, Karl Petry, who nurtures me with love and encouragement every day.

—Sueli Petry

Joint Acknowledgments

We are very grateful to all the staff at Norton who helped with our project, including of course our wonderful editor Deborah Malmud, our extremely diligent, gracious, and thoughtful copyeditor, Elizabeth Baird, and especially our Project Editor, Mariah Eppes, and Production Manager, Katelyn MacKenzie; both of whom worked with us from the very beginning to bring our efforts to fruition in the best possible way. They were also the go-betweens for the many other staff behind the scene at W. W. Norton, who made this new edition possible and brought it to fruition.

Preface

This book evolved out of a long interest in the clinical, research, and instructional value of genograms. Over the past fifty years, the use of the genogram as a practical tool for mapping family patterns has become widespread among health care professionals both in the U.S. and abroad. A dream we had when we first thought of writing about genograms now seems a real possibility: software to create a database for studying genograms as well as mapping them graphically. In the past decades genograms have become widely used in the fields of medicine, psychology, social work, counseling, nursing, and the other health care, human service, and even legal fields. This fourth edition of *Genograms: Assessment and Intervention* reflects the growing and now widespread use of genograms for clinical intervention, particularly the evolving use of family play genograms. The book attempts to better illustrate the diversity of family forms and patterns in our society and the many applications of genograms in clinical practice. The genogram is still a tool in progress. Based on feedback from readers and other developments in the field, we have expanded the book and slightly modified the symbols used since the third edition. We trust that the evolution of the genogram as a tool will continue as clinicians use genograms to track the complexity of family process.

While a genogram can provide a fascinating view into the richness of a family's dynamics for those in the know, it may appear to be a complex arrangement of squares and circles on a page to those who don't know the players in the drama. Our solution to this dilemma has been to illustrate our points primarily with famous families, about whom we all have some knowledge, rather than clinical cases. We are family therapists, not historians, and thus the information we have gleaned about these families is limited. Most of the sources have been biographies, newspapers, and the internet. Readers may have better information about some of the families than we were able to uncover from published sources. We apologize in advance for any inaccuracies in the material. Hopefully the descriptions sketched here will inspire readers to pursue further the fascinating stories of such families as the Eriksons, Fondas, Freuds, Kennedys, Robesons, and Roosevelts. Surprisingly, only limited family descriptions are available for many of history's most interesting personalities. We trust that future biographers will be more aware of family systems and use genograms to broaden their perspective on the individuals and families they describe.

Monica McGoldrick and Sueli Petry

1

Genograms: Mapping Family Systems

A *genogram* is a modern version of a family tree that maps much more than just your ancestry. It conveys who you belong to and the patterns of your family over several generations. It is by far the best way to explore and keep track of basic information about families from a systemic perspective. By using genograms, clinicians can offer deeper insights about the overt problems that people so often get stuck in: anger, depression, anxiety, and relationship cutoff or conflict. Genograms can also indicate patterns of a family's relationships and functioning much more readily than a written text or questionnaire.

Over the past 50 years, genograms have become the most widely used and practical framework for mapping and understanding family patterns. This book lays out the practical, theoretical, graphic, and clinical uses of genograms. Genograms appeal to us because they are tangible and graphic representations of complex family patterns.

They can help guide our clinical process with clients and they can also help us to better understand our own families.

What Is a Genogram?

Genograms record information about family members and their relationships over at least three generations. They display information graphically in a way that provides a quick gestalt of complex family patterns. This makes them a rich source of hypotheses about how clinical problems evolve in the context of a family over time. Genograms can also be an extremely useful tool for research on patterns, events, relationships, and sources of resilience in families over generations.

Genogram applications range from simply depicting the basic demographic information of a family (Turabian, 2017), which can be done in a 10 to 15 minute intake, medical, or nursing interview (Wright & Leahey, 1999; Libbon, Triana, Heru & Berman, 2019), to multigenerational mapping of the family emotional system using a Bowen Systems approach, completed over the entire course of therapy (as we do). Genogram interviews can help us diagram and clarify complex family patterns across multiple households and in challenging social contexts. They can also expand families' constraining narratives, offering new perspectives on life experiences and future possibilities, and help clients see problems that have been out of awareness and make connections to their presenting problems.

This book discusses the rules of genogram mapping as well as the interpretive principles upon which genograms are based. It also discusses how to develop and study hypotheses regarding individual, family, and larger cultural and community patterns. The genogram guidelines presented here are evolving, as is the mapping process itself, as our systemic thinking about families progresses. We define the symbols and conventions which make genograms the best shorthand map for summarizing family information and describing family patterns. The companion book, *The Genogram Casebook* provides a manual for the clinical use of genograms in systems oriented therapy. The other companion book, *The Genogram Journey: Reconnecting with Your Family*, previously called *You Can Go Home Again (1995)*, explains how to use genograms to make systemic change in your own family relationships. *The Genogram Journey* was written for a general audience, rather than for professionals, and uses the genograms of famous families, including Beethoven, the Marx Brothers, and the Kennedys, to illustrate multigenerational genogram patterns. It explains how to modify your reactivity to dysfunctional patterns, including traumatic loss, cutoff, conflict, and other problematic family patterns.

Genograms Map Who We Belong To

A systems perspective guides the use of genograms for clinical assessment and intervention. This perspective views family members as inextricably intertwined in their lives and in death, and views all members of society, like all the rest of nature, as interconnected. Neither people nor their problems (or solutions to problems) exist in a vacuum. As Paolo Freire said, "No one goes anywhere alone, even those who arrive physically alone. . . We carry with us the memory of many fabrics, a self [that is] soaked in our history and our culture" (1994, p. 31).

All human beings are inextricably interwoven into broader interactional systems, the most fundamental of which is the family. The family is the primary and, except in unusual instances, the most powerful system to which we ever belong. In this framework, "family" consists of the entire kinship network of at least three generations, both as it currently exists and as it has evolved over time (McGoldrick, Garcia Preto, & Carter, 2016). Family is, by our definition, those who are tied together through their common biological, legal, cultural, and emotional history, and by their implied future together. The physical, social, and emotional functioning of family members is profoundly interdependent, with changes in one part of the system reverberating in other parts. In addition, family interactions and relationships tend to be highly reciprocal, patterned, and repetitive. It is these patterns that allow us to make tentative predictions from a genogram.

A basic assumption here is that symptoms reflect a system's adaptation to its total context at a given moment in time. The behavior of members of the system reverberates throughout its many levels—from the biological to the intrapsychic to the interpersonal, i.e., immediate and extended family, community, culture, and beyond. Also, family behaviors, including problems and symptoms, derive further emotional and normative meaning in relation to both the socio-cultural and historical context of the family. Thus, a systemic perspective involves assessing the problem in relation to these multiple connections.

Families are organized within biological (including emotional), legal, and cultural structures and processes, as well as by generation, age, gender, and other factors. Where you fit into the family structure, as well as into the larger context, can influence your functioning, relational patterns, and the type of family you form in the next generation. Gender and birth order are key factors that shape sibling relationships and characteristics. Given different family structural configurations mapped on the genogram, the clinician can hypothesize possible personality characteristics and relational and functioning compatibilities. Ethnicity (McGoldrick, Giordano & Preto, 2005), race, religion, migration, class, financial situation, and other socioeconomic factors, as well as a family's life cycle stage (McGoldrick, Garcia Preto & Carter, 2016) and cohort or location in history (Elder, 1977, 1992; Phelps, Furstenberg, & Colby, 2002), also influence the family's structural patterns. These factors all become part of the genogram map.

Using A Genogram to Map Family Structure

Typically, the genogram is constructed from information gathered during the first meeting with a patient and revised as new information becomes available. The initial assessment forms the basis for treatment. It is important to emphasize, however, that clinicians typically do not compartmentalize assessment and treatment. Each interaction between a clinician and a family member informs the assessment and thus influences the next intervention. Integrating new information as one goes along greatly enriches the reliability of our knowledge about our patients and their families.

Genograms help a clinician get to know a person and his or her family. They are thus an important way of "joining" with families in therapy. By creating a systemic perspective that helps to track family issues through space and time, genograms enable an interviewer to reframe, detoxify, and normalize emotion-laden issues. Genograms can be extremely valuable when working collaboratively with clients to reframe negative life stories into narratives of resilience and transformation. Also, the genogram interview provides a ready vehicle for systemic questioning. In addition to providing information for the clinician, the genogram interview helps clinicians connect with clients and understand them from a systemic perspective. Throughout this book, especially in Chapter 3 on genogram interviewing, we offer suggestions about questions to ask to understand and clarify family patterns on a genogram. (Our companion book, *The Genogram Journey* includes an extensive list of systemic questions at the end of each chapter to facilitate understanding of the patterns explored in genogram work.) Genograms help both the clinician and the family to see the "larger picture"—to view problems in their current and historical context. Structural, relational, and functional information about a family can be viewed on a genogram both horizontally across the family context and vertically across the generations. A template for a 1-page genogram looks like **Figure 1.1: Template for a Genogram**.

Scanning the breadth of the current family context allows the clinician to assess the connectedness of the client and the immediate members of the family to one another. This overview may also indicate their connectedness to the broader system—the extended family, friends, community, society, and culture. This can help us evaluate the family's strengths and vulnerabilities in relation to their overall context. Family, in our definition, includes all those with whom we have a shared history and a potential future, not just those who are biologically related to us. So, we include on the genogram map itself the immediate and extended family members, as well as significant non-blood "kin," friends and pets who have lived

Figure 1.1: Template for a Genogram

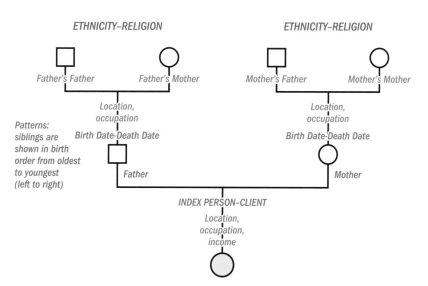

with or played a major role in the family's life. We also note relevant life events (moves, life cycle changes) and problems (illnesses, traumas, dysfunction) that may have affected family members (Holmes & Masuda, 1974; Holmes & Rahe, 1967). Current behavior and problems of family members can be traced on the genogram from multiple perspectives. The index person (the "I.P.," or person with the problem or symptom) may be viewed in the context of various subsystems (such as siblings, immediate family, triangles, and reciprocal relationships), or in relation to the broader community and socio-cultural context.

Genograms allow you to map the family structure, functioning, and relationships and to update the map as more information emerges. For a clinical record, the genogram provides an efficient summary, allowing a person unfamiliar with a case to quickly grasp a huge amount of information about a family and to scan it for potential patterns, problems, and resources. While notes written in a chart or questionnaire easily become lost in the record, genogram information is immediately recognizable and can be added to and corrected at each clinical visit as one learns more about a family. Genograms can also be created for any point in the family's history—showing the ages and relationships of that moment to better understand family patterns as they evolve over time. Soon software will allow clinicians to track the family's time-line or chronology, and to follow the details of key developments in relationships, health, and functioning over the entire life cycle of the family.

The graphic format of genograms makes it easier for us to grasp the complexity of a family's context, including their history, patterns, events, and coincidental stressors that may have ongoing significance for patient care. Just as our spoken language potentiates and organizes our thought processes, genograms' maps of relationships and patterns of functioning help clinicians think systemically about how events and relationships in their clients' lives are related to patterns of health, illness, relationships, and functioning in their families.

Gathering genogram information should be an integral part of any comprehensive, clinical assessment, not only to know who is in the family and how people are connected, but also to track the relevant facts of their current situation and history. The genogram is primarily an interpretive tool that enables the clinician to generate tentative hypotheses for further evaluation in a family assessment. It cannot be used in a cookbook fashion to make clinical predictions. But it can sensitize the clinician to systemic issues, which are relevant to current functioning and to sources of resilience.

Exploring Families in Social Context

It is also important to show the context around the biological and legal family in order to understand a family systemically. This includes adding friends, godparents, neighbors, and even those who are long dead if they are sources of hope and inspiration (or sources of pessimism and despair). It includes those people who live in clients' hearts, those who would offer a loan, if needed, and those who give strength and courage. It is this kinship network, not just the biological relatives, and not just those who are currently alive, who are relevant to know about if you want to understand clients and help them access their resources. Some of them may be the original authors of negative self-talk "scripts," which may be important to help clients revise or neutralize.

Genograms Challenge Individualistic, Linear Thinking and Foster A Family Systems Perspective

Many forces in our society pressure us not to notice key aspects of our history, such as the fact that women and people of color have been mostly ignored in our history books and have more difficulty succeeding in our society. Unwritten social "rules" supporting the status quo urge us not to think about these inequities, and not to think of human psychology from a systems perspective. We are pushed instead to operate as though the individual alone could and should define his or her own life.

Genograms challenge this approach. They require asking questions that go beyond "polite" conversation and reveal secrets our families have kept and that even our teachers may not want us to challenge. Thus, the study of genograms is, of necessity, an act of rebellion—guiding us to ask questions beyond what we have been told about our family's and our culture's history in order to seek a fuller understanding of ourselves. The exploration of genogram patterns requires thinking "out of the box."

For example, we may need to do our professors' genograms or those of the authors of our textbooks to determine whether we can trust their perspectives. As one illustration, our psychological progenitor Sigmund Freud (whose genogram we will be discussing in Chapter 8) always wanted to downplay family history. So creating genograms can be a challenge. But genogram exploration of family patterns over the course of the life cycle can be very healing—an antidote to such negativity. It can open us up to an appreciation of families' strengths and resilience in dealing with their problems and struggles. We are actually only here because our ancestors had the resilience and creativity to survive and push on, in spite of many hardships and setbacks they experienced.

Genograms Let the Calendar Speak

Families repeat themselves. What happens in one generation will often repeat itself in the next; that is, the same issues tend to be played out from generation to generation, though the actual behavior may take a variety of forms. Bowen termed this the "multigenerational transmission" of family patterns. His hypothesis was that relationship patterns in previous generations provide implicit models for family functioning in the next generation. Exploring such pattern repetitions on a genogram is one of our basic tools for assessment and intervention.

Genograms "let the calendar speak" by suggesting possible connections between family events over time. By scanning the family system historically and assessing previous life cycle transitions, patterns of illness, and earlier shifts in family relationships related to loss and other critical life changes, genograms place present issues in the context of the family's evolutionary patterns. When family members are questioned about the present situation in regard to the themes, myths, rules, and emotionally charged issues of previous generations, repetitive patterns often become clear. These factors provide the framework for hypothesizing about the current issues of a particular family.

In conjunction with genograms, we usually include a family chronology, which depicts the family history in chronological order. The chronology includes nodal and critical events in the family's history, particularly in relation to the life cycle, facilitating our ability to see repeating patterns (Elder, 1977, 1986, 1992; Stanton, 1992; Walsh, 1983; Nerin, 1986, 1993; McGoldrick, Garcia Preto, & Carter, 2016).

The Context for Assessing Problems: Belonging, Our Multiple Identities, and the Sense of Home

A genogram is a central grounding map, which can highlight multiple dimensions of experience, history, relationships, and functioning, but it always evolves in the context of larger societal features—culture, politics, religion, spirituality, socioeconomic class, gender, race and ethnicity—which organize each member of a society into a particular social niche.

We have increasingly focused our genograms on our multiple identities and the various contexts to which we belong. Our identity pertains to our sense of "home" or as Vaclav Havel (1991) spoke of it:

> The house we live in, the village or town where I was born, . . . my family, the world of my friends, . . . (my) social and intellectual milieu, my profession, my company, my work place. . . the country I live in, the language I speak, the intellectual and spiritual climate of my country. The Czech language, the Czech way of perceiving the world, Czech historical experience . . . (and) modes of courage and cowardice, Czech humor—all of these are inseparable from . . . my home. My home is therefore my . . . nationality . . . it is as essential a part of me as, for instance, my masculinity, another aspect of my home . . . It is also my Czechoslovakness, which means my citizenship. Ultimately, my home is Europe and my Europeanness and—finally—it is this planet and its present civilization and, understandably, the whole world. But that is not all: my home is also my education, my upbringing, my habits, the social milieu I live in . . . And if I belonged to a political party, that would . . . be my home as well . . . Every circle, every aspect of the human home, has to be given its due. It makes no sense to deny or. . . exclude any one aspect for the sake of another: none should be regarded as less important or inferior. They are part of our natural world, and a properly organized society has to respect them all and give them all the chance to attain fulfillment. This is the only way that room can be made for people to realize themselves freely as human beings, to exercise their identity."

A systemic approach involves understanding both the current and historical context of the family (see **Figure 1.2: The Context for Assessing Problems**). While families and societies are always moving along through time, they carry with them both historical patterns that have come down over the generations, and also horizontal factors that affect individuals, families, and societies as they move along through time (McGoldrick, Garcia Preto, & Carter, 2016).

At the family level, the vertical axis includes the family history, and the patterns of relating and functioning that are transmitted down the generations, primarily through the mechanism of emotional triangling (Bowen, 1978;

Figure 1.2:   The Context for Assessing Problems

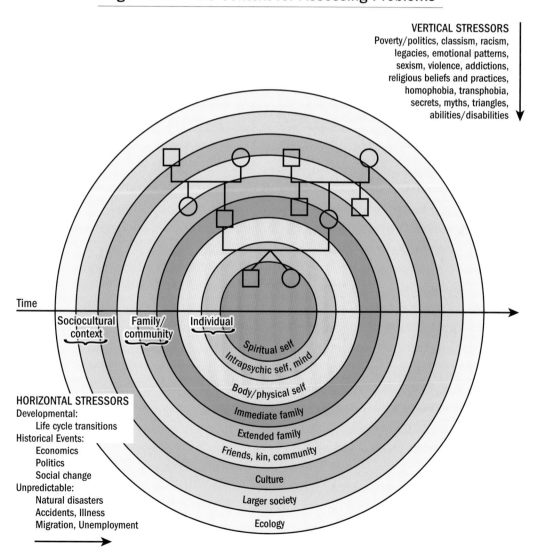

VERTICAL STRESSORS
Poverty/politics, classism, racism, legacies, emotional patterns, sexism, violence, addictions, religious beliefs and practices, homophobia, transphobia, secrets, myths, triangles, abilities/disabilities

Time

Sociocultural context   Family/community   Individual

Spiritual self
Intrapsychic self, mind
Body/physical self
Immediate family
Extended family
Friends, kin, community
Culture
Larger society
Ecology

HORIZONTAL STRESSORS
Developmental:
    Life cycle transitions
Historical Events:
    Economics
    Politics
    Social change
Unpredictable:
    Natural disasters
    Accidents, Illness
    Migration, Unemployment

McGoldrick, 2016; Titelman, 2007; Guerin, Fogarty, Fay, & Kautto, 1996: see also McGoldrick video: "Triangles & Family Therapy: Strategies and Solutions," www.psychotherapy.net).

These configurations are a major aspect of what we examine during a genogram assessment. The horizontal axis at a family level describes the family as it moves through time, coping with the changes and transitions of the family's life cycle. This horizontal flow includes both the predictable developmental stresses and those unpredictable events that may disrupt the life cycle process—early death, birth of a handicapped child, migration, chronic illness, job loss, and so forth.

At a socio-cultural level, the vertical axis includes cultural and societal history, stereotypes, patterns of power, social hierarchies, and beliefs, all of which get passed down through the generations, with variable penetration and expression. The vertical axis provides a closer assessment of the family's social cultural context by including a cultural and social history, patterns of power, social hierarchies, stereotypes, and beliefs that are passed down through the generations and have variable emotional effects on a person. Negative social and cultural stereotypes about the family's cultural group, particularly legacies of trauma, will have variable emotional and physical impact on families and individuals as they go through life. Examples of historical traumas that continue to affect present generations are the Holocaust's impact on both Jews and Germans, the impact of the system of slavery on both African Americans and white people (who have benefited from white supremacy), the impact of colonization on the colonized and the colonizers, the impact of crimes against LGBTQ people as well as on their heterosexual family and communities.

The horizontal axis relates to community connections or lack thereof, current events, and social policy, as these factors impact the family and the individual as they move through time. This axis depicts the consequences of society's "inherited" (vertical) norms of racism, sexism, ageism, classism, and homophobia, as well as ethnic and religious prejudices, manifested in social, political, and economic structures that limit the options of some and support the power of others (McGoldrick, Garcia Preto, & Carter, 2016). With enough stress on this axis, any family will experience dysfunction. Furthermore, stressors on the vertical axis may create additional problems, such that even a small horizontal stress can have serious repercussions on a system that is carrying along many vertical stressors.

For example, if a young mother has many unresolved issues with her mother or father (vertical anxiety), she may have a particularly difficult time dealing with the normal vicissitudes of parenthood (horizontal anxiety). Coincidences of historical events or of concurrent events in different parts of a family may not be random happenings, but may be interconnected systemically, though the connections are hidden from view (McGoldrick, 2011). The genogram helps the clinician to track the flow of anxiety down through the generations and across the current family context.

Most importantly, key family relationship changes seem more likely to occur at points of life cycle transition. Symptoms tend to cluster around such transitions, when family members face the task of reorganizing their relationships with one another in order to go on to the next phase (McGoldrick, Garcia Preto, & Carter, 2016). The symptomatic family may become stuck in time, unable to resolve its impasse by reorganizing and moving on. The history and relationship patterns revealed in a genogram assessment provide important clues about the nature of this impasse—how a symptom may have arisen to preserve or to prevent some relationship pattern or to protect some legacy or secret of previous generations.

Of the many relationship patterns in families, patterns of closeness and distance are of particular relevance. At one extreme are family members who are distant, in conflict, or cutoff from each other. At the other extreme are families who seem almost stuck together in emotional fusion: this can look conflictual, codependent, or just overly close to a detrimental extent. Family members in fused or poorly differentiated relationships are vulnerable to dysfunction, which tends to occur when the level of stress or anxiety exceeds the system's capacity to deal with it. The more closed the boundaries of a system are, the more immune it is to input from the environment, and consequently, the more rigid family patterns tend to become.

Family members in a closed, fused system tend to react automatically to one another, practically impervious to events outside the system that in general require continuous adaptation to changing conditions. Fusion may involve either positive or negative relationships. Fused family members may feel very good about each other or experience almost nothing but hostility and conflict. In both cases, it is the overdependent bond that ties them together. With genograms, clinicians can map family boundaries and indicate which family subsystems are fused and thus likely to be closed to new input about changing conditions.

Triangles: As Bowen (1978) and many others have pointed out, two-person relationships tend to be unstable. Under stress two people tend to draw in a third. They stabilize the system by forming a coalition of two in relation to the third. The basic unit of an emotional system thus tends to be the triangle. Genograms are one of the best maps for identifying key triangles in a family system, tracking how triangular patterns repeat from one generation to the next, and designing strategies for changing them (Fogarty, 1973; Guerin, Fogarty, Fay, & Kautto, 1996; Titelman, 2007; Kerr, 2019).

The Members of a Family Tend to Fit Together as A Functional Whole

The behaviors of different family members tend to be complementary or reciprocal. This does not mean that family members have equal power to influence relationships, as is obvious from the power differentials between men and women, between parents and children, between the elderly and younger family members, and between family members who belong to different cultures, classes, or races (McGoldrick, 2011). What it does mean is that belonging to a system opens people to reciprocal influences and involves them in each other's behavior in inextricable ways. This leads us to expect a certain interdependent fit or balance in families, involving give and take, action and reaction. Thus, a lack (e.g., irresponsibility) in one part of the family may be complemented by a surplus (over-responsibility) in another part. The genogram helps the clinician pinpoint the contrasts and idiosyncrasies in families that indicate this type of complementarity or reciprocal balance.

The History of Genograms

Despite the now widespread use of genograms around the world by family therapists, family physicians, and other healthcare providers, it took a generation for the agreed-upon symbols to be accepted by different healthcare fields, and even by family therapists. We actually do not know who first developed the genogram, but its widespread use was fostered most of all by Dr. Murray Bowen, from whom we learned of it. He said he did not know who had first developed it and he preferred to call it a "family diagram" rather than invent the new word "genogram." The earliest genogram drawing we could find was one drawn by Dr. Bowen at a presentation he gave at an American Orthopsychiatric Association conference in 1958, at a workshop called "Psychotherapy of the Family as a Unit," attended by various other early key figures such as Virginia Satir and Dr. Steven Fleck (Bowen & Butler, 2013).

In 1967, Dr. Bowen shocked the field by presenting his own family work at a research conference (later published anonymously by Jim Framo in 1972). That same year, Gordon published the first medical article about genograms, which were called pedigree charts, borrowing the term from the genetic pedigree (Gordon, 1972). The very first volume of the Georgetown Family Symposia papers, published in 1974, included several genograms in papers by Andres, Colon, and

Hall (Andres & Lorio, 1974). The next year Eileen Pendagast and Charles Sherman published a paper entitled "A Guide to The Genogram" in the journal *The Family*, a publication of the Center for Family Learning in New Rochelle, New York. In 1976 Phil Guerin and Eileen Pendagast included a chapter on genogram use in Guerin's text, Family Therapy, (1976). In 1978, a popular family medicine textbook included a chapter promoting the routine clinical use of "family trees" (Medalie, 1978). In 1980, a second medical journal article further broadened genogram awareness among family physicians (Jolly, Froom, Rosen, 1980).

In 1980 Betty Carter and I (MM) published a genogram format in our book *The Family Life Cycle*, which we copyrighted to Bowen, because of his central role in promoting genograms in clinical work which we were including in that text. That same year (1980), Jack Bradt, a psychiatrist who trained and worked with Bowen, published a small booklet called *The Family Diagram* (Bradt,1980), which also offered a format for doing a genogram, which he preferred to call a diagram or family chart as he believed it a more inclusive term.

Many of the early leaders in both family therapy and family medicine developed their own "favorite" symbols. Some resisted the use of the term "genogram" altogether, preferring to call the figures "family diagrams," as did many of Bowen's followers (discussed in Butler, 2008). Some, such as Virginia Satir, used somewhat different "family maps."

Some have critiqued genograms for their prioritizing the legal, biological, and emotional context of patients' lives. Australian therapist, Michael White (2006) believed that gathering genogram information was problematic, because it "privileged" certain family of origin experiences over other relationships, which might disqualify or fail to honor non-family connections. On the other hand, he and the others in the Narrative Therapy movement have conveyed strong interest in the histories of those who have been marginalized by the dominant society. We believe that it is precisely this aspect— articulating historical patterns—that is one of the most valuable aspects of genograms. They can reveal aspects of the family that have been hidden from family members—secrets of their own history. Such revelations help families to demystify and understand their current dilemmas and provide future solutions. Indeed, one of the most exciting aspects of genograms is the way they lead families beyond the one-dimensional, linear perspectives that have so often characterized psychological explanations. They actually teach people to think systemically, because as soon as family members and clinicians notice one pattern, their vision tends to expand and notice other patterns as well.

The very richness of the genogram graphic itself facilitates the ability to notice more than one pattern at a time. Genograms are by their nature more than genealogy charts. They include informal kinship connections as well, conveying what genograms are meant to show: to whom people belong, where they come from, who has influenced them in their lives, and what resources may be brought to bear to move forward.

Even among clinicians with similar theoretical orientations, there was only a loose consensus about what specific information to seek, how to record it, and what it all meant. It was for this reason that a committee of leading proponents of genograms from family therapy and family medicine decided in the early 1980s to try to work out a standardized genogram format.

The Importance of Agreeing on Genogram Symbols

If we are going to share systemic information about families, we can only do so with the help of agreed-upon symbols. Furthermore, symbols are only useful if we all know and can remember what they mean. There is no point creating a language with so many symbols that we cannot remember how to read them.

The genogram format presented in this book evolved through a collaboration sponsored by the North American Primary Care Research group, which took the lead in the early 1980s to create agreed-upon symbols, in order to facilitate family research and clinical practice. Systemic therapists realized they needed an agreed-upon language to share family information. It was the hope of evolving digital genograms that led me (MM) to participate in the effort to standardize genogram symbols: to facilitate family systems study and research.

Leaders in the fields of family therapy and family medicine worked together to agree on the standardization, which we published in the first edition of this book in 1985. Those involved included such key people as Murray Bowen from family therapy and Jack Froom and Jack Medalie from family medicine. While many of Bowen's followers still argue that genograms do not fit with Bowen's concepts (Butler, 2008), Bowen himself participated in working out the agreement on the choice of symbols. I myself (MM) worked with him directly on the agreement about which symbols would be included in the standardization. He and the other prominent clinicians using genograms became part of the committee organized by the North American Primary Care Research Group to define the most practical genogram symbols and agree on a standardized format.

Since that time, this format has become the standard for clinicians wanting to track family histories and relationships. Since the format was originally agreed upon and published in the first edition of this book in 1985, there have been a number of modifications recommended by different groups around the world. For those of us who see Bowen's concepts as the core of our orientation, genograms are a key tool for mapping factors that underlie Bowen's systemic concept of differentiation. We are still working to find ways to incorporate Bowen's concept of societal process into genograms—the emotional process in society, long explored by Elaine Pinderhughes (Pinderhughes, Jackson, & Romney, 2017) and others, as it intersects with family process in systems.

The format included in this fourth edition of *Genograms: Assessment and Intervention* continues to be a work in progress. We are aware that unless everyone using genograms can remember what the symbols stand for and the rules for where symbols are placed on a genogram, this will not be a useable language. While we have urged users to expand genograms with special codes for issues they want to track in their particular research, there will need to be general agreement about what the map represents for it to be of real value.

The expanded use of genograms will, of course, require further modification of the format and hopefully we will all become proficient at expanding our potential for mapping genograms as they evolve while at the same time recognizing, as Bateson (1979, p. 32) always said, "The map is not the territory." But maps can still greatly facilitate our ability to understand where we are, where we have been, and where we are trying to go.

For example, with computers we have greater potential for standardizing and color coding names, dates, locations, occupations, illnesses, and so forth, which has been an interest of therapists for many years (Bradt, 1980; Lewis, 1989; Jordan, 2004). We will also find ways of creating three-dimensional maps to zoom in on an individual's data or zoom out on larger family patterns and community or social data, which expands our ability to track individuals and families over time and space.

Multiple Applications of Genograms

The *New York Times* reported in 2006 that the Salzburg Music Festival, "pitying the poor opera goer, who is left to sort it all out," had offered a kind of genogram to help its audience follow the family relationships of a Mozart opera: "something between a schoolgirl's doodle and a molecular diagram sketching the characters' various love interests and misadventures with hearts, arrows and mere wisps of verbal descriptions" (Oestreich, 2006). If only they had known about genograms!

A colleague, Deborah Schroder (2015), has developed a most creative use of art-based genograms that she uses in family of origin therapy, and we ourselves, with our colleague Eliana Gil, developed the use of family play genograms described in Chapter 11 of this book.

Indeed, if you google "Star Wars family tree" or "Star Wars genogram" you will see that numerous people have been making genograms and family trees to facilitate understanding of the Skywalker family in Star Wars—Arturo Alvarado of www.genopro.com has even made an excellent little video to teach viewers about genograms using the Star Wars family, which is also accessible on YouTube! (https://www.genopro.com/genogram/examples/)

Many friends and colleagues who watch increasingly common multi-year long TV series are frequently asking for their genograms—whether we're talking about *Last Tango in Halifax, Downton Abbey, Doc Martin, Game of Thrones*, or *This Is Us*. So, we put together the genogram for *This Is Us* (**Figure 1.3: *This Is Us* Family**) to help newcomers connect to this fascinating four-generation family. Such genogram examples make clear why having a genogram can be so handy. Clearly, a verbal explanation of this family's relationships quickly becomes too complex to convey or hold in mind.

The story begins with a white family that has triplets. With the help of the genogram, (and assuming you understand the symbols!) you can easily see the triplets born to the parents, and that one died. An African American baby, who was born that same day and abandoned by his parents, was adopted by the family. The series moves back and forth through time and space, showing the intertwined family relationships. The specifics of their genogram make it much easier to track the family's relationships over time. Not surprisingly, there is a level of fusion between the two surviving triplets, Kevin and Kate, in which they can seemingly read each other's minds and have a nonverbal connection that mystifies others. Kevin and Randall, meanwhile, have always had a certain level of competition, having grown up sharing the same room and competing in athletics, school, and having different experiences of racial discrimination. The relationships have been deeply influenced by previous family experiences, including the secret that the adoptive mother had contact with the adopted son's biological father but never told him.

Because of the mind-boggling new field of genetic genealogy, we all suddenly have access to our genetic histories in ways no one ever imagined possible. As Adam Rutherford has entitled his book on the subject: *A Brief History of Everyone Who Ever Lived* (2017), we have a phenomenal amount more to learn about our systemic connections to each other. We are barely at the beginning of learning about our family and cultural heritage—from our distant connection to Genghis Khan or Marie Antoinette, to the closer realities of our cultural and racial heritage,

Figure 1.3: *This Is Us* Family—Showing Some Secrets and Relationships

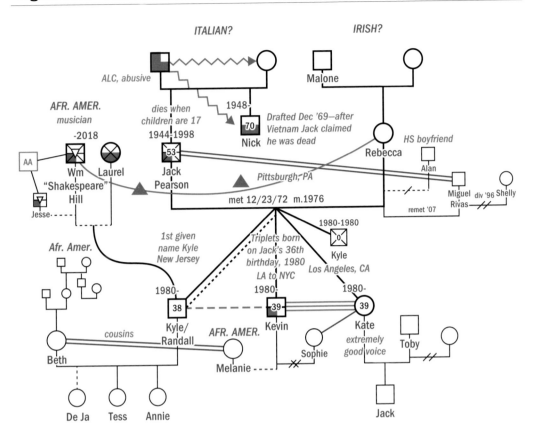

which may be deeply hidden by family lore (Jacobs, 2017; Harmon, 2006; Shapiro, 2019; and, for example: https://thegeneticgenealogist.com). Many of us have begun to expand our genograms through online DNA sharing, which allows us to connect to family members all over the world. Mapping out our family tree with the aid of computers will enable us to incorporate the complexities we are coming to know about our heritage. This may at times reveal secrets, such as that our parents or siblings are not who we thought they were.

Using Genograms to Depict Larger Societal Patterns

Literature on genograms has also focused on expanding their meaning to include the larger societal context, although the graphics to facilitate these expanded genograms have not yet been well developed. At times we may actually define on a genogram the resources and institutions of the community to highlight families' access, lack of access, or relationship with community resources (**Figure 1.4: A Genogram with Community Context**). A whole book has been written on "Community Genograms," although the graphics do not resemble genograms, and do not depict the three-generational family genogram map as a basic context (Rigazio-Digilio, Ivey, Kunkler-Peck, & Grady, 2005).

Difficulty depicting expanded genograms flows from the problems of showing multiple dimensions on one genogram graphic. This reflects the age-old problem that without sophisticated computer graphics, diagramming a genogram is always a tradeoff between the amount of information included and the clarity of the graphic. Rigazio-Digilio and her colleagues (2005) have suggested ways to depict the larger temporal and contextual community. These maps resemble eco-maps, illustrating various events and situations in a spherical grid that have come

Figure 1.4:   A Genogram with Community Context

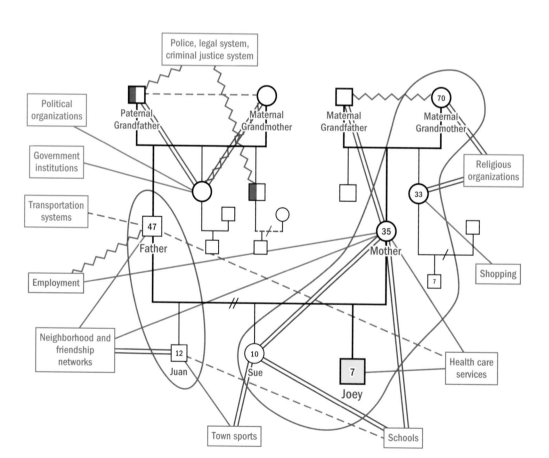

to shape clients' experiences over time. While not really genograms in that they are not really family maps, they do attempt to depict aspects of the context within which people live. We look forward to the continued evolution of genograms to help us better illustrate larger cultural factors along with specific family patterns.

There has also been much discussion of the "cultural genogram," which focuses specifically on the cultural aspects of a family's history, and religious or spiritual genograms, which focus on the ways that religion and spirituality play out in family patterns. Growing awareness of the profound impact of racism, sexism, and economic or social oppression on individuals and families has fortunately begun to lead to discussion of how genograms can help us take account of the traumatic impact of social injustice (Hardy & Laszloffy, 1995; Goodman, 2013).

Many have been attempting to expand genograms to take larger social structures into account. Scharwiess (1994) used a genogram with multigenerational, step-sibling, and half-sibling relationships to show multigenerational international connections evolved when East and West Germany were divided and then reunited more than generation later, having had to deal with their much different and more powerful "step-parents," Russia and the US, in the meanwhile.

One issue that needs expansion as we become a global society is the need to account for the culturally different family patterns around the world. In some cultures, women have been raised for centuries to leave their families of origin and thence forward live with and tend to the parents in the extended family into which they marry. In the U.S., family members too often become estranged from one another, and this is a problem clinicians try to help them resolve through reconnection, if at all possible. So, our understanding of how to map patterns in different cultural contexts needs to take into account that marriage, in-laws, elders, and sibling patterns have very different meanings in different cultures, and these cultural differences should be included in our conversation.

Genograms in Medicine and Nursing

Genograms have been viewed as a way to sensitize physicians, nurses, and other healthcare professionals to the relevant psychosocial issues of their patients; to enhance evaluation, diagnosis, and care of patients; to provide a framework for assessment and interaction with particular patients, such as the elderly, at a critical time in the health care process (like at the time of diagnosis of a serious illness); and to prevent problems or intervene with families to address them (Alexander &

Clark, 1998; Baird & Grant, 1998; Bannerman, 1986; Campbell, McDaniel, Cole-Kelly, Hepworth, & Lorenz, 2002; Christie-Seely, 1986; Crouch & Davis, 1987; Dumas, Katerndahl, & Burge, 1995; Garrett, Klinkman, & Post, 1987; Like, Rogers, & McGoldrick, 1988; Mullins & Christie-Seely, 1984; Olsen, Dudley-Brown, & McMullen, 2004; Shellenberger, Shurden, & Treadwell, 1988; Sproul & Gallagher, 1982; Troncale, 1983; Wright & Leahy, 1999, 2013; Zide & Gray, 2000).

Research has demonstrated that family has a powerful influence on health and illness, and that marital and family relationships have as significant an influence on health outcomes as biological factors (Rolland, 1994, 2018; Campbell et al., 2002; Siegel 2015, 2016). The value of family history in assessing risk for common diseases is becoming increasingly realized (Wattendorf & Hadley, 2005). The Human Genome Project and the resultant identification of the inherited causes of many diseases and the establishment of national clinical practice guidelines based on systemic reviews of preventive interventions make the need for such an assessment even more obvious (Wattendorf & Hadley, 2005). Because genograms provide information about family demographics, the history of serious illness, relationships, and genetic risks, detailed genograms are essential components of patients' medical evaluations (Campbell et al., 2002; Rolland, 1994, 2018).

It was family physicians who first developed the use of genograms to record and track family medical history efficiently, and who first proposed the standardization of genogram symbols (Jolly, Froom, & Rosen, 1980). Within the field of medicine, there has been widespread effort to incorporate genograms as a basic assessment tool. Scherger (2005) wrote about the need to encourage family physicians to offer truly family-oriented care, for which genogram information would be a major part. He argued powerfully for using new information technologies to help track and deal with families in a contextual way, advocating that it was the only serious way to provide appropriate care to families in our society. For that to happen, we will have to develop the technology to address families systemically and train physicians to use it, so they will not be overwhelmed by the morass of paperwork and insurance industry-driven services of our current system.

In a classic article in the *Journal of the American Medical Association*, Rainsford and Schuman (1981) wrote about the importance of genograms and family chronologies for tracking complex, stress-ridden cases, which often require the most attention from the health care system. Such families can be a tremendous drain on a system and require a comprehensive understanding of individual stresses on the family as a whole. The authors tracked each family member's stressful events and clinic visits over a seven year period, illustrating the importance of health providers developing a longitudinal picture of all family members in order to understand each member's clinical visit at a particular moment in time. Such multi-problem families show up at every entry point of the health care system: Emergency Rooms, social service agencies, schools, mental health clinics, and in the criminal justice system. It makes eminent sense to have clear and comprehensive ways of tracking their patterns. Genograms could allow clinics to track office visits in relation to other family stressors, not just for one patient, but for all family members. Such mapping of every assessment would make it a great deal easier to recognize when extra resources are needed to prevent the serious and costly ripples of dysfunction, especially in multi-problem families.

Michael Crouch (see Chapter 10), one of the most influential family physicians in the promotion of genograms, was also one of the first family physicians to write about the value of mapping one's own family for professional development, an approach that has been widely promoted by Bowen and his followers. Crouch even constructed a genogram depicting the field of family practice and family medicine (See **Figure 10.6: Family Practice and Family Medicine**) showing the potential of genograms to illustrate the history of systems other than families. Susan McDaniel, at the University of Rochester Medical School, has all their residents present their own genograms including their family's handling of illness and consider their own family illness issues when seeking consultation on a case. She and her colleagues wrote a medical care text in which all the authors discussed their own family history in dealing with illness before discussing their work on a case (McDaniel, Hepworth & Doherty, 1993).

Tracking the Genogram of Family Therapy

In appreciation of the value of understanding ourselves in historical and cultural context in order to figure where we might go in the future, and following the rich insights of Michael Crouch, we offer two "genograms" for the history of family therapy in the U.S. It now appears that there are ancestors from at least four different "cultural" groups that have contributed to family therapy practice in the 21st century.

The first grew in a huge burst of energy from the 1960s through the 1980s, out of a partnership of some psychiatrists and social workers who became excited about systemic ideas, and working with families to solve the problem of one member. Social work had lower prestige, but a history of trying to think systemically about social problems. The efforts of these two groups was greatly pushed forward by the deinstitutionalization of psychiatric patients, who had previously (before medication) often spent most of their adult lives in mental institutions.

In the decades following World War II, these psychiatrists evolved an interest in systems theory, which led them to explore the whole family context with regard to one person's problem. This was in contrast to the Freudian psychoanalytic focus on the intrapsychic processes of the individual, which had become the dominant ideology within psychiatry. Various psychiatrists, who were somewhat outsiders within psychiatry (which seemed to be the least prestigious specialty within medicine), became inspired by general systems theory, and began collaborating with social workers, anthropologists, sociologists, and others.

A further push toward systemic theory and practice came from the Community Mental Health Center Act of 1963. This act was championed by Eunice Kennedy Shriver, who had studied sociology and done social work for many years, inspired most of all by the mental health needs of her sister Rosemary. She convinced her brother John Kennedy to sign the Mental Health Center Act the very week before he was killed. (We will be discussing their genogram in this book.) The Mental Health Center Act was meant to serve the needs of those whose mental health care had so long been ignored within the dominant health care system, and the importance of family and community was prominent in this initiative.

My own history (MM) in family therapy began in 1966 at a newly opened community mental health center in Connecticut. Clinical social workers were the primary mental health clinicians in the 1960s, so they were natural allies for psychiatrists in dealing with patients. The most dynamic development of family systems theory and practice in the U.S. occurred during the late 1960s and 1970s (**Figure 1.5: Genogram of Family Therapy**).

The first systemic centers included the Mental Research Institute (MRI) in Palo Alto, which evolved from an earlier project led by the anthropologist and cybernetician Gregory Bateson, whose systemic ideas have had a most profound impact on the field. The MRI drew in some very creative men, including Don Jackson, Jay Haley, Paul Watzlawick, John Weakland, and Carlos Sluzki. There were very few women, but one key figure was the social worker Virginia Satir, who began the first family therapy training program ever in 1955 (Luepnitz, 1989), and became MRI's primary family therapy trainer in 1959. When looking back at the ancestors of the field, psychiatrist Harry Stack Sullivan has been given credit for the influence of his "interpersonal psychiatry" on systemic thinking. But one major influence on Sullivan's thinking, so he said, was the work of Jane Addams, one of the founders of the field of social work. Yet her role has been omitted from the history, which is one of the reasons that doing our genogram is so important.

The MRI soon developed a collaboration with the New York Family Institute that became the Ackerman Family Institute, led by Nathan Ackerman with sev-

Figure 1.5:   Genogram of Family Therapy 1960s through 1980s

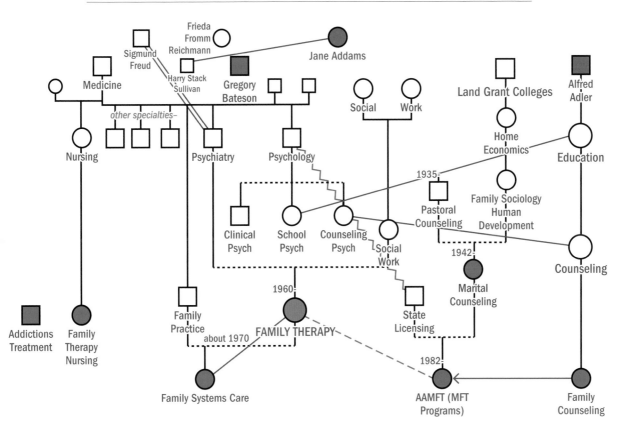

eral others including Kitty La Perriere and Don Bloch. Those two organizations founded a family systems journal, *Family Process*, which remains a leading systemic journal in the field.

Early family therapy leaders were mostly psychiatrists: Murray Bowen, Carl Whitaker, Ivan Boszormenyi Nagy, Salvador Minuchin, Dick Auerswald, and many others, who were drawn to systemic thinking. Many of the early innovators in the family therapy movement were clinical social workers (including Satir, Peggy Papp, Betty Carter, Olga Silverstein, Marianne Walters, Froma Walsh, Carol Anderson, Harry Aponte, Braulio Montalvo, and so forth) and a few psychologists (including La Perriere, Jim Framo, and Carolyn Attneave).

Interestingly, problems of addiction were not really included under the rubric of mental health problems then and that separation continues even until now. For the most part, addiction treatment seems to have evolved quite separately from interventions for other psychological problems, even though it would make sense to think of all the mental health problems that affect individuals (and thus families) from a similar systemic perspective.

A second "cultural" strand of today's family therapy has roots in Land Grant Colleges, established in 1862, which provided the first opportunities for women to receive a college education. Women's education gradually expanded beyond home economics to a focus on family and marriage, evolving a developmental perspective and eventually a focus on counseling. There was then a coming together of marriage counselors with pastoral counselors, especially from the South, that coalesced in a Marriage Counseling organization, which then changed its name to Marriage and Family Counseling and then to the American Association for Marriage and Family Therapy (the AAMFT) to credential therapists in marriage and family counseling or therapy.

A third "cultural" group that developed an interest in families and family therapy were counselors, who evolved mostly in the education departments of Land Grant Colleges. Interestingly, while Freud's influence was felt most in psychiatry and psychology, and somewhat in social work, Alfred Adler, an early psychiatric colleague of Freud's, became probably the first actual family therapist—that is, the first person we know of who convened families in order to solve the problems of an individual member. He did so as early as 1919, and his focus was usually one of the children.

Only recently, 60 years into the evolution of systems thinking and practice (and with many forces undermining family system theory and practice), does there seem to be a coming together of family therapy as it originally evolved with counseling of all sorts, including psychological, school, career, guidance, marital and couples counseling, pastoral counseling, addictions counseling, and so forth.

A fourth strand in family therapy evolved from the field of nursing, including, for example, Lorraine Wright and Maureen Leahey (2013), which still seems to be evolving systemic theory and practice.

Changes Since The 1990s

Healthcare, mental health, and psychological intervention have all been majorly reshaped since about 1989 by the powerful forces of Managed Care (HMOs), Big Pharma, and the insurance industry. In recent decades family therapy has been taking a back seat to other individually focused, primarily brief behavioral interventions, and there is an increased interest at the margins of mental health care in how physical exercise, yoga, the martial arts, and meditation contribute to mental as well as physical health.

To illustrate the systemic changes in the field since about 1990, we drew a second genogram to show the developments in the field since that time (**Figure 1.6: Genogram of Family Therapy since 1990**), adding collaborative and abusive relationships, which have been developing between insurance conglomerates, the pharmaceutical industry, and Managed Care and Health Maintenance Organizations, which have virtually taken over healthcare and the mental health field. Psychiatry abandoned it's "child." Family Therapy has become primarily what we might think of as a "step-wife" in arranged marriages to those three forces. Psychiatry has abandoned family therapy and systemic theory and practice altogether, as it has abandoned virtually all methods of intervention other than pharmacology.

Clinical psychology, which had developed Division 43 to focus on family psychology, never defined family psychology as a specialization within psychology and any systemic or family oriented focus has become de-emphasized in recent years. Social work, although the most natural "home" for systemic thinking and practice, has also abandoned family therapy. Meanwhile, marriage counseling seems to have "married" the licensing boards and has become the home of "officially labelled" family therapists, but not particularly of systemic theory or practice.

Figure 1.6:   Genogram of Family Therapy since 1990

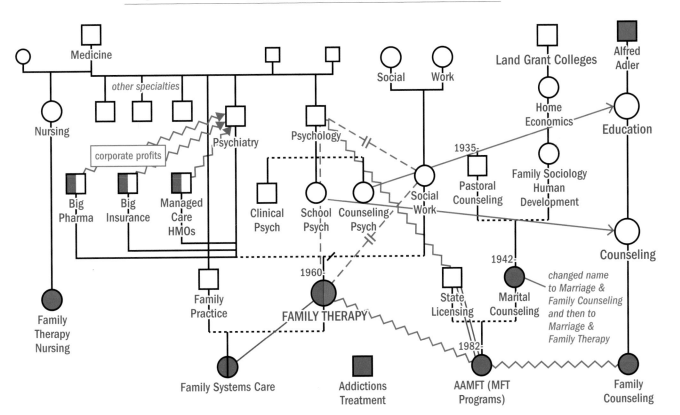

This preliminary attempt to map the evolution of family therapy's genogram is just a suggestion of the complexity of our field's history. Any genogram is just a preliminary map of the complexity of a family or system's evolution. It can never possibly convey the full complexity of organizational processes. But hopefully it can highlight the importance of our attempting to use genograms to map our organizational histories, expanding our contextual understanding of families, organizations, and social movements from a systems perspective.

Using Genograms to Explore Specific Patterns and for Family Research

While the genogram is almost as old as the fields of family therapy, family medicine, and family systems nursing, a focus on its enormous potential as a research tool has been slow in coming. This seems remarkable, given the ability of genograms to track and maintain so much family information in a relatively simple updatable graphic format, and given the fact that it is a tool widely used by clinicians for mapping their patients' histories and contexts.

We know that clinicians find genograms helpful for thinking systemically, and for mapping family patterns and "making sense" of client problems in context. Publications have made clear that the genogram is an effective and ever more widely-used clinical tool around the globe.

Bowen Systems Coaching

Obviously the first arena for genogram use has been in Bowen Systems Coaching, for which there has been burgeoning literature (Bowen, 1978; Carter, 1991; Carter & McGoldrick, 1976; Colon,1973, 2005, 2019; Crouch, 1985; Friedman, 1971,1987; Hall, 1987; Guerin & Fogarty, 1972; McGoldrick, 2004a, 2004b, 2011, 2016, 2019; McGoldrick & Carter, 2001; Pinderhughes, 2019; Titelman, 1998, 2003, 2007, 2015; Lerner 1984, 1990, 1994, 1997).

The clinical application of genograms has been expanding, and the literature affirms the therapeutic value of working collaboratively with clients to construct genograms. It encourages their voices to be heard, empowers them to make their own discoveries about their family processes, and affirms the recommendation to include genograms in the training of marriage and family therapists (Dunn & Levitt, 2000).

A wide range of uses and modifications have been proposed: family sculpting of genograms (Papp, Silverstein, & Carter, 1973; Satir & Baldwin, 1983; Banmen, 2002), cultural genograms (Congress, 1994; Hardy & Laszloffy, 1995), gender-grams (White & Tyson-Rawson, 1995), sexual genograms (Hof & Berman, 1986), family play genograms (see Chapter 11), and genograms with different life situations. We mention a few of these suggestions here to inspire readers about the rich clinical potential of genograms.

Spiritual and Religious Genograms

A number of authors have explored the possibilities of spiritual and religious genograms (Dunn & Dawes, 1999; Frame, 2000a, 2000b, 2001; Hodge, 2001a, 2005a, 2005b; Willow, Tobin & Toner, 2011).

Education & Career Focused Genograms

Many have focused on the value of genograms for career counseling (Doughhetee, 2001; Gibson, 2005; Granello, Hothersall, & Osborne, 2000; Magnuson, 2000; Malott & Magnuson, 2004; Brott, 2001; Moon, Coleman, McCollum, Nelson, & Jensen-Scott 1993; Okiishi, 1987). Genograms have been used as the basis for teaching illiterate adults to read, by having clinicians interview them about their genograms, transcribe their stories, and then teach them to read their own narratives (Darkenwald & Silvestri, 1992). Some have used work and career genograms to facilitate career decisions (Moon, et al., 1993; Gibson, 2005).

Life Cycle Stage Focus

Clinicians have also stressed the usefulness of genograms for working with populations at various life cycle stages, such as children (Fink, Kramer, Weaver, & Anderson, 1993), couples in premarital counseling (Shellenberger, Watkins-Couch, & Drake, 1989) and other couple and family situations (Foster, Jurkovic, Ferdinand, & Meadows, 2002), and the elderly (Bannerman, 1986; Erlanger, 1990; Golden & Mohr, 2000; Gwyther, 1986; Ingersoll-Dayton & Arndt, 1990; Shellenberger, Watkins-Couch, & Drake, 1989; Shields, King, & Wynne, 1995).

Healthcare

The most comprehensive discussion of this topic is in John Rolland's 2018 text *Helping Couples and Families Navigate Illness and Disability*. But many others have also talked about the relevance of genograms in healthcare. Ingersoll-Dayton and Arndt (1990) have written persuasively about the research potential of genograms for gerontological social workers assessing and intervening with older adults, or for professionals supporting caregivers of the elderly who are feeling burdened with their role. Hockley (2000) discusses their use for providing comfort for those in palliative and hospice care; others have emphasized their use for the identification of cardiovascular risk (Wimbush & Peters, 2000).

Olsen, Dudley-Brown, and McMullen (2004) have made a strong case for combining genograms, ecomaps, and genetic family trees (called pedigrees) to optimize healthcare assessments in nursing. While in our view, pedigree information can easily be incorporated onto genograms and is therefore not necessary to consider as a separate tool, such a comprehensive assessment makes absolute sense for multiple reasons. Olsen and her colleagues have laid out the specific uses of such an assessment to:

- Guide identification of risk factors
- Inform patient and family of clinical decisions vis-a-vis care management strategies, psychosocial support, and education for reproductive decisions; risk reduction, prevention, screening, diagnosis, referral, and long-term management of disease.
- Decide on testing strategies
- Establish patterns of inheritance
- Identify at-risk family members
- Determine reproductive options
- Distinguish genetics from other risk factors
- Enhance patient rapport
- Educate patients and families
- Examine communication patterns and barriers
- Explore emotional and behavioral patterns in an intergenerational context
- Help the family see itself as an interdependent group, connected in important ways
- Help family members see commonalities and uniqueness in other members
- Clarify options for change in a family (e.g., rearranging household membership)
- Prevent isolation of one family member as a "scapegoat," independent of whole family structure

- Portray an overview of family connections to each other and to outside institutions
- Demonstrate access to and patterns of resources, clarifying current resource patterns and defining what extra resources may be needed.

Therapy with Children in Foster Care

We and others have written about this and include two cases in Chapter 11 of this text. (Altshuler, 1999; Petry & McGoldrick, 2005)

Understanding the Impact of Larger Systems

Rembel, Neufeld, and Kushner (2007) have argued for the value of genograms, ecomaps, and ecograms, which depict the larger systems impacting the individual and family system (Brown, 2004; Franklin & Jordan, 1995; Gilbert & Franklin, 2003; Hodge, 2000, 2005b; Murray & Murray, 2004). Other suggested uses are for keeping track of the complex relational configurations seen in remarried families, for engaging and keeping track of complex, culturally diverse families, or for specific genogram interventions, such as with family play genograms (see Chapter 11).

Genograms Can Increase Accuracy of Clinical and Research Information

Olsen and her colleagues (2004) also laid out important issues around accuracy of information. Obviously accuracy increases with confirmation of one patient's memory with that of other family members, and with data incorporated from medical records. Clearly, the more a record is updated and checked over time, the more accurate it will become. This makes clear the value of using a genogram/ecomap/chronology which has been gathered over time and with input of various family members, as well as from healthcare, social services, and other sources, rather than starting fresh in every new encounter a person has with a therapist, nurse, or physician.

Ethical and Legal Implications

There are ethical and legal implications of such an assessment. Producing such an expanded account of a patient's interpersonal and ecological world raises issues of confidentiality and privacy and requires careful scrutiny. Information revealed about relatives and family members is confidential, and can only be released with the consent of that individual. Yet, patients should be encouraged to discuss genetic information with their relatives, particularly if the future health of those relatives or their children may be affected. Deciding who and what to tell are important considerations for patients and health care providers. Protecting privacy and confidentiality in research is also important. Of particular concern is the possibility that health insurance may be denied based on genetic information. Legislators have made an effort to protect patients' rights with the Health Insurance Portability & Accountability Act (HIPAA) of 1996 (Department of Health and Human Services), and more recently the Genetic Information Nondiscrimination Act of 2005 (S. 306, H.R. 1227), which prohibits using genetic information to refuse or cancel insurance coverage.

Modification of the Genogram Format and Function

Some have suggested modifications of the genogram format, such as Friedman, Rohrbaugh, and Krakauer's (1988) "time-line" genogram, Watts Jones' (1998) genogram to depict the "functional" family, Friesen and Manitt's (1991) attachment diagrams, Rogers and Holloway's (1990) self-administered genogram, and Burke and Faber's (1997) genogrid to depict the networks of lesbian families.

Some have wanted to illustrate organizations, such as a medical practice (McIlvain, Crabtree, Medder, Strange, & Miller, 1998). Others have creatively expanded the genogram concept with what they call a gendergram, to map gender relationships over the life cycle (White & Tyson-Rawson, 1995).

Using Genograms to Explore Culture and Immigration

Genograms have also been used to elicit family narratives and expand cultural stories (Hardy & Laszloffy, 1995; McCullough-Chavis & Waites, 2004; McGill, 1992; Shellenberger et al., 2007; Sherman, 1990; Congress, 1994, Thomas, 1998; Keiley et al., 2002; Kelly, 1990; Estrada & Haney, 1998), Makungu Akinyela (personal communication) developed the use of genograms to teach an African American Family course in the department of African American Studies at Georgia State University in Atlanta. In this course, students track their own family histories and place these in the context of literature on policy, history, migration, and cultural development of African American families. In taking this approach, students are able to see the connection between their own families' lived experience and the political, economic, and social context in which they have evolved. Yznaga (2008) describes the value of genograms for facilitating the intercultural competence of Mexican immigrants.

The most comprehensive exploration of expanding genogram mapping to include a more multicontextual perspective has been Celia Falicov's multidimensional ecosystemic comparative approach (MECA). Falicov expands the mapping of genograms with a rich understanding of the place of culture in clinical practice and training, including MECAmaps and MECAgenograms. These maps focus on four aspects of families: their ecological context, their family life cycle, their organization, and their migration/acculturation history (2012, 2015). She explores in wonderful detail the possibilities of including these multicontextual dimensions to map out families' cultural and life cycle experiences.

Using Genograms with Military Families

Weiss, Coll, Gerbauer, Smiley and Carillo (2010) have created a very useful exploration of the specific genogram issues for military families, including specific notations that may be relevant for working with them.

Using Genograms to Further Various Therapeutic Approaches

Genograms have also been used to identify therapeutic strategies, such as reframing and detoxifying family legacies (Gewirtzman, 1988), solution-focused therapy (Kuehl, 1995; Zide & Gray, 2000) and those for children growing up in foster care and in multiple homes and family constellations (McMillen & Groze, 1994; Altshuler, 1999; Colon, 2019). Wachtel (2016), who began from a psychodynamic perspective, talks about genograms as a "window into the psyche," a way to expand clients' worldviews and conscious and unconscious feelings. She finds they provide opportunities to address a person's most painful, conflicted, and vulnerable experiences in constructive ways, so that they can hear the input. Schutzenberger (1998) uses variations of genograms in transgenerational psychotherapy to explore hidden links in clients' family trees in therapy. Bill Nerin (1986, 1993), a follower of Virginia Satir and a proponent of family reconstruction, has used genograms and family chronologies as key components of work with students and clients to reconnect with their parents.

Chrzastowski (2011) has offered an extremely valuable discussion of the use of genograms in narrative therapy. She posits genogram analysis (and perhaps photographs of family members) as an opportunity to conduct remembering conversations that explore the stories of those with a preoccupied attachment (to help them gain some distance from their emotional reactivity) as well as those whose attachment styles are emotionally distant and avoidant (to help them reconnect through discussion). Genograms provide a unique opportunity, as Chrzastowski says, to explore and re-tell family stories.

Using Genograms to Explore Loss and Trauma and to Strengthen Resilience

In her 2016 book *Strengthening Family Resilience*, Froma Walsh offers an important discussion of "Resilience-Oriented Family Genograms," emphasizing "relational lifelines" and positive connections, including to peers, community, and pets, in a project she and John Rolland were involved in in Los Angeles to reduce gang violence. They offer a detailed appendix with guidelines for developing resilience-based genograms. Others have specifically focused on the value of genograms for addressing issues of trauma and loss (Jordan 2004, 2006; Goodman 2013; McGoldrick, 2004; Kuhn, 1981).

Using Genograms in Training

Much has been written about the value of students studying their own genograms as a key part of their clinical training. (Carter & McGoldrick, 1976 Magnuson & Shaw, 2003; McGoldrick, 1982; Soh-Leong, 2008; Kağnıcı, 2011, 2014). Aten, Madson, and Johnston Kruse (2008) developed a schema for creating a genogram of students' supervisory experiences to explore them as they work out their own preferences for becoming a supervisor.

Toward Future Developments

Computerized genograms will soon make it a great deal easier for clinicians to track family history. We will hopefully be able to explore an entire database of genograms for particular patterns: genetic patterns, illnesses, gender and sibling patterns of functioning, emotional triangles, loss or trauma in previous generations, correlations between various symptom constellations, and so forth.

A chronology will be able to show events for any particular moment in the family's history, or for a particular point in the life cycle in earlier generations. Genealogy software has been doing this for decades.

Furthermore, new software programs specifically designed for clinical work are emerging that will encourage the computer-savvy generation of therapists to use the graphics in their clinical work and in teaching. We have barely begun to realize the research potential of genograms. Even the standardization of genogram symbols and notation is still in its early developmental stages. We hope this book will stimulate more discussion about how the tremendous power of computer graphics can be deployed for genograms. With appropriate encryption, computerized genogram graphics attached to a database will have many possibilities for depicting specific issues one or two at a time, and then shifting graphics to show different moments in a family's history or different contexts and themes (education, health and illness, emotional relationships, etc.). Such possibilities will greatly increase our ability to study genogram patterns as families move through time, because they will be modified and corrected as patients get to know their healthcare professionals.

The potential for clinicians to add to the basic demographic, functioning, and relationship information on patients' genograms at each visit would be invaluable for healthcare and mental healthcare research. Given the practical value of the genogram as a map and its potential to track deeper layers of information, it could be easily adapted for specific research purposes. Using genograms for research would not require special research forms, but would rather be part of the everyday clinical chart, used to track individual and family history, perhaps adding particular information of interest to researchers.

The evolution of this tool will, however, require several developments:

- Computerization of genograms as a flexible graphic underpinned by a database that can be mined directly for research and lead immediately to feedback that is useful to clinicians and their patients.
- Addressing the issues of encryption and confidentiality, so that the privacy of health records can be protected.
- Facilitating the ease of record keeping and the accessing of genogram information so that clinicians will be inspired to keep careful note of new information and updates.
- Facilitating feedback to clinicians about research results, so they see the value of keeping careful track of patients, because they and their patients will benefit from timely research feedback.

A Caveat

Throughout this book, we make assertions about families based on their genograms. These observations are offered as tentative hypotheses, as is true for genogram interpretations in general. They are suggestions for further exploration. Hypotheses based on the genogram are not facts. Interpretations of genograms should be seen as roadmaps that, by highlighting certain characteristics of the terrain, can guide us through the complex territory of family life.

Many of the genograms shown here include more information than our discussion can cover. We encourage readers to use these illustrative genograms as a departure point for further developing their own skills in using and interpreting genograms.

Genograms are obviously limited in how much information they can display, although with computers, we will be able to include much more information than we can display at any one time. Clinicians always gather more information on people's lives than can ever appear on any particular genogram illustration. Computers will enable us to choose what aspects of a genogram we want to display for a particular purpose, while having the capacity to maintain the whole history in a computer database.

The genograms of famous people were created from available biographical materials and probably have many inaccuracies. Having spent years studying genograms, we are well aware of the difficulties of getting accurate information. On the other hand, we hope you will share our excitement about the richness they draw forth. For our errors, we apologize ahead of time.

2

Creating Genograms

Clinically speaking, gathering family information and constructing a genogram should always be part of a more general process of joining, assessing, and helping a family. Information is gathered as family members tell their story in the context of the problem for which they are seeking help. While basic genogram information can be collected in a structured format as part of a medical record, the information should always be gathered for a purpose that the participant understands, and treated with the greatest respect. Exploring a family's history is an intimate process, not mere technical fact-gathering. Any question you ask may lead to the most sensitive, embarrassing, or traumatic experience, so it is never something that can be manualized with a list of questions or thought of as just collecting "the facts."

The drawing itself, however, needs to conform to the conventions for mapping genograms, so that genogram symbols become a common language that allow clinicians to share their understanding. The value of a genogram is that its shared symbolic language is a shorthand for clinicians to map out the structure and detail of a person or family's demographics, relationships, and functioning. This chapter explains the graphic elements of the genogram and offers an example of how to build a genogram map for a case. Later chapters will explain in detail the underlying patterns to explore that pertain to specific family and cultural issues, as well as their clinical and research potential.

Genogram information can be obtained by interviewing one family member or several. Clearly, getting information from several family members increases reliability and provides the opportunity to compare perspectives and observe interactions directly. Although, of course, we then have to deal with the added complexity of trying to make sense of multiple versions of family history and figuring how to record the different versions.

Timing of Genogram Interviewing

Of course, seeing several family members is not always feasible, and often a genogram interview is done with one person. The time required to complete a genogram assessment can vary greatly. While the basic information can usually be collected in 15 minutes or less (Wright & Leahy, 1999), a comprehensive family assessment interview involving several family members might take one to two hours. It often takes much longer for family members to feel comfortable enough to reveal traumatic aspects of their history, so it makes sense to assume you won't get all the pertinent information in one interview. Asking about toxic issues such as sexual or physical abuse may not be possible during the first interview, especially when clients might be putting themselves in jeopardy by responding in front of another family member. Even a question of family income, while essential to a clinical assessment, may need to wait until some trust is established and the client realizes why such personal information matters.

Clinicians often prefer to spread the questioning out over time and develop the genogram as they progress in their work and trust with the family. What makes the genogram such a rich tool is that information can get corrected and expanded as the clinician learns more about the family history and context. Thus, over time, the genogram itself becomes a more accurate, comprehensive, and valuable map of the family's story.

Mapping the Family Structure on a Genogram

The backbone of a genogram is a graphic depiction of how different family members are biologically, legally, and emotionally related to one another from one generation to the next. A genogram is a construction of squares and circles representing people, and lines delineating their relationships. When making a genogram we usually go back to the grandparents of the index person, including at least three generations (four or even five generations if the index person has children and grandchildren).

Dealing with Complex Genograms

Since genograms can become very complex, there is no set of rules that will cover all contingencies. We want to illustrate how we have dealt with some of the common problems. First, it helps to plan ahead. Obviously, if three-fourths of the page is filled with the father's three siblings, a problem will emerge when we discover that the mother is the youngest of 12. So it helps to get an overview of the number of siblings and marriages in the parental generation before starting. The following questions will help in anticipating complexities and planning the graphic from the start:

- How many times was each parent married?
- How many siblings did each parent have?
- Where were each of them in the birth order?

These three questions can help you manage the space on your page. But there are, of course, times when a situation is just too complicated to fit on one letter-size page, and one has to make choices to show the key family members of the clients you are meeting, adding an extra page (or using larger flipchart paper) to keep track of a father's four other marriages and children he has participated in raising.

Generally, the index person is the focal point of the genogram, and details about others are shown as they relate to this person. The complexity of the genogram will thus depend on the depth and breadth of the information included. For example, if we add details for a nuclear family with many problems and traumatic events, the genogram is likely to get complex, crowded, and difficult to read. There are, naturally, limits to what the genogram can show, particularly regarding complex relationships and multiple marriages. Sometimes, in order to highlight certain points, the arrangement must be reorganized and redrawn to emphasize the key clinical aspects of the assessment. At a certain point this kind of complexity becomes impossible to depict on a genogram and you may want to create a special genogram to show:

- The key factors at the present moment.
- The key factors at the time of symptom onset.
- The chronology of a particular client or for a particular time period, such as when the symptoms began
- The key factors around a particular moment of trauma in the past.

Mapping Key Information with a Limited Number of Symbols

When fleshing out the history of the immediate and extended families, your initial concern should be getting basic facts on each family member. These are the vital statistics of the family, the type of objective data that can usually be verified by public records. There are specific places to put some of this information.

Demographic Information

Ethnic Background & Migration (Ethnicity is placed above the family members it pertains to and the wavy line for immigration is shown on the line above the person's symbol)

Age (inside the square or circle of the person)

Dates of Birth and Death (above left and right of the person's symbol)

Location (above the person's symbol, if different from that of the index person)

Income (above the person's symbol)

Occupation (near the person's symbol)

Educational Level (near the person's symbol)

Generally speaking, to make the language of genograms practical, the developers realized that only so many symbols could be created for a genogram map, or else it would get too complicated and no one would remember what the symbols stood for. We have tried to keep from expanding the symbols too much, so that people can learn the "genogram language" and keep the symbols in mind. For more details, the clinician must look beyond the basic genogram map. Thus, the symbols are meant to illustrate basic patterns and key life altering functioning and relationship issues. Beyond that, clinicians have to note other detailed information or develop their own special symbols for their particular projects and interests.

For example, there is no symbol for suicide, even though that is an extremely important fact in a family system, about which clinicians would generally want to know considerable detail. Some have suggested having symbols for suicide, but then we would have to have symbols for murder, disappearance, and other traumatic loss. Given the toxicity of suicide, which is generally the most traumatic of all deaths, the relevant facts surrounding suicide would be critical to an understanding of any family that has had this experience. Such additional family information, including about other suicides or suicide attempts in the family's network, should be noted on the family chronology and on the genogram. But all the details and all the implications can never be conveyed, so choices still always have to be made. This is a challenge for the clinician's skill and judgment. So we rely on having a few indicators for life-altering factors and assume clinicians will add other information that they consider essential as there is room for it on the genogram, without the map becoming unreadable.

Over the years a number of symbols have been added to genogram usage, including a symbol for immigration, for secrets, and a symbol for pets, who are often extremely important family members. Indeed, at times pets are the only ones that family members actually touch! And they often play a major role in the family's wellbeing or dysfunction, as when a pet is part of a person's therapy or when the pet is ill or dies.

For those working with specific populations, we encourage inventing specific additional symbols as necessary and practical, to make genograms more illustrative of the patterns that researchers and clinicians are focusing on.

Basic Symbols and Their Location on a Genogram

Figure 2.1: Basic Symbols shows the basic symbols and their possible location on a genogram:

- Males are squares, females circles, and those who identify as non-binary have a new modified gender symbol.
- A square outside a circle indicates a transgender man and a circle outside a square indicates a transgender woman.
- A triangle inside the symbol indicates gay, lesbian, transgender, bisexual, queer, intersex, or asexual sexual orientation.
- The person's name goes just below the symbol.
- The birth date goes above the person's symbol and to the left.
- The death date goes above the symbol to the right.
- The person's location and income go above the birth and death dates.
- An institutional affiliation such as AA, a religious or fraternal organization, or some other organization to which a person belongs is shown by a rectangle with the organization name inside connected by a line to the person's symbol.
- Pets (sometimes shown with a dotted line as with a foster child) can be shown as a kind of diamond shape.
- An immigrant is shown with 2 wavy lines above the symbol and a person who has lived in other cultures, but has not migrated altogether, has one wavy line.

Figure 2.1: Basic Symbols

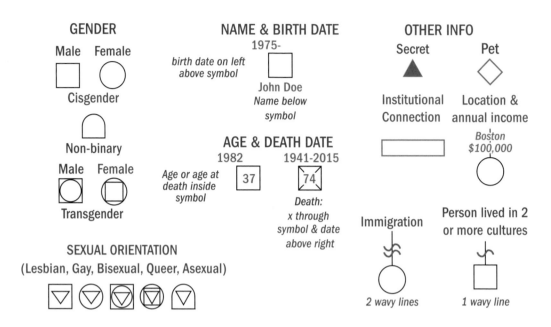

- A filled in triangle indicates a secret, whether about an affair, a cutoff, the parentage of a child, a suicide, or anything else. You will want to note what exactly the secret is about.
- The person's income and current location are typically written just above the birth and death dates (other financial information, such as indebtedness, is also relevant to include).
- Other demographic information on each individual, such as employment, functioning, or other notation goes near the person's symbol, wherever there is room.

Mapping Couple Relationships on Genograms

Couple relationships (**Figure 2.2: Couple Relationships**) are shown on a genogram by a line drawn down from the male partner and across and back up to the female (in a heterosexual couple). An LGBTQ couple would be joined with a solid line in the same way, if they are married.

Figure 2.2: Couple Relationships

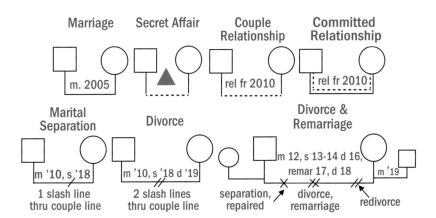

- The male partner (shown with a square) in a heterosexual relationship is always on the left and the female partner (shown with a circle) on the right. This holds for grandparents as well as parents.
- Paternal grandparents are always on the left and the maternal grandparents are always on the right for heterosexual couples.
- If a couple was together for some time, but was not married, they are connected with a dotted line.
- A dotted and solid line in parallel shows a non-married couple in a committed relationship.
- Separation of a couple is shown by one right slash through the couple line.
- Divorce is shown by two right slashes through the couple line.
- If a couple separated, then got back together, there would be a backslash through the slash, making an X on the couple line, showing that the separation ended.
- If a couple divorced and then remarried each other, there would be a backslash through the divorce line
- Once people have been married several times it often becomes impossible to keep the male on the left and the female on the right and the children in chronological birth order. At that point choices have to be made, prioritizing the key people you are working with and their key partners and children.

Figure 2.3: **Placement of Children in Relation to Parents**

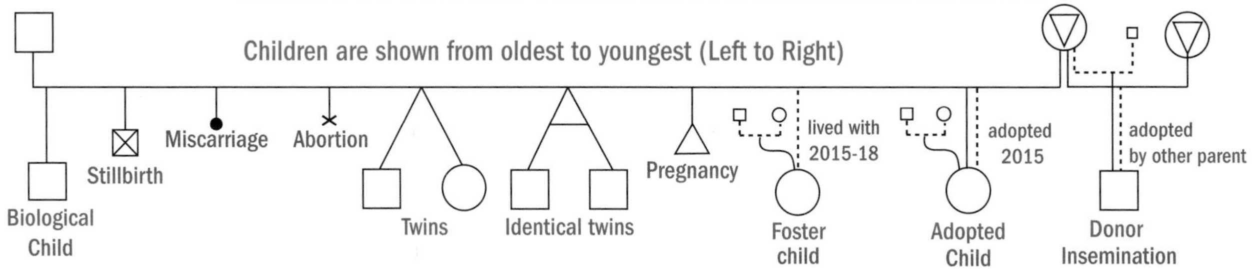

Mapping Children on Genograms

Children's placement on a genogram is essential for understanding their relationship to the siblings and adults in their lives (**Figure 2.3: Placement of Children in Relation to Parents**).

- Children descend from the parent line from left to right in order of birth.
- A biological child is connected with a straight line.
- A child who dies in infancy or childhood is shown higher and smaller than the other children to emphasize the loss.
- Miscarriage is shown by a small circle, abortion by a small x.
- Twins' connecting lines both descend from the same place on the line in order of birth, with a bar across if they are identical twins.
- A pregnancy is shown by a triangle (with a square or circle inside if the gender is known).
- A foster child is shown by a dotted line, on which the dates of living with the family can be shown.
- An adopted child is shown by a parallel solid and a dotted line to show the permanency of the connection. Again, the date of adoption can be indicated on the line to the child.
- A child born through donor insemination can be shown by a small line to the donor and the child hanging down from there through the couple line.

Symbols for Addiction and Other Physical or Psychological Disorders

Our symbols for illness show only that there is an addiction or a major physical illness. The symbols basically indicate that there is a life-altering problem, but the viewer must check for details to understand the exact nature of the problem (**Figure 2.4: Addiction, Physical, & Mental Illness**). In general, the nature of the illness should also be indicated near the symbol. Genogram software will obviously allow us to track illnesses, both physical and psychological, in much better detail. We can then choose to show particular illnesses for diagnostic purposes, or, on the other hand, hide details in order to track other family patterns more easily. If a person participates in therapy, AA or another recovery program, or indeed if they have any strong institutional affiliation, such as with a church, fraternal organization, or other group, this can be indicated by a line out to a box indicating the therapists or recovery program (See **Figure 2.1: Basic Symbols**). The dates of treatment can also be shown.

- We fill in the left side of the symbol to show physical or psychological illnesses.
- Addictions are shown by filling in the bottom half of the square or circle. If addiction is suspected but we are not sure, the bottom half of the person's symbol has slash lines rather than solid fill.

Figure 2.4:   Addiction, Physical, & Mental Illness

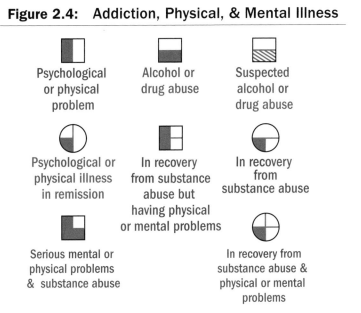

Psychological or physical problem

Alcohol or drug abuse

Suspected alcohol or drug abuse

Psychological or physical illness in remission

In recovery from substance abuse but having physical or mental problems

In recovery from substance abuse

Serious mental or physical problems & substance abuse

In recovery from substance abuse & physical or mental problems

- If someone is in recovery from an illness, we fill in only the lower left half, but the line runs through the whole symbol.
- Those in recovery from addiction have only the lower left half filled in, but again, the line continues all across the symbol.
- When a person has both an addiction and a mental illness, three-quarters of the symbol is filled in.
- When a person is mentally ill but in recovery from addiction, the left half is filled in.

Patterns of Functioning

Information about functioning, some of which will be clear from the demographics (education, occupation, state of health and relationships, etc.) includes more or less objective data on the medical, emotional, and behavioral functioning of family members. Objective signs, such as absenteeism from work and drinking patterns, may be indications of a person's functioning, though family members often start with vague descriptions, indicating that the family member is "weird" or "unreliable." It may take time for them to convey the full extent of the family member's dysfunction.

The problems families come in with have sometimes already occurred in previous generations. Numerous symptomatic patterns, such as alcoholism, sexual abuse, violence, suicide, and psychosomatic patterns are often repeated from generation to generation. Family functioning in relation to addiction or illness may have repeated itself across several generations. This transmission does not necessarily occur in linear fashion. An alcoholic father may have children who become teetotalers, but whose children may again become drinkers. By noting the pattern repetition, the clinician may help the family understand their present adaptation to the situation and potentially short-circuit maladaptive processes.

All families should be assessed for their resilience, strengths, and successes as well as their problems (Walsh, 2016), since it is through their strengths and resilience, rather than their dysfunction, that we can best help them deal with their problems. Indicators of highly successful functioning as well as dysfunction should be noted. The information collected on each person is placed next to his or her symbol on the genogram. The clinician might also indicate a global level of functioning on the genogram by each person's symbol, and track changes in the functioning over time on a family chronology.

We hope that in the future genogram software will allow us to track individual functioning in more detail, as well as track substance abuse (daily marijuana use,

Figure 2.5: Symbols Denoting Interactional Patterns Between People

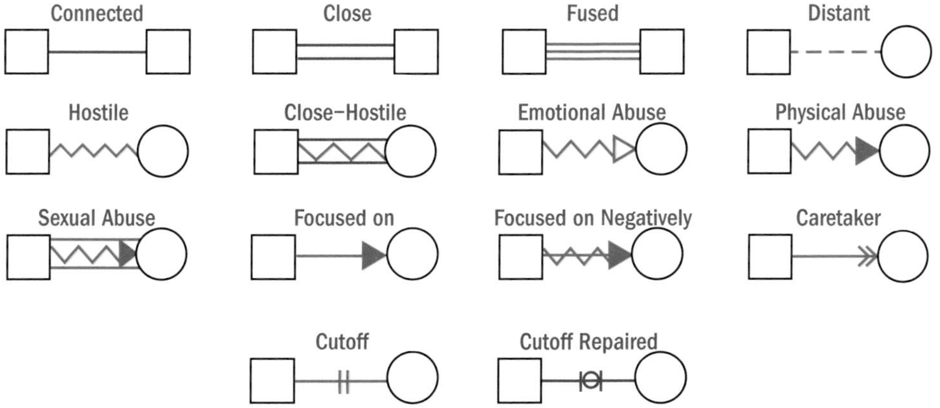

weekend binge drinking, prescription drug abuse with pain killers, and so forth), in order to follow the evolution of substance abuse problems over time.

Showing Relationships on Genograms

Relationship lines are the least reliable lines on a genogram because they are inevitably oversimplified. We cannot possibly indicate all the variations of relationships, which also tend to change over time. Nevertheless, there are some basic relationship lines indicating closeness, distance, conflict, and cutoff, and a few other significant patterns, such as abuse and caretaking. (**Figure 2.5: Symbols Denoting Interactional Patterns Between People**). Other important aspects of relationships (such as the power differential between people) are key factors we cannot yet convey on a genogram, along with more subtle issues of ambivalence and dependency.

The symbols we have show the following relationships.

- One straight line indicates that two people are connected. Two straight lines indicate they are close. Three straight lines indicates they are fused, that is, that their relationship is highly interdependent.
- A dotted line indicates a distant relationship, a zigzag line indicates conflict, and a zigzag line with 2 straight lines indicates a close-hostile relationship.
- A zigzag line with an arrow that is not filled in indicates emotional abuse.
- A zigzag line with an arrow filled in indicates physical abuse in the direction of the arrow.
- A zigzag line with a filled in arrow and two straight lines on the sides indicates sexual abuse toward the person to whom the arrow points.

- Other lines with arrows convey that one person is focused on the other. If the line is zigzag then the person's focus is negative toward the other person.
- A line with a double arrow indicates that one person is the caretaker of the other.
- A single line with two slashes through it indicates a cutoff.
- A single line with two slashes and a circle between them indicates a cutoff that has been repaired.

Family Relationships and Roles

It will, of course, be easier with genogram software to modify the information and relationship lines or illustrate stressors for any given moment in history. Indicating the timing of changes in relationship patterns is important for tracking family emotional process. Delineating the relationships between family members is the most inferential aspect of genogram construction. Such characterizations are based on the report of family members and direct observation. Although such commonly used relationship descriptors as "fused" or "conflictual" are difficult to define operationally and have different connotations for clinicians of various perspectives, these symbols are useful in clinical practice to convey the intensity of relationships. Relationships in a family do, of course, change over time, so this aspect of genograms, as indicated above, is one of the most subjective and subject to change. Furthermore, one might argue that any conflictual relationship implies underlying connection, and by that definition reflects fusion as well as conflict. However, the fused/conflictual lines are often used to illustrate a relationship with intense connection as well as overt conflict.

Cutoffs are the most important relationship indicators to depict, since they have such a powerful impact on a family. It is especially relevant to indicate the start and end dates on any cutoffs in a family, since it is likely to ripple out into other patterns of illness or other dysfunction. We think cutoffs, as with death, have a major impact on the whole family system. Murray Bowen used to say he considered cutoffs to be the most significant family variable influencing prognosis for the system (Kerr & Bowen, 1988). Cutoffs can also involve great conflict or silent distancing.

Relationship Questioning

It is helpful to get as many perspectives on family relationships as possible. For example, the husband may be asked, "How close do you think your mother and your older brother were?" The wife might then be asked for her impression of that relationship. The goal is to uncover differences as well as agreements about family relationships, and to use the different perceptions of the family to enrich the genogram picture for both the clinician and the family.

Common Relationship Questions

- Are there any family members who do not speak to each other or who have ever had sustained or recurrent periods of not speaking? Are there any who were/are in serious conflict?
- Are there any family members who are extremely close?
- Who helps out when help is needed?
- In whom do family members confide?
- All couples have some sort of marital difficulties. What sorts of problems and conflicts have you encountered? What about your parents' and siblings' marriages?
- How do you each get along with each child? Have any family members had particular problems dealing with their children?
- What are the power dynamics in your family's relationships? Are there certain family members who are intimidated by others? Are there certain family members who have more power to define what will happen in relationships? This refers not just to family members who have charisma or emotional power in the family, but specifically to family members who have more power because of their status in the family and/or in society, due to gender, race, skin color, money, socio-economic status, size, age, or sexual orientation.

Questions About the Family Role Structure

Labels or nicknames used by family members may be particularly instructive. Often family members have nicknames that describe or even constrict their position in the family, e.g., the tyrant, the super-mother, the star, the rebel, the responsible one, or the baby. Labels are good clues to the emotional patterns in the system. Questions that may elucidate the structure and complementarity of roles in the family could include:

- Has any family member been focused on as the caretaker? The problematic one? The sick one? The bad one? The mad one? The selfish one? The strong one? The weak one? The dominant one? The submissive one? The successful one? The failure? The savior?
- Who is or was seen as warm? Cold? Caring? Distant?

Sometimes it is useful to ask how members of the present family would be characterized by other family members, e.g., "How do you think your older brother would describe your relationship with your wife?" or "How would your father have described you when you were 13, the age your son is now?" Again, gathering as many perspectives as possible enriches the family's view of itself and introduces channels for new information.

Relationship patterns of closeness, distance, conflict, etc., may also repeat themselves over the generations. Genograms often reveal complex relational patterns that would be missed if not mapped across several generations. Recognizing such patterns can, it is hoped, help families avoid continuing the repetition in future generations.

Household, Key Information, and Position of Family Members on a Genogram

We start a genogram by building a three-generational map and expand from there as needed. We draw a line around the key household or households so we know who is living in the central family and other key factors about the immediate family situation.

Figure 2.6: Household, Key Information, & Position of Family Members shows a genogram for Alisa Bahr, a 30-year-old psychologist, who sought therapy in 2014. She was the middle of three children. Her older brother Joe had moved to San Francisco and worked in IT. The younger sister Ellen still lived with their parents, Sam and Betty, and their dog Muff (shown as a foster child).

- *Alisa is shown lower and larger than her two siblings* to convey that she is the Index Person or focus of our genogram.
- *Alisa's parents, Sam and Betty, are also drawn lower and larger than their siblings* (Sarah and Edna) to indicate they are part of the primary family.
- *Spouses of siblings and their children are drawn smaller and lower*, as, for example, Joe's partner, to indicate he is not part of the primary family.
- Sam's mother died years ago and his father had remarried a divorced woman with 2 children. *The father's second wife and her previous husband and children are also shown smaller than the father himself.*
- Prominent relationships are indicated: Sam and his father are quite cutoff.

Figure 2.6:   Household, Key Information, & Position of Family Members

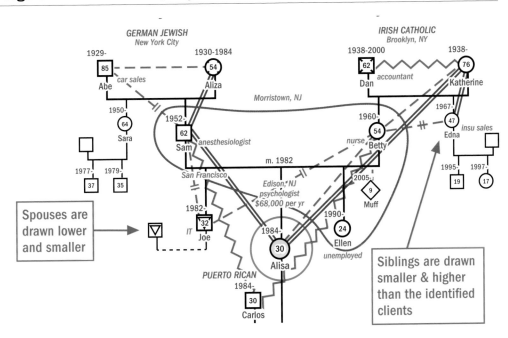

Betty, the mother, and her sister are cutoff, and she has a distant relationship with her mother.

- Key information about *cultural background* (shown above the earliest generation), *occupation, income, whereabouts, and relationships within the family*
  are indicated on the genogram
- The *key members of the household or households are encircled.* In this example
  the IP, Alisa, is living alone, and the parents are living with the younger
  daughter, Ellen, and their dog.

Information Relevant for Each Family Member

The following information would be relevant for each family member, although
we are not always able to include it:

- Dates of birth, marriage, separation, divorce, illnesses, and death (including cause)
- Sibling position

- Ethnicity/race, class, and religious background
- Any changes in social class through education, income, or marriage
- Current religious practices and changes in religion or spirituality
- Education and occupation
- Current whereabouts
- State of current relationships—closeness, conflict, cutoff

The genogram can map the family's evolution through time and broaden the family's historical perspective on their issues. As the clinician collects more information about family events, certain gaps are likely to appear in the history. Family members themselves often become so interested in their story that they begin their own historical research to fill in gaps and expand their perspective. They may learn more information by speaking to relatives, consulting family bibles, reading local or regional histories, or obtaining medical, genealogical, and other public records through internet resources such as Ancestry.com.

Building a Genogram

We will now illustrate the building of Alisa Bahr's genogram, as the clinician learns more about family members. We want to emphasize that there is no "correct" way to gather this information. While we want to learn about all the items mentioned above, clients' answers should inspire our follow-up questions, conveying first of all our interest in what they have already told us about their context and their problem. In general, we want to include, at a minimum, information going back to at least the grandparents of the Index Person or Identified Patient (IP), and include all members of generations below the IP: marriages, children, nieces and nephews, pets, friends, and kinship supports of the IP. The figures representing family members are connected by lines that indicate their biological and legal relationships.

If we are not creating the genogram with computer software (we generally use genopro.com genogram software—www.genopro.com/genogramformat—which has a beginning family template), we usually begin with a skeletal three-generational genogram format, as we showed in Chapter 1 (**Figure 1.1: Template for a Genogram**), to make constructing the genogram easier.

In addition to the genogram information itself we generally create a family chronology to track the timeline of family events and symptomatic patterns. We go back and forth between notations on the chronology, case notes that describe symptom development and other important family or personal information, and the genogram map itself. Computer software will, hopefully, soon facilitate this note taking and allow us to look at particular patterns one at a time while collecting the complexity into a database. But for now, we are describing the mapping itself and the systemic thinking about how problems evolve, and how healing also evolves by our thinking of our lives with a systemic perspective.

Colors and Sizes Used on the Genograms for This Book.

For this book we are using particular colors to convey certain types of material:

1. The Index Person (identified patient or IP) is generally filled in with yellow.
2. The basic text for names and dates and for the presenting problem is blue. The size depends on the person's position in the family (key person: large; other key family member or friend: medium; spouse or child of siblings, cousins, other spouses, etc.: small).
3. The additional general information (location, occupation, income and other general demographic information) is green.
4. Cultural and religious backgrounds are brown, as is the symbol for immigration and the boundary around the household.
5. Close connection lines are blue.
6. Negative connection lines are red—cutoff, distance, abuse, physical or mental illness, and other information about major problems in the family. Connections to other organizations are generally green.

We began building Alisa Bahr's genogram with a yellow symbol (shown in **Figure 2.7: Genogram with Index Person (IP), Presenting Problem, Occupation, and Location Added**). Alisa's name and the date of initial contact (9/4/2014) are shown in the upper left of the page and her presenting problem in the lower left. Her birthdate (1984) is shown above left of her symbol and her age, 30, in the circle of her symbol. The symbol of the Index Person or Identified Patient (IP) is sometimes shown as a double circle or a double square to emphasize that person's priority, but we find it easier to just make that person larger and lower than any siblings. Alisa's location, occupation, and annual income are shown just above her birth date.

Figure 2.7:   Genogram with Index Person (IP), Presenting Problem, Occupation, and Location Added

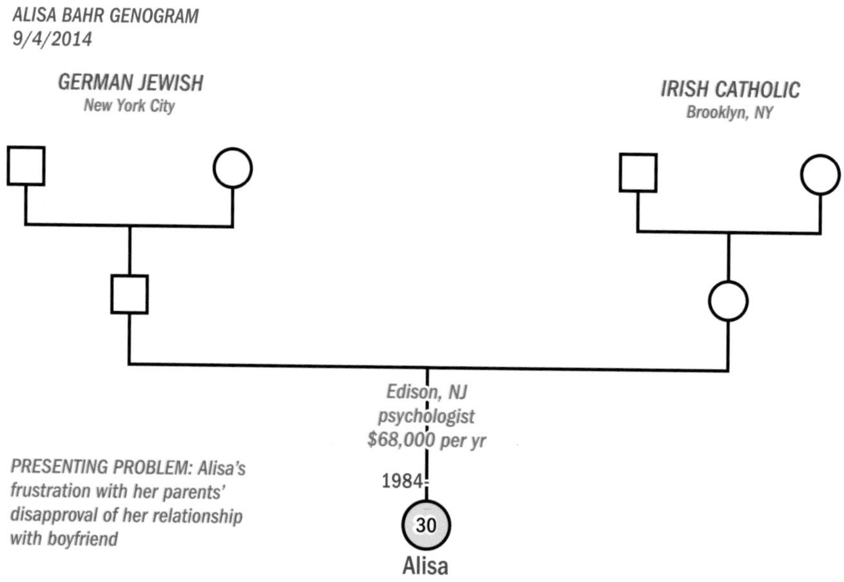

ALISA BAHR GENOGRAM
9/4/2014

GERMAN JEWISH
New York City

IRISH CATHOLIC
Brooklyn, NY

Edison, NJ
psychologist
$68,000 per yr

1984

30
Alisa

PRESENTING PROBLEM: Alisa's frustration with her parents' disapproval of her relationship with boyfriend

The presenting problem is shown here in red at the lower left, namely Alisa's frustration with her parents' negativity toward her boyfriend, Carlos. The date of the initial genogram is usually shown, as here, in the upper left corner. Alisa's work situation (she is a psychologist), her location (Edison, NJ), and her income ($68,000) are indicated just above her symbol and her birth date (1984).

In **Figure 2.8: IP's Cultural and Religious Background and Nuclear Family Added** you can see that Alisa's father's background is German Jewish, and her mother is Irish Catholic. You can also see the basic information about her immediate family and her boyfriend, Carlos. She is the middle of three siblings. Her older brother, Joe, is gay and lives in San Francisco. He works in IT. Alisa has a sister Ellen, six years younger, who lives with the parents and is unemployed. The father is an anesthesiologist and the mother a nurse and they also live in New Jersey, in Morristown. The line surrounding the parents and sister indicates their household, and the fact that they also have a nine-year-old dog, Muff.

Alisa has a circle drawn around her, indicating that her household includes only herself. Because Alisa and Carlos are not married, their couple connection line is a dotted rather than a solid line. Carlos is a social worker, which could mean his professional status may not be viewed as highly as hers, which might be a factor in her parents' negativity toward him. We also see that Carlos is from a Puerto

Figure 2.8:   IP's Cultural and Religious Background and Nuclear Family Added

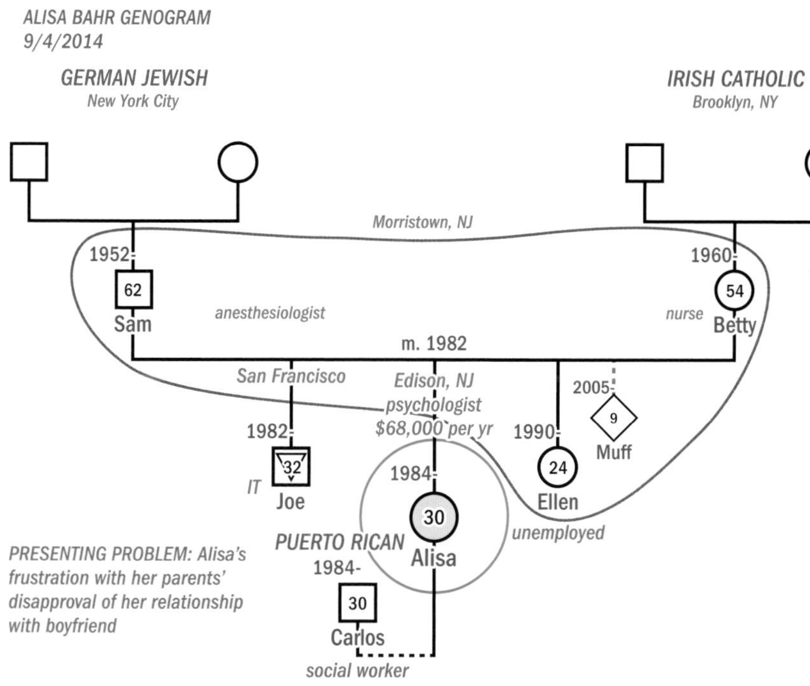

Rican background, which could be another source of Alisa's parents' negativity. We will want to get more genogram information to assess the meaning of cultural and educational issues for the family, since we can see the parents themselves were from different backgrounds from each other. We will probably want to ask how their parents dealt with the difference in their cultural backgrounds when they got together.

We may also notice that the parents were married the same year the first son was born, which could raise a question about the circumstances of their marriage. For this reason, many clinicians enter exact dates for marriages, births, and deaths, to allow checking out hypotheses that relate to the timing of major family events. If they had a premature pregnancy, they may fear that Alisa might also get pregnant before she intends to. There is also the issue that the oldest son is gay and lives on the opposite coast and the younger adult daughter is unemployed, which may suggest pressure on Alisa to be the "good daughter."

As you build a genogram you are continually developing hypotheses about the patterns you notice, which you check out as you go along. You never know whether people fit into the stereotypes we may have about family patterns, but hypotheses

Figure 2.9: Families of Origin

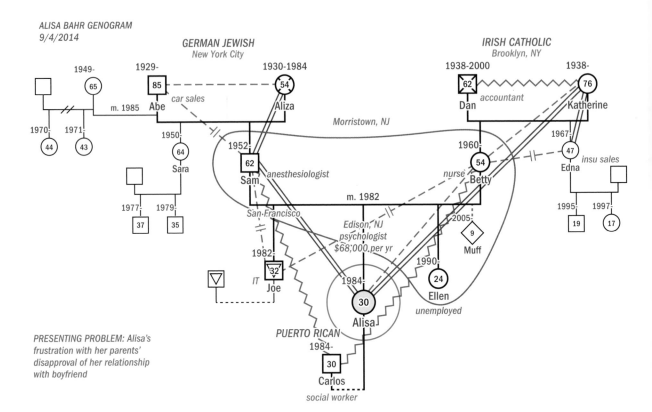

PRESENTING PROBLEM: Alisa's frustration with her parents' disapproval of her relationship with boyfriend

will help you build your inquiry and your understanding of how the presenting problem fits into the larger family situation.

Figure 2.9: Families of Origin adds Alisa's parents' families of origin. Alisa's father, Sam, was the younger brother of an older sister. He was, according to his daughter, extremely close to his mother, Aliza, for whom Alisa was named. Aliza died the very year Alisa was born and she was always "daddy's girl." Sam was never close to his father, who began dating very soon after his wife's death. Sam has had a virtual cutoff from his father ever since the father's quick remarriage to a divorced woman with two daughters. The father has lived in Florida with his new wife ever since his remarriage.

Alisa's mother, Betty, is the elder of two sisters, the other with whom she has apparently had lifelong conflicts and complete cutoff for the past 14 years. Betty saw her younger sister Edna as the favorite and herself as Cinderella—never appreciated for her successes and always in the shadow of her more attractive younger

Figure 2.10. Alisa Bahr Family with Functioning, Relationships, Secrets, and other Stressors

ALISA BAHR GENOGRAM
9/4/2014

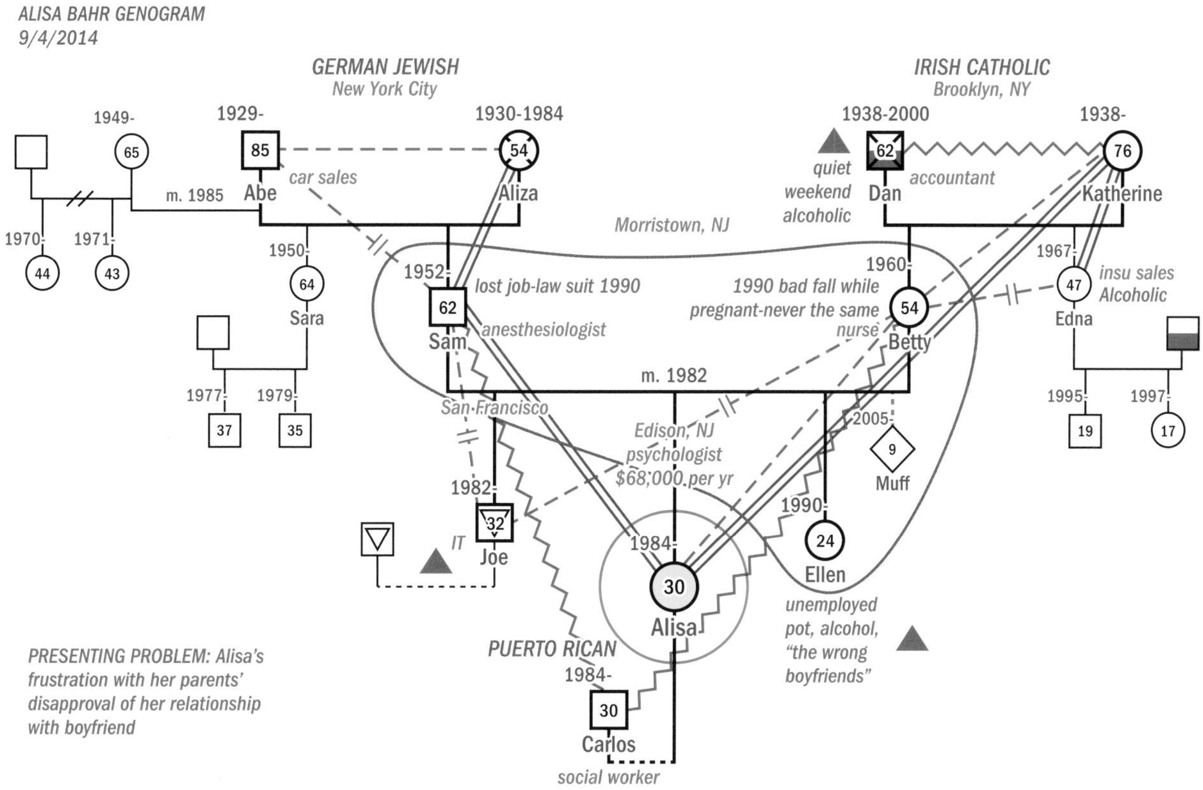

sister. Alisa has never felt close to her mother, but she has had a close relationship with her maternal grandmother, Katherine.

Next, we have added indicators of family functioning. (**Figure 2.10: Alisa Bahr Family with Functioning, Relationships, Secrets, and other Stressors**). We see that neither set of grandparents had a positive relationship with each other. The paternal grandparents were distant and apparently avoided each other, while the maternal grandparents were in an overtly negative relationship. Sam was close to his mother and never got along with his father, while Alisa was distant from her mother, whom she saw as preferring her younger sister and with whom she always felt competitive. Both sets of grandparents had been negative toward the parents' relationship, just as Alisa's parents were now negative toward her relationship with Carlos.

Other key issues include the parents' cutoff from their oldest son, Joe, whom

CHRONOLOGY 2.1: ALISA BAHR FAMILY CHRONOLOGY

1982   Sam and Betty met working on the same hospital unit and Betty soon became pregnant. Her Irish Catholic parents and her husband's German Jewish parents were all outraged and refused to attend the small wedding the couple arranged when Betty was 4 months pregnant.

1982   Joe born in December.

1984   April. Alisa's paternal grandmother, Aliza, died suddenly of an aneurism at age 54.

1984   June. Alisa Bahr was born and named for her grandmother Aliza.

1985   January. Alisa's paternal grandfather, Abe, remarried a woman with two teenagers and left the state for Florida, causing a serious rift with his son, Sam, Alisa's father.

1990   Sam, caught up in hospital politics, lost his job and had to sue the hospital where he had worked for 15 years.

1990   Betty had become pregnant with her third child and at 8 months of pregnancy fell in the bathtub. She has felt she was never the same since.

1990   Daughter Ellen was born.

2000   September. Brother Joe, age 18, left for college at Stanford in California, having come out to his parents as gay the previous year. The family rarely spoke of him, refused to deal with his homosexuality, and kept it a family secret.

2000   October 10. The maternal grandfather died suddenly at age 62. He had been an accountant, but a quiet alcoholic on weekends, though no one discussed this.

2000   November—at Thanksgiving. Betty had final break with her sister Edna with whom she had never been close. She felt her sister had finally insulted her one time too many.

2005   Ellen was found with marijuana at school and began missing class and getting drunk at parties. Her troubles would continue for many years and she never left home, having completed only one semester of community college and having only spotty employment and many relationships with "unacceptable" boyfriends when Alisa began therapy in 2014.

2014   Alisa Bahr, 30 year-old psychologist, sought help for frustrations with her parents' disapproval of her boyfriend, Carlos, a Puerto Rican social worker. She had been the parents' favorite, an excellent student and very successful throughout her growing up years. But her parents became very critical when she began dating Carlos, her first serious boyfriend.

they rarely even mention. Similar "secrets" relate to Betty's father having been a quiet alcoholic for years and to her cutoff from her sister Edna, which has been going on for more than a decade. In addition, the parents never discuss the dysfunction of their youngest daughter Ellen, who seems never to have launched and is still at home and supported by her parents. She has rarely held down a job and seems to smoke pot and have the "wrong" boyfriends most of the time.

The Family Chronology: It is at this point that we have enough information to map out a family chronology (**Chronology 2.1: Alisa Bahr Family Chronology**) to follow the timeline for the family. A family's chronology is not as easily apparent on a genogram, which maps the space and structure better than the timeline of history.

Alisa's parents, Sam and Betty, had apparently conceived Joe at a time when both sets of grandparents were strongly disapproving of their relationship and their wedding was kept secret. Each set of parents thought their child was too good for the partner. Neither set of grandparents attended the wedding. As mentioned, the paternal grandmother died just before Alisa was born, and the paternal grandfather remarried very shortly after and moved away, leading to his cutoff from his son, Sam, for whom his daughter Alisa became his adored middle child.

At the time that the third child, Ellen, was born, both parents were experiencing major stresses. The father had gotten caught up in some hospital politics, lost his job, and had to bring a lawsuit against the hospital where he had worked for 15 years. At the same time, Betty, eight months pregnant, fell in the bathtub and hurt her hip, after which she felt had never been the same.

The parents' family of origin history undoubtedly contributed to what happened in Alisa's family as she was growing up, which will surely influence the current family reaction to her developing a relationship with Carlos. Below we highlight some key patterns to note on a genogram with this family as the illustration. (A more detailed analysis of the work with this family is provided in *The Genogram Casebook* [2016] and in the video" Triangles and Family Therapy: Strategies and Solutions," available through www.psychotherapy.net.)

Key Patterns to Note on a Genogram

Incorporating Cultural Factors on Genograms

Genograms help us contextualize a person's kinship network in terms of culture, class, race, gender, religion, family process, and migration history. When we ask people to identify themselves ethnically, we are highlighting themes of cultural identity, connection, and continuity to make them more apparent. Genograms should always depict information on clients' problems from a contextual framework. All genograms should be cultural genograms, taking into account the cultural context in which clients are situated. Just as you ask the names, dates, and whereabouts of a client's family members, you should ask about their cultural background. Clients in the United States are often disconnected from their cultural history. Genogram tracking that places them in social class, gender, ethnic, racial, and religious context is thus part of helping them understand who they are, just as is questioning around sibling patterns, untimely loss, and multi-generational triangles.

> *All genograms should be cultural genograms, taking into account the cultural context in which clients are situated.*

By its nature, doing a genogram involves the telling of stories and emphasizes respect for the client's perspective, encouraging the multiple views of different family members. By scanning the family system culturally and historically and assessing previous life cycle transitions, the clinician can place present issues in the context of the family's evolutionary patterns of geography, migration, and family process.

Alisa's family represents typical multi-ethnic families in the U.S. that minimize their cultural issues. It was only when carefully questioned that Alisa mentioned her parents' reaction to Carlos as perhaps reflecting their prejudice against people of lesser ethnic/racial status. This was a parallel reaction to how her grandparents on both sides had reacted to her parents' relationship. Her German Jewish grandparents felt an Irish daughter-in-law would lower their status; her Irish Catholic grandparents felt a Jewish son-in-law would lower their status. The other side of those reactions was, of course, that somehow the families had survived the parents' marriage and adapted to cultural expansion over many years, providing a possible model for the parents to think more broadly about their daughter's boyfriend, Carlos.

Loss and Responses to Loss

Loss is the most difficult emotional experience we humans must deal with. As founding family therapist Norman Paul used to say, if you can track only one pattern on a genogram, let it be loss. We always try to explore issues of loss on genograms. In the Bahr family we can see at least two situations of cutoff following loss: first, when the paternal grandmother died suddenly at only 54, her husband remarried and moved into another family within five months, creating a cutoff from that point on with his son Sam.

Some years later, in 2000, the maternal grandfather died suddenly at age 62 and it was only two months later that his daughter Betty had a final cutoff from her sister Edna. Apparently Betty made no connection between the death of her father and cutting off her sister, a common dissociation in families that are inclined toward cutoffs. This cutoff happened also very close to the time that the oldest son was launched to college with virtually no emotional support from his parents. Cutting off a family member when one disapproves of his or her behavior seems to be a family pattern. This pattern was also reflected in both sets of grandparents refusing to attend Sam and Betty's wedding because they disapproved of their relationship and the pregnancy.

With this pattern in mind, it would seem an extremely good sign that Alisa sought therapy when her parents began showing disapproval for her relationship with Carlos. She did not, apparently, want to have a repeat of that kind of family disconnection. This would seem an excellent indication of her resilience: seeking outside help rather than shutting down.

Sibling Constellations

Sam, the father, was the younger brother of an older sister, while Betty, the mother, was the older sister of a younger sister. This could suggest that the couple might have managed to keep their marital connection by Betty being the "older" sister, and Sam the "younger" brother, though his career status as an MD while she was a nurse might suggest the male dominant/woman-as-handmaiden role doctors and nurses have often had within the medical system. Betty also did not grow up with a brother, and her closest immediate family relationship seems to have been with her father, who was a controlling presence. So her father/daughter relationship might have been replayed in her relationship with a husband who had a high-status job, even though he was a younger brother.

If we look at the sibling constellation of the three children, one might be surprised that the parents were so willing to disconnect from their oldest and only son. His place seems to have been taken by the success-oriented middle daughter, who was a herself replacement for a much-loved paternal grandmother. The grandmother's death was accompanied by the grandfather appearing to leave the family to join his second wife's family.

The youngest daughter in the Bahr family seems in many ways like more of an only child than a sibling, as she was born six years after her sister Alisa, so they would have been unlikely to grow up as chums. But this sister was also born into a very different family, whose hopes and dreams appear to have been dashed just as she was born: both financially, by the father's stress and job loss, and also by the mother's physical difficulties after hurting her hip in a fall. One might hypothesize that neither parent had much energy for this third child. Perhaps the first two children, who were barely two years apart, were very supportive to each other in childhood, as they were both extremely bright and talented.

Taking a Life Cycle Perspective

When we look at this family from a life cycle perspective, we can see that the parents had trouble at the transition to couplehood, so perhaps it is not surprising that Alisa comes in at this same life phase. In addition, her choice of partner is someone from a different culture, similar to her parents' choices of partners from different cultures. The transition to launching seems to have been a problem at some level for all three of the children in this family. Joe was launched prematurely, basically extruded once he told the parents that he was gay. He seems to have left home, almost never to return. The youngest child, Ellen, on the other hand, never truly launched, not having completed an education or achieved job skills to support herself. The parents seem to be continuing to support her without setting any clear boundaries for her participation in the family.

The Impact of Socio-Economics on the Family

Differences in siblings' education and social status can be an important stress on their relationships. In this case, Betty became much more successful that her sister. Edna married an insurance salesman, who had not finished college. She seems to have struggled in relation to her older sister's more affluent and successful career-oriented family. We might suspect that unless things change, Ellen will be in a similarly one-down position in relation to her siblings as she moves through life.

Creating Specific Genograms to Explore Issues or to Promote Resilience in a System

At times it is useful to create separate genograms to show particular kinds of information, perhaps one for basic demographics, one for relationship patterns, one for patterns of family functioning and creativity, one for the family's community connections, interests, and values, and others to provide snapshots of key points in the family's history, such as the point of symptom onset. We may even imagine that in the clinical chart of the future, all such genograms would be possible, allowing clinicians to track the resilience factors in their cases as they work to promote health of their patients.

As we have tried to emphasize, it is important to make sure that the context of the family is indicated on a genogram: their cultural, religious, socio-economic, and community values and connections, including work and friend relationships. While the complexity of these contextual factors is impossible to convey on a single graphic, some basic information about this context is essential. Computers will soon make tracking various dimensions easier by enabling us to show one or two dimensions at a time, or to move through time to show changes as they have evolved.

By asking about other contextual forces that have influenced the family, we can get a much broader range of responses. From sports on TV to credit card companies to belief in social justice to shopping or music to social status, it can be very helpful to inquire about broader issues that are relevant to the family.

Figure 2.11: Alisa Bahr Family with Value Connections shows issues Alisa described as important for different members of the family. Just asking clients about such interests can often lead to very helpful insights for intervention and reconnection. In this case, Alisa mentioned her father's love of golf—which she said no one shared with him. She then came up with music and work, which both her parents and grandmothers shared.

Then she thought of holidays, which had become a sore point, especially for her mother since the cutoff from her sister, but which had always been important before that. We tagged that as something she might work to expand, whether in creating new holiday rituals or by finding ways to revive the old enthusiasm. She then mentioned her involvement in PFLAG (Parents and Friends of Lesbians and Gays), which she had joined to support her brother, Joe, and had tried without success to get her parents to join.

Next she thought of her sister's interest in theater, one of the few positive interests she could think of regarding her sister, and something which she as well

Figure 2.11   Alisa Bahr Family with Value Connections

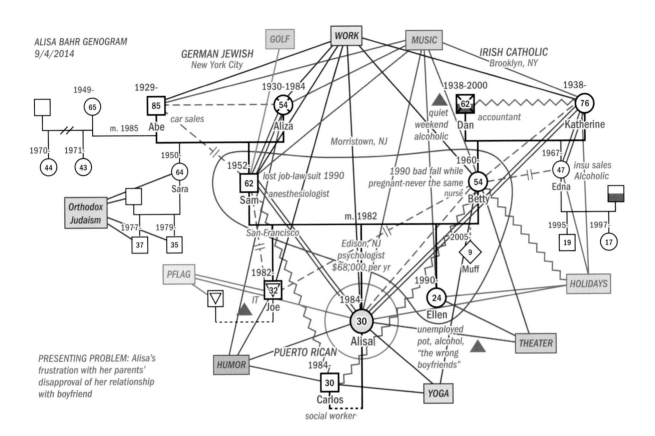

PRESENTING PROBLEM: Alisa's frustration with her parents' disapproval of her relationship with boyfriend

as her mother could potentially share with her. She then mentioned that her aunt Sara had become orthodox when she married her husband. This had created a separation on that side of the family, which she gradually realized she could try to build a bridge to cross. Then she mentioned humor, which she said was especially important for her father, and apparently for her paternal grandmother as well. She thought she and her brother Joe always had a connection through humor and that this could possibly be a link to connect them both with their father. It was only later in therapy that she realized that her sister Ellen also had a keen sense of humor and began to share with her in ways she had been missing for years.

Such interests can help families become aware of shared values and also point out values that may cause conflict, which may be an important issue for clinical intervention.

Contextual Influences May Include:

Institutional Affiliations: religious, business, political, community service, professional, military, self-help, or athletic institutions; fraternities; choir; TV; Internet social networks, chat, or hobby groups.

Physical/Psychological/Spiritual Activities: working out, hiking, church, meditation or yoga

Support Systems (those who support the family and those who are supported by the family): friends, community groups, neighbors, housekeepers, accountants, lawyers, chiropractors or other caretakers, hairdressers, God, children, pets

Business and Governmental Institutions: legal system, political system, welfare system, social services, credit card companies, insurance companies

Values or Interests: education, food, sports, humor, movies, music, art, outdoors, genealogy, stock market.

Community Connections: We want to understand clients' relationships to their community as well: What community institutions family members belong to, where they go to socialize, what connections they have with school, work, civic, community, religious, or fraternity/sorority groups. Are there groups from which they have felt excluded? Are there groups in which they feel at a disadvantage, such as if they are the only democrat in a republican family or the darkest skinned member of their family, the only one who has gone to college, or the only Jewish family in an Anglo community?

Indicating Cultural Background, Education, Occupation, Socio-Economic Situation, Religion, and Spirituality on Genograms

We can generally track a family's basic cultural background, educational, occupational, and financial information, and some basics of each person's interest in spiritual and religious issues without too much difficulty. But the details of family members' cultural patterns on these dimensions over the life cycle will be more complicated to track, though for some patients it will be crucial for understanding the current stress and helping them find solutions. It is important to begin to track these dimensions on the genogram even though the details will likely be too complicated to convey in their full complexity. (For more in-depth exploration of tracking issues on a genogram see Chapter 4: Tracking Family Patterns with Genograms).

Exploring Patterns of Functioning, Relationships, and Structure Over the Generations

Since family patterns are likely to be transmitted from one generation to the next, the clinician should scan the genogram for patterns that have repeated over several generations. Such repetitive patterns occur in functioning, relationships, and family structure, as we have suggested above for Alisa Bahr's family. Recognizing such patterns often helps families avoid repeating negative patterns or transmitting them into the future. Tracking critical events and changes in family functioning allows us to make systemic connections between seeming coincidences, such as anniversary reactions, and assess the impact of traumatic changes on family functioning, resources, and vulnerability to future stresses. This facilitates our attempts to contextualize these experiences within the larger family and community context. Such tracking enables the clinician to promote resilience based on past sources of strength, helping family members modify past adaptive strategies that have become dysfunctional (Walsh, 2016).

Attending to Missing or "Hidden" Information on Genograms

Information is always missing from genograms. There is no way one could include all the relevant information on a genogram in any case: it is just a map to track highlights and serve as a guide. But when family members actually don't have much relevant information, we can often help them piece together at least some information over time. Missing information in itself also provides clues to family secrets and cutoffs. For example, how have they dealt with things they did not know or understand? Did they discuss their questions or did the topics become toxic? When only partial information can be unearthed, we include it, of course. But when key information is missing, we can also begin to speculate about why.

Information that is kept hidden by family members may in fact be most important for understanding their psychology. So we always look for missing information on a genogram, not only to see how we might fill in the gaps, but also to see whether we can help the family modify patterns of secrecy, the uncovering of which may help them understand their family's story.

Issues Difficult to Capture on Genograms

Certain genogram patterns, while extremely important to the systems theory underlying genogram mapping, will remain very difficult to capture. These include the mapping of:

Triangles: While the theory of triangles is at the core of systemic understanding of family patterns, they are extremely difficult to map on a genogram. The best we can usually do is show one or two key triangles, even though by exploring any family story we are trying to assess for patterns of closeness and distance that tend to stabilize into triangles in a family and become problematic. (see Chapter 6 on Triangles in *The Genogram Casebook*, 2016.)

Family Members Involved in Family Business: It is extremely difficult to show the organizational relationships of a business in relation to the structural relationships of families, where numerous family members might serve on boards, as CEOs, managers, or as full or part-time workers within a family business. In particular, the complexities of power dynamics in a family business—which can be assessed most directly by answering the question of who makes how much money and who gets to participate in what decisions—would be extremely difficult to schematize on a genogram. At the same time family relationships are probably the best clue to understanding how the triangles in a family business run: with power tending to veer toward the males, the oldest, and not the in-laws. A "genogram" or organizational chart of the family business could help map out the overlapping and potentially conflicting lines of authority between a family and its family business.

Tracking Medical and Psychological Stressors and Family Members' Relationships to the Healthcare System: Family members have different healthcare needs and different relationships with care providers. It is very difficult to map members' relationships to the healthcare system because of the potential complexity of each person's medical or psychological history. Nevertheless, it is the most practically useful tool available for assessing patients in any healthcare setting. It is important to know, at least in outline, the health history of all family members connected to the Index Patient because of the resource role they may play in the health care, as well as the ripple effect of stress created by others' illnesses. Family members may be resources as caretakers, and previous generations may provide role models for handling the stress of illness, or they may amplify a patient's fears of reliving previous negative illness scenarios.

The complexities of these connections would be extremely difficult to convey on a genogram. We do, however make a point of including at least other current healthcare providers, previous therapists, and therapeutic organizations on a genogram because they are often central to the family's experience of help or frustration.

Cultural Genogram Issues: Even though they are at the foundation of all genogram understanding, cultural issues quickly become too complex to convey. Thus, while family members' cultural heritage and points of migration are typically shown, much of the complexity of cultural conflicts and issues can barely be hinted at on their genogram. It is difficult to show multiple dimensions for families who have grown up in more than one country, speak multiple languages, have migrated into multiple other cultural contexts, or who have experienced fluctuations from one social class to another. The ethnicity of a single individual can become prohibitively complex, not to mention that of the whole family. Frida Kahlo, for example, is ¼ German, ¼ Hungarian Jewish, ¼ Mexican, ⅛ Native Indian, and ⅛ Spanish. We have drawn a whole special genogram to illustrate that (**Figure 7.5: Kahlo–Rivera**). Furthermore, our nation's cultural heritage is getting more complex by the day as more and more people intermarry and have ever more multi-ethnic children. How do we show these complexities? We quickly reach a point at which it is extremely difficult to map the complexity in any handy graphic form.

Indicating Issues Regarding Sexuality on a Genogram: Obviously, it would be extraordinarily difficult to draw a graphic on a genogram that would represent all the sexual information one might want to gather. Mapping the sexual history of multiple family members on a genogram would very quickly become overwhelming, and there is probably no way we could make a clear graphic to show this complexity. Multigenerational patterns of family members having multiple known intimate primary relationships may be obvious on some genograms, but the subtler sexual issues would require special symbols and connection lines to depict. Nevertheless, such themes are important, and using a genogram format for organizing the tracking of sexual themes does seem to be the most efficient framework for assessing sexual history.

Family Secrets: We might be able to indicate who knows a secret and who does not on a genogram, but usually, when there is one secret, there are others. To show how particular secrets are kept or shared through a family would tax any mapping process, although computers may be better able to capture them to help us see more clearly how secrecy operates in families.

Particular Family Relationships: Complementarity, unequal power, patterns of avoidance, intrusion, over-functioning/under-functioning, over-responsibility/under-responsibility, scapegoating, dependence/independence, enmeshment/individualism/isolation are so complex they are difficult if not impossible to indicate clearly on a genogram.

Patterns of Friendship: Even patterns of friendship can quickly become difficult to manage on a genogram. It is easy enough to ask the members of a household to add their key friends, but once we ask about their parents' patterns of friendship it becomes more complex. What if the husband's mother always had a "best" friend but within the past year she has had a dramatic cutoff and it embroiled other friends and family? And what if the parents have many "couple" friends, but only a few with whom they have real intimacy? And then what happens to this network if the couple gets divorced? The graphic would rapidly become very crowded and hard to follow!

Relationships with Work Colleagues: The same problems emerge in mapping relationships with work colleagues. Over a whole lifetime these networks may tell a complex story, and if you add the stories of siblings' and parents' work relationships, the picture could quickly become jammed. Yet these relationships may be key stressors or resources at critical moments in the family history.

Spiritual Genograms: Religious or spiritual genograms are similarly complex, since each person in a family may have had a complex spiritual journey, changing religious beliefs and practices at different points through life, or giving religion or spirituality a different valence at each life cycle phase. So any particular graphic always highlights certain aspects of individual and family history while leaving others in the shadows. A number of authors have written about working with couples and families around their spiritual history (Walsh, 2009). Some have even drawn elaborate graphics of doves, bibles, and numerous religious symbols to illustrate religious visions, intensity of religious experience, and involvement in religious organizations. Practically speaking, however, even with a graphic artist and a very fancy computer to generate the graphic, the landscape of the genogram will quickly become overloaded when trying to track even one person's spiritual history, never mind that of the whole family. Nevertheless, some notation on any genogram about key religious or spiritual affiliations and experiences is essential, and the assessment of clients' spiritual and religious beliefs and history is necessary for effective clinical assessment and treatment. Furthermore, Hodge (2000) offers interesting genogram interview questions on whether clients have ever experienced angels, saints, demons, evil spirits, or the dead and, if so, what kinds of encounters they have had. Such experiences may help to understand a person's distress or sources of hope, but it would be a challenge to find ways to map these relationships on a genogram.

Community Genograms: Because of the multiple dimensions of family members' relationships with their communities, it is difficult to imagine a genogram that could visually depict a family's community connections in a meaningful graphic, although the issue of including community context in assessment and intervention with clients is extremely important (Rigazio-DiGilio, Ivey, Kunkler-Peck, & Grady, 2005). At best we can probably explore a few dimensions at a time (see Celia Falicov's brilliant discussion of multiple complex contextual dimensions in her 2016 book on Latinos). It is nevertheless worth trying to display a family's connections, resources, and problems in their community context. This is important because, as Rigazio-DiGilio and her colleagues (2005) point out, without some mapping of the community context, it is hard to help clients appreciate the multiple ways it influences their problems, and why it is therefore an important factor in finding solutions. If you do not take the larger context into account in assessment and in intervention, you marginalize it as a factor in human problems, and thus mystify clients about the nature of much of their distress.

In one of the classic attempts to contextualize genograms within an eco-map, Ann Hartman (1978, 1995) offered 14 larger context institutions (such as social welfare, healthcare, extended family, recreation) and five different types of connection lines: strong, tenuous, stressful, flow of energy toward family member, and flow of energy toward institution, organization, or group. Even with a small family, as mentioned above, the picture quickly becomes very crowded. So depicting social context is indeed challenging.

If you do not take the larger context into account in assessment and in intervention, you marginalize it as a factor in human problems, and thus mystify clients about the nature of much of their distress.

The difficulty of drawing comprehensive graphics is not a reason to ignore these important issues in genogram mapping, but rather to acknowledge the reality that the graphic dimensions can never cover the richness of genograms as a tool for clinical inquiry. This reality is similar to the well-known observation that a photograph of a spectacular vista or sunset can never come close to capturing the beauty and complexity of what the human eye sees.

Most of the writings about contextual expansions of the genogram refer to a clinical process in which the genogram map becomes the basis for a contextual inquiry about these various dimensions of life, rather than as graphic depictions. Computers will help us greatly with this because they can capture many complexities and changes over time. But the limitations of the complexity of any graphic remain.

In spite of the complexities that make it impossible to map all aspects of a family's context on a single graphic, we are at the start of a very exciting new era. With the help of computers, we will soon be able to make amazing three-dimensional maps that will enable us to track complex patterns in ways we can barely imagine. We will be able to zoom in and track details in greater depth on a particular dimension, and then compare patterns of thousands of genograms at a time, just as we are now able to do with the DNA patterns of people all around the planet. What is very exciting is that for the first time we will be able to examine complexities that go beyond the scope of an individual's ability to convey. We will be able to check out our hunches and intuitions about family patterns over a huge group of families to see whether our ideas are borne out. We will also potentially be able to see new connections between an individual's health, resilience and creativity.

Choices Always Have to Be Made

Genograms are necessarily schematic and never detail all the vicissitudes of a family's history. Some complex family situations may require more than one genogram. We want to remind you again that, choices must always be made between the importance of the information on the graphic and the amount of information that will make the graphic too complex to read.

We want to remind you again that sharing a family history is an intimate process. Genogram information should always be gathered for a purpose the participant understands and should be treated with the greatest respect.

3

The Genogram Interview

Mapping our connections through genogram interviewing could be the first step toward systemic healthcare, and can help us recognize our connection to each other and to the world around us. We believe that fragmentation within families and communities is responsible for many of the ills we witness in our society. If we embraced the simple postulate that "illness is a family affair" (Wright & Leahey, 1999, p. 261), we could begin to change the face of health and mental healthcare toward the systemic perspective that genograms offer. A genogram interview may be done in a few minutes, or over many hours, depending on the purpose. This chapter offers a framework for thinking about the layers of information on a genogram. We envision genogram interviewing as part of not just healthcare and mental health assessment and intervention, but also social services, education, and counseling services as well.

We have only begun to tap the clinical potential of genograms. They have been used in many ways—to assess, reframe, detoxify, unblock, and engage individuals, couples, and families, and to connect them to their history in order to empower and free them for their future. Genograms can be a powerful psycho-educational tool to help families understand their own patterns and learn to research their own family process. Creating genograms provides a unique chronicle, which is in itself a remarkable therapeutic intervention that allows families to view themselves systemically.

But it is crucial that those who use the genogram as a mapping tool recognize it as a shorthand for looking at patterns, not just a page of information to be gathered and put in a drawer. The power of genograms is in their ability to help clinicians understand a person's problems and sources of resilience and healing. Readers will want to modify their own ways of collecting genogram information to suit the context in which they are working.

As stated earlier, the basic genogram information can be gleaned in as little as two minutes (Wright & Leahey, 1999)! (A quick four-minute genogram of my (MM) family created with www.genopro.com/genogramformat is available on YouTube). Adding to the basic names, age, birth and death dates, and family structural information, we include ethnicity, occupation, education, religious affiliation, migration experience, relationships, current health status of family members, as well as information about other helpers and informal family resources. Adding all this information would, of course, take longer.

We offer the reader a framework for genogram questioning. This is not an outline for how to conduct an interview, which depends on its particular purpose and the flow of questioning as the interview proceeds. Rather we provide a framework for thinking about the questions to consider. A further guide to genogram questions is provided at the end of each chapter in *The Genogram Journey: Understanding Family Relationships* (McGoldrick, 2011), which offers a basic explanation of the theory of family systems undergirding genogram interviewing. The conversation itself must, of course, be built around the aims of the session and the relationship between the clinician and the individual or family.

Genogram Interviewing to Engage Families

A genogram interview is a practical way of engaging a whole family in a systemic approach to treatment. Especially in family crisis situations, it may help to include as many relevant family members as possible, so that both the clinician and the family members can share the basic story of the family and see the problem in context.

Genogram interviewing demonstrates interest in the whole family system. The process of mapping family information on the genogram immediately conveys the notion that a contextual view of the situation is necessary to understanding the problem. It also conveys a major systemic assumption: that all family members are involved in whatever happens to one member, and that the connection is ongoing from their past and toward their future.

Equally important, the genogram interview can build rapport among family members by exploring their relationships around key family traditions and issues of specific concern. Genogram questioning goes to the heart of family experiences: birth, love, illness and death, conflict and cutoff. Its structure provides an orienting framework for discussion of the full range of family experiences, and for tracking and bringing into focus difficult issues such as illness, loss, and emotionally charged relationships.

Genograms provide quick access to complex, emotionally loaded family material. Yet, the structure of the genogram interview allows the therapist to elicit such information in a relatively non-threatening way. Also, the genogram framework helps both the clinician and the family organize family experiences in ways that can lessen the toxicity of even the most painful traumas, by elaborating the context for the experiences over time and space. Memory and survival narratives can help participants overcome silence, secrecy, pain, and shame. Casual, matter-of-fact interviewing often leads family members to give straight-forward information. Even the most guarded people, who are quite unresponsive to open-ended questions, are often willing and able to discuss their families' experiences in this structured format. There is also something impressive about displaying the full range of information to the family in an organized, graphic way. Cognitive understanding of symptomatic behavior as it relates to emotionally charged relationships can increase family members' sense of mastery over their situation. Creating a family's genogram becomes a collaborative task that empowers them, since they are the experts on their own history and the therapist is only the recorder and witness of it. Creating a genogram also allows the clinician to give something back to the family, namely the graphic map of their story, and a nonjudgmental hearing of it. For many families, the richness of their history is an important affirmation, no matter how painful their experiences have been.

Some clinicians create and display the genogram on a chalkboard, whiteboard, large note pad, or computer screen. Genograms seem to possess a certain mystique, which may become a "hook" to engage families. Jack Bradt (1980), one of the early promoters of the use of genograms, used to draw them on a large pad he kept in his office and brought out whenever he saw a family. I (MM) often give a print-out of my computer-generated genogram to clients at the end of their first session. This invites their participation in the assessment, as I ask them to correct the genogram for the next meeting. They are often amazed and fascinated to see how much information about their history can be organized on a small page in this way.

The Family Information Net

The process of gathering family information can be thought of as casting an information net in larger and larger circles. The net spreads out in multiple directions:

- from the presenting problem to its larger context;
- from the immediate household to the extended family and broader social systems;

- from the present family situation to a chronology of historical family events;
- from easy, non-threatening queries to more difficult and possibly anxiety-provoking questions;
- from obvious facts about demographics, functioning, and relationships to judgments and hypotheses about family patterns;
- from pathology focused depictions of family problems to resilience-oriented re-descriptions of their family history and resourcefulness in contending with issues.

The Presenting Problem and the Immediate Household

In healthcare, genogram information beyond the most basic demographic data is often recorded as it emerges over the course of multiple office visits. In family therapy, family members usually come with specific problems, which are the clinician's starting point. In an educational setting where learning problems are the focus, the family's educational and learning history would obviously take priority. When there is a problematic occupational history, the previous occupational experiences would be highlighted.

At the outset, families are told that some basic information about them is needed to fully understand their problem. Such information usually springs naturally from exploring the presenting problem and its impact on the immediate household. In both healthcare and mental health settings, it makes sense to start with the immediate family, and the context in which the problem occurs:

- Who lives in the household?
- How is each person related?
- Where do other family members live?

The clinician gathers the name, age, gender, and occupation of each person in the household in order to sketch the immediate family structure. Other relevant information is elicited through inquiring about the problem:

- When did the problem begin? Who noticed it first?
- How has each family member responded? Who is the most concerned about the problem? Who the least? Which family members know about the problem? How does each view it?

- What solutions have been suggested or attempted by whom so far?
- Has anyone else in the family ever had similar problems? What solutions, including what medications, have been attempted by whom in those situations?
- Were family relationships different before the problem began? How have they changed?
- What other problems existed before or since this problem began? Relationship problems? Mood problems?
- Has the problem been changing? For better or for worse? In what ways? This is also a good time to inquire about previous efforts to get help for the problem, including previous treatment, medications, therapists, hospitalizations, and the current referring person.
- Have there been any medication prescriptions? What was the dosage? Was the dosage ever changed or were other medications added? For what reasons? After what assessment? With professionals known in what context and for what period of time? The specific history of medications, prescribed by whom and under what circumstances, is important to ascertain.

The Current Situation

Next the clinician spreads the information net into the current family situation. This usually follows naturally from questions about the problem and who it involves.

- What has been happening recently in your family? Have there been any recent changes in the family (e.g., people coming or leaving, illnesses, relationship, job or financial changes or problems)?

It is important to inquire about recent life cycle transitions, as well as anticipated changes in the family situation (especially exits and entrances of family members—births, marriages, divorces, deaths, or the departure of family members).

The Wider Family Context

The clinician then looks for an opportunity to explore the wider family context by asking about the extended family and cultural background of all the adults involved. The interviewer might move into this area by saying, "I would now like to ask you something about your background to help make sense of the current problem" inquiring about each side of the family separately, beginning, for example, with the mother's side:

- Let's begin with your mother's family. Your mother was which one of how many children?
- When and where was she born?
- Is she alive? If so, where is she now? How is her health? If not, when did she die? What was the cause of her death?
- What does she do? If she is retired, when did this happen?
- How far did she go in school and what has she done for work?
- When and how did your mother meet your father? Did they marry, and, if so, when?
- Had she been married before? If so, when? Did they separate or divorce or did the spouse die? If so, when was that?
- Did she have children by any relationship other than with your father?
- What is she like? How do you get along with her?

In like fashion, questions are asked about the father. The aim is to learn about the person and the family history and relationships. The clinician might then ask about each parent's family of origin, i.e., father, mother, and siblings. The goal is to get information about at least three or four generations, including grandparents, parents, aunts, uncles, siblings, spouses, and children of the index patient.

Obviously, you do not just go through a list of questions. Questions cannot be asked in a manualized fashion. Each response influences the next question. You take your cue from what the person tells you to learn more about the individual and about the relationships in the family.

Never forget that any question can lead to very painful answers regarding abuse, suicide, criminal behavior, mental illness, or an experience of racism. The clinician needs to be prepared to hold the answers with the deepest respect. This is never a superficial conversation. As the clinician you are dealing with the core issues of your patient's life. It is a profound responsibility.

Resistance in the Genogram Interview

When people come in with a problem, they may have a limited view of what is wrong and what needs to be changed. Their perspective is often rigid and non-systemic, based on the belief that only one person, the symptomatic one, needs to change. Any effort to move directly to other problematic areas in the family may be blocked by vehement denial of other family difficulties. One cannot simply ignore the family's agenda for the appointment and set out to gather all the genogram information in the initial session. Such a single-minded approach would likely alienate the family from treatment. Gathering information for the genogram should be part of a more general approach of joining with the family and seeking to understand their problems and their view of their lives.

Resistance is often sparked as clinicians touch on painful memories and feelings related to the information being gathered. For instance, if it comes out that a brother died in a car accident, a grandparent committed suicide, or a child was born out of wedlock, family members may seek to redirect the focus of the session. "Why open up old wounds," they may ask, "when we know that Joe here is the problem?"

Sometimes, seemingly innocuous questions provoke intense reactions. Resistance can show up in various ways. It may be direct and vehement. Or it may be subterranean, with family members becoming bored, restless, or disruptive. For instance, one client burst into tears after being asked how many siblings he had. The question had stirred up memories of his favorite brother, who had died in a drowning accident. Ostensibly simple questions may also unearth family secrets (Imber-Black, 1993, 1999). A question such as "How long have you been married?" may lead to embarrassment or concealment if the couple conceived their first child before marriage. Even questions of geography, such as "Where does your son live?" may be sensitive to a parent whose son is in jail, in a psychiatric hospital, or out of contact with the parent.

When you meet repeated resistance to discussion of family history, it may help to focus instead on the resistant person for a while. Allow the person to feel heard. Let him or her know you are concerned about the presenting problem. Be reassuring about where you are going. Let the family know that your aim in learning about their history is to help you understand their situation.

Sometimes family members are so resistant that you have to temporarily forego the genogram interview altogether. This is fairly rare and is probably a sign of unusually toxic multigenerational issues. In these instances, as you refocus on the presenting problem, you still seek to understand who is in the family and how they are involved with each other and with the problem. You will still be seeking to make connections between the current situation and past events and patterns. These connections help to remind people of their belonging to something larger than themselves.

Occasionally family members are so resistant to discussions of genogram information that we have to leave the subject until we find another way of engaging them. In those situations, after we have eventually succeeded in building a relationship with the family, we generally find that the resistance has come from specific anxieties about family experiences embedded in the genogram, such as the stigma of a parent who was abusive, committed suicide, or was in a mental hospital.

There are times when a client's discussion of their genogram becomes an avoidance of taking appropriate action in the present. This must be challenged, as when a parent ignores the immediate needs of children or avoids dealing with alcohol or drug abuse by sidetracking discussion to the genogram (or anything else, for that matter).

Constantly demonstrating the relevance of the larger family context to the family members' immediate concerns helps them realize that they are not alone. Eventually a family's resistance and concealment of information may be overcome as they begin to see the connections between their concerns and historical family patterns. You can often return to organized questioning for the genogram in subsequent sessions. For more detailed understanding of the clinical issues in using genograms, see the clinical genogram videos "Harnessing the Power of Genograms," "The Legacy of Unresolved Loss," "Couples Therapy a Systemic Approach," and "Assessment and Engagement in Family Therapy," available from www.psychotherapy.net, and the clinical companion book, *The Genogram Casebook* (McGoldrick, 2016). As we work with families and gain their trust, we can hopefully help them see the relevance of their genogram through linking their family experiences and history to the presenting problems for which they are seeking help. Ultimately, we hope to help family members themselves become "researchers" of their own genograms. The aim is to empower families to modify their relationships and shift dysfunctional patterns.

Dealing with a Family's Resistance to Doing a Genogram

As indicated above, when family members react negatively to questions about the extended family or complain that such matters are irrelevant, it makes sense to redirect the focus back to the immediate situation, until the connections between the presenting problem and other family relationships or experiences can be revisited. An example of such a genogram is illustrated on the videotape *The Legacy of Unresolved Loss* (available from www.psychotherapy.net). It shows an assessment for a remarried family whose teenage daughter's behavior was the presenting problem, demonstrating a family's resistance to revealing genogram information. Gentle persistence over time will usually lead to obtaining the information and demonstrating its relevance to the family.

Family's Beliefs About the Problem and About Possible Solutions

We always need to conduct interviews in ways that are sufficiently congruent with the family's beliefs so that they can connect with the recommended interventions. What are the family's cultural beliefs about the problem and about possible solutions? How might the interviewer respond to these beliefs in assessment and intervention?

Diplomatic Inquiry About Basics of Family History and Functioning

To understand family members' functioning and interests you will want to know the basics of their education and work history, finances, sexual relationships, and their history of oppression and other trauma. But it may be challenging for them to discuss some of these issues until they have developed a degree of clinical trust. This is why it is impossible to develop a manualized interview for learning any individual or family's story, and clinicians must be sensitive and patient, especially when learning about the more difficult areas of a family's history and situation.

Interviewers should monitor themselves when asking questions about cultural differences, class, gender, age, race, sexual orientation, religion, spirituality, life cycle stage, and other beliefs, remaining mindful of how their own issues may be an asset or a liability in understanding or engaging particular family members. It is easy to get caught in triangles with the family or with the family and other institutions, such as the referrer, other therapists, or the therapist's own work system. In particular, any ongoing therapeutic relationship a family member has with another therapist could lead to the development of triangles.

Socio-Cultural and Religious Background

It is essential to also learn about the family's ethnic, socioeconomic, political, and religious background in order to place the presenting problems and current relationships in context. This layer of questioning typically evolves naturally as questioning expands to the extended family. Asking about ethnicity and migration history helps establish the cultural context in which the family has operated, and offers the therapist an opportunity to explore the family attitudes and behaviors that have been influenced by such contextual factors. It is important to learn what the family's cultural and religious traditions are with regard to solving problems, health care and healing, and where the current family members stand in relation to their cultures' traditional values. Considering their cultural expectations about relationships with healthcare professionals is important, since this will set the tone for their clinical responses. Where there is a history of oppression, the family's history of dealing with other institutions will, of course, be a critical issue, especially if you are white and your client is a person of color.

Social class differences among family members or between family members and their healthcare professionals are also likely to create discomfort, which will need to be taken into account in the interview. Questions about class pertain not just to the family's current income but to their cultural background, religion, education, and social status within their community. Once the clinician has a clear picture of the cultural and religious factors influencing the family, it becomes easier to raise delicate questions geared toward helping them identify behaviors that, while culturally sanctioned, may be keeping them stuck. Examples include a woman sacrificing her own needs to devote herself exclusively to the needs of others (see McGoldrick, Giordano, & Garcia-Preto, 2005), and anyone dealing with racism, which is relevant for any person of color and an issue about which whites tend to be oblivious. Inquiring about ethnic and racial group matters should be done in particular with members of ethnic/racial minorities, since these topics are likely to be especially sensitive and difficult for them to discuss candidly.

By scanning the family system through a cultural and historical lens and assessing previous life cycle transitions, the clinician can place present issues in the context of the family's evolutionary patterns of geography, migration, and socio-cultural change. Among the relevant issues are:

Socio-Cultural, Socio-Political, and Socio-Economic Factors

Are sociocultural factors (social class, ethnicity, race, finances, language, educational level, employment potential, legal status, and so forth) impeding the family's functioning? What is the family's social location in terms of finances, education, and fit in their community? What has been their educational, occupational, and financial history? What has been their political history and did it cause suffering or conflicts for family members?

Cultural Heritage

Clients belong to their history, their present context, and to the future. When we ask people to identify themselves ethnically, we are helping them to recognize the cultural continuities and discontinuities in their history and to articulate the themes of cultural identity in their families. This line of questioning is, like all genogram exploration, a therapeutic intervention in itself, because it links individuals to their broader historical and sociological context. The questions are meant to be considered by the clinician and asked as they fit into a particular clinical conversation. The issues you will want to know about include:

When we ask people to identify themselves ethnically, we are helping them to recognize the cultural continuities and disconuitites in their history and to articulate the themes of cultural identity in their families. This line of questioning is, like all genogram exploration, a therapeutic intervention in itself, because it links individuals to their broader historical and sociological context.

- What ethnic, racial, religious, community, professional, or other traditions do clients consider themselves a part of?
- Have they lived in an ethnic enclave, or in a community in which they were viewed as outsiders?
- Have their spiritual and religious beliefs supported or minimized their acknowledgment of their ethnic heritage?
- When and under what circumstances did the family come to the US?
- How secure do they feel about their status in the US?
- When did they come to their present community?
- What languages did they speak at home? In their community? In their family of origin?

- What experiences have their racial or ethnic groups had of privilege or oppression?
- What burden may they carry for offenses their group committed against other groups?
- How have they been affected by harmful things their own groups have done, or by what was done against them?
- Have they perhaps been complicit in the wrongs done by their ancestors?
- How may they have given voice to their group's guilt, their own sorrow, or their own part in the harm done by their ancestors? What do they think would repair these wounds?
- What experiences have been the most stressful for their family members in the US?
- To whom do family members in their culture turn when in need of help?
- What are their culture's values regarding male and female roles? Education? Work? Success? Family connectedness? Family caretaking? Religious practices? Psychotherapy? Have these values changed in their family over time?
- Do they still have contact with family members in their country of origin?
- Has immigration changed family members' education or social status?
- How do they feel about their culture(s) of origin? Do they feel they belong to the dominant U.S. culture? How do they think their status with respect to the dominant U.S. culture has affected their family's life experience?

These discussions can remind the family of their resilience through the values of their heritage, their ability to transform their lives, and their ability to work toward long-range goals that fit with their cultural values. Questions that help to locate families in their cultural context may help them access their strengths and resilience in the midst of stressful situations. Questions that might help families feel the strength of their heritage could include:

- How might your great-grandfather, who dreamed of your immigration but never made it himself, think about the problem you are having with your children?
- Your ancestors survived being enslaved for hundreds of years. You are here because they had great strength and courage. What strengths do you think you got from these ancestors that could help you in dealing with your problem?
- Your great-grandmother immigrated at 21 and became a piece worker

in a sweat shop, but managed to support her 6 children and had great resourcefulness. What do you think her dreams were for you, her daughter's daughter's daughter? What do you think she would want you to do now about your current problem?

- Your father died of his alcoholism, but when he came to this country at age 18, he undoubtedly had different dreams for his future. What do you think his dreams were? How do you think he felt about the parents he left behind? What do you think he would want for you now?
- Are there some Latino political groups in your town which could help you fight for the resources you and your group have deserved from the United States for hundreds of years?
- How do you think the fact that you are Italian and your wife is Irish may influence the way you handle conflicts?

Finances

Many cultures consider discussing money taboo, but to understand families' experiences we must know where they are located socio-economically. We need to understand the financial pressures they are under in trying to solve their problems and support their members. Furthermore, one of the rules of understanding power in a family is to follow the money. That is, to know who controls it, and who is dependent on others for it.

We usually write the annual income of the immediate family members right above the birth and death dates, and note on the side of the genogram any indebtedness—especially credit card debt, which is a prevalent family problem in the U.S., as well as expected inheritance and financial obligations (explicit or expected) toward other family members. Debt or success may both be stressors on a family. For families that are from marginalized cultures, the first member to "make it out" of poverty or the lower working class often feels pressure from other family members—jealousy, resentment, or perceived obligation to help less fortunate family members. Families from upper middle or upper class backgrounds who have lost their resources may feel shame or be in conflict with their extended family. Any family struggling to meet basic survival needs (shelter, food, clothing, healthcare) is under enormous stress continually. Issues to explore include:

- How much income does each member generate? If there is an imbalance, how is the imbalance handled? How does the economic situation compare with that of relatives?

- Is there any expected inheritance? Are there family members you support or whom you may need to care for in the future?
- Are there resources being saved for future needs? Do you think they are adequate?
- Who controls the money? How are spending decisions made? Are these patterns different from the ways money was handled in each family of origin?
- Does anyone have a gambling or over-spending problem? How is that dealt with?

Belief Systems, Religion, and Spiritual Values

What are the primary beliefs that organize the family? What is their general worldview, and are they organized by particular myths, rules, spiritual beliefs, or family secrets? What is the history of the family's religious beliefs and practices, including changes in belief? What has been the impact of intra-family religious differences or those between the family and the surrounding community? Have any family members changed religion? How did other family members react to this change? How is the family's religious orientation viewed in the wider society? Have they experienced discrimination or abuse from others?

Language Skills and Acculturation of Family Members

Immigrant family members vary in how quickly they adapt, how much of their heritage they retain, and the rate at which they learn English. Speaking the language of the culture of origin generally helps to preserve a family's sense of cultural connection.

What languages were spoken while the children in the family were growing up? Are there differences in language skills and acculturation within the family that may have led to conflicts, power imbalances, or role reversals, especially if children were expected to translate for their parents?

Connections to Community

It helps to know how good family members are at maintaining friendships. How accessible are friends, neighbors, religious organizations, schools, physicians, community institutions, and other healthcare and social service resources, including therapists? When family members move away from an ethnic enclave, the stresses of adaptation increase, even several generations after immigration. The therapist should learn about the community's ethnic network and, where possible, encourage the rebuilding of informal social connections through family visits, letters, web chats, and through the building of new social networks.

Migration History

Why did the family migrate? What were they seeking, (e.g. survival, freedom from persecution, adventure, wealth)? What were they leaving behind (e.g. religious or political persecution, poverty)? Therapists need to be as attuned to migration stresses and ethnic identity conflicts as they are to other stresses in the family's history. Assessing such factors is crucial for determining whether a family's dysfunction is a "normal" reaction to a high degree of cultural stress, or whether it goes beyond the bounds of transitional stress and requires expert intervention. The stresses of migration may at times be "buried" or forgotten. The cultural heritage before migration may have been suppressed or forgotten, but may still influence the family's outlook, if sometimes subtly, as they try to accommodate to new situations. Many immigrant groups have been pressured by the dominant culture in the U.S. to abandon their ethnic heritage and thus have lost a part of their identity. The effects of this hidden history may be all the more powerful for being unseen. Families that have experienced trauma and devastation within their own society before even beginning the process of immigration will have a monumentally more difficult time adjusting to a new life than those who migrated for adventure or economic betterment. Specific areas to investigate regarding migration include:

The Pre-Migration History:

What was the situation in the country of origin politically and economically?

The Migration History:

How traumatic was the migration itself and did it entail losses along the way beyond the loss of the culture of origin?

The Post-Migration History and Culture Shock:

What experiences did the family have when they arrived in the U.S.? Did they have problems with language, immigration status, poverty? Was there loss of social status or job options? To what extent was there a shock of cultural values? Did they live in a supportive or an antagonistic community or were they isolated?

Migration and the Life Cycle:

How old were family members when they migrated? How old were the family members who remained in the homeland? How did the age at migration influence family members? Were certain children drawn into adult status because they learned English faster than their parents or because the family lacked the resources to treat them as children? Did the life cycle stage at migration bring about a reversal of the parental hierarchy, because parents were less able to negotiate the new culture than their children. Were grandparents limited by their inability to learn English? How did the family's life cycle phase influence their adaptation?

Questioning About Difficult Issues of Cultural and Social Location

Though cultural and socio-economic questions are extremely important, they are likely to be difficult to inquire about and require considerable clinical skill. In African American families, for example, it would be virtually impossible for issues of racism and skin color not to have had a major influence on family relationships (Boyd-Franklin, 2006), given the racist context in which African Americans have existed in the U.S. since our early history. African American cultures have tended to internalize racist ideology about skin color and family triangles are highly likely to have been influenced by these pernicious factors. White families tend to be extremely unaware of how their social location has been influenced by race until a family member chooses a partner of another race. However, the inequities of the racial arrangements of U.S. society affect all families, just as do class arrangements and the inequities of gender. The impact of racism, white supremacy, anti-Semitism, sexism, ageism, class hierarchies, and homophobia on families in the U.S. cannot be minimized and must be part of our assessment of all families (McGoldrick & Garcia Preto, 2005; McGoldrick & Hardy, 2019). The same goes for socio-economic factors.

The Informal Kinship Network

The information net extends beyond the biological and legal structure of the family to encompass common law and cohabiting relationships, miscarriages, abortions, stillbirths, foster and adopted children, and anyone else in the informal network of the family who is an important support. Information about everyone who has been important to the functioning of the family— friends, godparents, teachers, neighbors, parents of friends, clergy, caretakers, doctors, and so forth— is included on the genogram. Key support figures can be important emotional or spiritual resources for therapy, although it is obviously not possible to include all such information. In exploring such outside supports, the clinician might ask:

- To whom could you turn if you need financial, emotional, physical, and spiritual help?
- What roles have outsiders played in your family? Who outside the family has been important in your life?
- What is your relationship to your community?
- Did you ever have a nanny or caretaker or babysitter to whom you felt attached? What became of her or him?
- Has anyone else ever lived with your family? When? Where are they now?
- What has been your family's experience with doctors and other helping professionals or agencies?

For particular clients certain additional questions are appropriate. For example, the following questions would be important in working with LGBTQI clients (see Nealy, 2017; Burke & Faber, 1997; Laird, 1996a, 1996b; Scrivner & Eldridge, 1995; Shernoff, 1984; Slater, 1995).

- When did you first become aware of your sexual orientation as you now understand it?
- Who was the first person you told about your sexual orientation?
- To whom on your genogram are you "out"?
- To whom would you most like to come out?
- Who would be especially easy or difficult to come out to?

Tracking Family Process

Tracking shifts that occurred around births, deaths, and other transitions can lead the clinician to hypotheses about the family's adaptive style. Particularly critical are untimely or traumatic deaths and the deaths of pivotal family members. We look for specific patterns of adaptation or rigidification following such transitions. Assessment of past adaptive patterns, particularly after losses and other critical transitions, may be crucial in helping a family in the current crisis. A family's relationship to their past may provide important clues about family rules, expectations, patterns of organization, strengths, resources, and sources of resilience (Walsh, 2016).

The history of key problems is also important to investigate in detail with a genogram, focusing on how family patterns have changed at different periods—before the problem began, at the time of the problem's onset, at the time of first seeking help, and at present. Specific genograms can be done for each of these time periods. Computerized genograms that can be generated for all nodal points in time will be enormously helpful in this process, making it easier to show details for the key times of stress or symptom development.

Asking how family members see the future of the problem can also be informative. Viewing the family in historical perspective involves linking past, present, and future, and noting the family's flexibility in adapting to changes.

Questions could include:

- What would happen if the problem went away? How would your family be different?
- What do you foresee happening in your family if the problem continues? What is the worst thing that might happen?
- What changes do family members imagine are possible in the future?

Difficult Questions About Individual Functioning

As with all other areas of genogram assessment, inquiring about functioning requires clinical sensitivity, judgment, and tact, as it can easily touch a nerve in the family. To assess a family, we seek to understand the functioning, relationships, and roles of each family member. People may function well in some areas (e.g. school or work) but not in others (e.g. intimacy). They may vary greatly in their ability to manage stress. One family member with a severe illness may show remarkable adaptive strengths, while another may show fragility when under what appears to be minimal stress.

Assessing dysfunction, in particular around addiction, may be especially difficult, not only because of the patient's likely defensive response, but because other family members are so often intimidated and fearful of exposing problems. Family members should be warned that questions may be difficult and that they should let the interviewer know if there is an issue they would rather not discuss. That in itself may be problematic because clients may be uncomfortable articulating their discomfort with a particular question or line of questioning. The clinician will need to judge the degree of persistence to use if the family resists questions that may be essential to dealing with the presenting problem. Often it takes careful questioning and eliciting other family members' views to reveal the true level of a person's functioning, which is one reason it can be very helpful to involve multiple members in an assessment.

At the same time it may be necessary to interview family members separately around sensitive issues that arouse embarrassment or shame, although this may also increase resistance, if the most powerful person in the family fears being excluded from any part of the conversation. The clinician needs to be very careful when asking questions that could put a family member in danger if answered honestly, such as when physical abuse is suspected. Clinicians must always try to ensure that their questions do not put a client in jeopardy. A wife should never be asked about her husband's possible abusive behavior in his presence. The question assumes she is able to respond freely, which would not be the case if abuse had occurred, and her safety could be at risk if she answered the question in the husband's presence. Physical abuse can only be addressed jointly when there appears no risk of repercussions.

The following is a list of questions on individual functioning that require particular clinical sensitivity.

Serious Problems

- Has anyone in the family had a serious medical or psychological problem? Been depressed? Had anxieties or fears? Lost control? Has there ever been any verbal, physical, or sexual abuse?
- Has there been any child neglect?
- Is there any other serious problem that worries you? Have you ever sought help for it? If so, when? What happened? What is the status of that problem now?

Work

- Have there been any recent job problems, changes, or conflicts on the job? Unemployment? Under-employment? Do you like your job? Who else works in your family? Do they like their work?

Drugs and Alcohol

- Do any family members routinely use medication? What kind and for what?
- Who prescribed it? What is the family's relationship with any physician seen by family members?
- Do you think any members drink too much alcohol or have a drug problem? Has anyone else ever thought so? What drugs? When? What has the family attempted to do about it?
- How does the person's behavior change under the influence of alcohol or drugs? How does the behavior of others change when a member is drug involved?
- Has anyone ever been stopped for an alcohol or drug related legal offense (DWI)?

Trouble with the Law

- Have any family members ever been arrested? For what? When? What was the result? What is that person's legal status now?
- Has anyone ever lost his or her driver's license?

Physical or Sexual Abuse

- Have you ever felt intimidated in your family? Have you or others ever been hit? Has anyone in your family ever been threatened with being hit? Have you ever threatened anyone else in your family or hit them? Have you ever felt threatened in any other way within your family?
- Have you or any other family member ever been sexually molested or touched inappropriately by a member of your family or someone outside your family? By whom?

Given that physical battering has been called the number one health problem for women in the United States (McGoldrick & Ross, 2016), it is critical for clinicians to take extreme care when inquiring about power relationships in families. Couple relationships have many dimensions, all of which can involve abuse (economic, emotional, physical and psychological power, boundaries around the couple in relation to all other connections (work, friends, religion, family of origin, children, etc.), sexuality, chores, leisure activities, and childcare.

The complexity of these dimensions gives us a clue as to how carefully and thoroughly clinicians must proceed with their inquiries, since abuse is likely to be denied or minimized. We have found that in addition to the genogram, the Power Pyramid (**Figure 3.1**) is an extremely useful tool for assessing both violence and psychological abuse in the multiple domains of couple and family relationships. The pyramid can be given to partners in individual meetings to help them consider the power dimensions of their relationship. We suggest the clinician speak to the spouses separately about questions such as:

- Who generally makes the decisions?
- Who manages the money?
- How are conflicts resolved?
- What is each partner's attitude toward violence or intimidation in marriage?

Setting Priorities for Organizing Genogram Information

One of the most difficult aspects of genogram assessment remains setting priorities for the inclusion of family information. Clinicians cannot follow every lead the genogram interview offers. Awareness of basic genogram patterns can help the clinician set such priorities. As a rule of thumb, genogram information is scanned for the following patterns over the generations:

- **Repetitive Symptom Patterns.**
- **Over- and Under-Functioning.**
- **Repetitive Relationship Dysfunction** (Triangles, Coalitions, Conflicts, Cutoffs).
- **Coincidences of Dates**: e.g., the death of one family member or anniversary of this death occurring at the same time as symptom onset in another, or the age at symptom onset coinciding with the age of problem development in another family member.
- **The Impact of "Untimely" Life Cycle Transitions**: particularly changes in functioning and relationships that correspond with critical

Figure 3.1:   Power and Control Pyramid

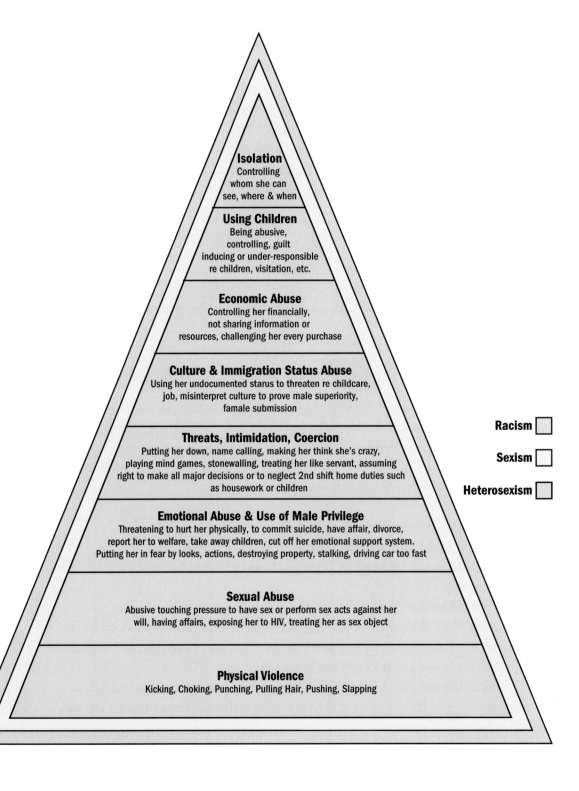

Isolation
Controlling whom she can see, where & when

Using Children
Being abusive, controlling, guilt inducing or under-responsible re children, visitation, etc.

Economic Abuse
Controlling her financially, not sharing information or resources, challenging her every purchase

Culture & Immigration Status Abuse
Using her undocumented starus to threaten re childcare, job, misinterpret culture to prove male superiority, famale submission

Threats, Intimidation, Coercion
Putting her down, name calling, making her think she's crazy, playing mind games, stonewalling, treating her like servant, assuming right to make all major decisions or to neglect 2nd shift home duties such as housework or children

Emotional Abuse & Use of Male Privilege
Threatening to hurt her physically, to commit suicide, have affair, divorce, report her to welfare, take away children, cut off her emotional support system. Putting her in fear by looks, actions, destroying property, stalking, driving car too fast

Sexual Abuse
Abusive touching pressure to have sex or perform sex acts against her will, having affairs, exposing her to HIV, treating her as sex object

Physical Violence
Kicking, Choking, Punching, Pulling Hair, Pushing, Slapping

Racism ☐
Sexism ☐
Heterosexism ☐

family life events and untimely life cycle transitions, e.g., births, marriages, or deaths that occur "off schedule."

- **Missing Information:** Awareness of possible patterns makes the clinician more sensitive to what is missing. Missing information about important family members or events and discrepancies in the information offered may reflect charged emotional issues in the family. Adult men and women may also know more about their mother's side of their families of origin than their father's side. Women may know more about their husband's family of origin than the husband does, reflecting society's expectations that women be more relationship-focused and men be more task-oriented.

Essentials of a Brief Genogram Interview

When conducting a brief genogram interview, clinicians will want to focus on the most essential information, such as age, occupation/education level, religion, ethnic background, migration date, and current health status of each family member. In addition, the clinician will want to ask questions such as:

- Who outside of your immediate family is an important resource to you?
- Who is stressful to you?
- Who referred you to us?
- What other professionals have been involved in helping your family?

Wright and Leahey (1999) recommend that the clinician think of at least three key questions to ask all family members routinely, depending on their clinical context. These questions might include:

- What are family members' most pressing concerns?
- What information might family members want shared with or kept from other family members?
- Who has been the greatest source of love or inspiration to family members?
- What are the greatest challenges family members feel they are facing?
- What question would the family members most want answered by the clinician?

They also routinely recommend that the clinician commend the family on at least two strengths or resources they have observed during even a brief interview. This is an extremely good idea, especially emphasizing patterns rather than one-time occurrences. Such commendations could include:

- Your family seems to have had a great deal of courage to face the problems you describe, in light of the resistance of others in your family to acknowledge these difficulties.
- You seem to be a family of survivors after all the problems you have struggled with: sexual abuse, violence, addiction, and mental illness.
- You seem very caring, in spite of the anger and despair that you have often struggled with.

Before concluding the interview, it is also important to debrief clients in case there are issues that have been raised about which they are distressed or which they feel need further clarification. It is also essential to note sources of resilience and hope so they are not left with only a problem saturated view of the discussion.

It is also important for the interviewer to validate the individual or family for sharing their story. We generally do this by offering clients a copy of the genogram we have created and asking them to review it for accuracy. This in itself may be a major intervention, because it enables clients to review the patterns in their family and gives them control over correcting the picture created. They may begin to see the systemic dimensions of their family once they see the "facts" depicted graphically.

In any case, it is the goal of any genogram interview to leave clients feeling understood and more connected to their immediate and broader social context than they were before. We always hope that people will recognize connections between their own distress and their relationships—present and past—and that these connections will promote a sense of hope for finding future solutions to their distress.

4

Tracking Family Patterns with Genograms

The power and richness of genograms lies in the patterns we can see, once we can look at a person or family through time and context. This chapter, the longest in this book, will try to convey some of the key patterns we track on genograms to better understand our clients' lives. We will look at the pile up of stressors, untimely and traumatic loss, resilience, and the power of secrets, as well as larger contextual factors of relationship cutoff, functioning and dysfunction, and the balance of caretaking needs and resources in a family.

Tracking Balance in the Family Structure, Roles & Functioning

Tracking roles, functioning, resources, and patterns of balance and imbalance in the family structure on a genogram speaks to the functional whole of a family system. Such tracking allows the clinician to develop hypotheses about how the family is adapting to stress. Family systems are not homogeneous. Contrasting characteristics are usually present in the same family. In well-functioning families, such characteristics tend to balance one another. Looking for contrasts and characteristics that "stick out," the clinician seeks to learn: How do these contrasts and idiosyncrasies fit into the total functional whole? What balances have been achieved and what stresses are present in the system due to a lack of balance?

Sometimes differences in family structure can be seen over a number of generations. There may be a contrast in the family structure for the two spouses, creating a graphically lopsided genogram. One spouse comes from a large family, with countless aunts and uncles, while the other is an only child of two only children. This could lead to both balance and imbalance. On the one hand, each spouse may be attracted to the experience of the other. One likes the privacy of a small family and the other the diversity of a large family. Or, the imbalance between the large number of relatives on one side and the paucity on the other may create problems.

One spouse may be used to playing to a crowd and engaging in multiple relationships, while the other seeks more exclusive, private relationships. Another issue involving structural balance occurs when one spouse comes from a family where divorce and remarriage are common and the other comes from a long line of intact couples. When a clinician sees this kind of structural contrast on the genogram, they will want to explore the spouses' different expectations about marriage.

In well-functioning families, members may take a variety of roles: caretaker, dependent, provider, spokesperson, comic relief, organizer, and so on. Sometimes it will be evident from the genogram that there are too many people in one particular role. An only child raised by a single parent, grandparents, aunts, and uncles might have difficulty functioning outside the context of "parental" approval. The opposite situation may occur when a single family member is in the position of caring for an inordinate number of family members, as happened to Ted Kennedy in 1969, at age 37. He was the youngest of the 9 Kennedy children, but became the only surviving male (**Figure 4.1: Kennedy Family, 1969**). First came the secretly arranged lobotomy of the oldest sister, Rosemary, in 1941. Then the death in World War II of the oldest brother, Joe, followed 4 years later by death of the oldest daughter, Kathleen, on a dangerous plane ride with her lover. Then in 1963 the whole nation experienced the tragic death of John Kennedy, the oldest surviving brother, who left two small children fatherless. Five years later came the national tragedy of the murder of the third brother, Bobby, who left 11 young children, the youngest of whom, Rory, hadn't even been born yet.

Since Ted was the sole surviving male member of his generation, he had a special role in the two fatherless households, as well as responsibility for his three children who had problems of their own. A clinician seeing such a family situation would want to explore what balance could be worked out and what other resources could be brought in to help take care of the many children involved. (This situation would have been even more difficult if it had occurred in a family without the Kennedy's abundant financial resources.)

Family members operate with different styles and at different levels of functioning. When patterns are balanced, the functioning of different family members fit together. We scan the genogram for contrasts and idiosyncrasies in functioning, which may help to explain how the system functions as a whole.

Any newly formed family needs to fit together different styles and ways of relating to the world. The result may be more or less complementary and growth-enhancing for the offspring. Certain imbalances in families may lead to family dysfunction. For example, we often see a complementary pattern of an alcohol or drug abusing partner married to a spouse who is an over-functioner (Bepko & Krestan, 1985; Steinglass, Bennett, Wolin, & Reiss, 1987). The non-abusing

Figure 4.1:   Kennedy Family, 1969

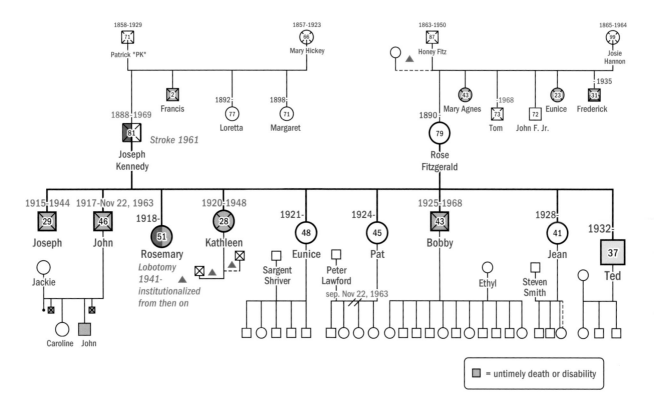

spouse is pressed to become over-responsible, to balance the under-responsible substance abusing partner. The willingness of one partner to be a caretaker and of the other to be taken care of may stabilize the relationship for a while. Since addictive behavior, by its nature, leads to and/or is a consequence of under-responsibility, the other partner may indeed take up the slack; but when that doesn't happen, children can be left in a vulnerable situation, often ending up having to take on adult roles prematurely. At times, the whole family may become organized in a complementary way around the dysfunction of one member.

Sometimes, when there is dysfunction in one area, the family will find ways to compensate for the difficulties. This seems to have been the case with the family of Alexander Graham Bell, the inventor of the telephone (**Figure 4.2: Alexander Graham Bell Family: Compensatory Functioning**). Both Bell's mother and his wife were almost totally deaf. Three generations of males in the family—Bell himself, his father and uncle, and his grandfather—all specialized in speech projection and elocution. Bell's grandfather wrote a classic text on phonetic speech, and both Bell's father and his uncle devoted themselves to teaching their father's methods. The family was a highly inventive one. When Alexander was a young teenager, his father suggested that he and his brother develop a talking machine. The instrument they developed replicated the mechanics of speech so well that it annoyed a neighbor, who thought he heard a baby crying. Some members specialized in speech and hearing, compensating for those who spoke with difficulty because they could not hear at all.

Determining whether there is balance in a system is essential when analyzing any family's patterns of functioning. Do extreme contrasts between family mem-

Figure 4.2: **Alexander Graham Bell Family: Compensatory Functioning**

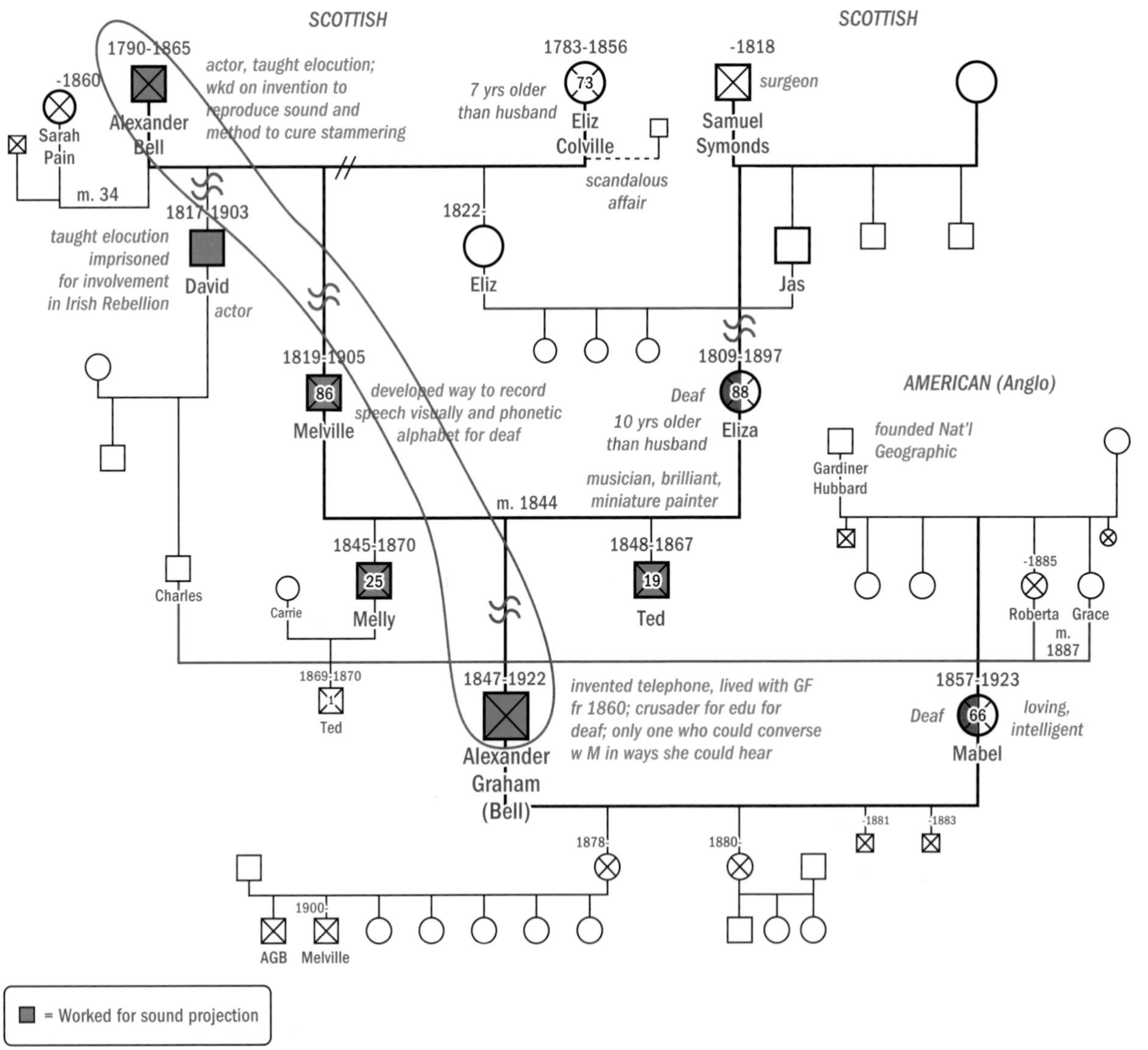

bers maintain the stability of the system, or are they pushing the family toward a different equilibrium? At times a system breaks down, not because of the dysfunction of one or two members, but because of the burnout of caretakers who previously balanced the system. In the case of chronic illness, family members are frequently able to mobilize themselves for support of the dysfunctional person in the short term, but over the long term they may not be able to maintain such behavior.

In other situations, outstanding functioning in one generation may be followed by remarkable failure in the next. This may be particularly true of successful families, where children may rebel against pressure to live up to the reputation of their parents. This is particularly likely with identical namesake "Juniors" and "III's." People may also come to believe that they are almost fated by family circumstance for the path they take in life.

Specific patterns of functioning may also be repeated across the generations. For example, a quick glance at the genogram of Carl Jung (**Figure 4.3: Jung Family: Patterns of Functioning over the Generations**) shows a preponderance of ministers, including Jung's father, maternal grandfather, one great-grandfather, three maternal grand uncles, all eight of his maternal uncles, and his paternal grandfather's brother-in-law, who was a famous theologian.

Next we can see that Jung's decision to become a physician was following his paternal grandfather (for whom he was named), one paternal uncle, his paternal great-grandfather and his third great-grandfather, all of whom were physicians.

Furthermore, we know that Jung was attracted to alchemy and the supernatural from his youth. In this, he was again following a pattern of many other family members who believed in the supernatural, including his mother, both maternal grandparents, and at least two of his grandfather's siblings. His maternal cousin, Helena Preiswerk, held séances as a medium in which Jung and many other members of his family participated.

Thus, it is perhaps not surprising that Jung became a physician with a profound interest in religion and in the supernatural. It fit with the predominant patterns of functioning in his family. One might be more surprised if he had ignored medicine, religion, and the supernatural, given the family patterns of functioning on his genogram. To this we might add that Jung's father served as chaplain of the mental hospital of Basel University for many years, just as Jung worked as a leading psychiatrist at one of Switzerland's most well known mental hospitals, the Burgholzi, for many years.

There was also a strong strand of psychosis, depression, and other psychological problems in the Jung family, including his mother, paternal great-grandmother, and a grand aunt and uncle. He himself had fears of inheriting the mental illness of his

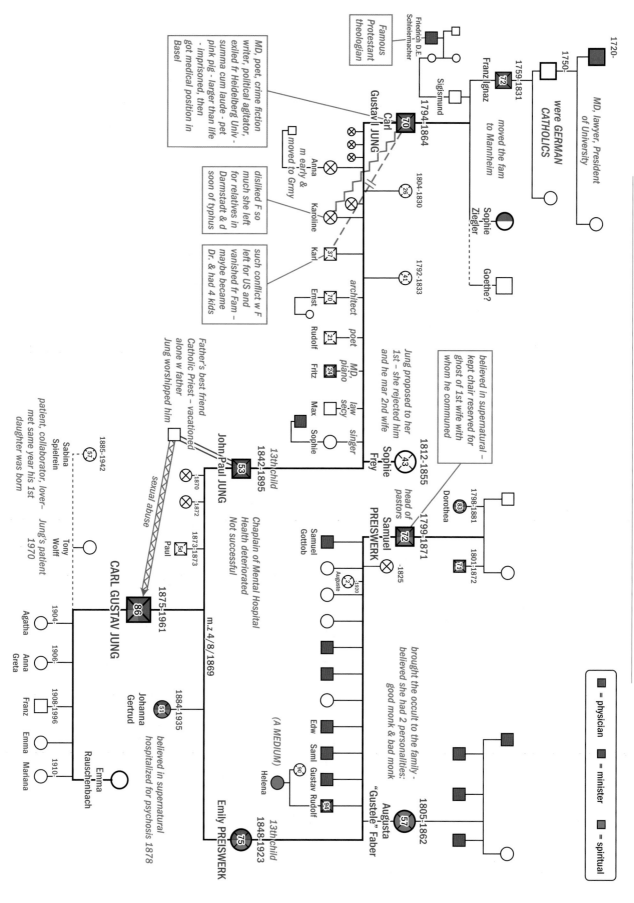

Figure 4.3: Jung Family: Patterns of Functioning over the Generations

mother and paternal great-grandmother, Sophie, and he did indeed suffer a break-down in 1913. He was also sexually abused by his father's closest friend, a priest, with whom the father used to go alone on vacation. While it is impossible to map out all the complexities of such functioning and career patterns, they are important and it can be worth making a special legend as we did here to help keep track. (We will be discussing the Jung family again in Chapter 6 when we explore family sibling patterns.)

Tracking Relational Patterns and Triangles on Genograms

The complexity of family relationships is infinite. In addition, of course, relationships change over time. In spite of such complexity, the genogram can often help us notice relational patterns that are worth further exploration. The smallest human system is, of course, a two-person system. The first and easiest relationships to analyze on a genogram are dyadic relationships. While the standard relationship lines depicting relationships on a genogram are necessarily oversimplified (because human relationships are incredibly complex and ever changing), stuck relationships typically fall into patterns of conflict and emotional cutoff at one end and intense closeness and fusion at the other. For this reason, the simplified relationship lines on a genogram can often help us assess functional and dysfunctional relationships and steer us toward a basic overview of the triangles we need to assess. We begin to learn about triangles by assessing how these dyadic patterns often form into three-person relationships, where two are joined in relation to the third, typically two in an over-close relationship and the other in a distant or conflictual relationship. While triangles, like many other complexities, are not always easy to show on a genogram, genograms are, paradoxically, one of the best ways to discover the typical triangles in a family and clarify triangular patterns that may need close attention. Understanding triangular patterns where two family members join against a third is essential in planning clinical interventions. "Detriangling" is an important clinical process through which family members are coached to free themselves from rigid triangular patterns. (For more in depth clinical discussion of triangles, see Chapter 5 and *The Genogram Casebook*, Chapter 6 on Triangles and Detriangling, and the video from psychotherapy.net "Triangles & Family Therapy: Strategies & Solutions").

If, for example, we see that in each generation the sons have conflictual relationships with their fathers and close relationships with their mothers, while daughters have conflictual relationships with their mothers and close relationships with their fathers, it may help to think how these patterns may really reflect triangles. If we look at the couple relationships, we might see that they too are distant or conflictual. The key point in genogram analysis is to notice how relationships are intertwined. If the closeness of mother and son relates to the distance between father and son and to the couple problems, which intersect with parent-child alliances, we can begin to notice the complementary pattern of marital distance, with intergenerational coalitions and conflicts, that are all part of a pattern of triangles. Obviously, a likely prediction would be that the son and daughter in the third generation, who are caught in cross-generational alliances and conflicts with their parents and with each other, may repeat the pattern of distant marriages and alliances and conflicts with their own children, unless they work to change it.

These fixed intergenerational patterns of triangling are well illustrated in the famous Jules Feiffer cartoon of the mother who says she hated her own mother and tried to do everything differently. Now her daughter has turned out (surprise, surprise!) just like her mother! In other words, systemically, dyadic relationships tend to be linked and to function together, which is one of the great advantages of studying genograms: to see how family members' relationships work together.

We can then begin to see sets of interlocking triangles. A father's closeness to his daughter may be a function of his distance from his wife, and may play a role in the mother's conflict with her daughter. The same could be hypothesized for any threesome in this system: the functioning of any two tends to be bound up with the other key relationships in predictable ways. The subject of triangles is one of the most important in systems theory (Bowen, 1974, 1975, 1978; Caplow, 1968; Fogarty, 1973, 1974; Guerin et al., 1996; Kerr & Bowen, 1988; McGoldrick, 2016).

While it would be impossible in this short book to explain all the complexities of systemic thinking that underlie the interpretation of relational patterns on genograms, looking at genogram patterns for triangles is an essential aspect of any family assessment.

Triangles tend to reduce tension in the initial dyad. Two family members may join in "helping" a third, who is viewed as needy or as the "victim." Or they may gang up against the third, who is viewed as the "villain" or scapegoat. It is the collusion of the two in relation to the third that is the defining characteristic of a triangle (Bowen, 1978). The behavior of any one member of a triangle is a function of the behavior of the other two.

And, as we are indicating, each triangle tends to be part of a larger systemic pattern of interlocking triangles as well. Thus, a child's tantrum with an overburdened mother is not only a function of the relationship between mother and child, but most likely also of the relationship between the mother and father, or between those two and an over-involved paternal grandmother, or a precocious older sibling, to mention just a few of the possibilities. In Bowen's conceptual framework, healthy development involves differentiation or maturity, which refers to a person establishing independent functioning in each relationship and not automatically falling into a pattern of relating to one person based on that person's relationship with a third person. Differentiation means reaching the point of relating on an individualized basis with each person rather than on the basis of the relationship that person has to someone else. Thus, a daughter would be able to have a close relationship with her mother, even if her father, to whom she is also close, is in conflict with the mother.

Tracking Families Through the Life Cycle and Critical Life Events

Families progress through transitions, or nodal points in their development, including, most likely: leaving home, forming a couple, the birth of children, child-rearing, adolescent child-rearing, launching, retirement, health, illness, and death. At each nodal point in the life cycle the family must reorganize itself in order to move on successfully to the next phase. Life cycle transitions can be very difficult for families that are inflexible or that are experiencing an overload of stresses. Regardless of the presenting problem, clinicians always need to assess whether the presenting problem reflects difficulties the family is having handling life cycle transitions. For example, at the point of forming a new couple, there are basic changes required not just by the couple but by all family members in the system in order to successfully integrate the new family members. The same is true when couples begin to have children. Space needs to be made to integrate the new person and family boundaries must shift. As another example, when children are small, parents can control them physically because of their size, but once they reach adolescence, physical control is no longer possible and families must change the very basic way they relate, transitioning from physical control to a different kind of psychological negotiation to help children continue their evolution to adulthood.

Timing of Life Cycle Transitions

The ages and dates on the genogram suggest what life cycle transitions the family is going through and whether life cycle events are occurring within normative expectations. If a couple is struggling in their dealings with in-laws, they may not be addressing the transitions of couplehood within the larger system. If they are struggling to maintain physical control of a teenager, they may not be making the transition to being a family with adolescents. There are also normative expectations for the timing of each phase of the family life cycle, such as the likely ages of family members at each transition point. While these norms and patterns are ever-changing and must not be regarded as fixed, the clinician must still track the family's experience with negotiating life cycle transitions.

We scan the genogram for family members whose ages differ greatly from the norm for their life cycle phase. The dates of birth, death, leaving home, marriage, separation, and divorce are all helpful in this regard. For example, if none of the children in a family left home as teenagers or married for the first time until their 40's, we would explore whether they have problems with leaving home or forming intimate relationships. One might ask a couple in which the husband is 27 and the wife 47 how they happened to get together and how this pairing might fit with their families of origin's patterns and in their community. A woman who has her first child at 43, a man who becomes a father at age 70, or a family in which three of the sons die before middle age, all suggest systems where deviations from the normative life cycle pattern deserve further exploration.

In all cultures, depending also on the time in history, there are generally preferable life cycle times for couples to marry. In American society, those who marry before the age of 20 or after the age of 35 tend to be at greater risk for divorce, although the normative time frame for first marriage has become dramatically later in recent years. Couples are increasingly marrying in their late twenties or even their mid-thirties. The possibility of preserving sperm and eggs is expanding the life cycle options for childbirth as well.

The time between meeting, engagement, and marriage, and between separation, divorce, and remarriage is also relevant. A short interval between life events generally does not allow time for family members to deal with the emotional shifts involved (McGoldrick & Carter, 2016). A very quick remarriage would suggest unresolved emotional issues and at least the possibility of an affair, trying to put a previous marriage behind, or seeking to stabilize the family without perhaps taking account of all the participants. One would wonder how family members, particularly the children, are adjusting to such rapid changes. If a parent has never discussed the transition with the children involved, or taken account of the time it takes for children to make such transitions, it is most likely s/he is attempting to short circuit the transition process.

Tracking these life cycle events gives the clinician a sense of the historical evolution of the family and of the effect of the family history on each individual.

• **Birth:** How did other family members react when a particular family member was born? Who attended the christening ceremony or bris? Who was named after whom and who "should have been"? Were there other family stresses around the time of the pregnancy or the birth?

- **Death:** How did the family react when a particular family member died? Who took it the hardest? The easiest? Who attended the funeral? Who wasn't there who "should have been"? Were there conflicts or cutoffs or other relationship changes over the will? Were there sudden or traumatic losses for which the family was not prepared? Were they able to access resources when needed? Was there a pileup of stressors around a death? (See also McGoldrick & Walsh, 2004; McGoldrick 2004a, 2004b; McGoldrick & Walsh, 2016).
- **Launching:** Were there particular struggles or conflicts around the time that family members left home? Did some family members not leave home in young adulthood and if so, how was that understood? Was there dysfunction or disability that impeded launching? Was there a need for caretaking of another family member? Was the pattern different for sons than for daughters?
- **Forming Close Relationships Through the Life Cycle:** Were family members able to develop close friendships from childhood on? Did they maintain close friends through adulthood and into their later life (Arora & Baima, 2016; Connidis & Barnett, 2018)? Did they have close working relationships? Did they belong to social groups that supported connections or with whom there were conflicts? Mentor relationships? Were there significant cutoffs from former friends? If so, when?
- **Work, Career Changes, Vocations:** We need to inquire about people's work, activities, hobbies and interests. Unemployment, changes in career, and military service and its impact may all be difficult to track, but can be important factors in a family's history.
- **Military Service:** Who served, and under what circumstances? Did the family move for military service? Were those who served able to talk about their military experiences? Did family members experience PTSD related to military service? Were they able to deal with the aftermath openly?
- **Forming Couple Relationships:** Did the family expand to include new members who partnered with those already part of the family? Or were there conflicts or cutoffs around the expansion of the family to include new members?
- **Caretaking:** Was there enough support for those who needed caretaking, both children and aging or disabled family members? Were there conflicts or over- or under-responsibility around caretaking of family members? Were there particular times of trauma and/or caretaking need? How did the family respond in those periods?
- **Moves and Migration:** When and why did the family migrate to this country or move from one place to another? How did they cope with the multiple challenges and losses created by moves or migration? How many generations of the family have lived in the U.S.? What was the context into which

they came and how did they manage the adaptation to new circumstances? How did they survive? Which members of the immigrant generation learned the language? How did language ability affect family relationships? What problems did family members have with their sense of belonging in different communities?

   • **Changes in Family Relationships:** Were there moments of cutoff for any significant relationship? If so, did it correspond to other stressors on the family? Were there particular periods when family came together or separated and did those relationship changes relate to other nodal events in the family?

Tracking Couples on Genograms: The Joining of Families

While we will be talking about couple relationships throughout this book (and Chapter 7 is devoted specifically to couples), there is good reason to begin the exploration of genogram patterns at this life cycle phase, because the joining of families when couples form is a time of many pattern readjustments that families have long taken for granted.

   Indeed, one of our musically talented students, Paula Schorr, wrote a song that became our Institute's theme song: *Let Me Do Your Genogram, Before I Commit to You!* The song conveyed the importance of each partner understanding the patterns on his or her own genogram and the partner's genogram, and thus having respect for the complexity of the joining of the two families' genograms. A genogram of the time of marriage or remarriage shows the coming together of two separate families, indicating where each spouse is in his or her own individual and family life cycle. In creating their new family, partners must find ways to negotiate issues pertaining to gender, culture, religious and socio-economic background, sibling constellation, and each family's history of untimely or traumatic loss. Other potential family issues include how to spend time as a couple, deal with money, have sex, regulate work/home boundaries, manage housekeeping, negotiate time, conflicts, and relationships with extended family, and so forth. Coordinating will be even more complicated if partners come from very different cultural experiences or are at different points in their own life cycles (e.g. A divorced woman with young children marrying a never married, childless man or woman).

   The genogram gives clues about the characteristics and patterns of each family—sibling constellations, cultural, religious, and socioeconomic background, and the loss and trauma history. It also indicates the emotional relationship history of family members, and the functioning and connectedness of each spouse in his or her own family of origin. For more in-depth understanding of clinical interventions with couples using genograms, readers are referred to the chapter on "Couples: Marriage, Divorce and Remarriage" in *The Genogram Casebook* (2016); it offers many case illustrations for dealing with the couple issues one encounters in therapy. In this discussion, we mean to offer primarily an awareness of the patterns to look for.

- Age and life cycle phase of each partner
- Sibling Constellation compatibility
- Stresses around time of couple meeting or making the decision to marry
- Similarities or differences in: culture, religion, socio-economic status, gender roles
- History of traumatic or untimely loss
- Relationship patterns of distance and closeness, triangles, cutoffs, conflict, fusion, abuse, codependence, etc.
- Patterns of functioning and style for dealing with stress and conflict: avoidance, denial, confrontation, emotional expressiveness
- Values in dealing with money, leisure time, housekeeping, boundaries in relation to work, friends and extended family, and inclusion of children in adult activities
- Secrets and Taboos

Genogram Patterns to Track for the Early Parenting Years

We urge readers to track patterns on their genograms using the following issues as guidelines. The early parenting years are stressful due to the new tasks of administrating family life, childcare, and relationships with extended family, teachers, friends, and their children and the multiple tasks parents must learn at this point in the life cycle.

- Closeness of each parent and others to the child
- Gender of the child in relation to hopes and expectations

- Traumatic or untimely loss or other stresses around time of birth
- Naming: Who is child named for—impact of that person's legacy.
- Three-generational triangles with a grandparent, parent, and child
- Secrets
- Relationships with community: friends, teachers, healthcare resources, and other social connections for children

Tracking the Family with Young Children

A genogram of the early parenting years often reveals stressors that could make this phase difficult. It may reveal particular circumstances surrounding the birth of a child and how those circumstances may have contributed to a child's special position in that family. Finally, the genogram will show the typical mother-father-child triangles of this period.

We may inquire about particular topics at this phase of the life cycle.

- Sibling patterns
- Gender inequities for daughters and sons, between the husband and wife, or in other relationships
- Similarities and differences in child rearing styles: strict or laissez-faire; affectionate, collaborative, or with strong generational boundaries
- Traumatic or untimely loss or other stresses related to finances, time, childcare, parental time as couple, children's developmental or learning problems
- Triangles with children, and each of the parents; and three-generational triangles with a grandparent, parent, and child
- Boundaries between the couple and children; between family and extended family; or between family and outsiders—other children, other families
- Secrets

Genogram Patterns for The Middle Childrearing Years

The main childrearing years of any family are characterized by an overload of tasks as parents try to manage their children and support their family, with the added tasks of dealing with the needs of the older generation, who are likely to begin having their own vulnerabilities and possibly need extra support. Issues to address may include:

- Sibling constellation patterns: distance apart in age, gender, disability, illness, special talents
- Gender inequities: between daughters and sons, husbands and wives, and other relationships
- Concurrent trauma, loss, or other stresses related to finances, illness, job stresses, caretaking burdens, parental time as couple, child developmental or learning problems
- Child rearing styles: strict or laissez-faire; affectionate, collaborative, or strong generational boundaries
- Triangles with children and parents and/or in-laws, three-generational triangles with grandparents
- Potential shifts in power as the older generation begins to age and may need extra support, which can create caretaking stress for the middle generation, sometimes referred to as the "sandwich generation" between needy grandparents and needy children.
- Boundaries between couples and children; between family and extended family; between family and outsiders—other children, teachers, other families
- Secrets

Families at Midlife: Adolescence, Launching, Young Adulthood, Joining as New Couples, and Moving On

Once children reach adolescence, the task is to prepare the family for a qualitative change in the relationships between generations, as the children are no longer so dependent on their parents. In the past, the launching phase (when children begin to leave home to be on their own) usually blended into marriage, since children often did not leave home until they married; but, in the 21st century in the U.S., this period of the life cycle is becoming prolonged, and we are talking about a whole extra phase of "adultolescence," as many young adults may not finish their education and become able to support themselves until they are in their 30s. Issues to discuss may include:

- Parent/child distance, adolescents/young adults revising their closeness to their parents, and parents' reactions to the distance.
- Gender inequities: different options and trajectories for daughters than for sons in terms of education, career, and couple relationships.
- Couples may need to renegotiate their own relationship and that with other friends and family as their children begin to launch
- Stresses related to finances and jobs can increase parental problems
- System can be overloaded when caretaking burdens of the older generation and when children's developmental problems interfere with their ability to launch
- Trauma of untimely losses and other stresses

The Later Chapters of the Life Cycle: Growth, Resiliency, Retrospection, Caretaking, Loss, Grief, and Legacies

The later phases of life are becoming the longest of the life cycle as we are having fewer children and living much longer than previously. Indeed, for the current generation, more than half of the healthy adult life cycle is spent not raising one's children. It is essential to track how family members manage this long stage of life. How active are family members physically, psychologically, intellectually, and spiritually and how emotionally connected do they stay with each other? What happens to couple relationships when child rearing is not a major focus? In the later years, how well do family members come to terms with death while focusing on the other aspects of life for themselves and for others? How well do they manage, when necessary, their increasing dependence while remaining as active as possible? How have partners managed the loss of a spouse and the need to create a new life? How have older adults in the family been at affirming and working out their emotional, spiritual and financial legacy so that it doesn't leave turmoil and cutoffs for the next generation and beyond? Issues to discuss may include:

- Parents/adult children revising and recalibrating their relationships in relation to caretaking needs of the older generation, reformulating relationships as adult children expand their families with partners, grandchildren, and in-laws
- Gender inequities: different options and trajectories for men and women in terms of caretaking responsibilities and financial resources
- Couples need to renegotiate their relationship as their children move on and they move toward retirement and have increased health needs
- Stresses related to changing finances at retirement and with healthcare costs.
- System overload with caretaking burdens for the older generation
- Trauma of illness, loss, death, and other stresses of aging

Tracking Families in Their Ability to Live Beyond Loss

As we said in Chapter 2, loss is the most difficult emotional experience we humans must deal with, and if you track only one pattern on a genogram, let it be loss (Norman Paul, personal communication, 1988; McGoldrick & Walsh, 2004) Exploring how the family has dealt with losses in the past is a key factor in how they are likely to deal with any trauma in the future. Tracking loss involves noting the specific factors relating to its time in the family's life cycle, which may place a family at greater risk for dysfunction. Factors to consider include:

- The timing of the loss in the three-generational life cycle
- The concurrence of multiple losses or of the loss with other life cycle changes such as births, marriages, and moves
- A history of traumatic loss and unresolved mourning
- The nature of the death
- The significance and function of the person in the family
- Whether the family was able to share the acknowledgment of the loss
- Whether the family was able to share the experience of the loss
- Whether the family was able to reorganize after the loss to recover from its disruptive impact
- Whether family members were able to reinvest in other relationships and life pursuits in the wake of the loss

Building Family Chronologies

A family chronology, that is, the timeline of important family events, is an essential tool to accompany any genogram, especially to track life cycle transitions, major traumas, and changes in relationships and functioning. Such a chronology is especially valuable for organizing demographic information for any individual or combination of family members you wish to follow.

It is also useful to make a genogram for particular nodal points, particularly around symptom onset, and to track major stress and illness in relation to concurrent events, or to events at the same point in the life cycle of other family members (Rolland, 2018; Barth, 1993; Huygen, 1982; Nerin, 1986, 1993; Richardson, 1987). Constructing a genogram for a particular key point in time can help clarify what was going on at that moment, who lived together, how old family members were, and what stresses they were experiencing, as we will show below for Erik Erikson and in Chapter 8 for Sigmund Freud. A chronology is also useful for tracking a particular family member's functioning, life transitions, and symptoms within the context of the family.

Assessing genogram patterns can also help clinicians understand how life events and changes in family functioning are interconnected. Since the genogram records many critical dates in the family's history, it is useful for the clinician to scan for coincidences of various life events and changes in family functioning. Often seemingly unconnected events that occur around the same time in a family's history are systemically related and have a profound impact on family functioning, even though family members may not even notice the connection (as can be seen below and throughout the examples in this book).

Tracking the Family of Erik Erikson: Secrets Over the Life Cycle

Taking a longitudinal focus on family patterns as people move through the life cycle helps us better understand their history. Let us follow some key life cycle points for Erik Erikson, whose work was itself focused on identity and life cycle development. Genograms can help people unpack layers of personal, familial, migratory, and cultural identity to better understand their history.

Erikson's mother, Karla, a Danish Jew, (**Figure 4.4: Erik Erikson's Genogram for 1902: The Year He Was Born**) was the fourth of six children and the only daughter in her family. Her mother died when she was 15 and her father died

Figure 4.4:   Erik Erikson's Genogram for 1902: The Year He Was Born

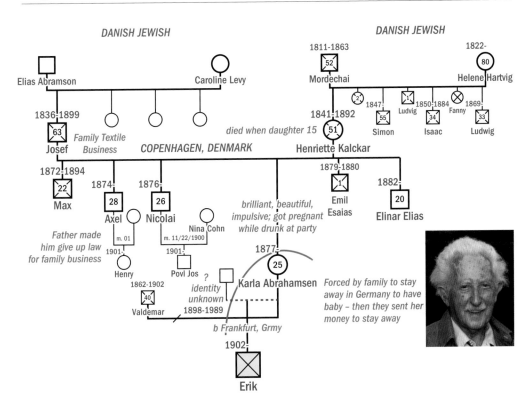

when she was 22. She had three older brothers, who were less than supportive, though the oldest died himself at age 22, two years after the mother. There were supposedly some aunts in the extended family who were watching over Karla, who became pregnant at age 25, possibly at an unsupervised party her brothers were having in the family home. She did not discover she was pregnant until she was on a trip to Germany, and was then told by her family not to return to Denmark, but to remain in Germany and have the baby there (Friedman, 1999). Thus, her son Erik began life as an immigrant in Germany, a place where he and his mother were completely isolated. The family then urged Karla to remain in Germany by herself with her baby. Her life as a parent thus began as a forced immigrant. Perhaps it is no wonder Erikson was preoccupied with the concept of identity all his life, growing up already extruded from family, and never having had the opportunity to feel secure in his own identity.

Exactly three years after Erikson's birthday, on June 15, 1905, his mother, Karla, married his German Jewish pediatrician, Theodor Homburger (**Figure**

Figure 4.5:   Erikson's Family, 1905: The Year of his Mother's Remarriage

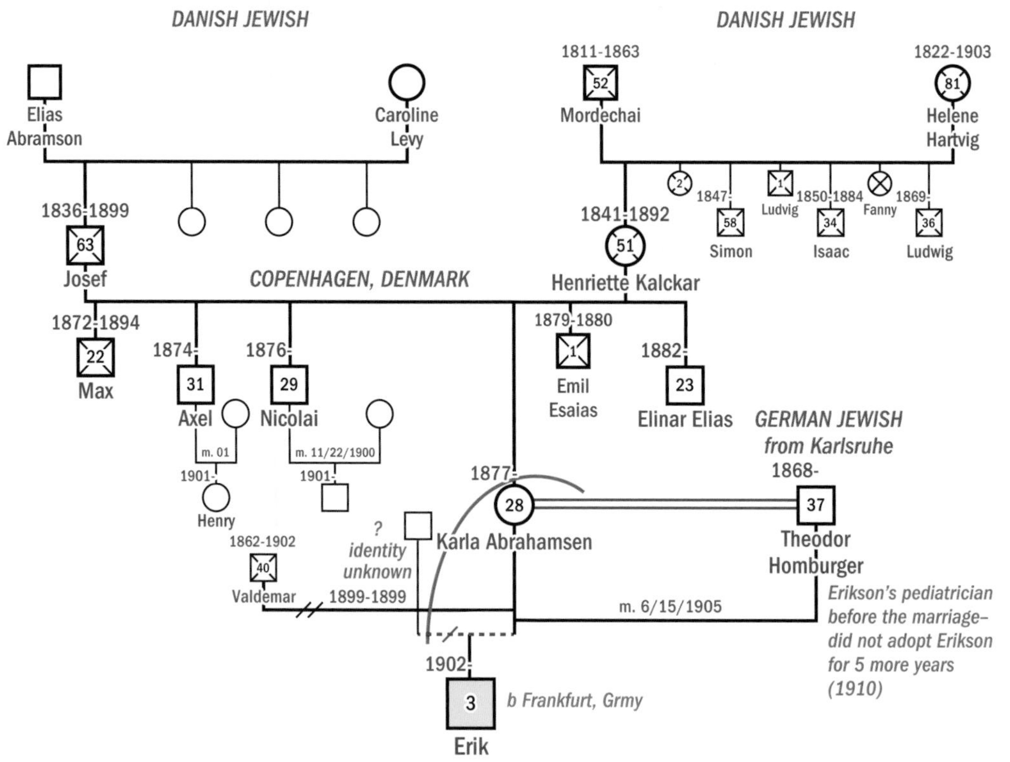

4.5: Erikson's Family, 1905: The Year of his Mother's Remarriage). This act took away even his birthday from him, making it also his mother's wedding day. Homburger apparently required Karla to tell Erik he was his biological father, though Erikson knew he was not. He later said, "(I) felt all along . . . doubt in my identity. . . all through my childhood years. . . I was quietly convinced that I came from a different background . . ." (Friedman, 1999, p. 33). Homburger's ambivalence about taking on a "father" relationship with Erikson is perhaps revealed in his having taken five years to complete the adoption papers to make Erik his son legally. Erikson's closest childhood friend, Peter Blos, said that, "Adoption was the great theme of Erikson's existence" (Friedman, 1999, p. 28). The issue was compounded by his mother acting as if Homburger was his real father, though Erikson knew perfectly well he was not, since he had been his childhood doctor! Erikson grew up to become a very tall, very blond man, making the charade that Homburger—a short, dark man—was his father even more unbelievable.

Erikson later created a woodcut (**Picture 4.1: Woodcut and Picture of Erik-**

Picture 4.1: Woodcut and Picture of Erikson at 3

son at 3) of his mother and her new husband on their honeymoon, on which he was taken along. It shows him miserable and alone, while the couple embraces in the background. Obviously, in his view, he had lost his beloved mother to her new husband and was not happy about it.

All his life Erikson sought to learn who his father was. His mother told him various stories but never the truth, and he continued all his life to be obsessed with this question. What he knew of his mother's family we do not really know, since she was extruded from living with or near them. Erikson's daughter later wrote about her father's search for his father:

> My father never knew . . . even who his father was. One of the saddest things about that, from my point of view, is that his mother refused throughout her life to tell him the identity of this all-important person. Her stated reason was that she had promised the man she married when my father was three that she would never divulge this information. But her explanation conveys a greater concern for someone else's wishes than for my father's aching need to know. (Erikson, 1999, pp 56–57).

It is perhaps not surprising that Erikson's theory of human development placed so much emphasis on autonomy and individuation rather than on relationships and connection. His mother was forced to manage on her own without the support of her family, just as she was becoming a parent. Then he had to accept losing her to her new husband, who came from a new country. He had to learn to manage for himself from early childhood, as the woodcut shows.

It is probably not surprising that Erikson continued to focus on autonomy, initiative, and industry as the stepchild in his remarried family, which included three half-sisters born over the next seven years (**Figure 4.6: Erikson Remarried Family Constellation, 1917**).

Erikson remained close to his mother, but did not become particularly close to his sisters, who were seven and ten years younger than he. (The sister closest in age to him died at age two). The family was required to speak German in the home, which left Erik with a lifelong feeling of regret that he had forgotten how to speak Danish.

As he grew up, he repeatedly questioned his mother about his paternity. When she finally acknowledged that Homburger wasn't his father, she told him he was

Figure 4.6:   Erikson's Remarried Family Constellation, 1917

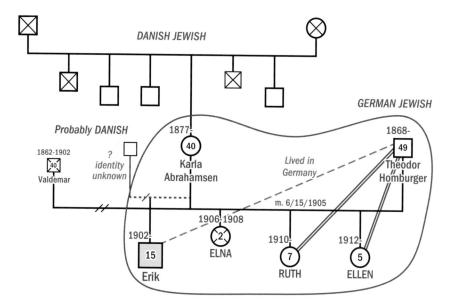

the son of her first husband, which couldn't possibly have been true, and he sensed that lie also. He talked constantly with his friend Peter Blos of the characteristics he thought his father might have. Throughout his life his mother gave him a variety of different stories, but never the truth. He said of the search, "if my father hadn't cared enough about me to want me . . . why should I look him up now" (Friedman, 1999, p. 39), but he could not stop wondering, even though he feared knowing the truth.

Erikson's widely accepted theory of human development appears to reflect some of the particularities and weaknesses of his own family and cultural situation that played out over his life cycle (McGoldrick, Garcia Preto, & Carter, 2016; Friedman, 1999). His model describes eight stages, each with a theme that contrasts healthy versus dysfunctional patterns:

Erikson's Eight Stages of Human Development

1. **Infancy**   **Trust vs. Mistrust**
2. **Early Childhood**   **Autonomy vs. Shame & Doubt**
3. **Play Age**   **Initiative vs. Guilt**
4. **School Age**   **Industry vs. Inferiority**
5. **Adolescence**   **Identity vs. Identity Diffusion (describes a sense of identity *apart from* one's family)**
6. **Young Adult**   **Intimacy vs. Isolation**
7. **Midlife**   **Generativity vs. Self-Absorption**
8. **Mature Age**   **Integrity vs. Despair**

Erikson's genogram may help us understand the limitations of this schema. He said the primary issue in the first two years of life was developing a trusting relationship with one's mother. His schema makes reference only to basic trust with one's mother, which, sadly, was all he had at that time of life himself. But in the first two years most children have a much more inclusive context for development, including their father and an array of other family members and caretakers who help them grow up, and they learn to trust many people beyond just their mother. Sadly, this was not the case for Erikson.

While Erikson's first stage focuses primarily on an interpersonal task—mother-child trust vs. mistrust—his next stages all the way to young adulthood focus entirely on the ability to manage for oneself alone: autonomy, initiative, and industry. And in adolescence, the focus is on identity *apart from* one's family, rather than *in relation to* one's family. The skills of "intimacy," the theme of young adulthood, would surely be difficult to achieve if one has been focusing on initiative, autonomy, industry, and identity apart from one's family for the previous 20 years, rather than on the development of interpersonal relationships or communication. Furthermore, the values that are considered dysfunctional in healthy development—shame, doubt, guilt, a sense of inferiority, and identity diffusion—seem to us essential for a healthy interpersonal ability for intimacy. Closeness requires a healthy sense of our interdependence and inferiority, knowing that at times we will do the wrong thing, causing shame and guilt, which can motivate us to change our behavior. We also need to have room for doubt in our ideas and actions in order to learn from others, and we need to have not just an independent sense of our identity apart from our family but an interdependent sense of identity in relation to our family, friends, community and others, in order to appreciate our basic human need for the support of others.

Later in Erikson's life he seems to have repeated the secret keeping that his mother and stepfather had forced on him in his childhood. His theory describes the phase of "generativity" as occurring *after* the phase of childrearing—the phase

Figure 4.7   Erik Erikson's Family, 1967: The Year Neil Died

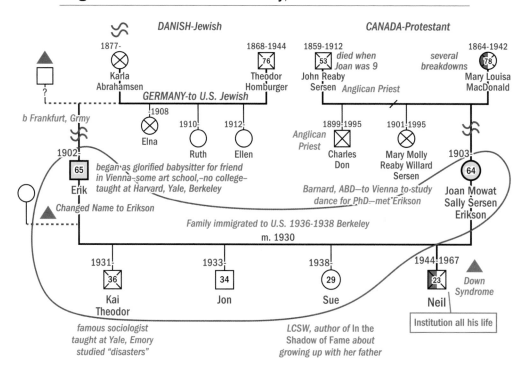

many would see as perhaps our most generative! Erikson and his wife, Joan, developed this part of the theory at a difficult time in their own lives, following the birth of their fourth child Neil, who was born with Down Syndrome (Trisomy 21) in 1944 (**Figure 4.7: Erik Erikson's Family, 1967: The Year Neil Died**).

Erik and Joan Erikson made the decision to keep the existence of their fourth child, Neil, a secret. He was put in an institution and they decided to tell their other children he had died, although, in fact, he lived to the age of 23. They rarely visited him. When their son Kai was 13 they told him about his brother Neil, but told him not to tell his siblings, a most unfortunate position to put one child in—to keep a secret from his siblings. Years later they told the other children of Neil's existence but never took them to visit. When Neil died, they were in Italy and did not return, telling Jon and Sue to handle the funeral and burial with people from an institution they had never known about. The people at the institution were surprised they wanted their brother buried in the children's part of the cemetery, since he was an adult, but, of course, they had never met him and had no idea. Surely this terrible secret of their family history influenced the parents' ideas about the life cycle, namely their concept that generativity does not refer to the period when one is bearing and raising children, but rather to the midlife period instead, as if to steer people away from the generativity of parenthood.

The Eriksons apparently characterized Neil as "a developmental aberration and wished that he had never been born" (Friedman, 1999, p. 22). Their sad story is not just about their personal failure to deal with the truth of their family's history, but reflects our society's pressure for success (and difficulty acknowledging shame, doubt, and a sense of inferiority). This leaves families with disabled children to feel invalidated, alone, abandoned, and pressured to lie about their lives in order to preserve an image of normalcy. In their daughter's memoir, she writes painfully about the anxieties that her brother's abandonment created in her. Both parents had felt abandoned in their own childhoods: Erikson never knew the truth about his father, and Joan, who lost her father at nine, said about his death that she had "lost what I never really had," (Bloland, 2005, p. 48) since she had grown up mostly away from her father anyway.

The Eriksons' painfully dreadful story reveals society's insidious pressure on families to distort their lives with lies and secrecy regarding any experiences that lie outside society's life cycle norms. Their story should surely lead us to question the assumptions of "normalcy" laid out by Erikson in the years when he was living a lie, pretending that he had a "perfect" family of five while secretly extruding the sixth member. Erikson was a leading theorist about children and his views of human development are still the most widely taught. The limits of his theory make clear the value of assessing families in life cycle context and tracking the power of secrets in families. Secrets may distort family process for generations and lead to imbalances in functioning between the external picture presented to the world and the internal realities of family relationships.

Genograms can help track the specific nodal points in a family's history. Specific genograms that track families at key points in the life cycle offer a snapshot in time to help us understand these nodal points, such as the time when Erikson was born, the time of his mother's remarriage, or the time when their son Neil was born.

These nodal points could be the focus for questioning to better understand what happened to create these circumstances. In the Erikson case, we do not know the details of what was going on in Karla's family when she became pregnant with Erik, though this moment would seem important to understand. Karla's mother had died nine years earlier and the oldest brother two years after that. Karla had had a one-night marriage (reportedly unconsummated) in 1898, at age 21, but having learned of her husband's criminal behavior, for which he had to flee, she contacted her brother from her honeymoon in Rome to come get her. The brother came, the husband fled, and she never saw him again. He died three years later. When Erikson was born, Karla gave her ex-husband's name as the father. Her own father had died the year after her one-night marriage, in 1899 when she was 22. Her two older brothers married the following year. So there must have been a sense that the family was disintegrating and there was not enough energy to support Karla in her launching. The supposed maiden aunts do not seem to have managed to do what was needed.

Were there other family stresses that led the Abrahamsens to extrude Karla when she became pregnant, rather than supporting her and her baby? What might have influenced her to become drunk and pregnant at a young age? If the story told to Erikson's biographer, (Friedman, 1999) is true, that Karla had become pregnant at a party given by the older brothers, they would seem to be implicated in her pregnancy. Did they indirectly contribute to her being abused and then blame her for shaming the family?

How did the parents die and what was the impact of their early loss on Karla and on the brothers? Did the brothers feel their own social status was threatened for some reason other than their sister's pregnancy? Did they mistreat her because of gender-related imbalances of power in the family, which would have been typical at that time? Who made the decision to pay her to stay out of sight? Did their stresses continue over the next few years, leading them to not let her come back even after the baby was born, "forcing" her to be alone with her child in a foreign country? We don't know the answer to any of these questions.

If we look at the decision to keep Neil a secret 40 years later in 1944, we can imagine the tragic difficulty the family must have experienced as the American immigrant parents of three other children. The reality of the war going on and the fact that Erikson was a half-Jewish immigrant would likely have figured in their dreadful decision to keep Neil's existence a secret.

Genograms can highlight the stresses on a family at a particular moment by showing who lived in the home and how old they were, allowing you to track details of family history around key points in time. It is very interesting that Erikson's daughter, Sue, who struggled all her life with her father's difficulty with intimacy, came to the conclusion that mature development requires one to be capable of having "authentic interpersonal encounters," in which you are "acceptable for who you are." (Erikson, 1999, p. 61). She herself pointed out the disadvantage of having to live a life where shame, doubt, guilt, a sense of inferiority, and identity diffusion must be viewed as indications of developmental failure. She said her mother had told her that neither she nor her husband had been able to seek help because of their public reputation. Erikson's theory made him unable to admit inadequacy, and thus be open to receiving help when needed. She says:

> When you have created a public image that denies your private experience of yourself—one that is, in important ways, the reverse of the shameful self—the contrast between the two creates feelings of personal fraudulence. I think my father suffered terribly because he could not in his intimate relationships be what his image suggested he would be . . . My longing to connect with my father was thwarted by his need to avoid feelings of inadequacy—by the defenses he had developed early on to ward off shame and depression. (Erikson, 1999, p. 61).

Using the example of her father, she makes very clear how essential the following qualities are for intimacy:

- The ability to acknowledge that you don't know everything, which means having a sense of your inferiority
- Realizing that you will make mistakes, for which you will have a sense of guilt
- The ability to doubt your ideas and actions, which fosters our ability to collaborate, learn from others, and to live in systemic harmony with others and with nature; rather than believing the myth that we can do it all ourselves
- A sense of your identity in relation to your family and others, not just apart from them.

By contrast, Erikson's mother, Karla was forced to survive completely on her own, and he in turn was forced to grow up without the normal developmental assets of family and community.

When Erikson came to the U.S. in 1933, he changed his name to Erik Erikson, which we might think of as "Erik, son of myself." Even in later life he felt like an outsider in that he never understood the culture of the U.S. It behooves us to be as inclusive as we can on our genograms by including as many layers of identity as possible. Coming from a Jewish family, the previous generations' migration and constant treatment as outsiders undoubtedly influenced his ancestors, and he had been a child who was extruded from his family and culture before he was even born!

Tracking Coincidences of Life Events

It is particularly helpful to track changes in a family's long-term functioning as it relates to critical family life events. We must examine genograms carefully for any pile-up of stresses, the rippling impact of traumatic events, anniversary reactions, and the relationship of family experiences to social, economic, and political events. This can help us assess the impact of change on a family and give clues to its vulnerability to future change.

Whenever several critical family experiences occur around the same time, it is wise to request details. It is particularly important to notice coinciding dates on the genogram, which may reveal hidden connections and emotional patterns in the system. Such "coincidences" may indicate a stressful period in the family's history. If nothing else, they pinpoint the critical periods for a family, which are likely to have left an emotional legacy. We are not talking here about one event "causing" another, but about the association of events that may have a systemic influence on the evolution of family patterns.

The Buildup of Stressors: Queen Elizabeth's "Annus Horribilis"

In 1992 Queen Elizabeth gave a speech referring to that year as the "annus horribilis," due to the multiple traumas that had plagued the Royal Family: the separation of one son, Andrew, from his wife, Sarah Ferguson; the divorce of Princess Anne from Captain Mark Philips; the ongoing rumors of marital problems between Charles and Diana, who announced their separation at the end of the year; and

Figure 4.8:   British Royal Family in 1992

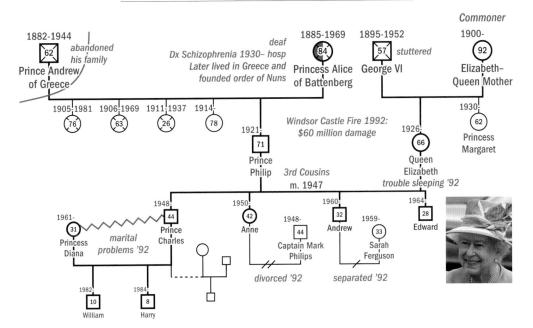

a horrendous fire at Windsor Castle that caused $60 million dollars in damage (**Figure 4.8: British Royal Family in 1992**).

In situations where there is a pileup of stressful life events, one must be on the lookout for emotional reactivity among all family members as well as other hidden stressors influencing the family. The stress of such a pileup may show itself in physical symptoms as well. Indeed, when the Queen gave her speech on the topic, she had lost her voice, due to a severe cold—perhaps a coincidence or perhaps a physical indicator of the stress she was describing. It was reported that she had difficulty sleeping for many months that year. As the Queen noted, her family's stress was compounded by stress in the country at the time. There had been months of worldwide turmoil and uncertainty, and Britain had had three years of severe recession. Millions were unemployed and there was a record number of personal bankruptcies and repossessed homes. There would be many more stressors for the Royal Family in the years ahead, including public knowledge of affairs and divorce for Charles, Diana, Sarah Ferguson and others, and most tragically Diana's sensationalized death five years later in 1997. One of the most important points to note about the build up of stressors is the family's ability to manage them, and how that ability may change over time.

Tracking Traumatic Coincidental Events: The Example of the Bateson Family

In some situations, coincidences occur over time, perhaps on anniversaries or influenced by a life cycle transition. For example, on the genogram of systems thinker Gregory Bateson (**Figure 4.9: Bateson Family Coincidences**) there are several striking coincidences.

- Gregory's parents were married shortly after the death of his mother's father, and triggered by that loss.
- Four years after the oldest son John was killed in World War I, the middle son, Martin, committed suicide in a most extraordinary way by shooting himself in a famous public space: Trafalgar Square in London, on John's birthday.

Figure 4.9:   Bateson Family Coincidences

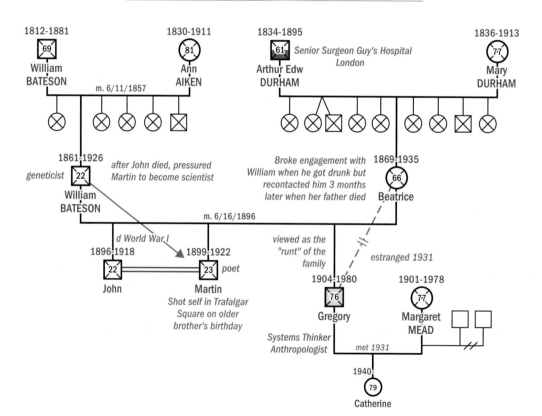

- Gregory met Margaret Mead a short time after he had become estranged from his mother.

Viewed systemically, these events look to be more than coincidence. Gregory's mother, Beatrice, had called off her engagement to the distinguished geneticist William Bateson after he got drunk one night. Her cutoff was a reaction influenced by her father's alcoholism. Three months later, her alcoholic father suddenly died, and Beatrice put a notice in the newspaper, hoping Bateson would contact her. He did and the couple married that spring.

The Batesons went on to have three sons. Cyberneticist and anthropologist Gregory Bateson was the youngest. He was thought of as the "runt" of the family, the least promising of the three, sickly in childhood and not a promising student.

John, the oldest son, was the one on whom the family's expectations fell. Brilliant and interested in science, he was to follow his father into biology. He and the middle brother, Martin, two years apart in age, were extremely close. Gregory, five years younger, grew up more on his own.

Then, tragically, John was killed in battle during World War I. A few days afterwards, the mother wrote to the middle son, Martin: "You and Gregory are left to me still and you must help me back to some of the braveness that John has taken away" (Lipset, 1980, p. 71). Following John's death, the father began to pressure Martin, as the next in line, to take his brother's place and become a zoologist. But Martin wanted to be a poet. Relations between the father and Martin deteriorated. When, in addition, Martin felt rebuffed by a young woman he admired, he took a gun and shot himself in Trafalgar Square on his brother John's birthday, April 22, 1922. His act was described as "probably the most dramatic and deliberate suicide ever witnessed in London" (Lipset, 1980, p. 93). Martin's choice to kill himself on his brother's birthday is a tragic example of an anniversary reaction, which we will discuss below. Was he trying to give his parents a message that he could never be a replacement for his older brother?

In the next generation, Gregory met and fell in love with Margaret just after becoming estranged from his mother. As in this instance, we often see that family of origin events trigger behavior in families in the next generation. Indeed, when trying to understand the timing of meeting a partner, the first suggestion would be to look to see whether there was some change in the person's relationships in the family of origin, possibly a change in a family member's health status, as when Beatrice reconnected with William Bateson, or a change in the relationship, as when Gregory met and fell in love with Margaret just after cutting off his mother.

Tracking Critical Life Changes, Transitions, and Traumas

Critical life changes, transitions, and traumas can have a dramatic impact on a family system and its members. Our own experience has led us to pay particular attention to the impact of losses on a family, especially untimely or traumatic losses. Families are also much more likely to have difficulty readjusting after a loss than after other family changes. Both Bateson brothers' deaths compounded each other in their impact on the youngest brother, Gregory. As Bateson's biographer noted, "Gregory had grown up unnoticed. His had been a vicarious, hand-me-down sort of youth. In part he had felt John and Martin were more able. . . Death now made Gregory sole heir to an ambiguous intellectual heritage in the natural sciences—personified by his father—and made him a central member of his family" (Lipset, 1980, p. 90). Though his response involved fleeing his mother and his home, he seems to have developed an amazing adaptive strategy in this situation: he became one of the greatest systems thinkers of all time—fulfilling in many ways the best hopes the parents could have had for their son.

Tracking the impact of family events must occur within the context of normative expectations for that life phase (McGoldrick, Garcia Preto, & Carter, 2016; Walsh, 2015). The age of family members and the family's structure at the time of a particular trauma is essential to consider. For instance, how children are affected by a critical event such as the loss of a parent depends on the child's level of emotional and cognitive development as well as on the supports the child has available.

An older child will, of course, have a different experience than a younger child, but the circumstances around the experience are critical to assess. Particularly traumatic for a family is the death of an infant or a young child. In researching the genograms of many famous people, we noticed how often they were born shortly before or after the death of a sibling: Beethoven, Ben Franklin, Sigmund Freud, C. G. Jung, Henry Ford, Thomas Jefferson, the Wright brothers, Frida Kahlo, Franz Kafka, Gustav Mahler, Eugene O'Neill, Diego Rivera, and Harry Stack Sullivan. One might attribute this solely to the higher child mortality rates of the past, or speculate that the death of a child makes the surviving child even more "special" to the parents. Or, perhaps, the child closest to the lost child feels impelled to do more for the family to make up for the loss, as seems likely to have been a factor with Gregory Bateson, whose life trajectory appears to have changed dramatically after the loss of his two brothers. In any case, it is essential to assess the family structure on any genogram to explore how children have been affected by any traumatic loss or series of losses, and always check what resources the child or family had to mitigate the stress.

A "good" event can also have a powerful impact on a family. The success or fame of one individual in a family may have profound repercussions for other family members. Not only might their privacy be lost, but children may feel they cannot get out of the shadow of the successful family member, just as children may find it difficult to deal with growing up in the shadow of a lost sibling.

Tracking Anniversary Reactions

Certain so-called coincidences can be understood as anniversary reactions, i.e., family members reacting to the anniversary of some critical or traumatic event. For example, a family member might become depressed at the same time each year around the date when a parent or sibling died, even without making any conscious connection. For Martin Bateson, for example, perhaps the anniversary of his much loved brother intensified his feeling of loss to the point of suicide, without his even realizing what he was reacting to. Family members frequently misremember anniversary dates for traumatic events, probably reflecting the intensity of the pain around the experience.

One traumatic event occurring on the anniversary of another can, of course, intensify the meaning of both events. An interesting "coincidence" along these lines was that both Thomas Jefferson and John Adams died on the 50th anniversary of the signing of the Declaration of Independence: July 4, 1826. It was almost as if both men waited until that anniversary to die. But their deaths on that day undoubtedly intensified the meaning of that anniversary for their families. As he died at age 90, Adams' last words were reportedly "Thomas Jefferson still survives," but he was mistaken. Jefferson had died five hours earlier at Monticello at the age of 82.

One of the best documented examples of an anniversary reaction is that of noted psychiatrist and internist, George Engel (**Figure 4.10: George Engel: Anniversary Reactions**), who described in detail his own anniversary reactions following the fatal heart attack of his identical twin brother (Engel, 1975). The temporal connections become evident on the genogram. George Engel had never lived apart from his twin brother, Frank, until the age of 23. He later wrote of their twinhood:

> I feel deeply the power and specialness our twinship afforded us . . . Actually, growing up we spent more time alone together than we did with any other person . . . At no time in our lives did we ever address one another as Frank or George, only as "Oth" (for other, derived originally from a finger game their father had played with them. (Cohen & Brown Clark, 2010, p. 10).

Figure 4.10:   George Engel: Anniversary Reactions

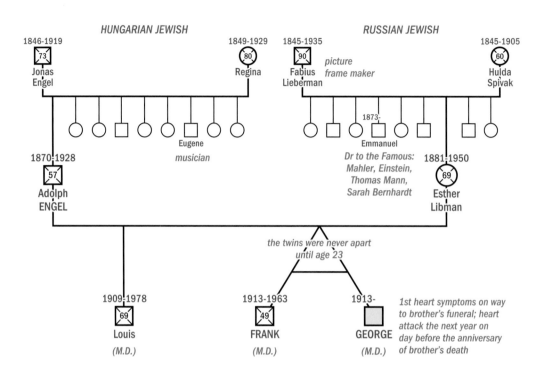

At 49 Frank died suddenly of a heart attack. George experienced heart symptoms on his way to his brother's funeral. The following year, Engel suffered a serious heart attack one year minus one day after the anniversary of Frank's death, seemingly in response to the stress of the anniversary. Engel later reported experiencing another type of anniversary reaction, an anniversary of age rather than date. Engel's father died of a heart attack two days before turning 58. As Engel approached this age, he found himself becoming more and more anxious. He repeatedly misremembered his father's age at death, fearing he would die at the same age. His experience led him to explore the psychological components of such family experiences and the mystifying way families often dissociate from such emotional processes, e.g., forgetting the day or the year of significant events. This illustration shows why it is so important for therapists to explore their own genograms and to recognize potential triggers in their own histories. We all have them, and one of the first places to look is at traumatic events and the anniversary of traumatic events.

Trauma may also set a family up for an anniversary reaction in the next generation. That is, as family members reach a certain point in the life cycle, they may expect particular events to recur. For example, if a man is cut off from his father when leaving home, he may expect his son to cut off when he reaches young adulthood. Or, a family in which the death of a key family member followed shortly after a marriage for two generations might become anxious around the next wedding. That particular life cycle transition might even become a toxic point for whole subsequent generations, with members consciously or unconsciously fearing to repeat the same events yet again.

Thus, it is important to scan genograms not only for coincidences in time and in date, but in age, and point in the family life cycle. Such coincidences point to the interconnectedness of events and the impact of change on family functioning. Once these are recognized, the family can be warned of the potency of particular anniversary reactions.

Tracking a Family in Historical Time: Social, Economic, and Political Events and Cohort

Of course, family events do not occur in a vacuum. Family development must always be viewed against the background of its historical context, that is, the social, economic, and political events that have influenced the well-being of the family, including poverty, oppression, war, migration, economic depression, and so forth. For example, within the U.S., a suicide in 1929 could suggest certain hypotheses about the stock market crash and the depression that followed; a marriage in 1941 might suggest hypotheses about the influence of World War II on the couple's relationship. It is important to connect the family events that appear on the genogram to the context in which they occur, and to consider what cohort a person is from, that is, when and where particular family members were born and how their era influenced their world view (Cohler, Hosteler, & Boxer, 1998; Elder, 1977, 1986; Phelps, Furstenberg, & Colby, 2002). We know, for example, that Eric Schmidt, Steve Jobs, and Bill Gates were all born in 1955 and came of age right at the time when it became possible to gain experience on a main frame computer (Gladwell, 2008). Those born earlier were probably too well-educated in previous methods to have the flexibility in thinking to create a new computerized world. Similarly, each generational cohort grows up with a particular popular music and historical story lines, as well as particular political experiences, all of which will influence how they experience their lives. Those who had a rocky time coming of age in the late 60s or 70s, were undoubtedly influenced by the Vietnam War, whether they participated in it directly or not. Millions of U.S. civilians (and some military personnel) were affected by observing and participating in the Vietnam War protest movement. People of every generation are influenced by the economic and political ethos of their era.

Figure 4.11:   Scott Joplin: Understanding A Family in Historical Context

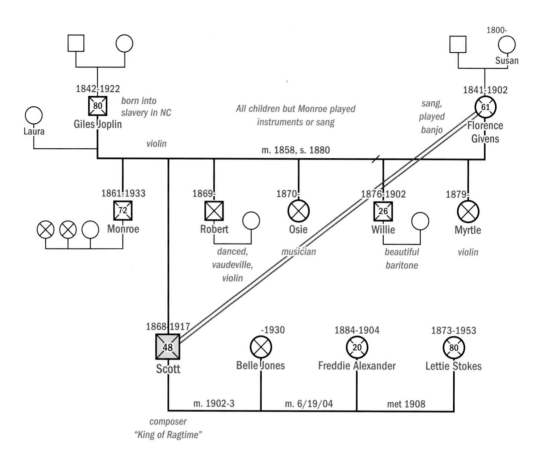

For example, Scott Joplin, (**Figure 4.11: Scott Joplin: Understanding A Family in Historical Context**), was the first African American composer to fully develop his compositions into an American idiom, and also the first of his family's children to be born after the end of slavery (1868). If we look at the Joplin genogram, we may wonder why Scott alone out of all his musical siblings became the famous composer, whose music is still widely listened to. Both parents and all of the siblings appear to have been very musical. He was extremely talented, but perhaps there were also historical patterns that contributed to his special development. We can see from his genogram that he was born eight years after the oldest son, followed in quick succession by his next brother. Then, the younger children were born at several year intervals. His older brother, Monroe, born in 1861, was the only one of the seven Joplin children who did not become a musician. The years between Monroe and Scott's births were the years of the Civil War. Scott was the first child born after the end of slavery, which perhaps made his birth special for the family (even though Texas, where they lived, did not acknowledge the end of slavery until 1870). It is also possible that there were other pregnancies between the first two brothers which we don't know about because we lack complete information about the family. If Joplin's mother, Florence Givens, lost children between Monroe and Scott, it could add to our understanding of Scott's apparent special position in her heart. She not only found a way for him to play the piano as a small child in the home of the family she worked for, but she also managed to buy a piano for him at the very time when her husband was leaving her for another woman. It has been suggested that Scott was triangled into his parents' relationship through his father's resentment of his mother's "over-encouraging" of him, and that this contributed to their separation (Haskins, 1978, p. 54). In any case, Joplin had a sense of his "specialness" from early on. He received considerable education, whereas his older brother Monroe apparently never went to school, though he did study music as did all the other Joplin children.

By the age of 16, Scott Joplin had organized a music group and before he was 25 he had become "The King of Ragtime." Sadly, his dream of seeing his two operas published and performed was largely unfulfilled because of the racism that blocked him from having what were thought of as "white" operatic works performed. His first opera went on a self-financed tour that quickly ended due to someone stealing the box office receipts: the score was confiscated, along with his other belongings, for non-payment of debts. He spent years unsuccessfully struggling to get his other opera, *Tremonisha*, performed; although its score was critically acclaimed, there was only one disappointing read-through performance, which Joplin paid for. The opera was largely unknown before its first complete performance in 1972. A few years later, Joplin was posthumously awarded the Pulitzer Prize for this opera. He had died penniless and tragically young at 48 in 1917. Joplin was ahead of his time in many ways. Although he is not known to have had any children within or outside of three short marriages, one must wonder how his descendants, if there had been any, would have felt about such acclaim coming 60 years late.

Tracking Social Class, Finances, and Downward Mobility on A Genogram

It is important to track information about the education, occupation, and financial status of family members, because this information indicates a tremendous amount about the stresses and resources that will impact them in any crisis. It can help to note how the family's socioeconomic status has evolved over time. At times we might want to create a genogram to specifically track a family's socioeconomic patterns over several generations.

Figure 4.12: Social Class Depicted on a Genogram depicts my (MM) Irish American family over four generations. In the immigrant generation, both of my father's grandfathers died at 50 and both families also lost several children. My paternal great-grandfather, Neal McGoldrick, had risen from poverty to great success. But shortly before he died, he apparently lost everything in a situation that left him feeling betrayed by other family members he had relied on. So, the loss was not just economic but emotional, leading to many cutoffs for the next two generations. The compounding of socioeconomic stresses and relationship cutoffs is common. When there are financial stresses, relationships become harder to maintain, and embarrassment, frustration, and shame are likely to contribute to cutoff. Could it be that my great-grandfather's financial debacle contributed to his stroke at age 50, six months later? I certainly think so.

On my paternal grandmother's side, her father's death at about 55 seems to have been just one of many stresses on the family. His wife, Mary McGuire Cusack, my great -grandmother, had apparently had a successful confectioners' business even before her marriage, but she had retired when she married. When her husband died, six children and 20 years later, she was perhaps unable to recover from the loss, which was compounded by her having already lost three babies. She ended up dying just a few months after her oldest son died suddenly at 37 in April of 1900, and after her only surviving daughter, my grandmother, had married. The middle brother, Ta, came into my grandmother's new marital household and remained there for the rest of his life. Could it be that their mother did not have the resources to support herself, as happened with my father's other grandmother? And could it be that Ta moving in was a financial as well as emotional decision? If so, they never discussed the reasons or the problems it created for my grandfather, to have a carefree uncle in the household who spoiled the children and had little responsibility, nor did they discuss what it meant that he never married or had his own family. In the next generation this pattern was

Figure 4.12:   Social Class Depicted on a Genogram

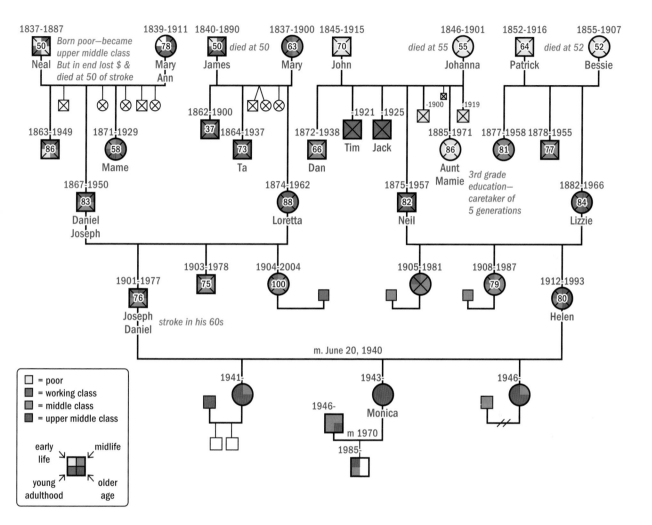

repeated when my uncle Raymond also never married, though he did move out of the parental home.

On my mother's side of the family, it was the women who died in their 50s. My mother's paternal grandmother died when the youngest of her seven children, a crippled son, was only 17. The only daughter in the family, my Aunt Mamie, ended up receiving only a third grade education, and became the caretaker of the family for the rest of her long life. She survived on family handouts and eventually on welfare, but she took care of five generations of the family's children!

Women are, of course, in a more vulnerable situation when there are economic difficulties, as well as when there are caretaking burdens, just as sons who do not become "providers" tend to be in special jeopardy. Only three of the seven of my maternal great-grandfather's children survived to middle age, and the families of the two sons in general did well in the next generation. My grandfather himself had only a fifth grade education but ended up becoming an Inspector in the New York City Police Department. He also started a police academy and wrote several books, so he moved up several stations in social class over his lifetime and was able to provide well for his three daughters. Indeed, the only one of the six children in my parents' families who did not get an Ivy League education was my father's youngest sister, who received a two-year "Normal School" education beyond high school and then became a teacher and the family caretaker. She didn't marry until age 50, the year after her father died, showing again the disadvantage daughters so often have in education and opportunities. In fact, the only situations throughout the family where I could find downward mobility (this has been my experience clinically as well) were situations of

1. Untimely death or serious illness and caretaking need.
2. Women on their own through singlehood, divorce, disability, or responsibility to care for others.
3. A cohort growing up in a time of war, economic or political disruption, or societal depression, who are unable to get an education or develop a career because of the societal disruption.

We know that women are more likely than men to move downward in social class after a divorce and that their children may have more difficulty maintaining their class status. Furthermore, women have been expected to be in the social class of their husbands, which can at times create unacknowledged stress when the husband is of a lower social class than his wife, much more so than if the wife comes from a lower social class than her husband. Thus, it is extremely important to track factors such as employment, number of dependents, and amount of income and debt. They are key to understanding how families have evolved.

Differences in resources may also become problematic when one sibling becomes more successful than the others. For example, if one sibling in a family becomes highly successful and others do less well financially or in social status, there may be an imbalance; an unsuccessful sibling may not be able to meet family expectations and may in turn resent the achiever. When resources (emotional as well as financial) are lacking, siblings may have conflict or cutoff, particularly around the caretaking of a parent or an ill sibling. Families may get caught up in struggles over who did more for the person in need.

When most siblings are doing well and only one sibling or one parent is in need, it is preferable to balance the responsibilities rather than to unduly tax one member. A wealthy sibling who contributes financially but not with time or emotional caretaking, for example, may add to a sense of imbalance in the family. Geographic distance of siblings from each other or from parents may also create imbalances, especially if only one sibling lives close enough to do the caretaking for a needy parent. He, or more likely she, may burn out and become resentful. Daughters are much more likely to be saddled with family caretaking burdens. Siblings who are not married or who do not have children may also be inequitably expected to do the caretaking for parents (especially for a single parent). All such imbalances in sibling responsibility for parents should be explored and inequities challenged. Otherwise they may create far-reaching negative effects on family relationships.

Tracking Migration

Migration has a profound impact on any family. Parents may have left their families and way of life out of desperation to create something better for themselves and their children. But the losses experienced may ripple in the family for generations. A family that migrates in the middle of the mother's child-bearing years may have two different sets of children, those born before and those born after the migration. The children born after the migration may have been raised in a much more hopeful context or, on the other hand, in a much more stressful family situation.

Maria Callas (**Figure 4.13: Maria Callas Family: Tracking Migration**) is an example of the stresses that the first child born after a migration can experience, where the move is often compounded by many other stresses. Immigration, and the subsequent stresses of dislocation, appear to have had a major impact on the Callas family. Maria's maternal grandfather, Petros Dimitriadis, disapproved of his daughter, Evangelika, marrying a pharmacist, George Kalegeropolis (whose name became Callas). But Petros died suddenly in 1916, after which his wife suggested Evangelika marry George, which she did two weeks after her father's death. The next year the couple had their first child, Jackie, a much-loved daughter. Three years later they had a son, who died at age three of meningitis. Just after this loss, George made sudden arrangements to move to the U.S. Evangelika was three months pregnant with her third child, who would become Maria Callas. Coincidentally, the family

Figure 4.13:   Maria Callas Family: Tracking Migration

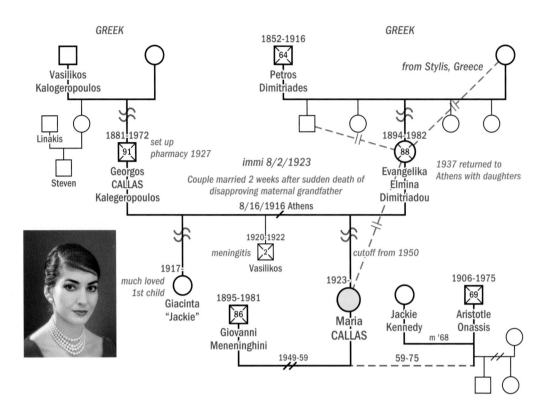

arrived in the U.S. on the very day of the sudden and traumatic death of President Harding. This must have added to the stress of the migration, since the father did not know English and had to take a job teaching Greek in a Greek neighborhood until he could establish himself and get a license as a pharmacist.

Maria was born four months after their arrival. Her mother was so disappointed in her being a girl that she refused to even relate to her for some time. The parents could not even agree on a name for her for several years. The father struggled but eventually established a pharmacy, though he lost it two years later in the Depression, just when Maria was starting school. Years later, Maria's sister, Jackie, powerfully described the insidious impact of the Depression on the family:

Do I truly remember . . . the Great Crash? Did I really see people throw themselves off high buildings? . . .Of course not, but it is difficult now to disentangle real life from the endlessly repeated newsreels which brought . . .images of a world gone mad. I doubt we children knew what was happening at the time. . . As the children of the rising professional classes, we were soon to be made aware that . . . many things formerly taken for granted were no longer to be relied on . . . I suppose each child thought him-or herself untouched by these strange events, until one evening . . .I came to the realization that financial disaster was upon us . . . Everyone was into . . . survival mode and Father began to sink into debt . . . It was the fulfillment of all (Mother's) prophesies. Father's new business had . . .eclipsed the loss of what might have been back in (Greece) . . .Now we were reduced to what we had been when we first arrived. The pharmacy had to be given up. . . When mother heard of the sale she dashed into the drugstore to confront Father as if he had been personally responsible for the financial instability of the Western world and when he turned his back on her and walked away, she rushed to the dangerous medicines cupboard, grabbed a handful of pills and swallowed them . . . Mother's self indulgent coup de theatre effectively marked the end of their marriage. From then on they would live under the same roof as irritable strangers. (Callas, 1989, pp. 42–43).

Jackie gives a strikingly clear depiction of the compounding stresses that the family faced after migrating to a new culture and experiencing the Depression, which clearly worsened the couple's longstanding conflicts. These stresses were surely exacerbated by the previous loss of their son as well as an accident when Maria was hit by a car at 6, while walking in the street. All these stresses undoubtedly contributed to Evangelika's suicide attempt. The family remained in turmoil and eventually the mother re-migrated with her daughters to Greece, leaving her husband in the U.S. The parents never managed to overcome the difficulties in their relationship with Maria, who, having been neglected in childhood by her very stressed parents, eventually became her mother's "ticket to success." She was forced to perform to help her mother achieve the dreams that she had never been able to realize for herself. **Chronology 4.1** illustrates the Callas Family Time Line for the immediate period around their migration.

We see in this brief illustration how the various problems in family relationships can be compounded by the stresses of migration: lack of language fluency, economic stress, accidents, and traumatic deaths.

In some situations a child born after migration may become the pragmatic, financially focused manager for the rest of the family, perhaps taking on a paren-

CHRONOLOGY 4.1: CALLAS FAMILY TIME LINE

1916   Parents married immediately after sudden death of maternal grandfather, who disapproved of their relationship. As soon as the grandfather died, the maternal grandmother urged Evangelika to marry Georgos Callas (Kalogeropoulos), a pharmacist.

1917   Couple's first baby born: Giacinta "Jackie"

1920   Son, Vasily, born

1922   Vasily dies of meningitis

1923   Spring. Evangelika becomes pregnant for the third time.
— Georgos makes secret arrangements for family to immigrate to U.S.—telling his pregnant wife, Evangelika, only at the last minute.
— Family arrives in New York at the very moment the U.S. is mourning the sudden and shocking death of President Harding at 58.
— Georgos has to become a low-wage Greek teacher until he can get a pharmacy license.
— December 2. Maria is born. Mother is so disappointed to have a girl that she refuses to see the baby.

1929   Maria, age 6, is hit by car and has anxieties from then on.
— The same year, Georgos loses his pharmacy in the Crash and has to rebuild.
— Evangelika is furious with husband's "failure" and stages dramatic suicide attempt.

1934   Maria wins a singing contest and Evangelika concludes that Maria is her ticket to success. From then on she devotes herself to daughter's success.

1936   Evangelika re-migrates back to Greece with her daughters, while Georgos stays in the U.S.

tal, caretaking role early on. In others, the effects of migration stress are long lasting and should be taken into account on any genogram, even as we move down the generations.

Tracking Family Caretaking

Caretaking is a major dimension of family life. Both early and later on in life, and at various times in between, family members need caretaking and dysfunction will follow if care is unavailable, handled poorly, or required for long periods of time without respite. To understand the politics of caretaking, it is useful to create a "Caretaking Genogram," which indicates who has needed long-term caretaking and who did that caretaking. We consider this issue so important that we have developed symbols to indicate the primary caretaker and others who take responsibility for taking care of family members in need. For example, in my own family (MM), virtually every member of my parents' and grandparents' generation required long-term caretaking (**Figure 4.14: Family Caretaking**), and virtually all of it was done by women. My mother cared for my father for 10 years after a

Figure 4.14:   Family Caretaking

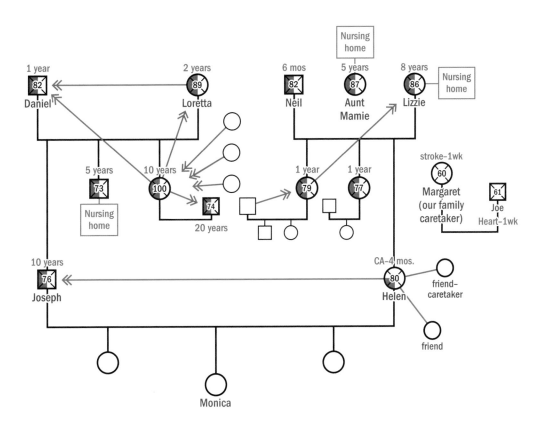

massive stroke, my aunt cared for her husband for the 20 years that he had serious emphysema, my paternal grandmother and aunt cared for my grandfather for the year that he was dying of cancer, and my aunt cared for my grandmother for several years before her death.

That same aunt, who had cared for her husband and both parents for so many years, lived to be 100, being cared for at home by a group of women caretakers. These caretakers were all women of color, illustrating the politics of caretaking, which is a seriously undervalued job in our society. Thus, we need to pay particular attention to caretaking patterns on clinical genograms. Families themselves may not mention caretaking issues, because we have all been socialized not to appreciate the caretaking requirements of family life. Because caretaking is not valued work within our society, it often goes unnoticed—done by those with the least power and status in the family and in the larger culture. At the same time, it has long been known that one of the primary reasons families seek help is not just the appearance of a symptomatic family member, but the burnout of the caretaker, who is no longer able to manage the task. Thus, intervention may require assessment of the whole genogram to tap into sources of resilience and resources that can be utilized to help the family get on track again.

One can also use a genogram of a family at a particular moment in time to show how the caretaking requirements may have affected the family. For example, in my own family (MM), as indicated by **Figure 4.15: Family Caretaking Over Time**, there have been a number of points in the life cycle when caretaking issues were primary. As can be seen, the losses were luckily timely, so children did not lose their primary caretakers. It can be an enormous problem for a family when a primary caretaker of children needs caretaking him or herself. But the strain on women was extensive, possibly affecting triangles elsewhere in the system. The first period of caretaking in my mother's life (from 1957-66) was a time of great strain in my relationship with her. I was a teenager, which is often a stressful time between parents and their children in any case. But the difficulties can be amplified if there are other stresses at the same time.

During the second major caretaking period (1969-78) in my mother's life, when my father had a stroke and she had to care for him, not only did her role change but also her power in the system. She became an effective leader for us all, where previously her leadership skills had been seriously circumscribed by her role as "wife" to my father. During that earlier period, she had much responsibility without much power. When she became our father's caretaker, she had responsibility, but for the first time, she also had control of her own money. In spite of her financial and personal burdens, she became more loving and less defensive. It

Figure 4.15:   Family Caretaking Over Time

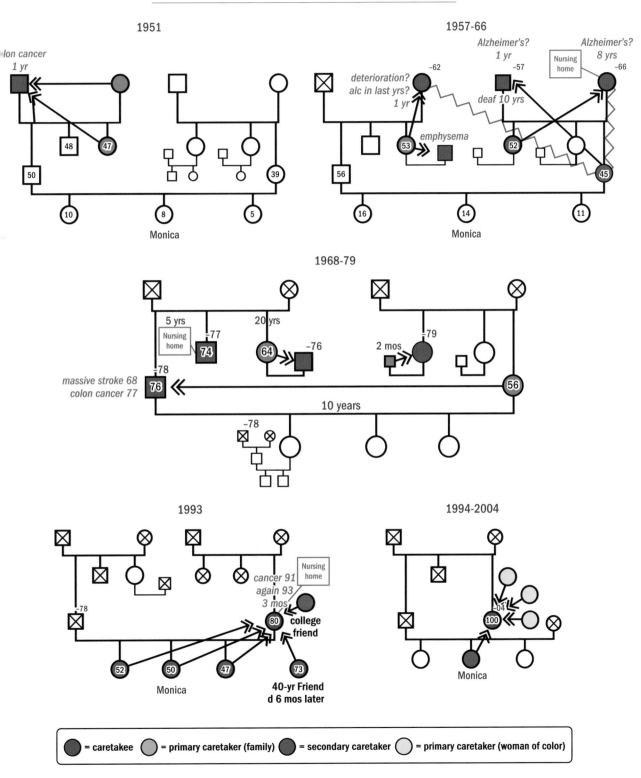

1951

1957-66

1968-79

1993

1994-2004

= caretakee   = primary caretaker (family)   = secondary caretaker   = primary caretaker (woman of color)

was only by exploring these caretaking patterns in relation to gender, power, and the life cycle that I was able to make sense of many of the dynamics in my family.

Creating caretaking genograms for my own family greatly increased my sensitivity to future caretaking. Thinking about who did the caretaking in our families in the past can lead to an awareness about who may be there to care for us in the future, which may make us more thoughtful in our interpersonal relationships. Walsh (2016) recommends that we foster caregiving as a team endeavor, involving both male and female family members and encouraging siblings to share the burdens and blessings of caretaking.

In many cultures it is daughters-in-law who, having the least power in the family structure, who must do the caretaking of mothers-in-law. The politics of gender contribute to the conflicts so often found in these relationships. In our society, such problematic relationships may be most pronounced in families of Asian heritage, where daughters were traditionally raised to leave their families of origin at marriage and become incorporated into their husbands' families, leaving them with marginal status. In the dominant society of the U.S., it is more often daughters than daughters-in-law who have this caretaking responsibility. However, challenging such skewed expectations may be essential for preserving sibling relationships, which have been shown to be a primary resource throughout adult life (Cicirelli, 1995; McGoldrick & Watson, 2016). Where the daughter has been overburdened with caretaking of aging parents or in-laws, having a family session or strategically coaching a daughter or daughter-in-law to challenge the rules may do a great deal to rebalance family relationships more equitably and functionally.

Tracking Specific Themes on a Genogram

There are any number of subjects on which "themed" genograms can be created: spirituality, religion, ethnicity, race, sexuality, caretaking, health and illness, education, hope and resilience, values, humor, work, pets, hobbies, clubs and organizations, etc. The essential issue is that tracking family patterns over time rather than just focusing on an individual is crucial for understanding human experience in the context of history.

Career Guidance Genograms

Gibson (2005), for example, recommends the use of genograms in guidance programs to help children view their career aspirations in context from the time they are in elementary school. She suggests that children begin to develop a work/

career genogram for their families in 4th or 5th grade, and evolve it as they move through middle and high school, hopefully using their understanding of their family's career history to develop their own aspirations. Obviously, if you are the first person in your family to go to college or to embark on a particular career path, it is much different and often much more difficult than continuing in an already established family path. Developing career counseling genograms with children as they grow up can help them to see their path in relation to their family heritage. It may also help young people see that their interests and choices are more connected to the legacies of the past than they realize.

One Greek psychologist I worked with around marital issues was reluctant to discuss family of origin, even though he saw that I kept a genogram. He said his parents were uneducated immigrants and knew nothing about him or his life as a psychologist. One day his mother came for a session and when I asked her what she thought about her son's life, she said, "It didn't surprise me at all that he became a psychologist. His father was a barber, and barbers are always listening to people's problems." Having established that bridge, we went on to have a nuanced discussion of her own and her son's life experiences.

Sexual Genograms

While it is extremely difficult to map issues of sexuality on a genogram, using sexual as well as cultural genograms (Hof & Berman, 1986; Hardy & Laszloffy, 1994; McGoldrick, Loonan, & Wolsifer, 2006) can be very helpful in understanding sexual symptoms, fears, and relationship problems. Sexual problems evolve within the context of relationships as we move through the life cycle and must be considered within this context. Therapists will surely benefit from constructing their own sexual genograms to highlight values they bring to their therapeutic work. Onto the basic genogram framework are added particular aspects of the individual, couple, and family history that have relevance to sexual history: health and psychological history, sexual and intimate liasons of family members, and sexual themes such as open discussion or avoiding discussion of sex, passing along sexual information on family members, etc. Constructing sexual genograms is an extremely useful way to help couples understand themselves and each other in a sexual and cultural context. It will help clients become aware of the values they have grown up with and recognize how these influence their sexual values, behaviors, and anxieties.

Below is a list of Sexual Genogram Questions (amplified from Hof & Berman, 1986 and McGoldrick et al., 2006) to help clinicians focus on sexuality from a cultural perspective.

Sexual Genogram Questions

- What overt and covert messages did partners receive from their families regarding sexuality? Intimacy? Masculinity? Femininity? What might other members of the family say about these issues?
- Who was most open sexually? Emotionally? Physically? Who was most closed? How did that affect other family members?
- How was sexuality or intimacy encouraged? Discouraged? Controlled? Taught? Did previous generations differ in the messages they gave?
- Were there ways that members of your family did not conform to the sexual or intimacy mores of their religious background? What was the impact of this?
- Were there secrets in your family regarding intimacy, sex, incest, or other sexual abuse? Inappropriate touching? Unwanted pregnancies? Extramarital affairs? Pregnancy before marriage? Abortions? Marriage of cousins?
- Were you or any other of your family members ever sexually abused in any way?
- What questions might you have been reluctant to ask about sex or intimacy regarding your family's genogram? Who might have answers? How could you approach people?
- How was the concept of birth control dealt with?
- How was erotic material from social media, books, or magazines dealt with? How was pornography dealt with? How do you deal with sexual media now in your relationship?
- What were the rules about monogamy in the relationships you saw? Was attraction to other people and talking about it alright?
- Were extramarital affairs or visits to prostitutes tolerated or discussed? How are these issues dealt with now in your family?
- Were there family members in previous generations who had an intimate relationship you would want to emulate or not emulate?
- How do you feel your family members' sexual or intimate relationships were influenced by their ethnicity? Patriarchy? Poverty? Success? Gender? Sexual orientation? Immigration? Language difficulties? Race?
- Have members of your family married out of their ethnic, class, or religious background? How did that impact others in the family? How do you think that impacted their sexual and intimate relationships?
- How do the values of your religious or cultural background influence your own views on sexuality and intimacy?
- Were there people in your family whose patterns of sexuality or intimacy

did not conform with your family's cultural or gender norms? How did others in your family react to them?

- How would you want to change the messages you give the next generation regarding sexuality and intimacy from the messages you received in your family?
- How were the norms in your family similar to or different from the norms in your partner's family of origin? How do you think those differences may affect your sexual and intimate relationship?
- How do you think you have done as a couple navigating the differences? What shared values have you arrived at about sexual issues?
- How did factors such as prejudice or oppression affect your family and personal development as a sexual person?
- What were your first sexual experiences like? How old were you? How did you feel about them then? How do you feel about them now?

Religion and Spirituality

Religion, or at least religious practice, is more likely to change in each generation of a family, at least in the 20th and 21st centuries in the U.S. Thus, religious genograms may be difficult to draw, because each family member may have a long spiritual trajectory over his or her life cycle. Furthermore, the point at which a conversion occurs may coincide with other life cycle events in ways which are important to assess. Hodge (2001, 2005) discusses a number of tools for spiritual assessment in clinical practice, from the spiritual life-map, which tracks the spiritual life cycle of an individual along a timeline, to the spiritual genogram, which illustrates the patterns in a family across the generations, to spiritual ecomaps and ecograms, which depict clients' current and historical spiritual relationships.

The following questions gleaned from our own experiences and the literature on spiritual genograms may be helpful to clinicians when discussing spirituality and religion with a client. Mapping the responses graphically will take all the creativity a therapist or client can muster!

Genogram Questions on Religion and Spirituality

- What meaning does religion or spirituality have for you in your everyday life? In your family's life? In times of danger or crisis?
- What religious or spiritual rituals or beliefs did you grow up with? Have you changed these? What or who influenced the development of your sense of spirituality?

- Are your religious/spiritual beliefs a source of connection or conflict between you and other family members?
- Who understands or shares your religious/spiritual framework?
- Do you participate regularly in religious services or other religious practices?
- What are your sources of hope?
- What are your beliefs about God?
- How do you deal with transgressions that violate your conscience? How do you find ways to forgive?
- Have you had premonitions concerning life events?
- What does your religion say about gender roles? Ethnicity? Sexual orientation? How have these beliefs affected you and your extended family?
- What role do music, prayer, reading, finances, group participation, or good works have in your spiritual practice?
- Have any of your family members felt disillusioned about religion or had serious conflict with each other about religion?
- Have you or any of your family members changed religions? If so, how did their families respond?
- Have you had spiritual experiences with friends or relatives who have died? Have you had encounters with spirits, ghosts, angels, or demons? Did you ever feel the intervention of a spirit on your behalf?
- While religion and spiritual practices have, throughout world history, been a primary resource for families in all kinds of distress, therapists have often ignored this dimension in their clinical assessment. But it is very important to track spiritual and religious practice, belief, and change in families as key markers of family process. We know that religious beliefs have a strong impact on clients' responses to illness and other stresses, and on recovery from addiction. Shared spiritual beliefs can either join or alienate family members.
- Other religious issues to track on a genogram include conversions, disaffection or expulsion from a religious community, and family conflicts that center on religious differences. Bill Clinton, for example, whose parents seem to have had little interest in religion, was first baptized at the age of nine with one of his best friends, and has had a very strong religious practice ever since. In his autobiography he discusses having been in the Masonic youth organization, DeMolay, but deciding against becoming a Mason, which he said would have been "following the long line of distinguished Americans going back to George Washington and Benjamin Franklin." His explanation was that this was "probably because in my twenties I was in

an anti-joining phase . . . Besides, I didn't need to be in a secret fraternity to have secrets. I had real secrets of my own, rooted in Daddy's alcoholism and abuse" (p. 45). Both Bill Clinton and George Bush became Born Again Christians, for different reasons and at different periods of their lives.

- The particular function of a person's connection to a religious or spiritual community as well as the meaning of one's distancing from a community of origin, is always worth exploration.

Fraternal Organizations

Often linked to religious and spiritual groups are fraternal organizations, such as the Masons, Elks, and the Odd Fellows. Many have religious as well as political origins. Most have been exclusively male, and have included secret rituals, or indeed been kept entirely secret, requiring members to tell no one about their membership. Fraternities and sororities have also often been part of university organizations and are often referred to at the college level as "Greek Life" because of the Greek letters that signify the organizations. Such societies, having religious as well as political and social underpinnings, may also have a strong political and power influence on business, friendships, and family relationships.

George Washington kept all diaries and letters from the early age of 14 (amounting in the end to more than 20 volumes), but never once mentioned "Christ," though he was a nominal Christian. However, like most of the founding fathers, he was deeply invested in the fraternity of Freemasons, which was a major building block of the American Revolution and of Washington's and other founders' views of government (Johnson, 2005, pp. 10-11).

In the 2004 presidential election both candidates (John Kerry and George Bush) were members of Skull and Bones, an elite secret society at Yale University, where members receive a large financial bonus for joining, but must promise to keep their fraternal and religiously connected secrets until death. While Kerry was descended from one of the founders of the society, Bush (**Figure 4.16: Bush Family Connections to Yale and Secret Society Skull & Bones**) was one of at least eight members of his immediate family who went to Yale, almost all of whom were also in Skull and Bones. This list included all four sons of his father's generation and the only daughter's husband, his paternal grandfather, great-grandfather, and one of his two daughters. For several generations, many of the closest friends of the Bush family were also members of Skull and Bones, who were also connected in political, financial, military, and national intelligence (CIA) circles. Without understanding the power, privilege, and social connections that come with membership in such societies, it would be impossible to have a good clinical assessment of such a family system.

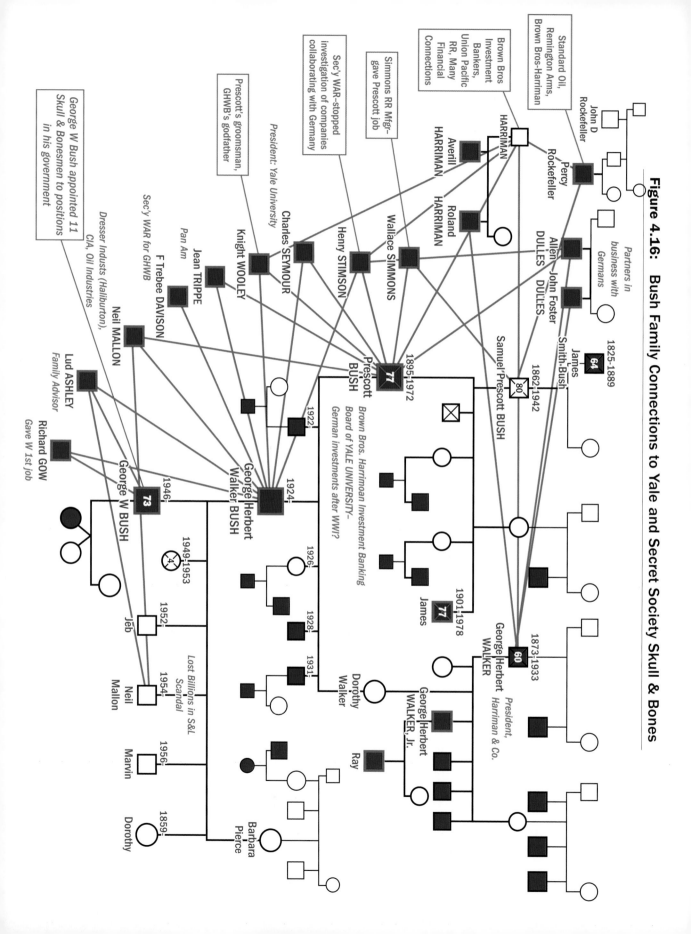

Figure 4.16: Bush Family Connections to Yale and Secret Society Skull & Bones

Within African American society, sororities and fraternities and other fraternal organizations such as Jack and Jill, Links, and others have had a powerful influence over the past century. Given the extrusion of African Americans from so many of our societal institutions, such organizations have been major social supports and connectors throughout the life cycle of those who belong (Graham, 2000).

Such fraternal relationships, like less secret religious communities, can have profound if unseen influence on families. All fraternal organizations to which family members belong should be noted on a genogram. They are key resources as well as influences on affiliations, beliefs, and behavior.

Ethical Genogram Questions

Paul Peluso (2003) has proposed the use of ethical genograms, which could lead to useful questions including the following:

- What are the toughest moral or ethical decisions you or members of your family have ever had to make, or should have made? How were these decisions or decision points handled?
- What kind of behavior was considered unethical? What happened when there were infractions in your family's moral code? Were there conflicts in your family over moral or ethical rules?
- Have you changed your values regarding any of the ethical rules you were taught growing up?
- How did issues of power and money fit into your family's moral code?
- How did your family's moral code compare to society's legal code? Were there people in your family who broke the law? How did others respond if this happened?
- Were there family members who transgressed the family's moral code? How did others respond if this happened? Harshly, leniently, consistently, inconsistently?
- What were the strongest family values in your family regarding ethical behavior? Honesty? Loyalty? Chastity? Fairness? Respect? Justice?

Tracking Missing Information and Discrepancies

Also of interest in exploring genograms is missing information. Why might a person know nothing about his father? Why are aunts and uncles omitted from his mother's side? What does missing information tell us about cut-offs, conflicts, or painful losses in a family? Often, filling in the missing information can lead to opening up new options for the client in terms of potential resources and clarification of the family drama that have eluded understanding. In the Fonda family, for example, Henry Fonda's wife, Frances—who was from a prominent New England family—committed suicide in a mental hospital, while Henry had begun an affair with the woman who very shortly after the wife's death became his next wife.

In spite of many biographies written about the Fonda family, we found it impossible to create even a basic 3-generational genogram for the family of either Henry or his wife Frances. She did have a younger sister who was raised in an institution and died of pneumonia at 15, and a younger brother who seems to have died in early childhood, and several other siblings. Frances's hospitalization and suicide must surely have traumatized all her siblings, and their children Yet, as far we could ascertain, neither the wife's father, nor her siblings, nor Henry's siblings even attended her funeral. Although Henry's sister, Harriet, and her husband, John, played a critical role in his son Peter's life, as mentors, guardian angels, and parental replacements, when Henry and his wives were inaccessible, the other aunt, Jayne, is also almost never mentioned.

Henry Fonda went on stage on Broadway the night of his wife's suicide and did not tell either of his children, who learned about it later from a movie magazine. When families withhold crucial information, it may be extremely important to create genograms to help them learn about their family's identity and history.

Peter Fonda later wrote movingly about his inability to learn the truth of his family history, which had been "sanitized" over the generations, and which he felt blocked from discovering, though he was sure there were explanations for the mystifying experiences he had growing up. At 20 he decided to go to live with his aunt Harriet, about which he writes: "I wanted to say good-bye to the dark, silent, booby-trapped thing that had been my 'family'" (Fonda, 1998, p. 133). Of his father's seemingly inaccessible history he says, "Things happened to him that we will never know. He was never beaten. But something happened to him that made him very quiet, very shy, and he let those qualities define his personality. They were the makeup and costume that he wore in real life. Somewhere, he found it was easier to say nothing. Easier on his heart, I mean. . . The deeper the emotion, the deeper he hid it. I say more about our father, because I know more about him. But I'll never know enough" (p. 496). Discussing his difficulty learning his family history he says:

> Such deafening privacy extended to my mother's family, of course. All I knew of my maternal grandparents—and they were both alive until I was in my late twenties—is that my grandfather was a debilitated (and debilitating) alcoholic,

who would come home some nights completely blasted, and mow the lawns, stumbling around and screaming invectives at the injustices of civilized people. My grandmother was patient to a fault with him, as she was with us during the years of our mother's gradual disappearance. . . I doubt I would believe a story told me by any remaining elder from either side. Too much time has passed, with too much opportunity to revise and sanitize the truth, and I hardly want to bother Harriet with my questions, now that she's in her nineties. My father's autobiography, as told to someone else, was full of so much sanitation that it had little base in reality. . . . Dad was too shy, too intensely private, to truly expose the part of his history that mattered to him. (p. 116)

From a systems perspective, one might want to help a person with this family experience create a genogram to explore the missing information in detail (some of which could, of course, be recovered through genealogical sources) to try to break through the "sanitized" version of their family's history. Such missing information often becomes the very focus of clinical investigation, since it is precisely what has been hidden that is probably most important to understanding the participants. As one of Nabokov's characters put it: "Remember that what you are told is really threefold, told first by the teller, retold by the listener, and concealed from them both by the dead man of the tale" (Nabokov, 1959, p. 52).

There are also often problems with discrepant information. For example, what happens if three different family members give three different dates for a death, or conflicting descriptions of family relationships? Discrepancies are common on genograms and need to be indicated somehow, if their implications might have emotional significance for the family. Bradt (1980) long ago suggested using color-coded genograms to distinguish the source of information. Hopefully, software will soon make it easier to track discrepant information.

When discrepancies exist, especially in complex families with multiple marriages, intertwined relationships, many transitions and shifts, and/or multiple perspectives, it is a challenge to create a genogram—but we urge clinicians to make the effort to map out the complexities of human experience. Skill, ingenuity, improvisation, and perhaps additional pages will often be needed!

Exploring Family Constellations with Genograms

By examining relational structure, family composition, sibling constellations, and various family configurations, clinicians can form many hypotheses about themes, roles, and relationships that can be checked out by eliciting further information about the family. The interpretive principles for evaluating genograms are based on the principles of family systems theory. For further elaboration of ideas outlined here, the reader is referred to literature on Bowen theory (Bowen, 1978; Kerr & Bowen, 1988; Kerr, 2019; Toman, 1976; Lerner, 1984 1990, 1994, 1997, 2002, 2005, 2012), and the writings of other family theorists who affirm the value of understanding family history in solving current problems.

The first area to explore on a genogram is the basic family structure, that is, the structural patterns revealed by the lines and symbols on the diagram. Examining this graphic structure allows us to hypothesize about family roles, relationships and functioning based on household composition, sibling constellation, and unusual family configurations.

Family patterns also tend to intensify when they are repetitive from one generation to another. Family members in similar structural arrangements as the previous generation are likely to repeat the patterns of that generation. For example, a mother who is the youngest of three sisters who herself then has three daughters will probably find herself over-identifying with her youngest daughter. A family that has experienced separation and divorce for three generations may view divorce as a norm.

Household Composition

Household composition is one of the first things to notice on a genogram. Is it a couple household, a traditional nuclear family household, a single-parent household, a multi-household family, a multi-family household, an extended family household, or a household that includes outsiders? Because assessing who lives in the household is so important, we suggest encircling the households on the genogram. This helps you see at a glance who lives together and consider how the structure, power arrangements, and finances may affect the relationships.

> *Because assessing who lives in the household is so important, we suggest encircling the households on the genogram. This helps you see at a glance who lives together and consider how the structure, power arrangements, and finances may affect the relationships.*

Traditional Nuclear Family Household

These days, 62% of children in the U.S. grow up in a household with both birth parents, although in 4% of those families the parents are not married (Zill, 2015). Twenty-three percent live with their birth mother only and 4% with their birth father only. By itself, these types of household structures might not attract attention. However, if the family is under severe stress or there is serious marital conflict, the clinician will want to explore what strengths have helped to keep the family together and what additional resources may be needed or may be accessible, since such structures tend to be less flexible under stress than more extended family units. In addition, nuclear family structures can be expected to have certain predictable parent-child triangles, with one parent allying with a child against the other parent or against another child, parents joining in relation to a "sick" or "bad" child, or siblings joining together in relation to fighting parents.

Single Parent Households

A single parent household, in which one parent is raising children alone, may be formed by a single parent bearing or adopting children or after a divorce, separation, death, or desertion by the other parent. Seeing a single-parent structure on the genogram should cue the clinician to explore stresses related to loss as well as loneliness, economic stress, overload of tasks with child-rearing strains, and so forth, depending on levels of support from extended family and other resources including neighbors, godparents, and friends.

Multigenerational Households

Often single parents live in three-generational households because of the number of tasks required in raising children. Such households can generally provide more flexible support—much needed in a single-parent situation—but they can also lead to typical triangle patterns that are important to assess. Another factor is whether other family members are in and out of the household. For example, in a three-generational household with a single parent, there may be other siblings or grandchildren who spend a good deal of time in the home and you will need to assess the grandparents' level of connection and relationship with the single parent and with the child/ren.

The example of Bill Clinton conveys some of the difficulties that can arise with the changing constellation of a multi-generational single-parent household over time. **Figure 5.1: Bill Clinton Early Household Changes** shows the first years of President Bill Clinton's life. During his first year, 1946, he lived with his mother, Virginia, who was 23 when he was born and lived as a single parent in a household with her own parents. Newly widowed, and with no real job skills or money, she had few resources. Luckily, her parents were available, although the most common triangle of such three-generational households soon developed: The parent feels like an outsider living in the grandparents' household, while the grandparents tend to develop a tight relationship with the grandchild. As Clinton's mother described the relationships:

Figure 5.1:   Bill Clinton Early Household Changes

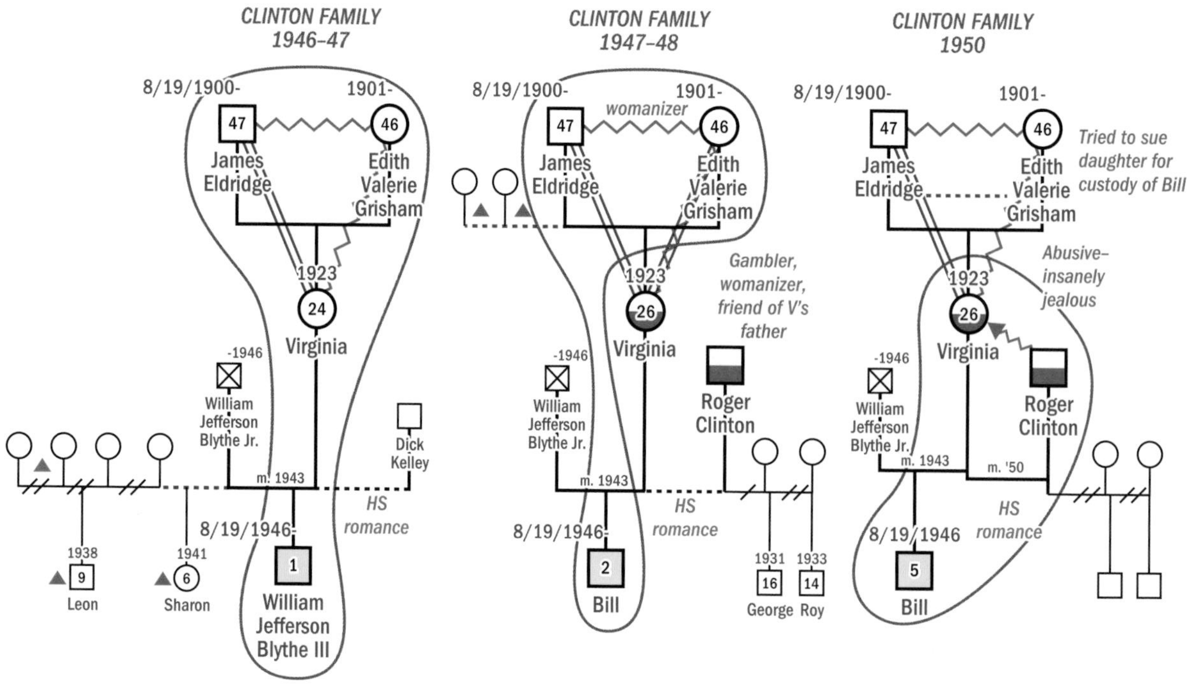

Mother . . . was totally involved in showing me how mothering was done. She meant well, but I felt like a lowly student nurse again, . . . while. . . my mother played God. . . When mother wasn't monopolizing (Bill). . . I would take him out for a spin in his carriage. (Clinton-Kelly, 1994, pp. 61–63)

The next year Virginia decided to go to New Orleans to finish school, leaving Bill with her parents. Her relationship problems intensified when she returned the following year:

Mother increasingly rubbed me the wrong way. I was 25, 26, even 27, and still living with my parents. It was a blessing, of course, that I had somebody to take care of Bill during the day. But there's always a price to be paid for such a service. Mother had already grown incredibly attached to Bill while I was in anesthetist school, and now, with me working, she still held sway over him. She would dress him and feed him and walk him and buy him things. Nothing was too fine or too expensive for her beloved grandson. (pp. 77–8)

Such problems are predictable in single-parent structures, and clinicians should inquire about these typical triangles whenever we see them on a genogram. Also of interest would be the impact on the family (particularly on the children) of the loss of the other parent and the associated difficulties managing the conflicts between the single parent and the grandparents, as well as the feelings about the missing parent. In Bill Clinton's case, he described being happily unaware of such triangles in his early childhood:

I was in the care of my grandparents. They were incredibly conscientious about me. They loved me very much, sadly, much better than they were able to love each other or, in my grandmother's case, to love my mother. Of course, I was blissfully unaware of all this at the time. I just knew I was loved. Later, when I became interested in children growing up in hard circumstances . . . I came to realize how fortunate I had been. For all their own demons, my grandparents and my mother always made me feel I was the most important person in the world to them (Clinton, 2005, pp. 9–10).

Often single parent households are part of larger multi-household networks, sometimes called bi-nuclear families (Ahrons, 1998) or multi-nuclear families, in which children are part of several different family structures at the same time. Such families require children to develop complex adaptive skills to deal with the different contexts they must negotiate in each home.

Parent-Child Triangles

Two parents may resolve tension by joining together to focus on their child. Regardless of the specific emotional pattern displayed (anger, love, clinging dependency), it is the joining together of two people in relation to a third that defines triangular relationships, one of the key patterns to track on a genogram, as we have discussed already. Genograms are an extremely handy tool for recognizing such triangles, because structural patterns, life cycle information, and specific data on dyadic relationships help to make obvious the threesomes who are likely to become triangulated. Three people in a relationship is not a triangle, but what we might just call a triad. Triangulation refers to the interdependent functioning of a threesome such that the relationship of each dyad depends on the third. If one person in a triad chooses to side with another in one conversation, this does not necessarily suggest they are in a triangle. However, if this relational pattern occurs regularly, it probably is.

Figure 5.2:   O'Neill Family Conflicts & Triangles

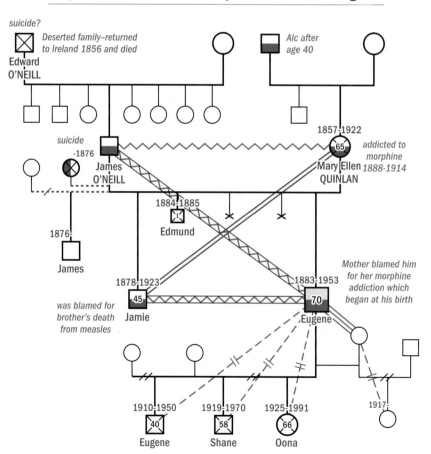

Sometimes intense sibling rivalry will appear, as shown on the genogram of Eugene O'Neill (**Figure 5.2: O'Neill Family Conflicts & Triangles**). The brothers had an intense and competitive relationship throughout their lives. Such intense sibling conflict on a genogram generally reflects parental issues, the conflict between the children both deflecting and reflecting the parental conflict. Indeed, the O'Neill parents had a difficult and tense relationship throughout their marriage. Perhaps the tension between the brothers was exacerbated by the fact that Jamie was blamed for the death of the middle brother, Edmund, whom he had accidentally exposed to measles as a young child. Eugene, the third brother, born after the second brother had died, was later blamed for the mother's addiction to morphine, which she began using at the time of his birth. The sibling conflict undoubtedly reflected not only the parental conflict, but also served as a distraction from the parents' many other individual and couple problems.

The genogram of Eleanor Roosevelt (**Figure 5.3: Eleanor Roosevelt Triangles**) presents an example of another common parent-child triangle. Although both of Eleanor's parents died by the time she was 11, she held on to the memory of having a special relationship with her father all her life, while feeling her mother was harsh and insensitive to his predicament. Her father was irresponsible and alco-

Figure 5.3: Eleanor Roosevelt Triangles

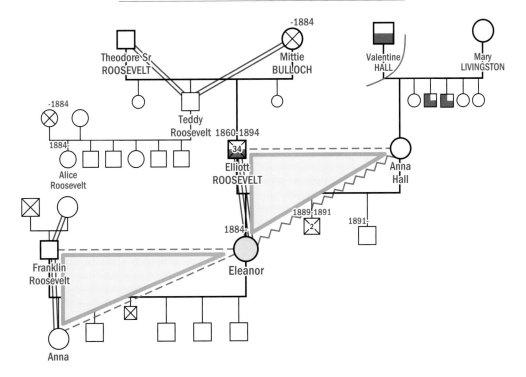

holic, and her mother separated from him and had him committed to an asylum. But to Eleanor, he was the hero and her mother the villain.

When parents are in severe conflict, such triangles are common. Children are often caught in loyalty conflicts between them, as Eleanor was, feeling her mother was cold, cruel, and mean. Although her father had at times abandoned her while he went drinking, and made endless promises he did not keep, Eleanor remembered only his love. She carried his letters with her for the rest of her life. This type of parent-child triangle is extremely common in cases of divorce and remarriage (see below). In the next generation, this triangle was repeated with Eleanor's daughter, Anna, an oldest like Eleanor, who preferred her father, Franklin, and saw Eleanor as overly harsh. Throughout her adolescence especially, she had a stormy relationship with Eleanor, which did not change until her father contracted polio. Eleanor later felt the ultimate betrayal when Anna participated in entertaining FDR and his girlfriend behind Eleanor's back at the White House and at Camp David. Fortunately, in later life Eleanor and Anna reversed this pattern of mother-daughter cutoff and became close (see McGoldrick, 2011).

Triangles in Families with Foster or Adopted Children

Parent/child triangles are particularly common when one or more of the children is a foster or adopted child. Tension between the parents—perhaps reflecting their disappointment at not being able to conceive a child together—may be present before the child is even adopted. This may lead the couple to focus intensely and negatively on the adopted child, who may be treated as an outsider, serving to distract the family from other concerns.

In many ways, families with foster or adopted children are like remarried families in that there are two families involved: the adoptive family and the biological family. This is true whether the biological parents are known or not, since people can triangulate a memory or idea as well as actual people. For example, consider **Figure 5.4: Adopted Brothers**. In this case, two sons were adopted from different families. When the older son Brad became a father, he decided to reconnect with his biological parents. His biological mother had contacted him when he was in college, but his adoptive parents had been so upset about it that he did not see her again for seven years.

But then, after he had married and was hoping for children himself, he realized he wanted to learn more about his biological family and why they had given him up for adoption. Brad re-contacted his mother, who helped him contact his father,

Figure 5.4:   Adopted Brothers

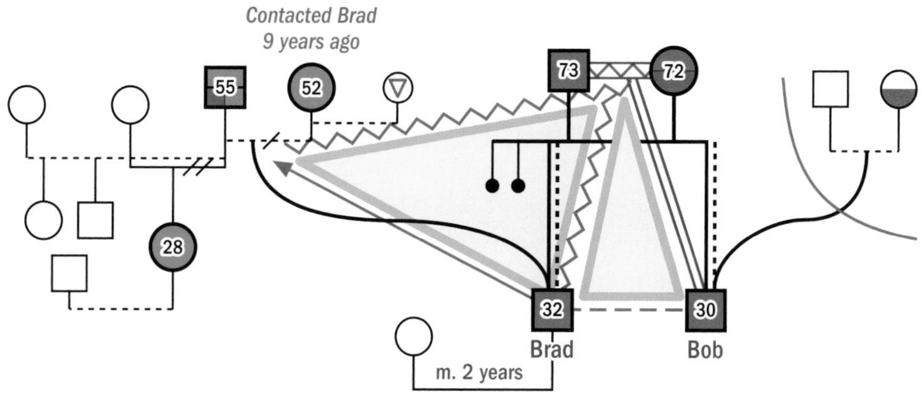

who had since had three other children with two different women. His father then took him to meet one of his half sisters, but when he told his parents, they became extremely angry, saying his contact was a betrayal of all they had done for him. This activated an interlocking triangle between Brad, "the bad brother," and Bob, "the good brother," who had never expressed interest in contact with his biological family. It took considerable work and time for Brad to help his parents realize that reconnecting with his biological parents did not change his relationship with them, his adoptive parents. He also had to work to maintain his connection to his brother, who had fallen into the "favorite son" position because he did not contact his biological parents.

Adoptive children may fantasize that their biological parents would be more loving or generous. The adoptive parents may also participate in triangles of blaming the biological parents in absentia for their own difficulties with the adoptive child ("bad" genes). If there are biological children as well, triangles between the foster/adopted and biological children are also common.

Multigenerational Triangles

As mentioned earlier, triangles can cross many generations. Probably the most common three-generational triangle is one in which a grandparent and grandchild ally against the parents. Seeing this on a genogram suggests the possibility of a triangle where a parent is in the role of an ineffectual outsider to a cross-generational alliance. Such multigenerational triangles are common when one parent is absent and most likely occurs when a single mother and her children share a household with her parents, as happened in Bill Clinton's family (**Figure 5.1**). The mother may lose power as the grandparents take over child-rearing responsibilities, or as a grandparent-grandchild alliance forms against her.

Family Boundaries: Open and Closed, Insiders and Outsiders

There also tends to be a correlation between the level of intensity of the relationships within a family and a family's relationships with outsiders, i.e., the more closed the system is to relationships outside the family, the greater the intensity of relationships within it. Thus, if one sees on the genogram patterns of fused relationships or intense triangles in the immediate family, one might investigate the family's boundary with the outside world.

For example, the fusion we described above between Eugene O'Neill and his third wife Carlotta (**Figure 5.2**) was intensified by their cutoff from their children, their extended families, and all others in a "two against the world" stance. O'Neill had required his second wife to cut off her daughter when she married him and now he cut off his children when they divorced. He and Carlotta became isolated and fused with each other as they cut off previous friends as well as their children.

As another example, Steve Jobs, whom we will discuss below, neglected his oldest daughter, Lisa, essentially from the time she was born. But when he decided to marry and had his first child, he invited Lisa to live with him, requiring, however, that she have no contact with her mother if she accepted! Such rigid boundaries suggest insecurities, which are unlikely to be resolved by such cutoffs.

The Brontë family (**Figure 5.5: Brontë Genogram: Loss & Boundaries**) developed a similar pattern of fusion and cutoff, which seems to have been strongly influenced by loss. The mother died a painful death in the home when the six children were still small. The two oldest sisters died the first time they left home for school. After they died, the other children were brought home to continue their schooling. Charlotte Brontë, the third child, became the oldest of the four surviving children and ended up being the only one of the four to have relationships outside the family and the only one able to leave home. The other three siblings all died one after another in young adulthood, almost as though their fusion made it impossible for them to live without each other. Any time the other three tried to leave home, something went wrong and they were forced to return. The sole son, Branwell, went away to art school, but never enrolled. He returned home and soon became an addict and an alcoholic, leading a miserable life until he died still in the household. From the day of his funeral the second youngest sister, Emily, seems to have caught a cold, and never left the house again. She died soon afterwards. The youngest sister, Anne, followed soon after that. Such a genogram raises questions about the reason for the strong boundaries around the family. None of the siblings except Charlotte ever left home for more than a brief period. Indeed, when Charlotte, the sole survivor of the six children, first told her father she wanted to marry, he became enraged and fired her fiancé who was his curate. Later he agreed to the marriage only if Charlotte and her fiancé promised never to leave him (McGoldrick, 2011). She did marry and soon became happily pregnant on a trip to Ireland, but felt drawn back and soon died while still pregnant. In the previous generation, the parents, Patrick Brontë and Maria Branwell, had married in a double wedding with a cousin who married Patrick's close friend. On the same

Figure 5.5:   Brontë Genogram: Loss & Boundaries

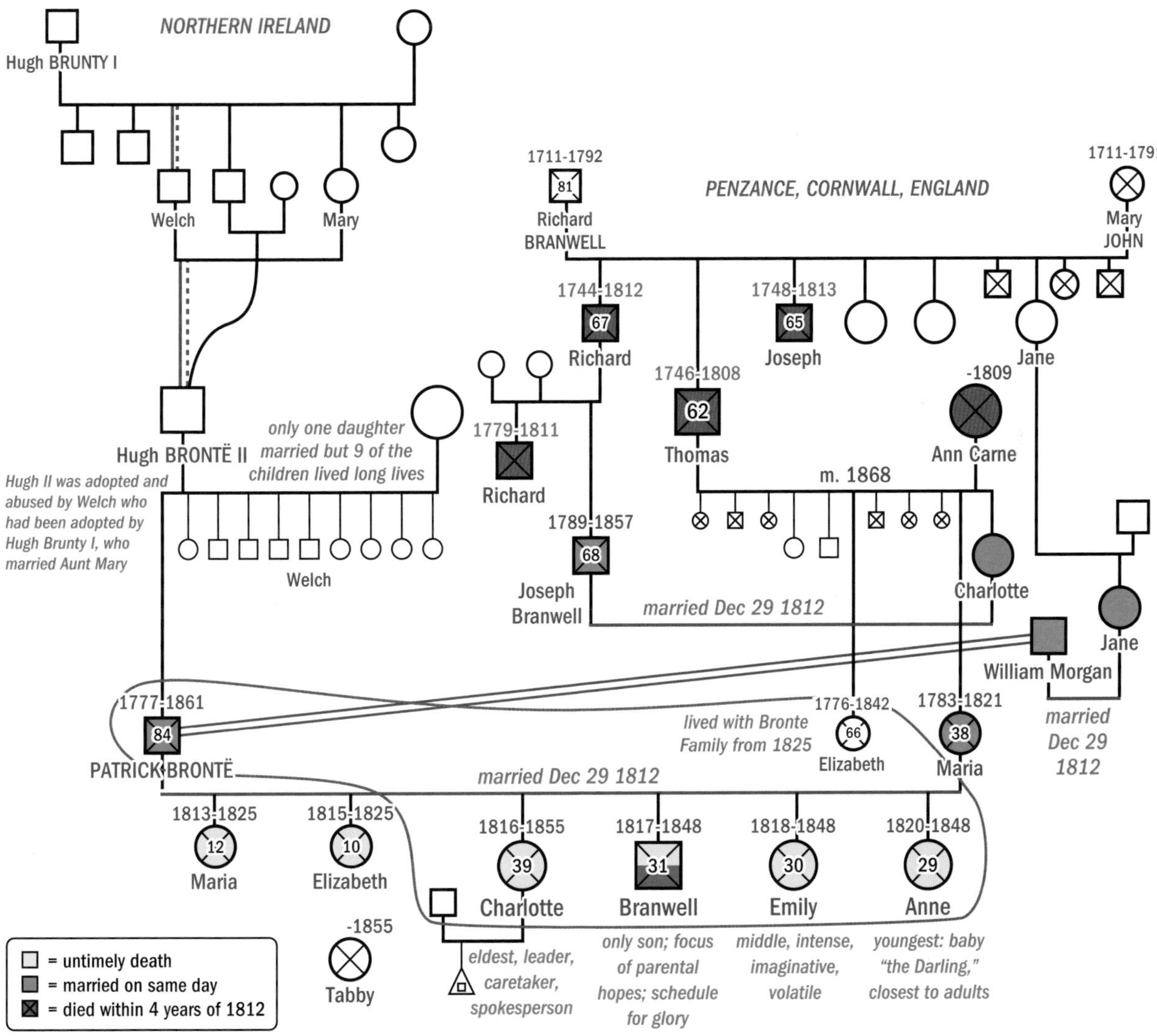

day two of her other Branwell cousins married each other. These three weddings seem to have followed closely after a series of deaths that had ended the Branwell family's successful mercantile business. It was almost as if there was a shutting down of the family, which seemed to continue in the next generation.

Triangles Over Time

To better understand family processes, it helps to track family triangles over time. Let us consider the British Royal Family in the last generation (**Figure 5.6: Royal Family Triangles**). When he was young, Prince Charles was apparently very close to his mother, but not to his father. In 1971, at age 22, he first met and became interested in Camilla Shand (Parker Bowles), at which time she supposedly joked: "My great-grandmother was the mistress of your great-great-grandfather. I feel we have something in common." They did have a lot in common and began dat-

Figure 5.6:   Royal Family Triangles

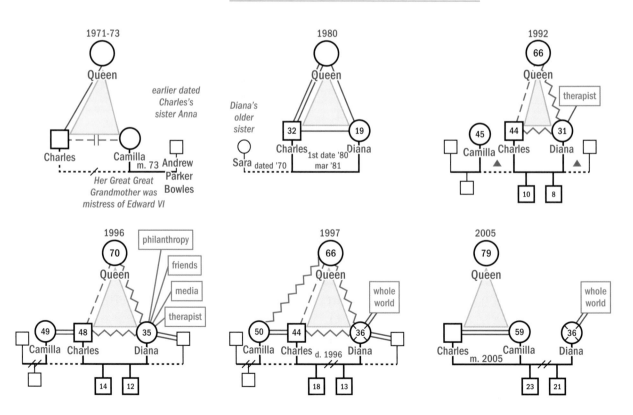

ing. But while Charles was away for a long stay on a navy ship, Camilla became engaged to Andrew Parker Bowles, who had previously dated Charles' sister Anne.

It was not until 7 years later (in 1980) that Charles first dated Diana, who was who was 19 at the time. He was now 32. (Charles had earlier briefly dated Diana's older sister Sarah.) His mother approved of Diana, and the couple were married within the year. But once they were married, Diana became unhappy and symptomatic, depressed and bulimic. Her dreams were not coming true. Charles was also unhappy and went to his mother for support. But she seems not to have helped. He was now having serious marital problems. Meanwhile, Diana went to therapy and her therapist conveyed that she was stuck with a very difficult family. Diana began to feel better. She became involved with affairs, friends, philanthropic work, and the media. Meanwhile, Charles met Camilla again.

Before long, the whole world became involved in their relationship, mostly on the side of Diana. Soon after the couple's divorce in 1996, Diana became engaged and then died tragically in 1997.

Once she died, the negative triangling against her stopped. It is extremely common to glorify someone who dies an untimely death. It took Charles another eight years (2005) to finally marry Camilla, whom he had loved already for 30 years. He was, apparently, no longer concerned about his mother's ongoing disapproval, and his mother seems to have come around to appreciating his relationship with Camilla. If we look back in the Royal Family to triangles in previous generations, Charles' great grandfather's affair with Camilla's great grandmother lasted for more than 12 years, ending only with his death; at which both his wife and his mistress, Alice Keppel were present. The two women seem to have had a certain level of reconciliation. Other triangles in the royal family played out for similarly long periods of time. Queen Victoria, Charles' great-great-grandmother, was alienated from her mother from the time of her wedding until her mother's death, 21 years later. Charles' mother was cut off for 30 years from her uncle, who had abdicated to marry a divorced woman. Their relationship—which has often been compared to Charles's with Camilla—and his exile from England lasted for the rest of his life. Thus, triangling patterns often continue over long periods in families, though the participants may change places. The precedents of such triangles have an extraordinarily long history within the Royal Family, and it remains to be seen what will happen in the next generations.

Actually, going back for the past five generations to Queen Victoria, we see similar patterns in each generation over the heir to the throne (**Figure 5.7: British Royal Family: Five Generations of Triangles**). Victoria was so well known for her rigidity and rules that the very term "Victorian" refers to her high standards. Her oldest son, Bertie, who did not become king until he was 61, was known since his youth for his love of the wild life. Queen Victoria blamed him for his father's

Figure 5.7: British Royal Family: Five Generations of Triangles

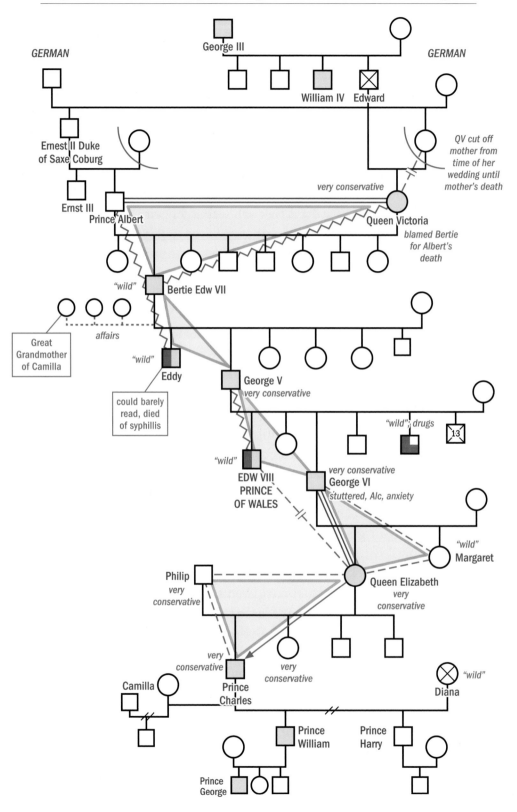

early death. Albert's oldest son, having gotten into a dissipated life from his youth, died at 25, which many said was fortunate, because he would have been incapable of ruling. The throne was left to his very conservative, prudish younger brother, King George V. George would not even meet with anyone who was divorced. King George V's older son again preferred life on the wild side, to the extent that he abdicated to marry the twice-divorced American Wallis Simpson, and was replaced by his younger brother, the conservative George VI (Queen Elizabeth's father), who took the rigid position of never letting her uncle return home with his wife. In the next generation there was the "good" Queen Elizabeth and her wild and rebellious sister Princess Margaret, who fell in love with Captain Peter Townsend, a married commoner 16 years older than she, who was in charge of her father's stables. Eventually she was told by her sister, the queen, that she could marry him but would lose her support and position in the Royal Family, and she gave in to the family pressure. Thus, there were significant triangles in every generation with either a "good" child and a "bad" child or a "good" parent and a "bad" parent. So the triangles that Diana and Charles became involved in were part of a much longer story.

Remarried Families

An increasing percent of children in the U.S. will spend some part of their childhood in a stepfamily, so it is essential to understand the particular dynamics when a new parent and perhaps new half or step-siblings are brought into a family. The children of the previous marriages may all live in the same household, they may be divided among households, or they may move back and forth between households. In any case, re-formed families, whether they formally marry or not, have to deal with specific issues, including custody, visitation, jealousy, favoritism, loyalty conflicts, and stepparent or step-sibling conflicts.

It is essential for clinicians to do an accurate genogram to be sure of who is part of the family, including aunts, uncles, grandparents, and informal kin who participate in each child's life, and to explore the impact of the divorce and remarriage on each family member. The relational patterns and triangles inherent in this type of family are reflected in Bill Clinton's family as they moved through time (**Figure 5.8: Bill Clinton: Remarriage, Separation, and Divorce**).

Indeed, the man who was married to Bill Clinton's mother and was supposedly his father, William Jefferson Blythe, Jr., was apparently in Italy at the time Virginia got pregnant with Bill. This man had already been married several times before marrying Virginia, who learned of these previous marriages only many years later, when she was already dying herself.

Figure 5.8:   Bill Clinton: Remarriage, Separation, and Divorce

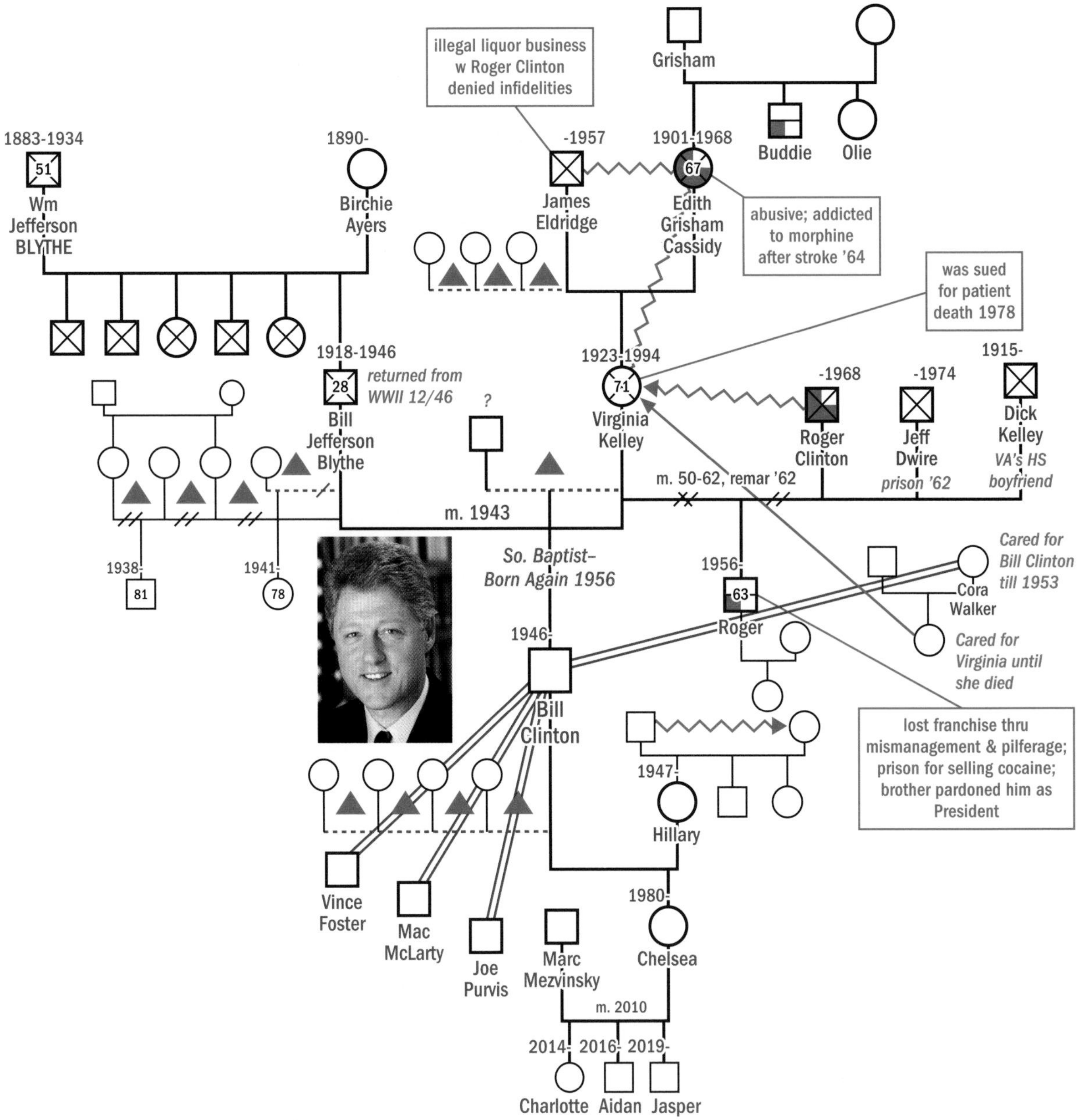

In mid-life, Bill Clinton became aware that he had two other half-siblings from Bill Blythe's earlier marriages. He met with his half brother, Leon, but not with his sister, Sharon (Clinton, 2005). Blythe was apparently a mysterious charmer, constantly reinventing himself. There are many discrepancies about his life. Even his birthdate is open to question. His family and his gravestone say he was born February 27, 1918; but his military records and marital records say he was born February 21, 1917. His wife, Virginia, said she met him when he was passing through Shreveport, but military records show he had been there for two months before they met. He did not tell Virginia that he had already married in December 1935, divorced the following year, and had a son, Henry Leon Blythe, in 1938. Nor did she know that he had married again on August 11, 1938, and divorced a second time nine months later by a judge's ruling, listing the reason as "extreme cruelty and gross neglect of duty" (Maraniss, 1995). Virginia also knew nothing about a third marriage in 1940 to his first wife's younger sister, apparently to avoid marrying a fourth woman who claimed to be pregnant with his baby. There is even another birth certificate, filed in Kansas City in 1941, for a daughter, Sharon Lee Blythe, born to Wanetta Alexander, a waitress whom he also married that year in Missouri.

Blythe was not the only one in the family to reinvent himself with new versions of his history, covering over the discrepancies and contradictions. Clinton's maternal grandfather, James Eldridge, always denied that he was in the illegal liquor business with his daughter's second husband, Roger Clinton, although he was. He also denied his wife's continuous accusations of marital infidelity, which were well known in the community. And Bill Clinton's mother Virginia seems to have told various versions of events in her own life. Such lies and self-reinventions can have a powerful impact on a child growing up, as they did for Clinton himself. Of his lost father, he wrote in his autobiography:

> All my life I have been hungry to fill in the blanks. Clinging eagerly to every photo or story or scrap of paper that would tell me more of the man who gave me life . . . Whatever the facts . . . given the life I've led, I could hardly be surprised that my father was more complicated than the idealized pictures I had lived with for nearly half a century . . . My father left me with the feeling that I had to live for two people, and that if I did it well enough, somehow, I could make up for the life he should have had. And his memory infused me, at a younger age than most, with a sense of my own mortality. The knowledge that I, too, could die young drove me both to try to drain the most out of every moment of life and to get on with the next big challenge. Even when I wasn't sure where I was going, I was always in a hurry (Clinton, 2005, pp. 5–7).

It can be a challenge to map the fluctuating structure and living arrangements in families with multiply changing partners, not to mention conveying the psychological complications. Bill Clinton's mother remarried 1950, when Bill was four. Her second husband, Roger Clinton, had also been married before. Virginia later divorced Clinton, had a brief marriage in between, and then remarried Roger

Clinton again a few months later. Such patterns convey, of course, something of the instability of a couple's relationship, but also key information for understanding children's anxieties and survival strategies.

It is important in addition to attend to structures that include godparents or other kinship networks, and to assess how the relationship patterns may be affected by these structures. Aunts, uncles, cousins, foster children, and housekeepers may be part of the household. Babysitters, close friends, or other "outsiders," may be especially important to families that experience disruption, often becoming members of the informal extended kinship network, and should be included on the genogram. For example, the Clinton genogram includes the housekeeper/caretaker Cora Walker, who worked for Clinton's family from 1953, and whose daughter Maye then cared for his mother, Virginia Clinton, until she died 41 years later in 1994. It is also important to include friends, especially in such disrupted families. Bill Clinton's genogram shows his friends from earliest elementary school: Vince Foster, Mac McLarty, and Joe Purvis, who, in fact, came with him 50 years later to the White House.

With a three-generational household, the clinician should always explore issues around cross-generational boundaries, alliances, and conflicts, particularly those reflected in conflicts around parenting. In the case of Virginia Clinton, she had always adored her father, but found her mother overpowering. Their conflicts over custody of Bill almost led to a court battle. Once Virginia remarried she had the resources to support Bill, but a friend said she and her mother competed for Bill for their entire lives. As with most children, his only wish was, apparently, that they would each realize he needed both of them (Gartner, 2008).

The clinician should also explore the roles and relationships of extended family members living in or near the household. Relationship issues will vary according to the individual's role and structural position in the family. A spouse's parent, brother, sister, aunt, uncle, or cousin may seem like an intruder to the other spouse, while a foster or adopted child is likely to become involved in predictable triangles as the "special" one or the "problem" one, depending on the child's own qualities and those of the family. It is important to consider the reverberations in both the immediate and extended family caused by the entry or even extended visit of other family members.

In Vitro Fertilization

We can also indicate the complexities of the networks of children conceived by donor insemination on a genogram, as in **Figure 5.9: In Vitro Fertilization**, which illustrates a lesbian couple with a child born to one of them, Sue, and

Figure 5.9:   In Vitro Fertilization

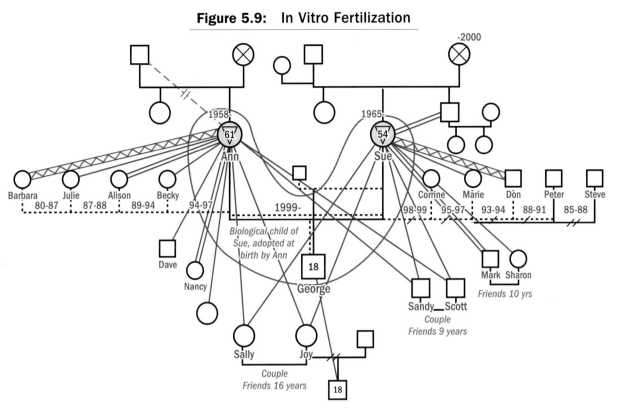

adopted by the other, Ann. The very small square indicated as the child's biological father is a sperm donor. The parents' previous relationships are also shown on the genogram. Sue had been married and divorced several times and Ann had had several live-in partners. Burke and Faber (1997) have suggested using a "genogrid," an adaptation of the genogram, to help to depict the liaisons, long-term bonds, and social networks of lesbian couples. The genogrid distinguishes historical influences, primary emotional and social relationships, and intimate relationships.

Children Raised in Multiple Households

When the "functional" family is different from the biological or legal family, as when children are raised by a grandparent or in an informal adoptive family, it is useful to create a separate genogram to show the functional structure (see Watts Jones, 1998).

When children have lived as part of several families—biological, foster, or adoptive—separate genograms may help to depict the child's multiple families

Figure 5.10:   Louis Armstrong's Living Situations Before Leaving Home

New Orleans Home for Colored Waifs

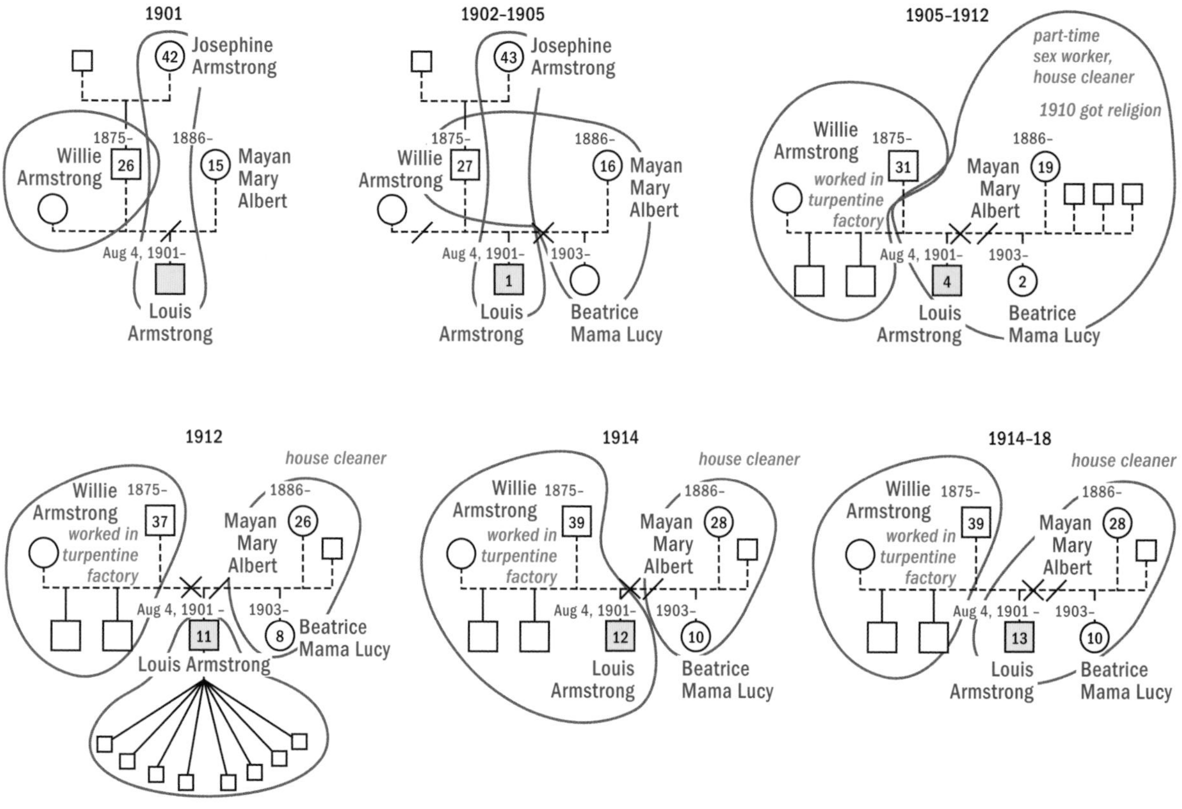

over time. **Figure 5.10: Louis Armstrong's Living Situations Before Leaving Home** shows Louis Armstrong's family in New Orleans for the year he was born, 1901. Louis Armstrong, perhaps the greatest jazz musician of all time, was an extraordinarily inventive and creative musician, who grew up in poverty and in shifting living situations from earliest childhood. Luckily he found support for his phenomenal talents from a relatively early age and through his powerful intelligence, was able to develop his talents. Soon after he was born he went to live with his father's mother, Josephine Armstrong, as his parents separated and his father went to live with another woman. The next year, however, his parents got back together and in 1903, Louis' sister, Beatrice, was born. But Louis remained with his grandmother until 1905, when his parents separated again and he and his sister, who was always called Mama Lucy, moved in with their mother. They lived with her and a number of boyfriends over the next several years. Then in 1912, when Louis was 11, he shot off a gun on a holiday, got arrested, and was sent to the New

Orleans Home for Colored Waifs. He remained there for a couple of years until about 1914, when he went to live with his father and half-siblings. But soon he went back to live with his mother, and stayed with her until 1918 when, at the age of 17, he moved to Chicago to work with King Oliver's band. Mapping out all the family constellations he lived in helps us to see his resilience and talent for improvisation and creative collaboration.

Genograms may become complex when children have been adopted or raised in a number of different households. When working with a person who has had this experience, it is helpful to map out the multiple households as a way to clearly show the complexity of their heritage. This goes beyond a chronology, actually creating a map to show who the person lived with. **Figure 5.11: Peter Fonda's Living Situations Before Adulthood** maps the 11 places and family connections actor Peter Fonda lived in before he was 20. It shows the traumatic changes of his father leaving, his being sent away to boarding school at six, the family briefly coming back together in 1947, and then his mother going to a mental hospital. It shows his attachment to his dog intensifying when his mother was hospitalized and after she then killed herself. His grandmother then had his dog killed and the family split again—he and his sister each went to separate schools, while their father went off with his new wife and added a new baby. Then the father left the new wife and baby and went off with yet another wife. As you track the changes, you can see how very many losses Peter experienced: his mother, his father, his grandmother, his sisters, his dog, his nanny, Katie, and his stepmother, Susan. Creating such a map makes the repeated losses powerfully clear. It is helpful in trying to understand anyone's development who has lived through so many changes to map out the actual chronology of moves. Even though such situations can be very complicated, mapping them conveys the trauma of the child's situation and can help a family realize the impact such shifts have on a child. For complex situations, it is worth creating a genogram for any difficult period of time to track the changes in detail.

Triangles with Pets and Objects

Triangling occurs with objects as well as people. A spouse's investment outside the family may be in an affair, work, hobbies, alcohol, the internet, etc., but the impact is similar, except that there is obviously no feedback loop from the inanimate third point in the triangle. What often happens with triangling an inanimate object, as with triangling a person, however, is that the closer the person gets to the affair, the job, or the internet, the more negative the spouse is likely to become toward both the person and the object of his or her "affection." In reaction, the more

Figure 5.11:   Peter Fonda's Living Situations Before Adulthood

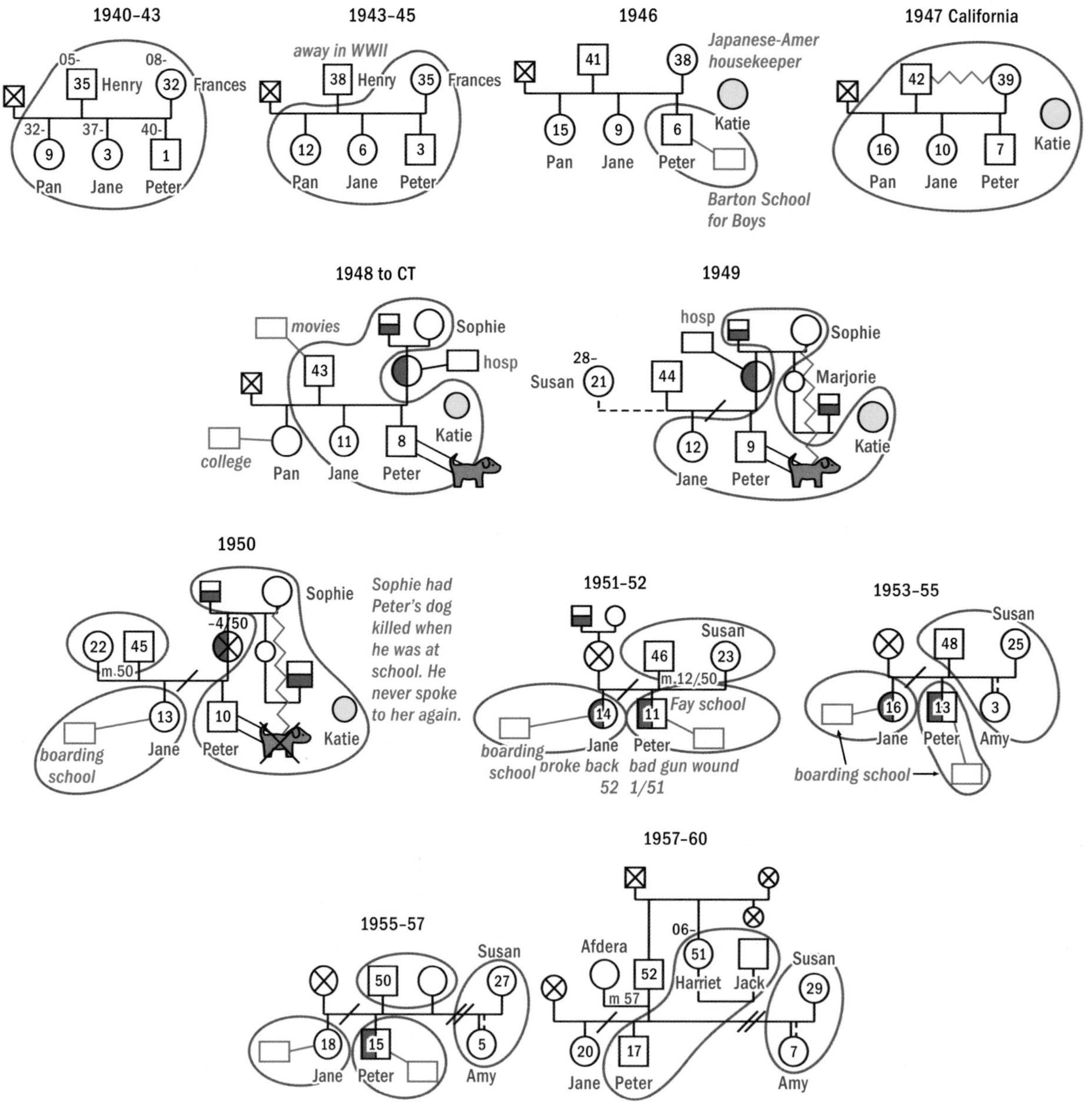

negative the spouse becomes toward the partner's preoccupation with the object, the closer the partner may move toward it, to avoid the spouse's complaints. Such triangles should be noted on a genogram. Family members may also triangulate with the family dog, the resulting pattern being that the closer the person is to the animal, the more negativity is created at the other end of the triangle.

As we have seen, Peter Fonda was extremely attached to his dog (**Figure 5.12: Peter Fonda: Triangle with Dog**), especially after he lost his mother to mental illness and then suicide. He felt very much alone, since his father was gone and he was living with his grandmother. The grandmother was, however, very bothered by the dog, and one day had it put to sleep while Peter was away. He never forgave her. Surely her reaction reflected other family traumas that she could not deal with—her daughter's mental illness and suicide, the stress of her alcoholic husband, and then being left by her son-in-law to deal with her grandchildren in the aftermath of their mother's suicide.

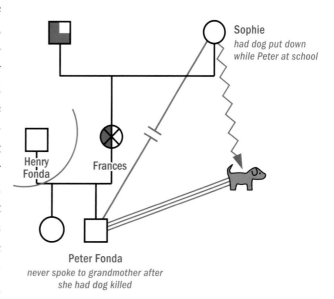

Figure 5.12:   Peter Fonda: Triangle with Dog

Sophie
had dog put down while Peter at school

Henry Fonda

Frances

Peter Fonda
never spoke to grandmother after she had dog killed

The dog undoubtedly became the scapegoat. The dog himself was probably reacting to the family stresses, as pets do, and this may indeed have been difficult for the grandmother to handle. Thus, triangles at times intensify lines of closeness and hostility in a family.

Richly Cross-Joined Families

Problems may arise when there are multiple intermarriages in the family, such as cousins or step-siblings marrying. There comes a point when the clinician must resort to multiple pages or special notes on the genogram to clarify these complexities.

Sometimes a genogram may be confusing because of the multiple connections between family members, as when two members of one family marry two members of another. It has been said that everyone on earth is connected within "six degrees of separation," that is, that within six connections each person becomes connected to each other.

Indeed, every family reaches a point of complexity at which we cannot illustrate all the details at once. Computerized genealogy programs often deal with the complexity by showing just one branch of a family at a time, but there are occasions when the complexity is exactly what we are trying to unravel, so we need to explore whole larger patterns at once. The family of Charles Darwin is one of the most richly cross-joined families we have ever seen! **Figure 5.13: Darwin Family Genogram** shows parts of multiple generations of this multiply intermarried family, which surely influenced Darwin's interest in evolution. There were multiple intermarriages over many generations in the family. Darwin's mother and his wife Emma's father were siblings, so he and Emma were first cousins. In addition, the parents of those two siblings were already 3rd cousins!

In Charles' generation there were multiple marriages of first cousins, in addition to himself and his wife. His sister Caroline married Emma's brother Josiah III, Emma's brother Henry married another first cousin Jessie, and another brother Hensleigh married a first cousin Fanny, though Charles' brother Erasmus had a lifelong love for Fanny as well. And then Charles sister Emily married the husband of Emma's sister, Charlotte, after Charlotte died.

This family included many creative members beyond just Charles and his Wedgewood in-laws, creators of the famous Wedgewood china. Darwin's paternal grandfather, Erasmus Darwin, was a well-known physician, natural scientist, inventor, and poet. The family also included the scientist and inventor Frances Galton and the composer Ralph Vaughan Williams. But there were also family members with serious physical and psychological fragility, which was a great worry to Darwin, who feared that the genetics of cousins marrying cousins was causing these disabilities.

Once a family has so many complexities, it is harder to notice the details of each particular part of the family. For example, Darwin was the second youngest of six children, three older sisters followed by his brother, Erasmus (Raz), who was born on the anniversary of their uncle Erasmus's suicide, and who was in love all his life with his first cousin Fanny. Raz would eventually die of opium addiction.

Darwin's mother died when Charles was only eight, having already become an invalid. He remembered hardly anything about her except her deathbed. He thought this was because his older sisters, in their grief, never wanted to even mention their mother's name. Charles was mainly cared for by his second sister, Caroline, whom he remembered mostly for his feeling of, "What will she blame me for now?", though he also thought of her as clever, kind, and always trying to improve him (Darwin, 1958, p. 22). He described himself as a "naughty boy," who was not very good at his studies except that he adored collecting. He said he was given to "inventing deliberate falsehoods" mainly for the sake of creating excitement (Darwin, 1958, p. 23).

Darwin felt humiliated by his physician father's critical attitude toward him. He remembered his father saying, "You care for nothing but shooting, dogs, and rat-catching, and you will disgrace yourself and your whole family" (Darwin, 1958,

Figure 5.13: Darwin Family Genogram

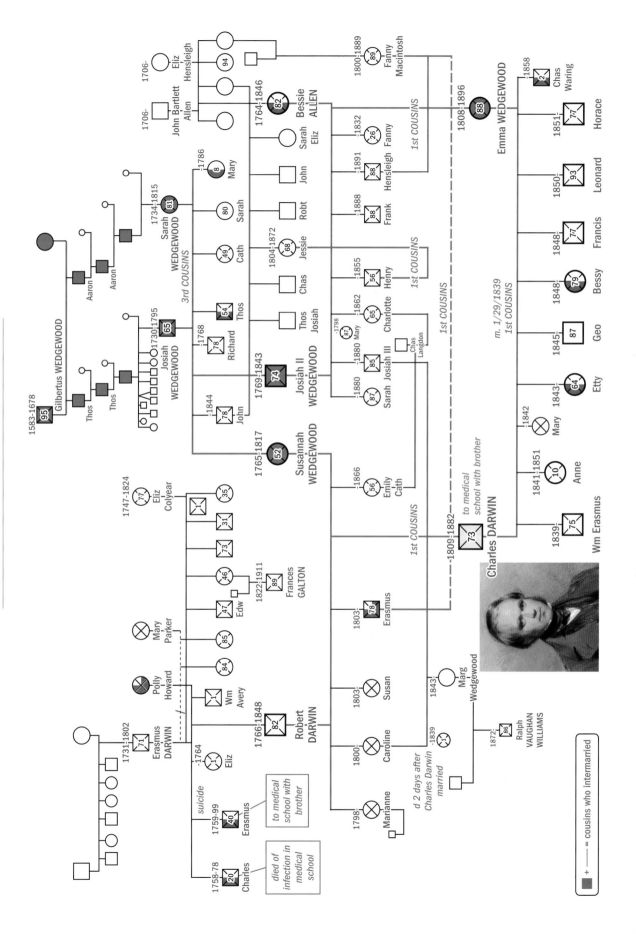

p. 27). Yet, he greatly trusted and admired his father, viewing him as a great diagnostician and the best judge of character he ever met.

The father, Robert Darwin, was the fourth of five children of the brilliant doctor and adventurer, Erasmus Darwin, with his first wife, and the only one to survive. Two children died as babies and a third son, also named Charles, contracted an infection during an operation while in medical school and died. The fourth child, also named Erasmus, later committed suicide, as mentioned, on the same day that Charles' brother Erasmus was later born. Charles Darwin's grandfather had several more relationships and another seven children, but Robert's experience as the sole survivor from the first group seems to have been set.

Robert Darwin's oldest brother, Charles, had been sent to medical school at Edinburgh accompanied by his next younger brother Erasmus. But Erasmus instead became a successful lawyer, who, however, got into debt and committed suicide by drowning himself at the age of 40, four years before his brother Robert's oldest son, Erasmus, was born. Robert himself became a respected physician. He named his second son Charles for his brother who had died tragically in medical school.

When Charles Darwin was 16, his father, Robert, arranged for him to accompany his 22-year-old brother Erasmus to Edinburgh to study medicine, a repeat of what had happened in the father's own family. Like his uncle before him, Charles did not take to medicine. He tried theology before deciding he most wanted to go exploring and to sign on to a five year boat trip to South America. His father totally disapproved. He said he would agree only if Charles could find a single "sane person" to vouch for the idea. Charles found his maternal uncle, Josiah Wedgewood, who later became his father-in-law. The trip was a definer for Darwin in his search to understand evolution. Upon his return he soon decided to marry his Uncle Josiah's youngest daughter, Emma.

To make his decision whether to marry, he decided to create a list of pros and cons. The cons included: that he would miss the conversation of clever men at clubs, he would have the expense and anxiety of children, and perhaps he would quarrel with his wife! The pros included: that he would have an object to be beloved and played with, who would be "better than a dog anyhow" (Johnson, 2018, p. 12).

Charles seems to have made the right decision. He had an extremely close relationship with his wife throughout their lives. At the same time, he had begun to develop his theories about evolution, and asked his father whether he should share his doubts about Christianity with her. His father recommended against it, but Charles told Emma anyway. Emma wrote a note to Charles saying she was very disturbed by some of his opinions and wanted to ask him, but didn't really want him to answer, and he didn't. But he carried her letter with him for the rest of his life, and wrote on the outside for her to find after he had died: "I have kissed this many times and cried over it." But they had never again discussed the issue of evolution and its implications that challenged Christianity.

Interestingly, as Darwin later procrastinated about publishing his theory and research on evolution, he made a clear agreement with Emma that if he died before publishing it, she would carry out the publication, which she agreed to do (p. 64).

The couple had 10 children. Two died in infancy. Several others were invalids for much of their childhood. Charles feared inbreeding was the cause of their problems and ill health. The tragic death of their second oldest child, Annie, at 10 in 1851, was something neither parent ever got over. It was a great blow to the last vestiges of Charles' personal religious faith. Neither parent attended her funeral, nor could they bear to mention her name for the rest of their lives.

At the same time, Darwin was extremely gratified by his family. In his autobiography, he wrote:

> "I have indeed been most happy in my family, and I must say to you, my children, that not one of you has ever given me one minute's anxiety, except on the account of health. There are, I suspect, very few fathers of 5 sons who could say this with entire truth. When you were very young it was my delight to play with you all, and I think with a sigh that such days can never return. From your earliest days to now that you have grown up, you have all, sons and daughters, ever been more pleasant, sympathetic and affectionate to us and to one another. When all or most of you are at home (as, thank heaven, happens pretty frequently) no party can be, according to my taste, more agreeable, and I wish for no other society." (p. 81).

Hypotheses About Darwin's Genogram

Whenever we do a genogram, we are always trying to notice patterns and develop hypotheses to understand the family. We might wonder about several dimensions of the Darwin story. For example:

What role did his sibling position perhaps play in his life journey? We might say that by being the younger brother of an older brother, preceded by three sisters, he was probably allowed a certain latitude to be inventive that would be much less likely for an oldest son. In fact, his father only sent him to medical school to accompany his brother; so perhaps it is no wonder that once he got there (in addition to the fact that he was only 16 at the time) he chose to attend only the classes he wanted to and did not take the official program too seriously.

Darwin's later choice to take a five year voyage would probably also not have been an option for an oldest son, whose parents would surely not want to have him at such a distance for so long, especially without a discernible life plan. To add to that pattern we might notice that Darwin was actually the younger son of a younger son of a younger son for at least three generations.

What role might the early mother loss and having strong-minded, interesting fathers have played? Perhaps the early loss of their mothers made both Robert and his son Charles Darwin become seekers. Both Charles and his father had fathers who were strong, interesting characters. The early mother loss plus their fathers' other preoccupations after the loss of the mother may have expanded the possibilities of both Charles and his father to pursue their own interests. In Charles' case it was his hobby of collecting. Erasmus Darwin's intense pursuit of his varied interests was most similar to that of his grandson. In all cases these were men of intriguing and outsized personality from families of free thinkers.

What about the Wedgewood side of the family? The Wedgewood side of the family were similarly free thinkers. Charles was closest to his mother's brother Josiah, also a younger brother. Darwin's maternal grandfather, Josiah Wedgewood, was the youngest of 12 children. He too had lost a parent (in his case his father) when he was only nine. He was another of the most creative, innovative, artistic men of the age. Coming from a family of potters, he began working for his oldest brother, but was eventually forced to go out on his own, after which he made some of the most creative changes in the family's pottery business. It was Josiah Wedgewood's creative developments that made Wedgewood the famous pottery it became. He loved to experiment and his work was original, characteristics not appreciated by his older brother, who was running the business. In addition, Josiah had had small pox in his youth, which enfeebled him, especially in his knee, forcing him away from spending full days at the potters' bench. This led him to investigate other aspects of the business and thus to develop the creative, artistic, and utilitarian changes in the pottery which made it what it became. When his older brother refused to use his ideas, he moved on and began working with others. He eventually became the Queen's potter, developing many creative ideas along the way.

What role might the closely cross-joined inbreeding in the family have played in Charles' trajectory? Family inbreeding was a great worry to Charles Darwin. We might hypothesize that families that repeatedly marry inward—cousin to cousin—are, as Darwin is often described regarding his choice of a wife, seeking a special familiarity in a spouse, and also perhaps reserving their adventures for other aspects of life. In Darwin's case, his wife was someone he had known all his life and felt extremely comfortable with. This may have been an important factor for him, since he seems to have realized quite early that the radical nature of his research would be a serious challenge and threat to a wife and to the whole society in which he lived. And it was!

Perhaps at another level, Darwin's anxieties about having married his first cousin and the implications of in-breeding for the next generation also drove his study of human evolution.

What role might his lifelong pattern of illness and disability have played in his accomplishments? Might there be something to the many losses and serious dysfunction? There were numerous dysfunctions and losses in the Darwin-Wedgewood families that Charles' own experience resonated with. His mother died when he was eight and he barely remembered her. Apparently after her death the children's feelings were bottled up. Both Charles and Emma were so devastated by the loss of their daughter that neither parent attended her funeral or ever visited her grave. Although Charles was with her when she died, he could not bear to stay for the funeral. Darwin's paternal grandmother had a serious alcohol problem. His daughter Etty (Henrietta) was a lifelong hypochondriac. His daughter Lizzy was said to behave strangely. His maternal uncle Thomas Wedgewood, a talented developer of photography, an opium experimenter, and apparently gay, had a mental breakdown. He died a chronic invalid at the age of 34 (Wikipedia, 2019) . Charles' uncle Erasmus committed suicide and his brother Erasmus became an opium addict (Desmond & Moore, 1991).

On the other hand, his uncle Josiah Wedgewood who had been enfeebled by smallpox and could not stand at a potter's wheel all day, was driven to extraordinary creativity with new methods for pottery. Might Darwin's brilliance in scientific thought have been similarly fostered by his long history of physical illnesses, which limited his health and mobility?

What patterns might have contributed to Darwin's exceptionally good relationship with his wife and children, which were not typical for men of the era? We have no hypotheses about this one, but genogram investigations always begin with the questions!

What patterns might have related to his creative pursuit of radical and highly threatening research, which challenged the dominant religious beliefs of the entire society? Certainly, the free thinking nature of both grandfathers contributed to his adventurous mind, both of whom were innovators that broke the bounds of tradition. They were an extraordinary family of talented and creative artists and scientists, which included the composer Ralph Vaughan Williams and the scientist Frances Galton in later generations.

Unusual Family Configurations

As the clinician scans the genogram, certain structural configurations may "jump out," suggesting critical family themes or problems. The genogram of Elizabeth Blackwell, the first woman physician in the U.S. (**Figure 5.14: Blackwells: Unusual Family Configurations**), illustrates several interesting unusual family configurations:

* This amazing family included Elizabeth Blackwell, the first woman physician, and Antoinette Brown, the first woman minister in the U.S., as well as numerous other successful woman physicians, ministers, artists, and suffragists.
* Yet, as so often happens, patterns of success and failure coexist in the same family. Along with the preponderance of successful women, a fifth sister was an invalid, and the pattern was repeated in the next generation in the family of Samuel Blackwell and Antoinette Brown: two daughters became physicians, one a minister, one an artist, and the fifth, Grace, was an invalid;
* Three sons in the first U.S. generation, who were strong feminists themselves, married extraordinary women in their own right. Samuel married Antoinette Brown, the first woman minister as mentioned, Henry married Lucy Stone, one of the most important early suffrage leaders in the U.S., George married Lucy's cousin, Emma Lawrence, another early suffrage leader. The fourth son, Howard, re-emigrated back to Britain, never married, and died at age 35.
* None of the five sisters ever married, nor had any of the father Samuel's

Figure 5.14: Blackwells: Unusual Family Configurations

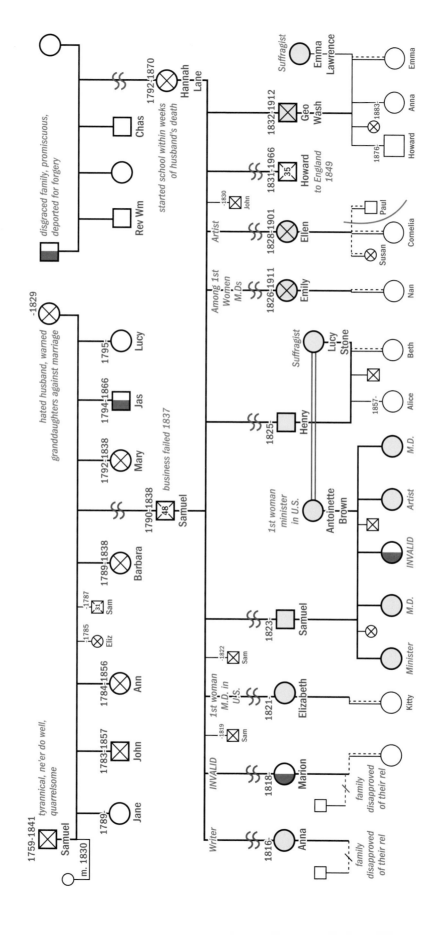

five sisters in the previous generation, and only a few of the 14 women in the third generation.

• The unmarried daughters adopted seven children and their brothers adopted two more. Only one of these children was male and that one was given back because he did not fit in to the family.

The Blackwells were a remarkably creative, resilient family who show a dramatic pattern of strong and successful women. The role of gender in this family of extraordinary feminists (several of them men!) is worth exploration. It would be fascinating to know the rules and attitudes that influenced this pattern. Some of these patterns have been suggested by Horn (1983), who says that the family viewed marriage negatively and actively discouraged the daughters from marrying. Two of the three sisters-in-law, Lucy Stone and Antoinette Brown, became best friends in college at Oberlin, resolving never to marry, but to adopt and raise children. When they met the extraordinary Blackwell brothers, however, they changed their minds. One is forced to wonder whether deeper forces are at play in some families, in which certain members seem to absorb negative energy, which is lived out through sickness or anger, freeing others for creativity and achievement.

The parents believed in equal education for women. In a family like this, one can't help asking about the underlying gender constraints and empowerment mechanisms. The family discouraged the one daughter, Marion, when she became interested in a young man who was a friend of her brother's. When Marion fell in love, Elizabeth wrote to discourage her, "The idea of your union seems to me now utterly impossible," offering herself as a substitute companion for her sister's romantic interest (Hays, 1967, p. 53). Only one other sister, Anna, ever became engaged, in her case to a "handsome, wealthy, educated, amiable, and fascinating man," but the family closed ranks against him, writing very strong letters to dissuade her from the marriage (Hays, 1967, pp. 52-3).

A different kind of unusual configuration is demonstrated on the genogram of Thomas Jefferson, the third President of the United States (**Figure 5.15: Thomas Jefferson**). Jefferson has an extraordinarily convoluted genogram, involving marriages and liaisons from within the same few families, both slave and white. Such configurations were a common occurrence in the era of slavery. White slave owners frequently fathered children with their slaves and then denied this parentage, making it very difficult for African Americans to know their history (Pinderhughes, 2019). The cutoffs and conflicts produced by this exploitation of African Americans, as well as by the systematic effort to suppress the cultural and family history of African Americans throughout our history, has been a shameful part

Figure 5.15: Thomas Jefferson

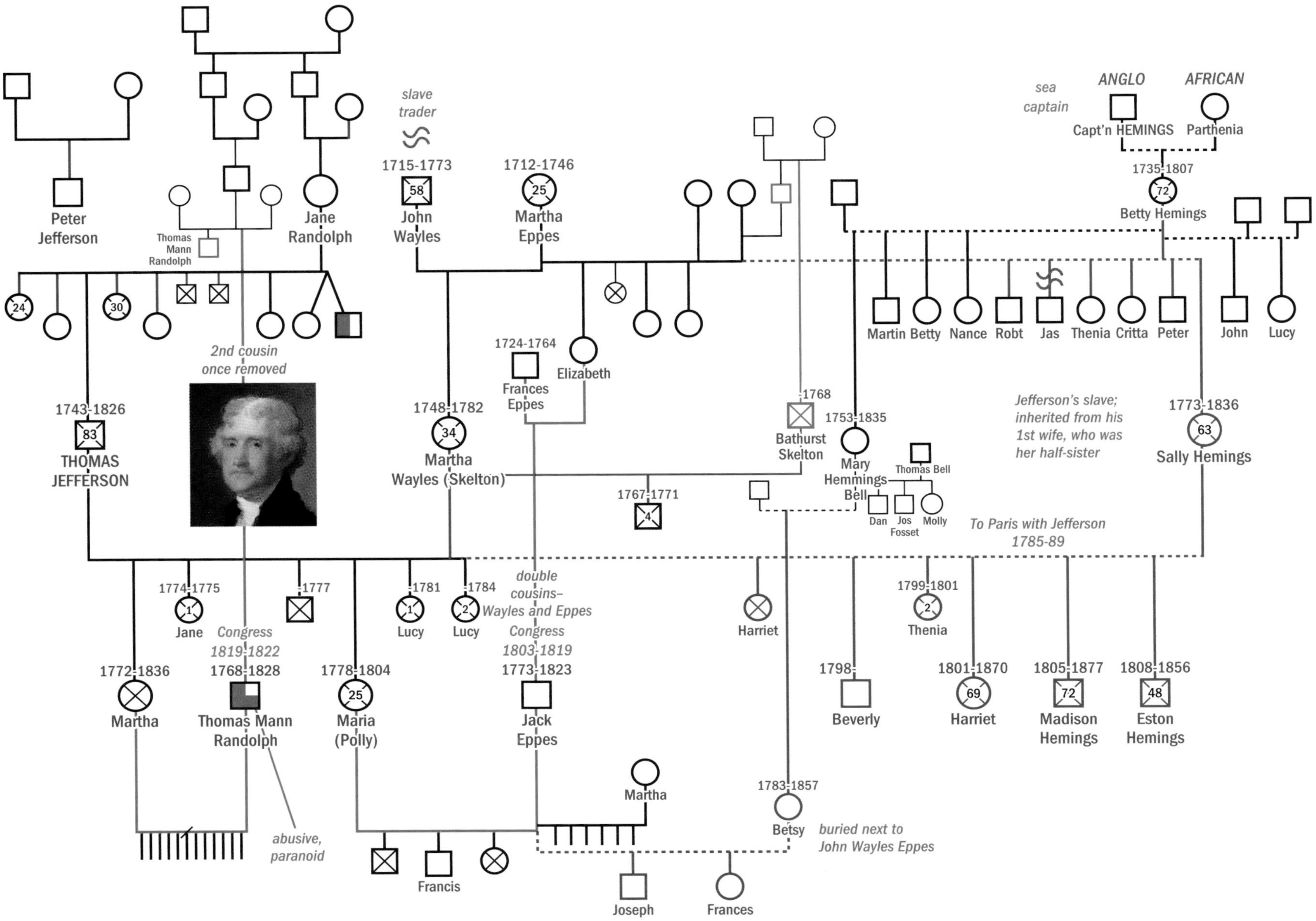

of our national heritage. Facing this history is an important part of healing and changing such patterns of exploitation. Making sense of this interracial configuration is a challenge. As Pinderhughes has said:

> The invisibility of African Americans in the recorded history of the United States has led to a pervasive ignorance for everyone, Black or white, about African Americans and their contributions to the building of our country . . . With no power to affect the writing of American history and few resources to disseminate our story, it has remained invisible or distorted by negative stereotypes, and we have until recently remained unable or unwilling to challenge the distortions, untruths, and omissions that have been accepted about our past . . . But we are coming to realize that knowledge of the past, even if painful, can nourish a people's strength. This realization has stimulated us to unseal these memories and reclaim the truth, no matter how cruel and shocking, so that the festering wound can begin to heal and so that we can better cope with the present and build the future. (2019, p. 427)

Historians have been extremely reluctant to face the truth of this history for families like that of Thomas Jefferson, in which there were many interconnected secret rapes and relationships. Jefferson's white family, along with numerous white historians, went to great lengths to cover up this part of the family history for more than 200 years. Historians have only recently been forced at long last to confront their own racism by the DNA tests performed on descendants of Jefferson and his slave, Sally Hemings. It is often necessary to carefully reassess the history we have been told in order to understand the truth of the relationships on our genograms.

Indeed, Jefferson's father-in-law, John Wayles, a slave trader himself, had a long secret relationship with his slave Betty Hemings, by whom he had six children. Wayles had owned Betty's mother, who became pregnant by a white ship captain who wanted to buy her freedom, but Wayles' father-in-law, Frances Eppes, had refused to sell her.

Jefferson inherited Wayles' slaves, including Betty and her daughter Sally Hemings, and had a 38-year secret relationship and seven children with her (shown in blue green on the genogram). Sally was the half-sister of his first wife, Martha Wayles Jefferson, who had died young.

Jefferson's daughters both married cousins (lines shown in red to indicate the cousin connection); Martha married the nephew of her paternal grandmother, and Maria (Polly) married John Wayles Eppes, a cousin on her grandmother's side, who had married her mother's half-sister. In the third generation of such relationships, Jefferson's son-in-law, John Wayles Eppes, after his wife Polly died, had a long relationship with one of Sally Heming's nieces, Betsy Hemings, with whom he had at least two children, although he remarried during their relationship. When Betsy Hemings died, she was buried next to him.

In addition, Thomas Jefferson's wife Martha's first husband, Bathurst Skelton, was the younger brother of her stepmother's first husband (the two brothers are shown in light green). Jefferson's family clearly had a tendency to turn inwards for their relationships and became a very richly cross-joined family.

To add complication to complexity, Thomas Mann Randolph's father, Thomas Mann Randolph Sr., got married for a second time in 1790 at the age of 50 to a 17-year-old named Gabriela Harvie. She bore him a son whom he again named "Thomas Mann Randolph" as if to erase his first son, who had the same name, Thomas Mann Randolph (Gordon-Reed, 2008). Such complexities can often reveal patterns in a family that become clinically relevant as we try to explore the more obvious dysfunctions they present at intake.

Children Growing Up in Multiple Families: Foster Care, Adoption, and Orphanage Experiences

Many children grow up in multiple settings because their parents divorce, die, remarry, or have special circumstances that require the child to live for a while or even permanently in a different setting. Genograms can be particularly useful for tracking children in multiple foster placements. Clinicians have often failed to make full use of genograms in such circumstances to track children through the life cycle, taking into account the multiple family contexts to which they belong. The numerous different family constellations children may live in are otherwise extremely hard to keep in mind. The more clear clinicians are in tracking the actuality of this history, however complex, the better able they will be to validate the child's actual experience and multiple forms of belonging. Such genograms can begin to make order out of the multiple household changes children may go through when sudden transitions or shifts in placement are necessary because of illness, trauma, or other loss.

Dr. Fernando Colon, a family therapist in Ann Arbor Michigan, has long been one of the strongest advocates for the relevance of family history for children who have lived in foster care. Colon himself grew up in several foster homes after the loss of his mother (**Figure 5.16: Fernando Colon: Foster Care**). As an adult he

Figure 5.16: Fernando Colon: Foster Care

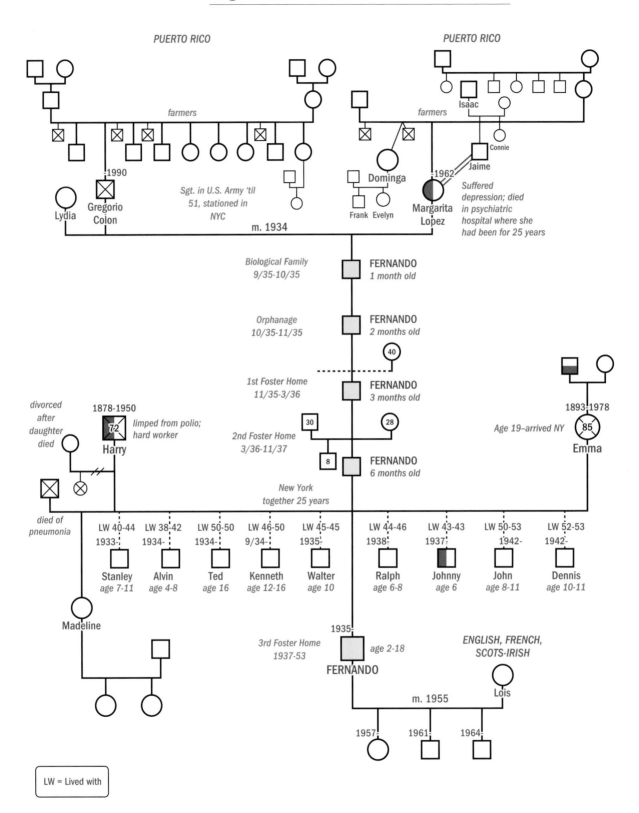

LW = Lived with

put much effort into exploring his own genogram (Colon, 1973, 1998, 2005) and helping others to think contextually about child placement and foster care (Colon, 1978). He has made a clear case for the importance of foster family genograms for understanding both the past and the future of foster children through the life cycle. Throughout his life, Colon maintained ongoing connections with the biological grandchildren of his third foster mother. They shared holidays and frequent other visits with their grandmother, his foster mother. They had much in common through this shared history, a history which is so often not acknowledged in our foster care system and in our society at large. One of the most powerful aspects of genograms is the way they can steer us to the rich possibilities of complex kin relationships, which continue throughout life to be sources of connection and support. It is not just our shared history that matters, but current connections that strengthen us and can enrich our future. Colon published his full story (2005) with illustrative pictures and genograms. He grew up mostly in foster homes from earliest infancy. He had experience in virtually every sibling constellation during his childhood years, a factor that probably increased his flexibility in dealing with multiple relationships as an adult. He was the youngest of three, the oldest of three, the middle of three, the older of two, the younger of two, but rarely an only child, although as the one child who remained with the family for his entire childhood, his position was a special one. At the same time, the three brothers who stayed for long periods of time (four years each) not surprisingly had more significance for him, especially because they were all close to Fernando in age. Less evident from the ages alone was the extremely special relationship that Fernando and his foster mother had with his brother Johnny, a child with severe developmental disabilities, who lived in the family for only four months. Both Fernando and his foster mother became very attached to Johnny through caring for him, and Fernando remembers clearly how hard Johnny tried to learn to say Fernando's name, and how he and his mother cried when they had to let Johnny go.

Whether relationships have been good or bad, beneficial or injurious, they are not to be dismissed. And most of the time they are not all positive or all negative, but rather some of each. Organizing family data on genograms has enabled people to put many fragments of their lives back together in a meaningful whole. As an adult, Fernando undertook a remarkable endeavor to find and reconnect with his family in Puerto Rico and in the U.S., which has continued over the past 30 years. Though his father had told him his biological mother had died, he found the town where she lived and went there, discovering that she had spent years in a mental hospital and that he had missed her by only a few years. He also discovered that he was related to almost everyone in the town.

Although the foster care system at that time operated on the principle that children were never to have contact with a previous family once they moved to a new home, Fernando's foster mother did not believe in that kind of cutting off. She made great efforts to reverse the process. In the early days of placement, one of his foster brothers, Kenneth, was especially depressed. Kenneth was one of five brothers, and, in spite of the regulations, his foster mother took him to see his brothers, after which he began to adjust to his new home. Colon's experience is an awesome lesson to anyone who is unable to see beyond the cutoffs that may occur in a family. *No* relationship should be discarded, because you never know who may be connected to that cutoff. Colon, by making creative use of his genogram, stayed connected to his foster family throughout his life and reconnected richly and rewardingly with his families of origin.

The accepted practice of severing any family ties, is, in our view, a tremendous tragedy. It has often led to therapists being drawn in to replace other relationships in a person's natural system. As Colon's own family demonstrates so well, such cutoffs leave people depressed, bereft, and weakened. A cutoff of one person tends to lead to multiple cutoffs of other family members and to the loss of many potentially rich relationships. It weakens the entire fabric of one's life. Doing the genogram can counter this tendency to oversimplify and cutoff, by making clear the enormity of the losses, as one scans the numerous people involved, and opens up the rich possibilities for connection and meaning.

As Colon's story shows, connections with others who have grown up in the same foster family may last a lifetime and reconnections at later life cycle stages may be particularly meaningful. This is one more illustration of the importance of creating genogram maps—to bear witness to the truth and complexity of people's lives, no matter how traumatic their experiences may have been.

Adoption Experiences: Steve Jobs

Here's to the crazy ones. The misfits. The rebels. The troublemakers. The round pegs in the square holes. The ones who see things differently. They're not fond of rules. And they have no respect for the status quo. You can quote them, disagree with them, glorify or vilify them. About the only thing you can't do is ignore them. Because they change things. They push the human race forward. While some may see them as the crazy ones, we see genius. Because the people who are crazy enough to think they can change the world, are the ones who do.

— Apple Inc. commercial.

We know Steve Jobs as the creator of Apple, one of the pioneers of the computer revolution. Not only was his life defined by his having been adopted, but also by his cohort: He was born on Feb 24, 1955, which was, according to Malcolm Gladwell (2011), the pivotal year for computer developers. Bill Gates was born the same year, as well as Eric Schmidt, CEO of Google, who ran Novell, one of Silicon Valley's most important software firms. Internet guru Bill Joy was born in November 1954.

Steve Jobs (**Figure 5.17: Steve Jobs: Adoption**) was the son of Abdulfattah "John" Jandali, an immigrant from a prominent Syrian Muslim family, who was a political science graduate student in Wisconsin. His mother, Joanne Schieble, was an undergraduate, the daughter of a Wisconsin German and Swiss farming family. His mother gave him up for adoption at birth, because her father disapproved of her relationship with Jandali.

Jobs was adopted by a couple in California—Paul Jobs, whose family had also been Wisconsin German farmers, and Clara Hagopian, who was of Armenian heritage. So Steve Jobs was raised by parents who were of backgrounds very similar to his biological parents, though their social status was quite different.

Joanne's father died soon after she gave up her son, and she and Jandali went on to marry and have a second child, a daughter, Mona Simpson, who has become a well-known writer. The parents later divorced, and Joanne remarried a man named Simpson.

Jandali was apparently the youngest of three sons in a wealthy family from Homs, Syria. He completed his PhD in 1956 and later taught at several universities, including the University of Puget Sound in Tacoma, Washington. He then, apparently, lost his academic position when he abandoned a group of students he was leading on a trip to Egypt, gambling away their money and disappearing. He eventually resurfaced in the restaurant and casino business in Nevada, where he has remained. His second wife had grown children when he married her, and they lived in Reno. After her death he married for a third time in 2008.

Steve's adoptive father, Paul Jobs, was a high school dropout, but an excellent mechanic. His adoptive mother, Clara Hagopian Jobs, was a bookkeeper who was married previously to a soldier who died in World War II (that was not talked about and thus we have drawn a triangle near it on the genogram). Steve grew up with a younger sister Patricia, who was also adopted, in a working class neighbor-

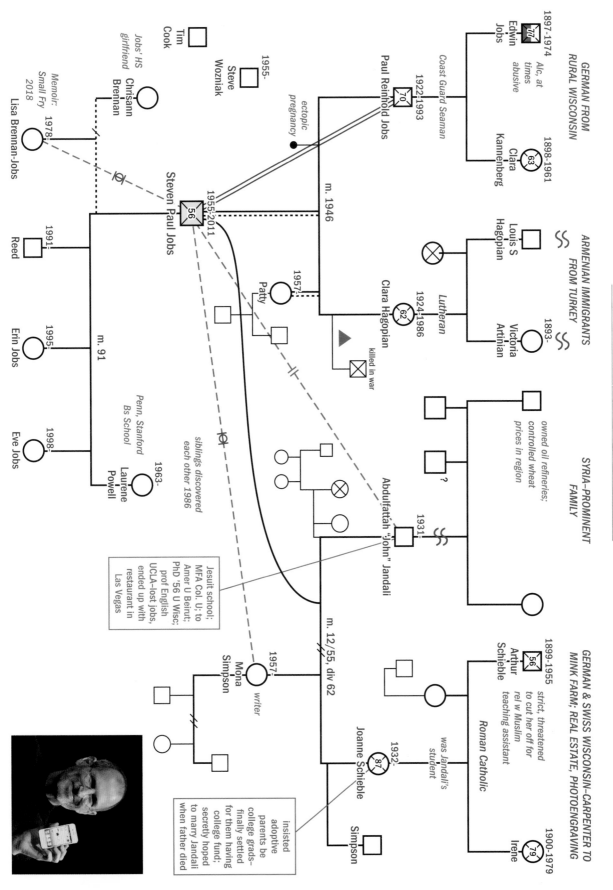

Figure 5.17: Steve Jobs: Adoption

GERMAN FROM RURAL WISCONSIN

Edwin Jobs
1897-1974
77
Alc, at times abusive

Clara Kannenberg
1898-1961
63

Paul Reinhold Jobs
1922-1993
70
Coast Guard Seaman

ectopic pregnancy

m. 1946

ARMENIAN IMMIGRANTS FROM TURKEY

Louis S Hagopian

Victoria Artinian
1893-
Lutheran

Clara Hagopian
1924-1986
62

killed in war

Steven Paul Jobs
1955-2011
56

Patty
1957?

SYRIA—PROMINENT FAMILY

owned oil refineries; controlled wheat prices in region

?

Abdulfattah "John" Jandali
1931-

Mona Simpson
1957-
writer

m. 12/55, div 62

Steve Wozniak
1955-

Tim Cook
Jobs' HS girlfriend
Chrisann Brennan

Memoir: Small Fry 2018

Lisa Brennan-Jobs
1978-

Reed
1991-

Erin Jobs
1995-

Eve Jobs
1998-

m. 91

Laurene Powell
1963-

Penn, Stanford Bs School

siblings discovered each other 1986

Jesuit school; MFA Col. U; to Amer U Beirut; PhD '56 U Wisc; prof English UCLA–lost jobs, ended up with restaurant in Las Vegas

GERMAN & SWISS WISCONSIN–CARPENTER TO MINK FARM; REAL ESTATE, PHOTOENGRAVING

Arthur Schieble
1899-1955
56
strict, threatened to cut her off for rel w Muslim
Roman Catholic
teaching assistant

Irene
1900-1979
79

Joanne Schieble
1932-
87
was Jandali's student

Simpson

insisted adoptive parents be college grads—finally settled for them having college fund; secretly hoped to marry Jandali when father died

hood in California. Paul and Clara had to promise Jobs' biological parents that they would make sure their son went to college. They saved for years for this, though in the end Jobs attended Reed College in Oregon for only one semester. He barely attended class, but was allowed to stay on auditing classes with the College President's permission, including one in calligraphy, which appears to have had much influence on his later emphasis on fonts and the look of letters in Apple computers.

All his life, Jobs seems to have suffered from feelings of rejection for having been given up for adoption. Yet, when he himself had his first child, Lisa, by his high school girlfriend, Chrisann Brennan, he denied paternity. Interestingly, both he and Chrisann were 23, the same age his mother was when he was born! He did not acknowledge Lisa for years. Chrisann was eventually forced to bring a paternity suit to get him to support his daughter. It was still years more before he began to spend any time with Lisa, and he pressed her to cutoff her mother in order to connect with him. It was not until 1987 that he became involved with her. Jobs' biographer, Walter Isaacson, quotes Lisa's mother as later saying that being put up for adoption left Jobs "full of broken glass . . . He who is the abandoned becomes the abandoner" (Isaacson, 2011, p. 5). He was a complex personality, possessing phenomenal energy, enthusiasm, and charisma in his creative endeavors, and on the other hand capable of coldness and cruelty to others, with hardly a hint of regret.

Jobs grew up close to his adoptive father Paul, who taught him a lot about working with electronics. The two of them spent many hours in the family garage, where Jobs learned a great deal about hard work and mechanics. Later, he gave his father much credit for the perfectionism of his design sense, saying his father would insist that even the back of a bookcase should be perfect, just like the part you see.

Because of his high intelligence, Jobs struggled in school, often feeling bored. By high school his father realized he was much more intelligent than he was himself, which was a hard moment for both of them.

Having been bullied earlier in his school life, Jobs had few friends his own age in high school. His friends were those interested in math, science, electronics, pot, and LSD. He lived in Silicon Valley, which was full of engineers, and where a neighbor turned him on to Heathkits. He joined a Hewlett-Packard Explorer's Club and eventually needed a part for something he was making. He looked up Bill Hewlett of Hewlett Packard in the phone book and called him. He got the part and also a summer job.

In personality he was arrogant and difficult. But he was also brilliant and creative, continuing throughout his life to reinvent himself and his computers until the very end.

He began developing video games for Atari. Two years later, he and his future partner, Steve Wosniak, started Apple Computers. Jobs was only 21. His father let them use his garage and helped them in their business. Wosniak became the designer of very user-friendly computers and Jobs was in charge of marketing. Their business did extraordinarily well.

As an adult, Jobs decided to make the effort to find his biological mother, and did so. She told him about his sister Mona, whom he then met also, but when she suggested they find their father he was unwilling. Later Mona found their father, but Jobs said he had decided from whatever information he had found about the father that he did not want to meet him. It turned out that some years earlier, Steve and the father had actually met, when Jobs happened to go to the father's restaurant. Neither realized at the time that they were related. Jobs made the decision not to meet his father again, a decision which, from a systems perspective, is regrettable.

In 1990 he met his future wife Laureen Powell, an MBA student at Stanford, who appears to have been an extremely positive influence on him. Together they had three children.

An article about Jandali from the *Daily Mail* in Britain says that:

"In the months leading up to Steve Jobs's death, Mr. Jandali became overcome with guilt for abandoning his son. But he admitted that after all this time he was too proud to make the first move to arrange a meeting. Mr. Jandali . . . said he did not call Mr. Jobs for fear he would wrongly think he was after his money. He said at the time: 'This might sound strange, . . . but I am not prepared, even if either of us was on our deathbeds, to pick up the phone to call him.'" (www.dailymail.com, Nov 7, 2012).

This quote suggests that father and son both had the same reluctance to face some aspect of their identity, which we would hope Jobs' children do not carry on into the next generation. To understand the reluctance, we would need to know much more about the family Jandali came from and the role he played. Was he the only one to come to the U.S.? How did he go from being a son of a wealthy oil family in Syria to being a college professor of political science in Wisconsin, to a restaurateur and then casino owner in Reno? And what about the rest of the family? Were there siblings who also immigrated to the U.S.? How did they fare? We may wonder now what has happened to the Jandali family in Syria. They come from Homs, which became a primary opposition stronghold and experienced a major attack in 2011. What has happened to the family in the past few years? Have they become part of the opposition in Syria? Have they become refugees? Have others come to the U.S.?

There are also more specific family questions we might ask: Were others as brilliant as Steve? Were they as interested in beautiful, streamlined, simple things? Were any as quirky in their eating habits or driven by spiritual quests or as difficult in their personal relationships as Jobs? Did any of the rest of the family abandon children? And why did Jobs repeat the same abandonment with his daughter Lisa that had been such a painful part of his own history? The interesting and transformative aspect is that Lisa herself has written a remarkable memoir, *Small Fry* (Brennan-Jobs, 2018), which is blunt about her experiences growing up in relation to her father, but very clear-sighted and thoughtful about her life. Though at some point she did the same cutoff of her mother in spite of her father's refusal to relate to her for many years, she conveys a profound understanding of her own evolution through her still young life. At the point when Jobs told Lisa that to be with him and his family, she would have to cut her mother off, Lisa did it. She says:

> "I'd leave my mother. . . having stolen her youth and energy, having driven her to a state of perpetual anxiety, without support or resources, now that I was flourishing in school and beloved by my teachers, I cast her out and picked him, the one who'd left. I chose the pretty place, when she was the one who'd read me books of old stories with admonishment not to believe in the trick of facades." (Brennan-Jobs, 2018, p. 235).

But she reconnected with her mother and went through many more complex and painful trials with her father, developing positive connections with her stepmother and aunt as well as other key family supporters who filled in gaps that her father left (such as cutting off her support when she was in college, yet demanding her fealty when he wanted it). She appears to have worked continuously to build her connections and understanding of her own and her parents' stories.

Our view would be that it is never time to shut the door to possibilities for learning your history. Perhaps one day Lisa or another of Jobs' children will make the effort to reconnect with the father's family. They would probably learn a lot about themselves from knowing about their grandfather and his family as well.

6

Exploring Sibling Constellations with Genograms

E xploring sibling constellations is a key aspect of genogram work. Many factors influence sibling patterns, including the timing of a child's birth in history and in the family's evolution; gender; distance apart in age (identical twins being the ultimate siblings); sibling constellation; loss; temperament; abilities and disabilities in the siblings; ethnicity; and life circumstances (Cicirelli, 1989, 1995; Bank & Kahn, 1997; Kluger, 2011; Leman, 2009; Mathias, 1992; McGoldrick, 1989; McGoldricik & Watson, 2016; McNaron, 1985; Norris & Tindale, 1994; Richardson & Richardson, 2000; Sulloway, 1996). The importance of sibling constellations has long been appreciated, beginning at least with the insights of Alfred Adler (1959) and later Walter Toman (1976). Our siblings are, as both Adler and Toman long ago pointed out, our earliest experience of peers. So, it's natural that the oldest would tend to become a leader, a youngest might expect to be taken care of, and a middle child might become a mediator, a rebel, or get lost in the pack.

There also tend to be sibling pairings, or at other times deep sibling conflicts. An important question to consider is the amount of time brothers and sisters spent together when young. Two children who are close in age, particularly if they are of the same gender, generally spend a lot of time together. They share their parents' attention and are often raised as a pair. Siblings born more than 6 years apart generally spend less time with each other and thus have fewer shared experiences; they grow up at different points in the family's evolution, and are, indeed, generally more like only children (Toman, 1976).

But these are just generalizations and may not apply in a particular situation. You have to explore each family to see how the patterns play out. When Bill Clinton's parents divorced in 1962, Bill, who had never been adopted by his stepfather, decided to change his name officially from Blythe to Clinton to connect him to his half brother, Roger Clinton, to whom he felt a deep sense of loyalty and caring. He seems to have done this because of his wish to protect his brother from his stepfather's abusive, alcoholic behavior. So even when siblings are 10 years apart in age as Bill and Roger were, we must never discount the importance of sibling, half-sibling and step-sibling relationships.

At present, sibling patterns in the U.S. and around the globe are undergoing significant changes, primarily because of the lower birthrate and changing family structural patterns that have followed the increasing availability of birth control, the women's movement, and the entry of more women into the paid work force. In today's world of frequent divorce and remarriage, families often have a combination of siblings, step-siblings, and half-siblings, who may live in different households and only come together occasionally. There are also more only children, whose closest sibling-like relationships will be their playmates. In addition, more often than in previous generations, there are two-child families, where relationships tend to be more intense than when there are multiple siblings. Clearly, the more time siblings have with one another and the fewer siblings there are, the more intense their relationships are likely to be. In large sibling groups, subgroups tend to form according to gender and distance in age. Two brothers born 18 months apart may form a dyad, and their two younger sisters born five and seven years later may form a second subsystem.

While Adler saw sibling constellation as a key factor in development, Freud ignored it completely, writing an entire autobiography without even mentioning that he had any siblings, though as we will see he had eight. Adler's ideas about family constellation seem to have derived from his personal experience. As psychiatric historian Henri Ellenberger described his thinking:

According to Adler, each one of the children in a family is born and grows up with a specific perspective according to his or her position in relation to the other siblings. From the outset, the position of the oldest brother is better than that of the younger ones. He is made to feel that he is the stronger, the wiser, the most responsible. That is why he values the concept of authority and tradition and is conservative in his views. The youngest brother, on the other hand, is always in danger of remaining the spoiled and cowardly family baby. Whereas the oldest will take his father's profession, the youngest may easily become an artist, or then, as the result of overcompensation, he will develop tremendous ambition and strive to be the savior of the entire family. The second child in a family is under perpetual pressure from both sides, striving to outmatch his older brother and fearing to be overtaken by the younger one. As for the only child, he is even more disposed to be spoiled and pampered than the youngest one. His parents' preoccupation with his health may cause him to become anxious and timorous. Such patterns are subject to modifications according to the distance between siblings and according to the proportion of boys and girls and their respective position in the family. If the oldest brother is closely followed by a sister, there comes a time when he will fear being outdistanced by the girl, who will mature more rapidly than he. Among many other possible situations are those of the only girl in a family of boys, and of the only boy among a constellation of girls (a particularly unfavorable situation, according to Adler) (Ellenberger, 1970, pp. 613–14).

This appears to fit very closely with Adler's own family experience. (**Figure 6.1: Alfred Adler Sibling Constellation**). He was a middle child, the son of two middle children, and he even married a middle child. Adler was himself sickly as a child. He had rickets, nearly died of pneumonia at age five, and was twice hit by moving vehicles. He felt that he was always in his older brother Sigmund's shadow. Indeed, though Sigmund eventually became very successful in real estate, in his earlier life he was forced to leave school because the father was not doing well enough to support the family and he needed to help out, while Alfred was able to continue his schooling and become a doctor. Adler's biographer Hoffman (1940) described the brothers' relationship as one of "relentless competition." (According to Ellenberger (1970), there had been an oldest brother, Albert, who died as a baby). As can be seen on the genogram, Alfred was followed closely by his sister, Hermine, with whom he apparently had little relationship in adulthood, though they were close in childhood. Very possibly he grew up with a fear of being outdistanced by her. When Alfred was four, the third little brother, Rudolf, died in bed next to him, which must have been very traumatic, even though child deaths were common in their time and situation.

The fourth brother, Max, seems to have been "born to rebel" (Sulloway, 1996) and was apparently very envious of Adler. He distanced from the family, moving to Rome and converting to Catholicism. The youngest child, Richard, was a typical youngest. He seems to have been spoiled and never quite able to take care of himself. He lived with his mother until her death, aspiring to be an artist and musician, but always had trouble supporting himself, living at times with Alfred and receiving support from him and from the oldest brother, Sigmund.

Missing information is always of interest on a genogram. In Adler's case, in spite of his explicit belief about the importance of sibling relationships for determining behavior, his biographers have given only sketchy and conflicting infor-

Figure 6.1: Alfred Adler Sibling Constellation

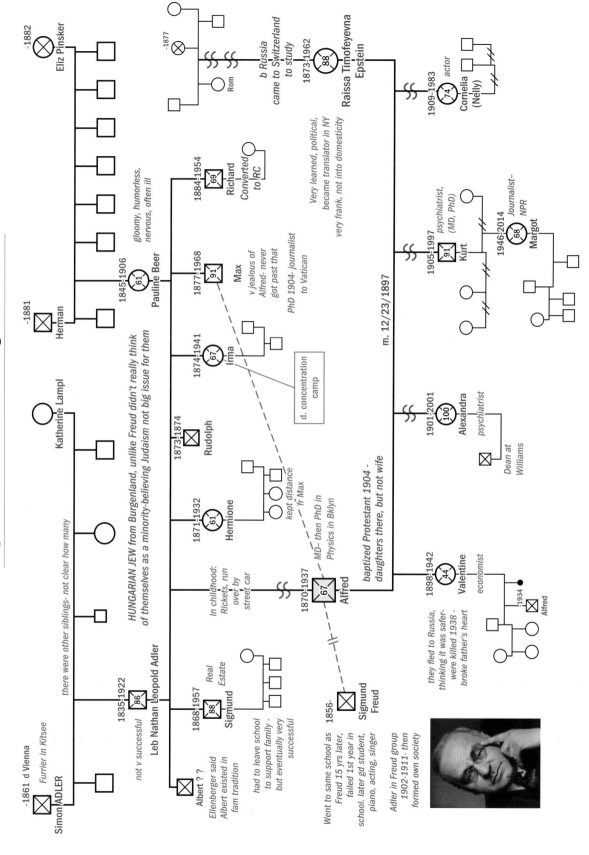

mation about his own sibling constellation (see bibliography section on Adler). We know even less about the sibling or family patterns of Adler's parents, a fact that is true also for Freud, Horney, and Jung, in spite of the great interest there has been in their work and their psychological make-up. Clearly, biographers have yet to take a systemic view of history (McGoldrick, 2011).

Sibling position can have particular relevance for a person's emotional position in the family of origin and with a future spouse and children or relations at work. An oldest child is more likely to be over-responsible, conscientious, and parental, while the youngest is more likely to be child-like and carefree. Often, oldest children will feel special and particularly responsible for maintaining the family's welfare or carrying on family tradition. They may feel they have a heroic mission to fulfill in life. In addition, sometimes the oldest will resent younger siblings, feeling they are an intrusion on his or her earlier exclusive possession of the parents' love and attention. The oldest child's experience is very different from that of the youngest, while middle children may feel caught in between and may have a need to find their niche and define themselves as different (Sulloway, 1996). Birth order can also profoundly influence later experiences with spouses, friends, and work colleagues, though, of course, it does not guarantee a particular type of personality. There are many other factors that influence sibling roles, such as temperament, ability and disability, physical appearance, ethnicity, intelligence, talent, gender, sexual orientation, and the timing of each birth in relation to other family experiences—especially deaths, moves, illnesses, and changes in financial status.

Twins

Twins and other multiple births are becoming more common because of fertility drugs and the development of modern medical resources. Prior to fertility drugs, about one person in 50 was a twin, although about one in eight pregnancies began as twins (Wright, 1995). Twins have a special relationship that is exclusive of the rest of the family. The grip twins hold on our imagination perhaps relates to the fact that their very existence challenges our sense of uniqueness (Wright, 1995). They have been known to develop their own language and maintain an uncanny, almost telepathic sense of each other. When one twin dies the other may experience lifelong guilt. Even fraternal twins often have remarkable similarities, because of their shared life experiences.

The major challenge for twins is to develop individual identities. Others may not understand how intimately they are connected—often seemingly able to read each other's minds. On the other hand, since they do not have their own unique sibling position, there is a tendency for others to lump them together (especially identical twins) and they may have to go to extremes to distinguish themselves from each other.

Different Roles for Brothers and Sisters

Brothers and sisters generally have very different roles in a family. Sisters of sisters also tend to have very different sibling patterns than sisters of brothers. Research indicates that, because of society's preference for boys, the segregation of boys and girls in their socialization is quite extreme from early childhood (Maccoby, 1990). In co-ed situations, boys tend to ignore or mistreat girls, whose wishes do not get equal attention. If a brother is older, he is often favored and catered to. If the brother is younger, he may be envied and resented by the sister for his special status.

The example of Princess Diana, while particular to her family's situation, also reflects general gender problems that exist the world over (**Figure 6.2: Princess Diana's Family: Different Roles for Brothers & Sisters**). Diana was the third daughter in a family whose status depended on producing a son who would become, upon the death of his father, the ninth Earl of Althorp, inheriting an estate worth about $140 million dollars. If the parents did not produce a son, they would have to leave the estate, so they were desperate. Their third child had been a boy, born the year before Diana, but he died shortly after birth. When Diana was born, the parents were so disappointed they did not even bother to register her birth (as happened also with Maria Callas, born after the loss of her parents' two-year-old son). Diana was the only one of her siblings who did not have a royal godparent. As she described it, "I was a disappointment. My parents were hoping for a boy. . . they hadn't even thought of a (girl's) name for me." (Campbell, 1998, p. 1). Although she was finally given the name of the one ancestor who almost married into the royal family, her position probably led to both her sense of inadequacy and her carefully cultivated aura of being special. As the third girl in a family that required a son and had just lost one, she would definitely need to be "different" to find a niche, and different she became. Her position was greatly alleviated, of course, when her younger brother was born three years later. Indeed, he became, not surprisingly, her favorite (the more so because the parents divorced soon afterwards) and the two siblings became each other's primary refuge. But years after the parents hostile divorce, conflictual remarriages, and Diana's own publicly aired problems with her husband, she asked her brother—who had just become

Figure 6.2:   Princess Diana's Family: Different Roles for Brothers & Sisters

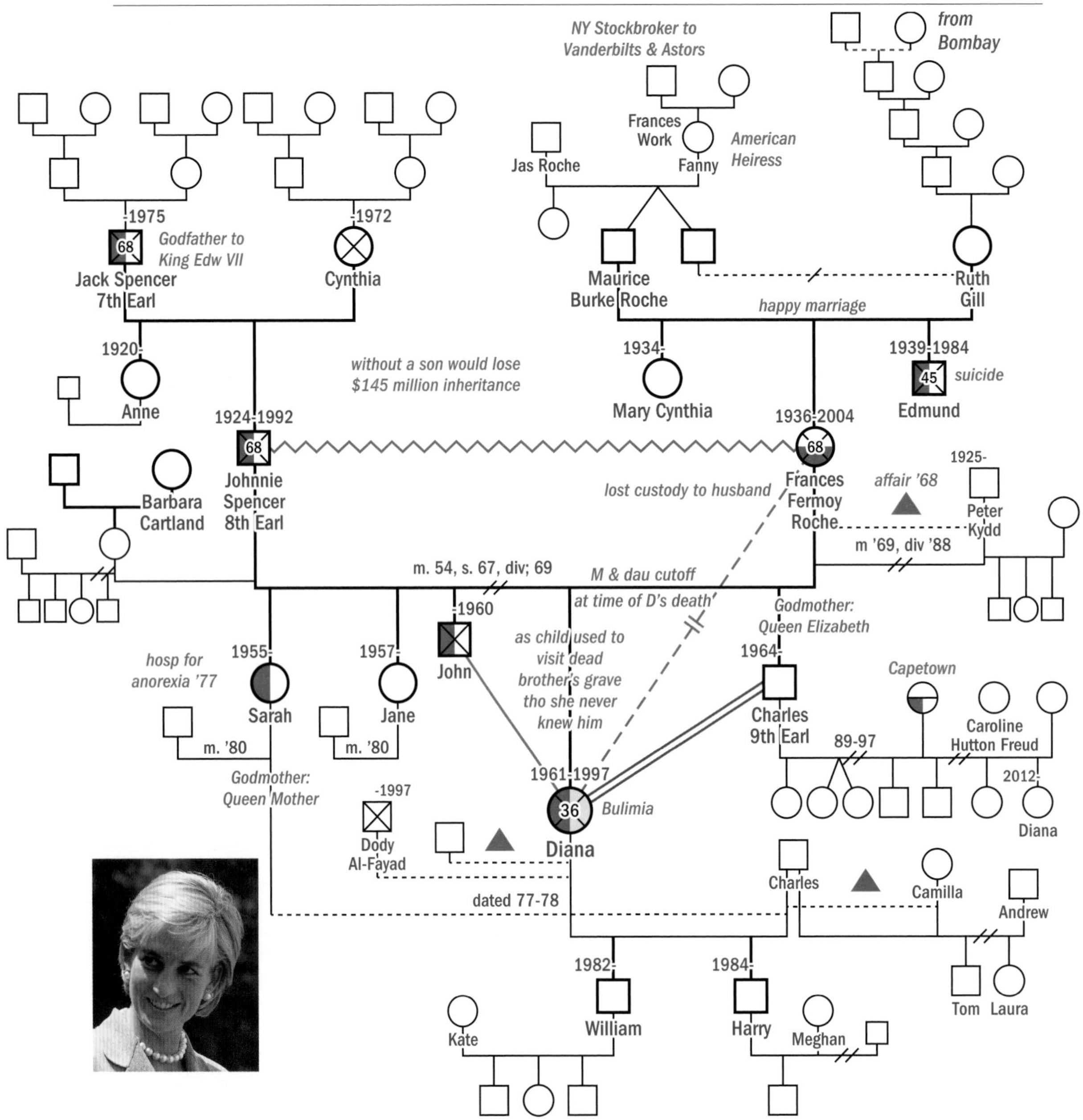

the ninth Earl of Spencer upon the father's death in 1992—if she could come back to the family home with her children. He refused. The year 1992 has already been discussed as a terrible year for the British Royal family (page 122) but it was also a terrible year for Diana's own family. Diana's conflicts in her family continued and she was completely cutoff from her mother at the time of her death. The mother was not allowed to attend the funeral. Her brother did allow Diana to be buried at the family estate, which has since become a major memorial to her. Charles, the youngest child and only surviving son of three older sisters, was raised to become the 9th Earl of Spencer. One wonders how he and his two surviving sisters will manage.

In early childhood, sisters are often caretakers of one another and of their brothers, as well as rivals and competitors for parental attention. Parents may, with the best of intentions, convey very different messages to their sons than to their daughters, as in the case of Jackie Robinson. Jackie, the remarkable Brooklyn Dodger who integrated major league baseball, saw his middle daughter, Sharon, very differently from his sons. (**Figure 6.3: Robinson Family: Different Roles for Brothers & Sisters**). Jackie's wife, Rachel, had had the same sibling constellation as Sharon—middle daughter surrounded by two brothers—which tends to intensify the pattern.

Figure 6.3 Robinson Family: Different Roles for Brothers & Sisters

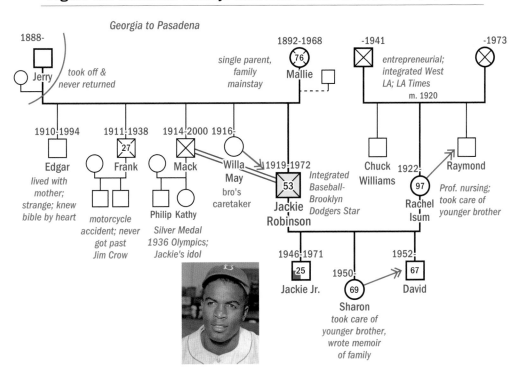

She was just such an ideal and perfect child in our eyes and in the opinion of virtually everyone who came in touch with her, that she sometimes seemed a little too good to be true. While fathers may be crazy about their sons, there is something extraordinarily special about a daughter. It's still the same—our relationship—perhaps even deeper. . . Rachel had been brought up with the same family pattern—a girl in the middle of two boys. She was the busy, loving, but not necessarily always happy, mainstay of her family, who took care of her younger brother. With a kind of grim amusement, I recall our assumption that Sharon was strong enough to cope well with whatever confronted her. We took her development for granted for many years. She rarely signaled distress or called attention to her problems by being dramatic. (Robinson, 1972, p. 242)

Sharon herself fell into many of the typical sister behaviors, in spite of both parents' efforts to the contrary and in spite of the fact that her middle-daughter mother was a highly dynamic and successful woman and role model of strength. Sharon later wrote a memoir describing her experience:

At times Jackie (her older brother), would hold me down and tickle me until I cried. Despite all this, I easily fell into the role of my brother's protector. . . In spite of my mother's warnings to the contrary, I was running up and down the hill in our backyard fetching water and food for my brothers, while they sat on the bank of the lake fishing. (Robinson, 1996, p. 88)

There are many reasons for the complexity of sister relationships: the familial bonds, the length of these relationships, the caretaking responsibilities sisters tend to be given, and their competitiveness for male attention and approval. Historically, our society has generally denied the importance of sister relationships. In most of our legends and stories, a man stands between sisters, who must compete for his attention (Bernikow, 1980). Mothers are, of course, hardly mentioned at all, unless derisively, as in *Cinderella*. Older sisters in literature are usually depicted as evil, while the youngest is the infantilized baby and favorite—"Daddy's Girl"— receiving his love and wealth in return for her loyalty and willingness to be his "love object." The influence of this negative mythology on how women in families see each other is an important issue in clinical assessment. Conflict between women should never be accepted at face value, but should be assessed in terms of who benefits when women cannot be each other's allies (McGoldrick & Watson, 2016). There is indeed also often a special intricacy and intimacy in sister relationships.

It is also important to assess sibling gender roles (and all other gender roles) in relation to culture. In many societies, daughters are raised to take care of others, including their brothers. Some groups, such as Irish and African American families may, for various historical reasons, overprotect their sons and underprotect their daughters (McGoldrick, Giordano, & Garcia Preto, 2005). Anglos, for example, may believe in brothers and sisters having equal chores. Other groups have less similar expectations, requiring daughters to do more home chores, including waiting on their brothers. In any case, it is essential to pay attention to how gender roles influence sibling patterns, and thus influence other relationships in life.

Unlike oldest sons, who typically have an unacknowledged feeling of entitlement, oldest daughters often have feelings of ambivalence and guilt about their responsibilities. Whatever they do, they may feel it is not quite enough and that they can never let up in their efforts to caretake and to make the family work right.

The Influence of Loss on Sibling Patterns

Patterns of loss are also important, usually affecting the siblings closest in age most of all. Carl Jung, whom we discussed in Chapter 4 (**Figure 6.4: Jung Family: Influence of Loss on Sibling Patterns**) is an example of a functional only child because of prior losses. Since the first two babies died at birth and then a third baby boy, Paul, lived only five days, Carl, the 4th child born, became the first and oldest surviving child. His sister, Johanna, was not born until nine years later, so Jung's experience was surely more that of an only child than a sibling.

But another factor contributing to Jung's position in the family was undoubtedly that both of his parents were the 13th and youngest children of their families, which was at the time thought to be an auspicious sign (Bair, 2003, p. 7). From a systems perspective the marriage of two youngests (especially when they each have many siblings) might tend to leave their children having to be adults before their time, as both parents might be likely to under-function in caretaking, having been the babies in their own families.

Indeed, Jung's parents seemed to be an extremely ill matched pair. His mother had serious psychological difficulties and was hardly able to function as a mother to her children. She was reportedly preoccupied with spiritual issues rather than with the practicalities of her family and her life. The father, though intelligent and having apparently had good prospects as a theologian, became a poor functioning minister, never managing to support his family very well. It would undoubtedly have been quite different had these two parents been the oldest of 13 children

Figure 6.4:   Jung Family: Influence of Loss on Sibling Patterns

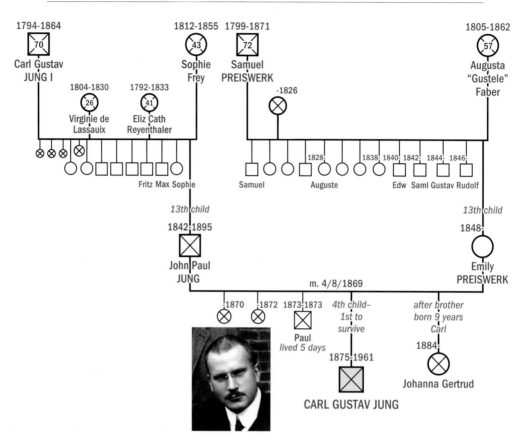

instead of the youngest. Two oldest children would likely have butted heads and struggled for leadership, but it is likely they would have worked hard to teach their son Carl to be a leader as their oldest surviving child.

Especially when there have been traumatic losses and parents are unavailable or unable to provide for their children's nurturing needs, siblings often come to rely greatly on each other. Jane and Peter Fonda (who both became successful actors, and whose genogram was discussed regarding Peter in Chapter 5), were three years apart, but because their mother was withdrawn and committed suicide in a mental hospital when they were still in their teens, they had to fend mostly for themselves. They experienced the early emotional loss of their father as well, because he was emotionally distant and usually away working. After their mother's traumatic suicide, they were shifted into multiple living situations. As often happens for siblings in such traumatic circumstances, they became each other's anchor in a painful and unstable world. Peter later wrote:

"Jane and I pulled together. . . . We began to carve holes in the wall between our rooms so we could talk at night. We had (still have) our very secret word that we could whisper into our little holes" (Fonda, 1998, pp. 14-15). "Moving a family, uprooting and relocating, no matter how close or great the distance is one of the most stressful things in life. . . . I felt that Jane and I had been sent into exile . . , hauled along on some unspoken crusade of our parents" (p. 35). "Jane became my savior. . . she was there for me at every critical moment. Sister and brother, brother and sister" (p. 39).

It was Jane who was there for him when at age 10 he shot and injured himself while his father was on his third honeymoon. It was Jane, then just starting college, who came for him when he was expelled from school at 16 and had no other guardian. He said of her "I really didn't have anyone else but Jane. She meant everything to me" (p. 54). He described her importance in his life many years later: "I needed her approval as much as I needed anything. Jane had always been just slightly below Dad on the need-of-approval scale and as we were closer and more in touch with each other, her blessing was the more important one" (pp. 292-293).

At one crisis in her life, when she was over 50, Jane made Peter promise to spend five days alone with her. She said she needed to talk about their childhood together, to know all the little details he remembered, so she could try to put the crazy, broken pieces of the puzzle of their early life together, and she feared losing him before they could do it (p. 474).

Oldest Sons and Daughters

In general, oldest children are likely to be the over-responsible and conscientious ones in a family. They tend to make good leaders, since they have experienced authority over and responsibility for younger siblings. But being the first-born can be a mixed blessing. As the answer to parents' dreams and the beginning of a new family, the first-born may receive an intensity of attention denied to the children that follow. But the burden may at times be heavy. Oldest children tend to become leaders of others and to assume responsibility for them, working hard to elevate the group to an elite position. George Washington (**Figure 6.5: George Washington: An Oldest Son**), is an outstanding example of this. He grew up as an oldest, although he had two much older half-brothers, whom he did not get to know until adolescence, because they were in England at school and then in the military or elsewhere working. One of them, Lawrence, became his guardian after his father died when George was 11, but died himself when George was only 20. Such father loss typically adds more pressure on the oldest son, of course, to become the "man of the house." In addition, George's mother, to whom he was never close, had been the youngest of many children. She was orphaned at an early age and seems never to have functioned very well. Such a pattern likely intensified Washington's role as the leader in his family, contributing to his leadership ability, which was a major factor in the formation of the United States. At the age of 20, Washington joined the Virginia Militia, quickly distinguishing himself to become Commander in Chief of all Virginia forces within three years. He had a truly remarkable ability to lead his men into battle and emerge unscathed. A brilliant leader, he kept a single-minded focus on his objectives and his obligation to support his men and accomplish his goal, regardless of the personal sacrifices involved.

Figure 6.5:   George Washington: An Oldest Son

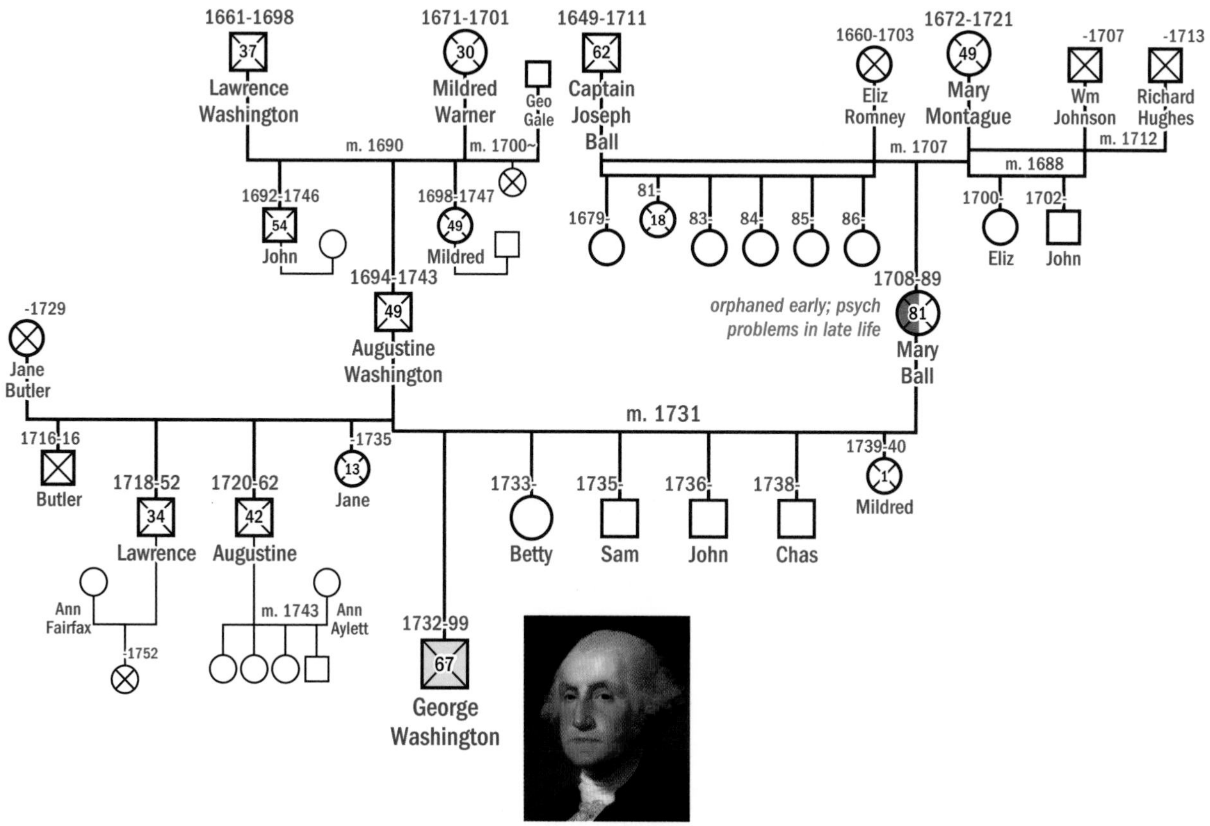

The oldest daughter often has a similar sense of responsibility, conscientious-ness, and leadership as her male counterpart, without receiving the same privi-leges or the same expectations to excel. Thus, oldest daughters are often saddled with the responsibilities of the oldest child without the power or enhanced self-esteem. Famous oldest sisters include Margaret Mead, Hillary Clinton, and Elea-nor Roosevelt.

When siblings are all female, oldest sisters may have certain privileges and expectations urged on them that would otherwise go to an oldest son. But when a boy follows an oldest girl in the family line-up, he may become a functional oldest, especially in a cultural context where sons are preferred and where a daughter does not have similar options.

Middle Children

Middle children in a family are "in between," having neither the position of the first as the standard bearer nor the last as the "baby." Not surprisingly, they may show characteristics of either the oldest or the youngest, or both combined. Though becoming a rarity in the U.S. because we are having fewer children, they serve many important functions in a family (Sternbergh, 2018; Salmon & Schumann, 2012). A middle child, unless he or she is the only girl or only boy, generally has to struggle for a role in the family. While the child may escape certain intensities directed at the oldest or the youngest, he or she may have to fight to be noticed. Middle children thus run the risk of getting lost, especially if all the siblings are of the same gender. On the other hand, they often develop into the best negotiators, more even-tempered and mellow than their more driven older siblings and less self-indulgent than the youngest. They may even relish their invisibility.

Martin Luther King (**Figure 6.6: Martin Luther King: Middle Child**) is an example of the best a middle child can be in terms of ability to play multiple roles and bring others together. His brilliant ideas of non-violent group resistance are a good fit with his middle sibling position, since a sibling in the middle does not have might on his/her side and appreciation of the power of joining forces comes naturally to middle children. Unlike the youngest, who would be unlikely to make a good leader, middle children may become outstanding collaborative leaders because they can draw multiple factions together through cooperation and medi-ation. In Martin Luther King's case his father was a surviving twin and a middle child, but also the oldest son, as King was himself. King's mother was a middle but functional youngest because the two youngest children died early.

Figure 6.6:   Martin Luther King: Middle Child

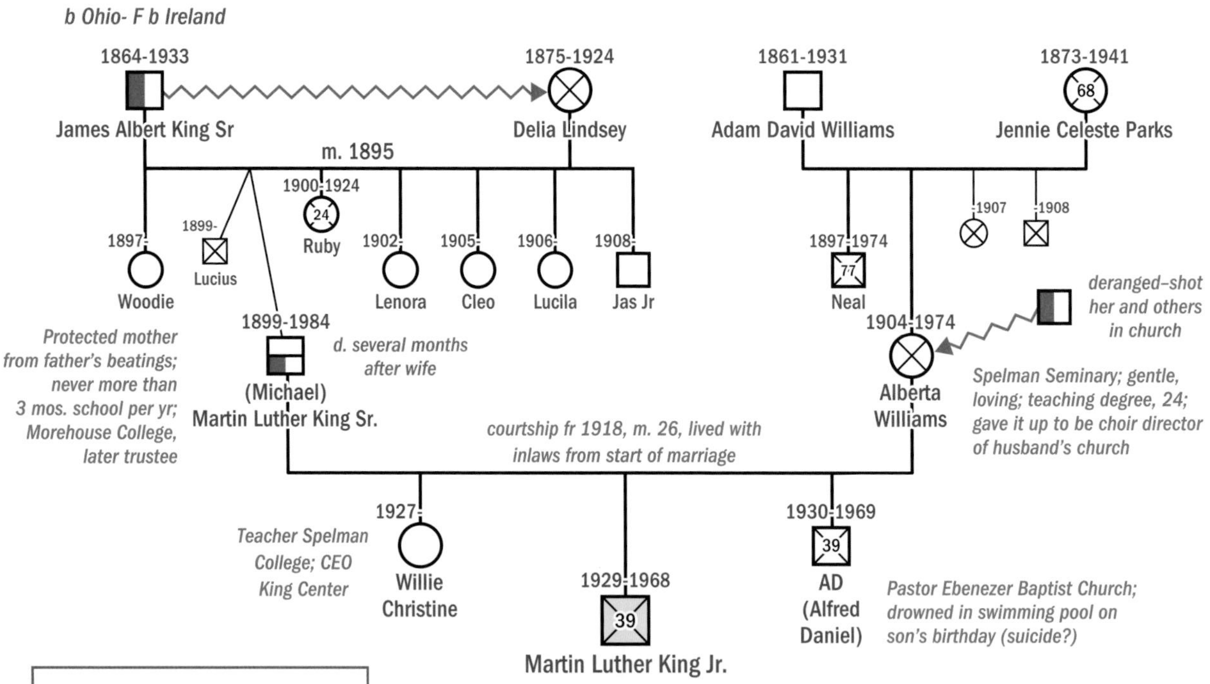

b Ohio- F b Ireland

1864-1933 — James Albert King Sr

1875-1924 — Delia Lindsey

1861-1931 — Adam David Williams

1873-1941 (68) — Jennie Celeste Parks

m. 1895

1897 — Woodie
Protected mother from father's beatings; never more than 3 mos. school per yr; Morehouse College, later trustee

1899- — Lucius

1900-1924 (24) — Ruby

1902- — Lenora

1905- — Cleo

1906- — Lucila

1908- — Jas Jr

1899-1984 — (Michael) Martin Luther King Sr.
d. several months after wife

1897-1974 (77) — Neal

1907 / 1908

1904-1974 — Alberta Williams
deranged–shot her and others in church
Spelman Seminary; gentle, loving; teaching degree, 24; gave it up to be choir director of husband's church

courtship fr 1918, m. 26, lived with inlaws from start of marriage

1927- — Willie Christine
Teacher Spelman College; CEO King Center

1929-1968 (39) — Martin Luther King Jr.

1930-1969 (39) — AD (Alfred Daniel)
Pastor Ebenezer Baptist Church; drowned in swimming pool on son's birthday (suicide?)

KEY EVENTS

1936 Suicide attempt after brother accidently knocked maternal grandmother down
1941 2nd suicide attempt after maternal grandmother died while he was at parade despite parent prohibitions, much questioning—esp of "emotional" religion—during adolescence and young adulthood
1956 house bombed
1956 MLK arrested & jailed

Middle children are under less pressure to take responsibility, but they need to try harder to make a mark in general, because they have no special role. In the family of Paul Robeson, who was a youngest, to be discussed (**Figure 6.7: Paul Robeson Family**), there were three middle children, who all played out variations of the middle child role. The oldest brother, William Drew, was named for the father and followed in his footsteps, attending the same college, Lincoln University, before going to medical school. The second oldest, Reed, was also brilliant, but too overtly angry to survive easily as an African American in their community. He became the "lost" middle child and the rebel. Paul felt he learned toughness from his brother Reed, who, as you can see on the genogram, was also surrounded by three miscarriages, which may have intensified the difficulty of his position in the family, as losses tend to do, especially for those children born closest to the loss. The third son, Ben, became an outstanding athlete and even-tempered role model for Paul. He became a successful minister like their father, and was the mediator in the family. The fourth child and only daughter, Marion, became a teacher like their mother and was noted for her warm spirit. She too was a mediator and connector. For Paul, Ben and Marion—those closest to him in age—were the most important mentors—"reserved in speech, strong in character, living up to their principles—and always selflessly devoted to their younger brother" (Robeson, 1988, p. 13). This support was all the more important because the children's mother died tragically in a fire when Paul was only six. Both Ben and Marion were willing to do without the limelight to facilitate the relationships of others.

Figure 6.7:   Paul Robeson Family

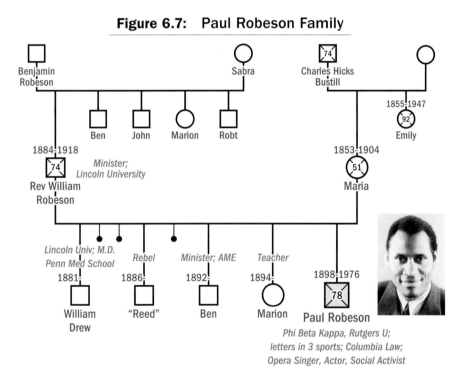

There were lessons also from Reed, who carried a little bag of stones for self-protection, in case he encountered a dangerous situation. Robeson admired this "rough" second-oldest brother, and from him learned to give a quick response to racial insults and abuse. Paul had a special feeling for this brother, who did not live up to the father's high expectations of the Robeson children. He later wrote of Reed:

He won no honors in classroom, pulpit or platform. Yet I remember him with love. Restless, rebellious, scoffing at conventions, defiant of the white man's law. I've known many Negroes like Reed. I see them every day. Blindly, in their own reckless manner, they seek a way out for themselves; alone, they pound with their fists and fury against walls that only the shoulders of many can topple. . . . When. . . everything will be different. . . . the fiery ones like Reed will be able to live out their lives in peace and no one will have cause to frown upon them. (Robeson, 1988, p. 14)

Although Reverend Robeson disapproved of Reed's carefree and undisciplined ways and eventually turned him out of the house for his scrapes with the law, Paul saw Reed as having taught him to stand up for himself. Reed, like many middle children, probably expressed feelings that others did not have the courage to express, in his case the rage against racism. In the famous biographical play about Robeson, Paul says there was one conversation he and his father could never finish—about the night his father turned Reed out, fearing he would set a bad example for his younger brother. Paul imagined getting together with his father and brother Ben to go looking for Reed and bring him home. He imagined defending Reed to his father:

"Aw Pop, don't change the subject. . . Reed was not a bad influence. Only horrible thing he said to me was, 'Kid, you talk too much.' All he ever told me to do was to stand up and be a man. 'Don't take low from anybody, and if they hit you, hit 'em back harder.' I know what the Bible says, Pop, but Reed was your son too! You always said you saw yourself in me. Pop, you were in all your sons." (Dean, 1989)

This dramatization expresses eloquently the varied roles different siblings take in a family and how much it matters if one is cut off, even though some in the family may not recognize these effects.

Youngest Children

The youngest child often has a sense of specialness, which allows self-indulgence without the overburdening sense of responsibility that comes with being the oldest. This may be more intense when there are several siblings. The younger of two probably has more a sense of "pairing" and twinship—unless there is a considerable age difference—than the youngest of five. Given their special position as the center of attention, youngest children may think they can accomplish anything, and sometimes they can. The youngest may feel more carefree and content to have fun rather than achieve. Less plagued by self-doubt than their older brothers and sisters, they are often extremely creative, willing to try what others would not even dare consider. Freed from convention and determined to do things their own way, the youngest child can sometimes make remarkable creative leaps, leading to inventions and innovations, as with the famous youngests Thomas Edison, Benjamin Franklin, Marie Curie, Paolo Freire, and Paul Robeson (for more detailed discussion of these families, see McGoldrick, 2011; Sulloway, 1996). Interestingly, Elizabeth Warren was the youngest and only sister of three brothers, and Nancy Pelosi the youngest and only sister of five brothers!

Youngests can also tend to be spoiled and self-absorbed, and their sense of entitlement may lead to frustration and disappointment at times. In addition, the youngest often has a period as an only child after the older siblings leave home, which can be an opportunity to enjoy the sole attention of parents, or it can lead to feelings of abandonment by siblings and of being ignored by parents.

Since the youngest has older siblings who have often served as caretakers, he or she may remain the "baby," a focus of attention for all who came before, expecting others to be helpful and supportive. At the same time, youngest children may feel freer to deviate from convention. Youngests may even feel compelled to escape from being the "baby," which may cause a rebellion, as with Edison and Franklin, who both ran away from home in adolescence.

A younger sister tends to be protected, showered with affection, and handed a blueprint for life. She may either be spoiled (more so if there are older brothers) and have special privileges or, if she is from a large family, she may be frustrated by always having to wait her turn. Her parents may have simply run out of energy for her, the more so if they had wished for a son and then gave up on that hope. She may feel resentful of being bossed around and never taken quite seriously. If she is the only girl, the youngest may be more like the princess, and yet the servant to elders, becoming, perhaps, the confidante to her brothers in adult life and the one to replace the parents in holding the family together. Youngest daughters may be the most likely to wind up being caretakers of their elderly parents, sometimes due to staying in the home longer before launching, or never marrying. This can make them "it" when aging parents became ill, disabled, or feeble.

Paul Robeson (**Figure 6.7: Paul Robeson Family**), whose family we discussed above, was a brilliant and creative youngest, the multi-talented star in his family, the more extraordinary because the family was African American, living in a racist society. An outstanding athlete in every sport, Phi Beta Kappa and valedictorian of his college class, lawyer turned world famous singer, actor, and then political speaker, Robeson was deeply aware of the importance of each of his siblings in his life. He said everyone lavished an extra measure of affection on him and saw him as some kind of "child of destiny. . . linked to the longed-for better days to come" (Robeson, 1988, p. 16). This is a common role for a youngest, especially when the family has experienced hard times, as the Robesons did.

Only Children

Only children are becoming more common in the U.S. as small families become more the norm. In the past it was quite uncommon for people to grow up as only children.

Only children may have the seriousness and sense of responsibility of an oldest and the conviction of specialness and entitlement of a youngest. At the same time, they tend to be more oriented toward adults, seeking their love and approval, and in return expecting their undivided attention. Their major challenge is how to get along "up close and personal" with others their own age. They tend to be more socially independent, less oriented toward peer relationships, more adult-like in behavior at an earlier age, and perhaps more anxious at times as a result of the attention and protectiveness of their parents. They often maintain very close attachments to their parents throughout their lives, but may find it more difficult to relate intimately with friends and spouses.

An extreme version of this, increasingly common in China and other quickly developing countries, is the only child of two only child parents (**Figure 6.8: Only Child of Only Children**), especially impactful when the culture has previously had large extended families. The family may develop an intense focus on the single child who becomes the focus not only for the parents, who in earlier days would have had several children, but also the focus of affection, hopes, and expectations of the four grandparents! In China this can become an extremely intense problem, where parents are sometimes both working far away from home and where grandparents are forced to retire in their mid-fifties and are very focused on their grandchildren, most of all on their grandsons (Miller, 2019). Children often struggle under too much weight in such situations, as parents and extended family place too much pressure on them to achieve and meet the needs of all the family.

In any case, the only children as "legacy delegates" of their parents, may be

Figure 6.8:   Only Child of Only Children

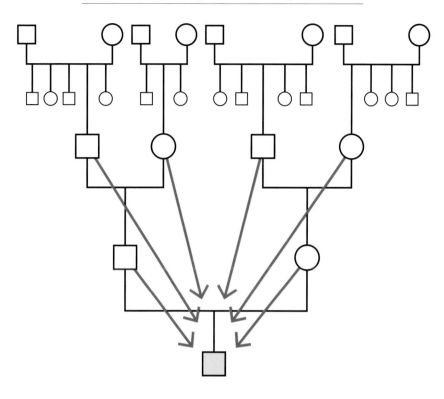

expected to fulfill all the hopes and dreams the parents have for them. An only child of successful parents may feel great pressure to measure up to high expectations. In less fortunate families, only children may be seen as the family's last chance for redemption or respectability—expected to do what the parents could not. Only children are also especially vulnerable to being triangled. They are the only option for "spreading out" chronic anxiety in such a family system. An only-child son may become the mother's confidante and quasi-partner. An only-child daughter may be induced into being the father's ally. Such families may even be vulnerable to incest urges and behaviors, although incest certainly occurs in multiple child families as well.

Indira Gandhi, the second Prime Minister of India, illustrates the experience of many only children (**Figure 6.9: Indira Gandhi & Her Father Nehru**). She grew up quite isolated and lived primarily in the presence of older people, becoming her father's confidante early on. She clearly had the sense of mission and responsibility of an oldest, but as a leader she was autocratic and led a rather isolated existence, keeping her own counsel. Both her father and paternal grandfather were functional only children as well. Her father, Jawaharlal Nehru, was eleven years older than his next sibling and her grandfather, Motilal Nehru, also a leader of India, was many years younger than his older siblings. He was raised in the home of his adult brother, because their father died before Motilal was born. The illnesses of both Jawaharlal's mother and Indira's mother undoubtedly compounded their isolated roles as only children and their connection to each other as father and daughter.

Figure 6.9:   Indira Gandhi & Her Father Nehru

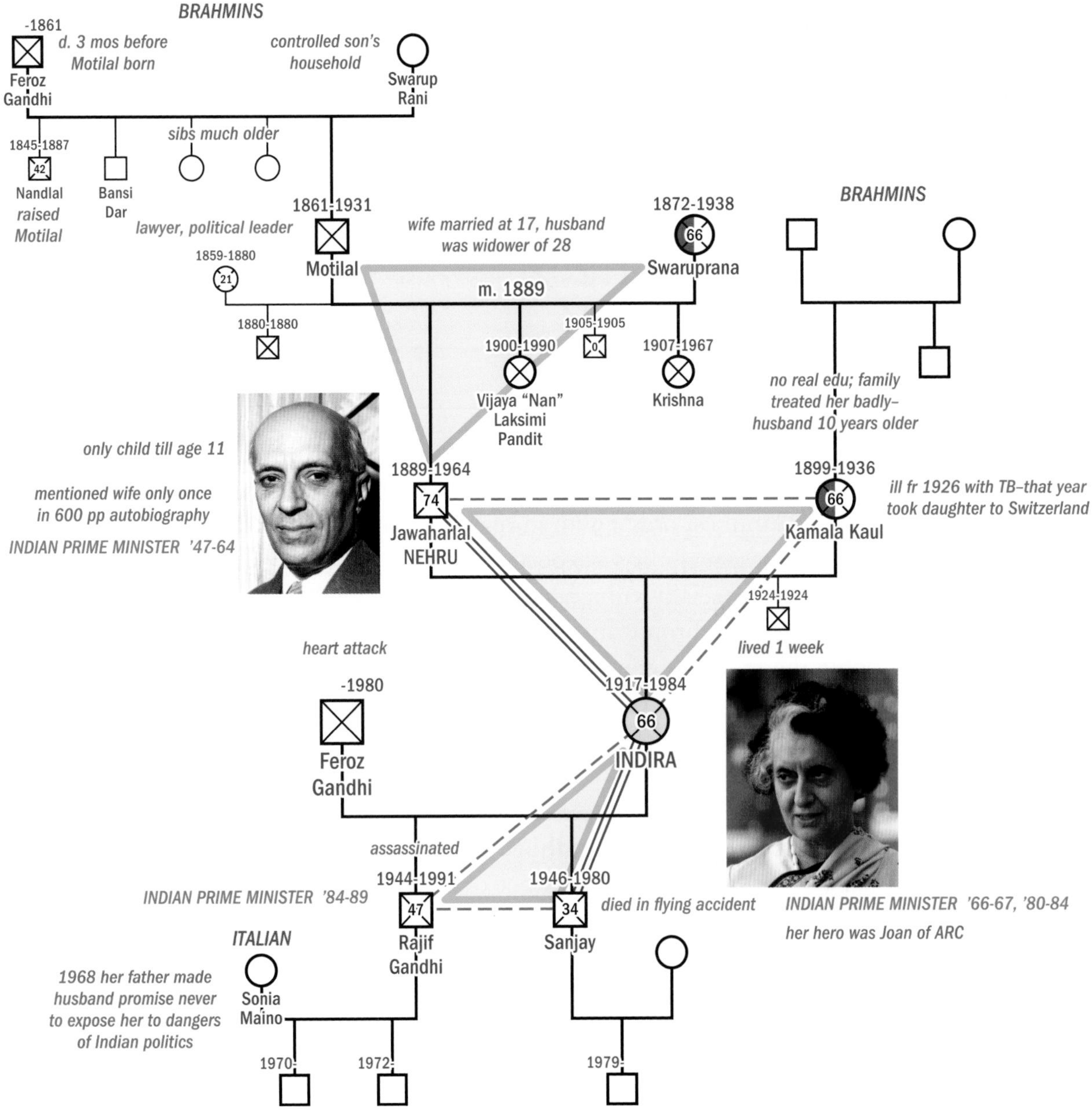

BRAHMINS

-1861
d. 3 mos before Motilal born
Feroz Gandhi

controlled son's household
Swarup Rani

1845-1887
42
Nandlal raised Motilal

Bansi Dar

sibs much older

1861-1931
lawyer, political leader
Motilal

1859-1880
21

1880-1880

wife married at 17, husband was widower of 28

m. 1889

1872-1938
66
Swaruprana

BRAHMINS

1900-1990
Vijaya "Nan" Laksimi Pandit

1905-1905
0

1907-1967
Krishna

no real edu; family treated her badly– husband 10 years older

only child till age 11

mentioned wife only once in 600 pp autobiography

INDIAN PRIME MINISTER '47-64

1889-1964
74
Jawaharlal NEHRU

1899-1936
66
Kamala Kaul

ill fr 1926 with TB–that year took daughter to Switzerland

1924-1924
lived 1 week

heart attack

-1980
Feroz Gandhi

1917-1984
66
INDIRA

INDIAN PRIME MINISTER '84-89

assassinated

1944-1991
47
Rajiv Gandhi

1946-1980
34
Sanjay

died in flying accident

INDIAN PRIME MINISTER '66-67, '80-84

her hero was Joan of ARC

ITALIAN

1968 her father made husband promise never to expose her to dangers of Indian politics

Sonia Maino

1970

1972

1979

Sibling Position and Parenting

We always want to scan genograms for the sibling constellations across generations. A parent may over-identify with a child of the same gender and sibling position. One father who was an oldest of five felt that he had been burdened as a child with too much responsibility, while his younger brothers and sister "got away with murder." When his own children came along, he spoiled the oldest and tried to make the younger ones toe the line. A mother may find it difficult to empathize with a youngest daughter if she felt envious of her younger sister. Parents may also identify with one particular child because of that person's family resemblance to another person.

Intergenerational problems related to sibling constellation may arise when parents' identification with a particular child is so strong that they perpetuate their old family patterns, as when a mother who hated being bossed around by her older brother is always accusing her son of tormenting his younger sister. In other situations a parent's own experience is so different that they may misread their children. A parent who was an only child may assume that normal sibling fighting is a sign of their children's pathology.

Sibling Relationships in Adult Life

Sibling relationships can be a very important connection in adult life, especially in the later years. However, if negative feelings persist, the care of an aging parent may increase sibling strain. At such times siblings who have been apart for years may need to work together in new and uncomfortable ways. The child who has remained closest to the parents, usually a daughter, often gets most of these caretaking responsibilities, which may bring long buried jealousies and resentments to the surface.

Once both parents have died, sibling relationships become truly independent for the first time. This is when estrangement can become total, particularly if old rivalries have continued. Strong feelings can be fueled by unresolved issues and conflicts. But the better the relationships siblings have, the less likely it is that traumatic family events will lead to conflicts and cutoffs.

Factors That Influence Sibling Constellation

We must not assume, however, that the hypotheses about sibling constellations apply to any particular family. Sibling constellation predictions may be influenced by a number of other factors which will impact whether or not people fit the characterizations. For example, how the sibling pattern fits into the constellation of cousins may modify or intensify certain sibling patterns. A son who has one sister but 6 girl cousins may have his special position as an only son exaggerated. The same intensification may exist if a child lives with relatives in a multigenerational household. Examples include when an only child has not only two parents but also two grandparents and an aunt and uncle living in the household, or where there are multiple household changes and children grow up in different constellations. When living situations are complicated, it is helpful to draw lines encircling the different households. This is especially important in multi-nuclear families, where children spend time in different households. Jackie Bouvier Kennedy and her sister Lee always seem to have lived in multiple contexts (**Figure 6.10: Jackie Kennedy's Complex Cousin and Sibling Constellation**). But this was more true after their parents' official separation when Jackie was seven, and even more so after her mother remarried when she was 13 and had two more children and various stepchildren.

But Jackie Kennedy's is also an example of a family in which it's essential to know not just the changing sibling constellations, but also how the sibling constellation is embedded in the cousin constellation. This genogram indeed challenges our power to show all the dimensions of a multiply-remarried family with changing circumstances at once. (Remember, there's only so much you can show on any one genogram! Beyond a certain point of complexity it will become too difficult to read and thus not useful as a map.)

During the school year, Jackie and her sister lived in New York City with their mother and maternal grandparents. The maternal great-grandmother, an immigrant from Ireland, was thought "uncouth," and kept upstairs in the grandparents' home for decades, during the years Jackie's mother and her sisters were growing up. That great-grandmother died just the year before Jackie was born. The grandparents never separated, but also never spoke to each other, though they sat together at meals.

The household constellation changed after Jackie and Lee's mother remarried, when Jackie was 13 and Lee was nine. Jackie and Lee then had step-siblings, and soon two much younger half-siblings. Jackie became very attached to several of these siblings, especially her slightly older step-brother Yusha, on whom she seems

Figure 6.10: Jackie Kennedy's Complex Cousin and Sibling Constellation

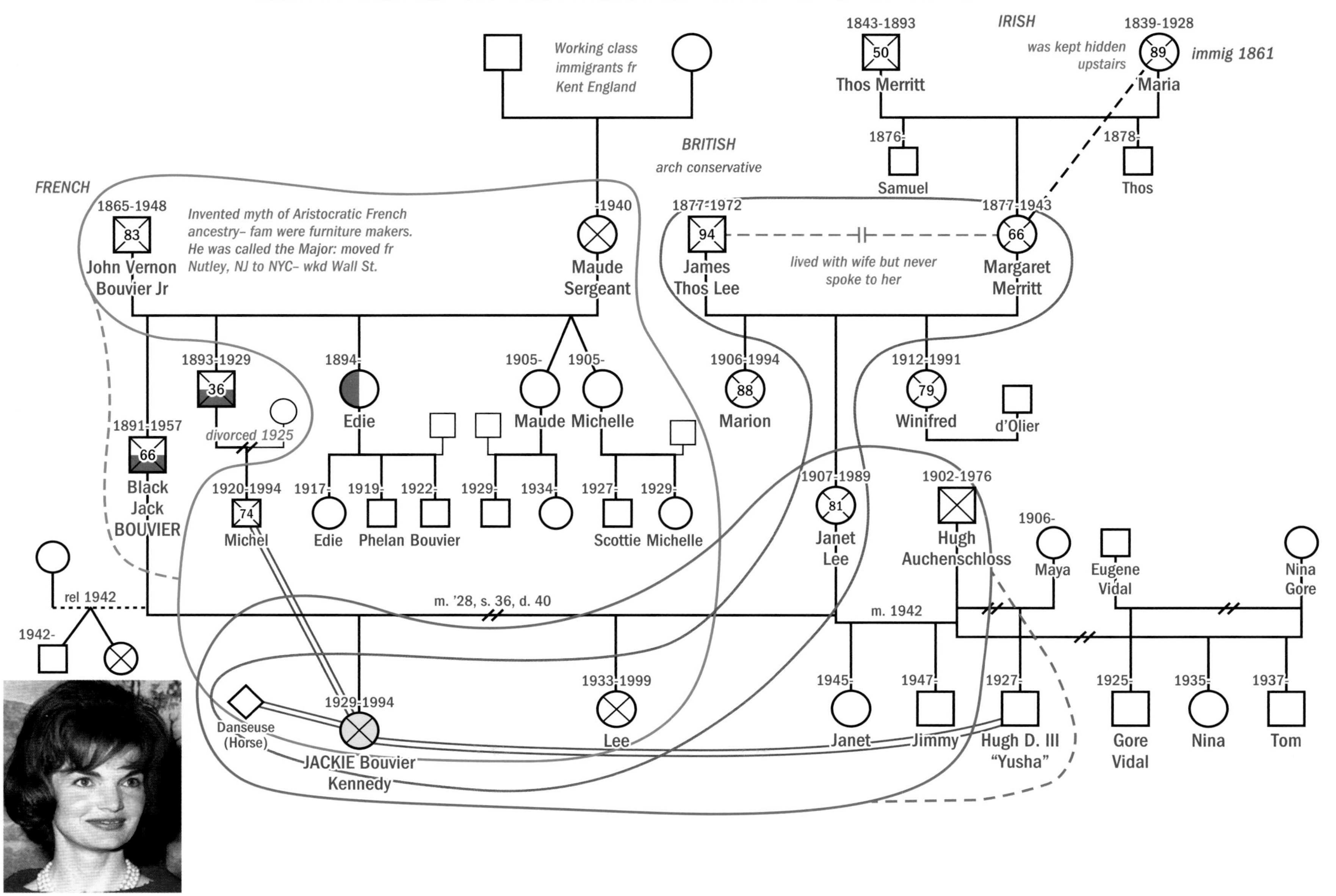

to have had an early adolescent crush for several years. It is interesting that Jackie never distinguished between her full sister and her half- and step-siblings.

During the summers, Jackie and Lee spent time with their father's large family on Long Island. This included grandparents, cousins, aunts, uncles, and Jackie's beloved horse, Danseuse, but their father appeared only occasionally. In this constellation, Jackie was one of three cousins born in the same year. She had a special preference for several older male cousins, above all her cousin Michel, nine years older, whom she even remembered in her will. Michel's special role in the family had intensified when his mother divorced his alcoholic father in 1925, creating great distress throughout the family, who felt they were losing the sole male Bouvier of the next generation. The sense of the fragility of the male line had begun in the previous generation, when there were only four males out of 12 children, and only one of them lived to marry and have children himself. Five of the siblings never married, though they lived a long time.

"Aunt and uncle power" can also influence a sibling constellation, giving special extra care and attention to certain nieces or nephews, which may influence sibling patterns. Aunts and uncles may play an important role in conveying their own unfulfilled dreams to their nieces and nephews in the next generation, especially namesakes, which were more common in previous generations.

Other experiences in a family's history may also modify sibling patterns. For example, Richard Burton (**Figure 7.2**) grew up in a complex family situation after the early death of his mother. His oldest sister, Cis (Cecilia), 19 years his elder, had recently married and became the primary mother figure for him and for many of the other siblings. As Burton described it, his older sister, "Cis was wonderful, but she was not my mother" (Bragg, 1990, p. 69) His older brother became a father figure, his other older sisters were like aunts, and Cis' daughters were like little sisters. His cousins became like brothers, while his real aunts were like mothers. He had, as he thought of it, "many alternative worlds. . . . Complexity, elaboration, alternatives, parallel lives, that was the way it had always been; that was the "norm" (Bragg, 1990, p. 69).

So we must always explore sibling constellation, like any factor in family life, while keeping the complex context of family patterns in mind. Out of temperament or necessity, siblings may often play non-sibling roles and non-siblings may play sibling roles, as they did for Burton. Indeed, the empirical research on sibling constellations is at best inconclusive, because there are so many other factors that can change or moderate the influence of sibling position. Nevertheless, an awareness of sibling constellation can provide clinically useful normalizing explanations of people's roles in their family, as well as indicate other factors to explore when predicted patterns are not found. In addition, adult siblings, often ignored by clinicians, can be extremely important resources in therapy and healthcare.

The Child's Sibling Position in Relation to that of the Parent

The child's position in the family may be particularly highlighted if it repeats the position of the same-sexed parent. Thus, a man who is the oldest son of an oldest son may have specific expectations placed on him that do not apply to his younger brother. If a man's relationship with his father was charged, there is a good chance that in the next generation the relationship with his son in the same ordinal position may also turn sour. This is more likely in cultures with strong rules governing sibling functioning in relation to birth order (McGoldrick & Watson, 2016).

John Quincy Adams, oldest son of John Adams (see **Figure 6.11: Adams Family: Naming and Functioning**), broke a three-generational family tradition of naming the oldest son John by naming his first son after George Washington instead. George Washington Adams was born the year his grandfather, John Adams, left office after not being elected for a second term. John Adams had served as Washington's Vice President and felt Washington had never given him credit for all he had done. Names or nicknames may give genogram hints about the family's "programming," but the clinician needs to explore the naming patterns to understand their meaning.

At the age of 29 George Washington Adams committed suicide, shortly after losing the family money and having a son out of wedlock, and just about the time his father, John Quincy Adams, lost an election for a second term as President of the United States. As can be seen on the Adams genogram, the family had a multigenerational pattern of both high functioning and very dysfunctional children. John Adams (1735-1826), the 2nd U.S. President, was an oldest and clearly had the role of leader, not just in his family but for our nation. He was the son of another John Adams (1691-1761). His oldest son, John Quincy Adams (1767-1848), had been preceded by a sister, who had a strong relationship with the parents. But parents generally have different expectations for daughters. John Quincy Adams became our 6th U.S. President, but played a less prominent leadership role, and, like his father, was elected for only one term. Interestingly, he later served for many years in Congress, an unusual role for a former president. He was an outstanding and collaborative congressional leader, especially important in the antislavery movement, perhaps suggesting that he was more comfortable with leading from a slightly less dominant position. His two younger brothers were seriously dysfunctional and alcoholic, causing enormous pain to their parents.

John Quincy, having named his first son George Washington, named his second son John. This son too succumbed to alcoholism and was a huge disappointment. His third son, Charles Frances Adams, became the family historian and seems to have fared the best of that third generation. To an extent, he managed

Figure 6.11:   Adams Family: Naming and Functioning

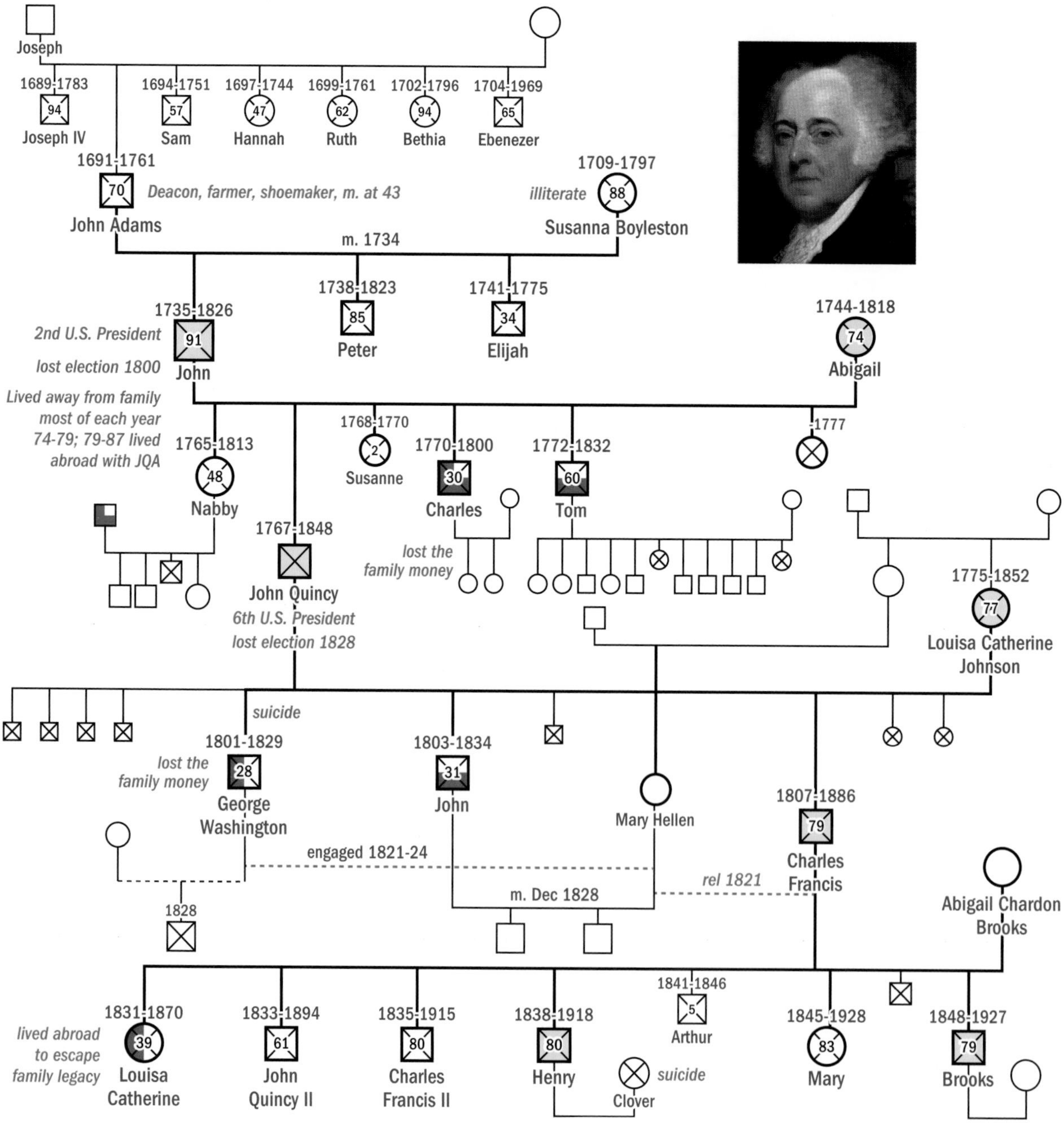

to shift the family pattern for his children. None of Charles Frances' sons experienced alcoholism, great failure, or early death. The only early deaths in that fourth generation were the women. The oldest daughter, Louisa Catherine, was considered the most brilliant of all the children. But she was resentful and rebellious, feeling she could have become President if she had been male. The family was reportedly dismayed that their first child was a girl (Nagel, 1987). She attempted to escape the family pressure and legacy by marrying in Europe and remaining there, where she apparently led a hedonistic, almost suicidal existence. She died in an accident at the age of 39. The other tragic woman of this generation was Clover, the wife of Henry Adams. She was a gifted photographer who committed suicide at the age of 42, having apparently struggled much with the gender constraints of her time. The youngest sister, Mary, having been a disobedient and stubborn child, became the most conventional of the fourth generation of Adams, mostly submitting to family ways, though in later life she became addicted to morphine. The oldest son, John Quincy Adams II, felt oppressed by the family legacy and the burden of being the oldest son. He wanted to be left alone, but was continually pressed to run for office. He dealt with this by trying to avoid running for any office unless he was sure he wouldn't win. He later burned his diary and letters, having earlier handed over the family finances to his younger brother, Charles, who eventually lost the money in the crash of 1893, and then cut off his siblings.

The Timing of Each Sibling's Birth in the Family History

When a child is born at a critical point in a family's history, there may be special expectations for that child, in addition to the typical expectations for that sibling position, as in the Adams family. These expectations may exaggerate a sibling position characterization (as with the oldest who acts super-responsible) or modify the usual sibling roles (as with a middle or youngest who functions as an oldest or only child). Particularly critical are untimely and traumatic family deaths and transitions. A child born around the time one of the grandparents dies may also play a special role in the family.

The Child's Characteristics

A child with special characteristics may also shift the expected sibling patterns in a family. For example, children may become functional oldests if they are particularly talented, or if the oldest is disabled in some way. If an older child has a disability, s/he may also be treated as a youngest.

The Family's "Program" for the Child

Parents may have a particular agenda for a specific child, such as expecting him or her to be the responsible one or the "baby," regardless of that child's position in the family. Children who resemble a certain family member may be expected to take on that person's role. A child's temperament may be at odds with his or her sibling position. Most difficult are situations in which children cannot fulfill the sibling role that is structurally ordained for them. Children may struggle valiantly against family expectations—the oldest who refuses to take on the responsibility of the caretaker or family standard bearer, or the youngest who strives to be a leader. Cultures differ tremendously in the expected roles of birth order and gender. Asian cultures, for example, tend to have highly stratified expectations for children, depending on their birth order and gender, while Jewish and Anglo families tend to be relatively democratic. In some families, it will be the child most comfortable with the responsibility—not necessarily the oldest child—who becomes the leader.

Naming patterns of siblings are often significant signals of family "programming." For example, Gregory Bateson was named for one of his father's heroes, Gregor Mendel. Though he was the youngest son, he was perhaps being "programmed" to aim at great accomplishments as a natural scientist.

Names sometimes reflect special circumstances. Ossie Davis was named Raiford Chatman Davis for his paternal grandfather (Davis & Dee, 2000), but when the county clerk asked for the name for the birth certificate and the mother said "R.C. Davis," the clerk thought she said "Ossie Davis." Because the clerk was white and the mother was black, in the racist context of rural Georgia, she did not dare to challenge him, so Ossie was his name from that time on.

Family Constellations Are Not Astrology

As William Shakespeare has Cassius say to Brutus in his play *Julius Caesar*, "The fault, dear Brutus, is not in our stars, but in ourselves, that we are underlings." Family constellations do not predestine our lives, but they do influence them in ways that are sometimes predictable, other times surprising. The clinician can best use family constellation information to form hypotheses about a family's roles and relationships, which must then be tested and revised as one's understanding of a particular family's complexities deepens.

Exploring Couple Constellations with Genograms

Couple relationships always evolve in the context of what has come before in their families and influences what will come later, so it makes sense to view them in at least a three generational context (see especially *The Genogram Casebook*, Chapter 8, for clinical perspectives on working with couples using genograms, McGoldrick (2016b) for a life cycle perspective on couples, and McGoldrick & Carter (2016) for discussion of the remarriage cycle of couples through divorce and re-coupling.

Sibling Position and Coupling

Sibling relationships often pave the way for couple relationships—for sharing, interdependence, and mutuality—just as they can predispose partners to jealousy, power struggles, and rivalry. Since siblings are generally one's earliest peer relationships, couples may be most comfortable in relationships that reproduce the familiar sibling patterns of birth order and gender. Generally speaking, couples seem to have less conflict when the partners complement their original sibling pattern, e.g., when an oldest pairs with a youngest, rather than two oldests marrying each other. If a wife has grown up as the oldest of many siblings and the caretaker, she might be attracted to a dominant oldest, who offers to take over management of responsibilities. But as time goes along, she may come to resent his assertion of authority, because by experience she is more comfortable making decisions for herself.

All things being equal (and they seldom are in life!), the ideal couple relationship based on sibling position would theoretically be a husband who was the older brother of a younger sister, and a wife who was the younger sister of an older brother. Of course, the complementarity of caretaker and someone who needs caretaking, or leader and follower, is no guarantee of intimacy or a happy marriage, but it may ensure familiarity with the role one has had previously.

Eleanor Roosevelt, an oldest, who was raised more as an only child, and her cousin Franklin, who was an only (though he did have a half-brother who was a whole generation older), are a good example of two strong-willed spouses whose marriage seems to have survived because of their ability to evolve separate spheres **(Figure 7.1: Franklin & Eleanor Roosevelt: Sibling Constellation & Marital Patterns)**. Leaders in their own separate worlds, they came to live apart except for holidays. Early in the marriage, Eleanor generally subordinated herself to Franklin and to his powerful mother, Sarah Delano, who played a major role in their lives. However, as Eleanor became more self-confident and developed interests of her own, she began to show the determination of an oldest.

Crisis came when Eleanor discovered letters revealing Franklin's affair with Lucy Mercer. Apparently, it was Franklin's mother Sara who negotiated a contract between them for Eleanor to return to the marriage. (This contract is the only document in the entire Roosevelt archive that is not open to the public.) Since oldests and only children are generally oriented to parents, Sara may have been the only one who could have kept them from separating—and she did. It is interesting that the pivotal person here, Sara Delano Roosevelt, was a middle child of 10, of whom only five survived through young adulthood. Thus, she probably inherited both an excellent mediating ability and also a specialness as the survivor of all the siblings who died early.

The Roosevelts remained married but lived separate lives, with politics as their common ground. After Franklin's paralysis due to polio, Eleanor became essential to his political career. She nevertheless had her own intimate relationships, her own political views and activities, and her own living space in a separate house at Hyde Park, which she shared with her friends.

If we look at the sibling constellations of their parents, we can see that Eleanor's parents were a poor match. Her mother, Anna Hall, was the oldest of six, while Eleanor's father, Elliott, was the younger brother of an older brother, surrounded by two sisters. While Elliott's brother, Theodore Roosevelt, became President of the U.S., Elliott fell into alcoholism and dysfunction, abandoning his family and dying by the time Eleanor turned 10. Her mother had already died when Eleanor was only eight, so she ended up being raised in the household of her maternal grandmother, where she was like an only child and felt like the orphan she was. Her middle brother died at four, the year after her mother, and her youngest brother Hall was born when she was seven. Eleanor was obviously forced to function very independently, as she needed to do much later in her mar-

Figure 7.1   Franklin & Eleanor Roosevelt: Sibling Constellation & Marital Patterns

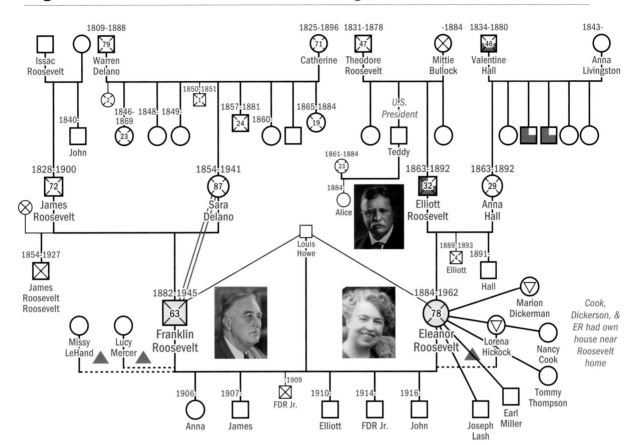

riage. She developed a rich array of friends, colleagues, and interests, as did Franklin, who had grown up in a tight relationship with his mother, Sarah Delano, and with a much older father, who had been 54 when Franklin was born. He died by the time Franklin finished high school, so his mother moved with him when he began college at Harvard.

A very different couple were Richard Burton and Elizabeth Taylor (**Figure 7.2: Richard Burton & Elizabeth Taylor: Marriage of Two Youngests**), well known actors who married and divorced each other twice. They provide a dramatic example of two youngest children who competed to be "junior," both seeking a caretaker. Burton was the second youngest of 13 children, but was treated like a youngest, since his youngest brother was reared apart. In very large families, several of the younger children will often have the characteristics of a youngest. Elizabeth Taylor was the younger of two, with an older brother, whose needs were often sacrificed to her stardom, which, of course, solidified her special position.

Figure 7.2:   Richard Burton & Elizabeth Taylor: Marriage of Two Youngests

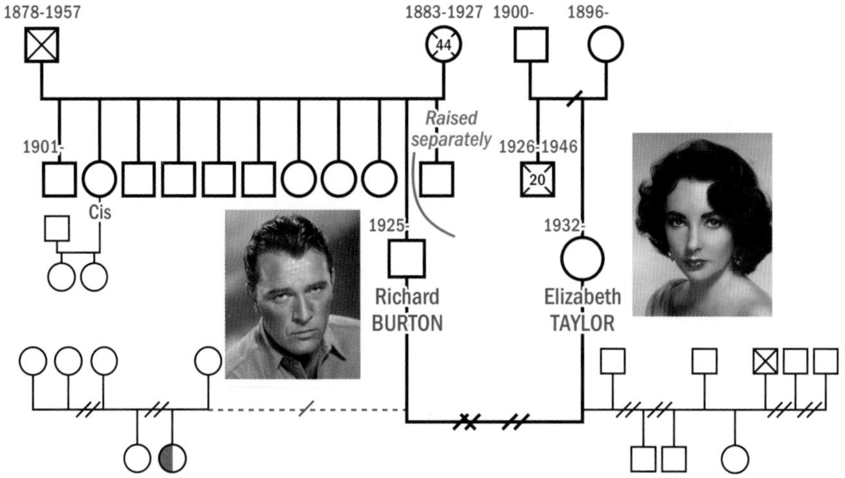

Burton and Taylor were known for their histrionic love quarrels, each outdoing the other in their demanding and childish behavior.

There are, of course, many other possible sibling pairings in marriage, and assessing any genogram for the compatibility of sibling constellations is well worth the effort. Only children tend to marry each other, but this has the particular difficulty that neither has the experience of intimate peer sharing that one has with a brother or sister. Two only children who marry may either try to fuse into one, or to seek more separateness than other spouses. Middle children may be the most flexible, since they have had experiences with multiple roles.

Of course, spouses from complementary sibling constellations may also have problems, and it is important to check any particular family more closely. A case in point is Margaret Mead, an oldest, who married Gregory Bateson, a youngest (**Figure 7.3: Gregory Bateson and Margaret Mead: An Oldest Married to a Youngest**). Their sibling positions seem clearly reflected in their personality styles. Bateson was a youngest, and was forced to take over the legacies of his two older brothers after they died. As their daughter, Catherine, describes their relationship:

> Margaret's approach must have been based on early success in dealing with problems, perhaps related to the experience of being an older child and amplified by years of successfully organizing the younger ones. Gregory's experience was that of a younger child with relatively little capacity for changing

what went on around him. Instead he would seek understanding. Indeed, he had a kind of abhorrence for the effort to solve problems, whether they were medical or political. (Bateson, 1984, p. 176)

Mead's and Bateson's respective sibling positions and problem-solving styles did not lead, however, to a complementary helper/helped relationship, but rather to struggle and disappointment in one another. Margaret's role as the senior partner

**Figure 7.3:   Gregory Bateson and Margaret Mead:
An Oldest Married to a Youngest**

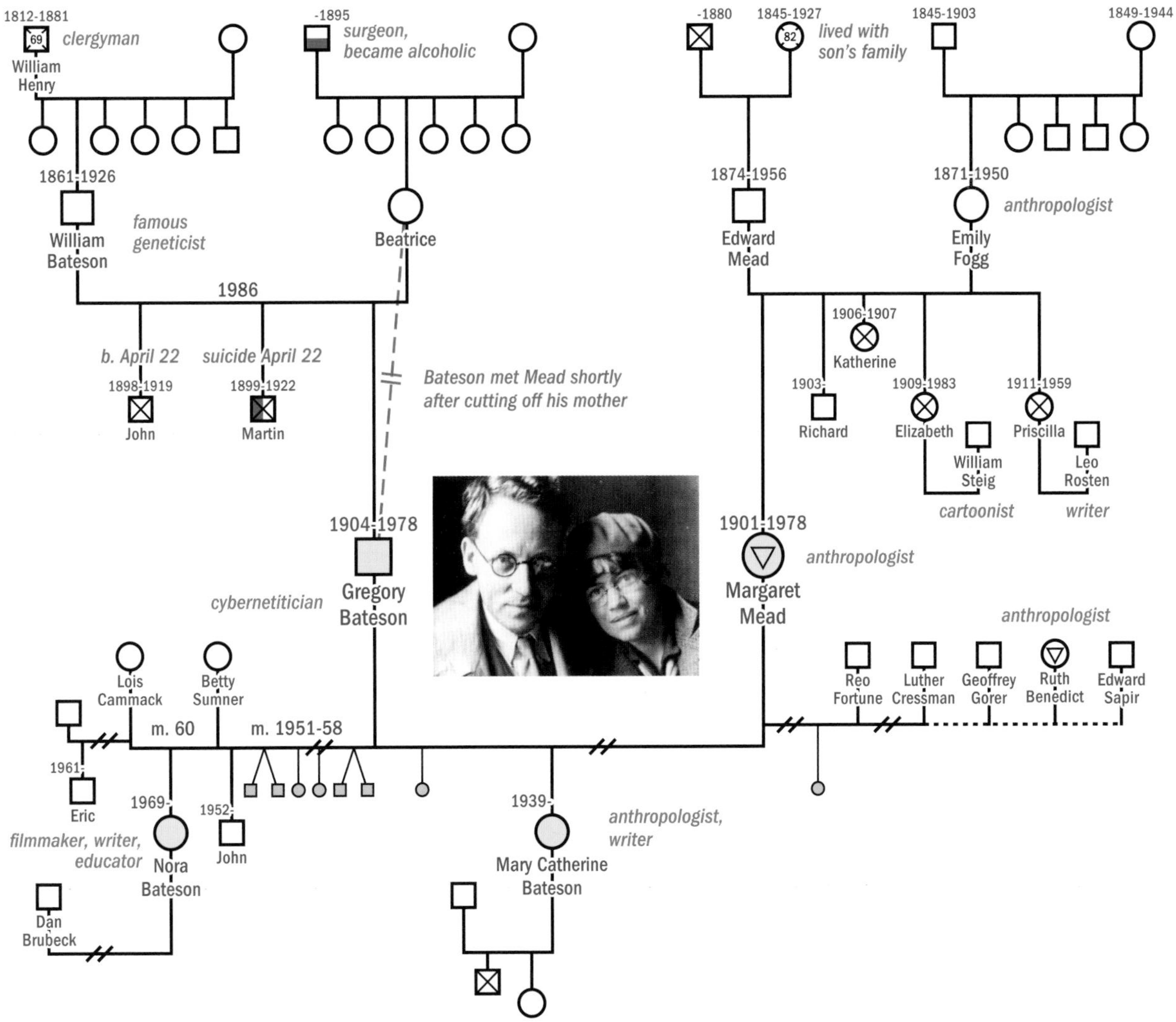

1812-1881 *clergyman* William Henry   -1895 *surgeon, became alcoholic*   -1880 1845-1927 *lived with son's family* 1845-1903   1849-1944

1861-1926 *famous geneticist* William Bateson   Beatrice   1874-1956 Edward Mead   1871-1950 Emily Fogg *anthropologist*

1986

b. April 22 1898-1919 John   suicide April 22 1899-1922 Martin   *Bateson met Mead shortly after cutting off his mother*   1906-1907 Katherine   1903 Richard 1909-1983 Elizabeth William Steig *cartoonist* 1911-1959 Priscilla Leo Rosten *writer*

1904-1978 *cybernetitician* Gregory Bateson   1901-1978 Margaret Mead *anthropologist* *anthropologist* Reo Fortune Luther Cressman Geoffrey Gorer Ruth Benedict Edward Sapir

Lois Cammack Betty Sumner m. 60   m. 1951-58

1961 Eric *filmmaker, writer, educator* 1969 Nora Bateson 1952 John   1939 Mary Catherine Bateson *anthropologist, writer*

Dan Brubeck

was emphasized by her being three years older than Gregory. (Her mother, also an oldest, had been similarly three years older than her husband.) Catherine Bateson describes her parents' relationship:

> "In the marriage she was the one who set the patterns, for Gregory lacked this fascination with pervasive elaboration. . . . His life was full of loose ends and unstitched edges, while for Margaret each thread became an occasion for embroidery." (p. 27)

> "It was Gregory, more than anyone else, who lashed back at her for trying to manage his life. . . . She would see a problem and her imagination would leap to a solution." (p. 111)

> "(He) began with his rebellion against Margaret, a rebellion shot through with resentment against his family and especially against his mother." (p. 160)

> "It may well be that the suicide of his brother Martin in 1922, which followed on heavy-handed parental attempts at guidance and led to a period of increasing efforts to shape Gregory's choices as well, was an ingredient in his anxiety about problem solving and indeed about any effort to act in the world." (p. 176)

This description of Bateson reflects his position as a youngest, waiting to be taken care of, yet rebellious against the one who does it—Margaret, an oldest. As discussed in Chapter 4 (Genogram 4.2), the expectations of Bateson's sibling position were changed by the traumatic deaths of his two older brothers, thrusting him at age 18 into the position of an only child and replacement for the losses endured by his family. The shift in Gregory's sibling position in early adult life may thus have contributed to the incompatibility between him and Margaret, even though their birth positions were complementary.

There is some similarity between Gregory, whose role as the only surviving child in his family intensified to the point of a toxic cutoff from his mother, and Margaret Mead's father, an only child, doted on by his mother from the time of his father's death when he was six. While the intensity of his mother's pressure in adolescence led Bateson to cut her off, Edward Mead's closeness to his mother from early childhood led him to bring her into his marital household, where she lived for the rest of her life. Such patterns of fusion or cutoff are thought to be systemically emotional equivalents. That is, at times one gets caught and remains too connected to the other, or, on the other hand, one cuts off to deal with the emotional difficulties of maintaining one's sense of self in an emotionally intense relationship.

Sibling Constellation, Coupling, and Gender

In addition to complementary birth order, it seems to help in coupling if partners have had siblings of the opposite sex. The most difficult coupling might be the youngest sister of many sisters who marries the youngest brother of many brothers, since neither would generally have had much experience of the opposite sex in a close way, and they might both play "the spoiled child," waiting for a caretaker. They would also likely have difficulty making decisions, both waiting for someone to take charge.

Mapping Couple Relationships with Multiple Partners

Often each partner has had multiple other partners. It can be quite a challenge to depict or even track the relationships and the children from each pairing. One famous genogram that depicts such complexity would be King Henry VIII's of England and his six wives (**Figure 7.4: Henry VIII and His Wives**). To make things even more complicated, Henry's first wife, Catherine of Aragon (daughter of King Ferdinand and Queen Isabella) had originally married his older brother, Arthur, to whom she had been engaged since age three. Their marriage was meant to solidify the alliance between England and Spain. Arthur died after a few months, still only 15 years old. Henry then married Catherine and had five children with her, but only one, Mary Tudor, survived. Mary later became Queen of England. Henry proceeded to have affairs as well as five more marriages. He had a son Henry Fitzroy with a mistress Bessie Blount in 1519 and then set aside his first wife Catherine because she had not produced a living son. His second wife was Ann Boleyn, with whose older sister he had also had an affair (and possibly two children). It becomes hard to map out all the relationships and impossible, of course, to include the siblings and families of origin of everyone, not to mention difficult to know the exact truth of the relationships people wanted to keep secret!

The fate of Henry's six wives' is itself very tragic and goes like this: divorced,

Figure 7.4: Henry VIII and His Wives

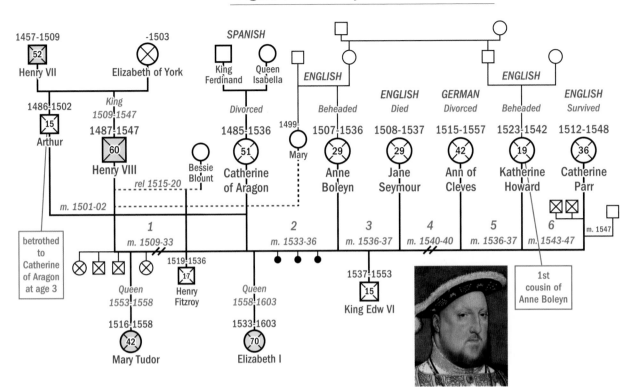

beheaded, died, divorced, beheaded, survived, with various affairs in between, only two of which are shown on Figure 7.4. You can see Henry's older brother Arthur on the left, and then his wives and key affairs in chronological order, with numbers added to indicate their order. After his first marriage to Catherine of Aragon and his affair with Elizabeth Blount, whose son Henry Fitzroy survived only to the age of 17, came his affair with Mary Boleyn, and then his second marriage to Ann Boleyn, who whose daughter Elizabeth later ruled England for 45 years.

Henry was disappointed not to have a son, and after Ann had 3 miscarriages he had her beheaded and moved on to Jane Seymour. She had a son, Edward VI, but she died the next year. Edward survived only to age 15. Jane was followed by three more wives, Ann of Cleves (whom Henry also divorced), Catherine Howard (whom he also beheaded), and finally, his last wife, Katherine Parr, who outlived him long enough to marry a fourth time, having herself been married twice before she married Henry.

Mapping such couple complexity is indeed difficult, but it helps to track couples' histories as best you can. This genogram also showed an extra complexity—two of Henry's wives were first cousins (Ann Boleyn and Katherine Howard). It is always a judgment call how much complexity one can add without making the graphic too complex. If you are working with a couple, you will want to include much more detail about each of their individual families of origin.

But in terms of multiple remarriages, the rule of thumb is that, when feasible, the different marriages should follow in order from left to right. If we are talking about a living couple, the current partner is usually shown closest to the spouse. So, if Henry VIII were alive and still married to his last wife, we would probably sacrifice the chronological order and show him closest to her, with his previous wives on his left and her previous husbands on her right.

Marriage and divorce dates also help to make the order of couple relationships clear, as well as indicating the time between separation, divorce, and remarriage, which may at times be remarkably long or short. Although not included in most of the example genograms, ideally we record the exact dates of birth, death, and marriage. These come in handy in the case of anniversary reactions, and can be a clue to such events as "shotgun weddings" and out-of-wedlock births. However, when each spouse has had multiple partners (and possibly children from previous marriages), mapping the complex web of relationships can be difficult indeed. Patterns of couple relationships and parenting can get very complicated if each partner has had multiple other spouses, who themselves have had other partners and children in different relationships. If spouses have had other partners, it may be helpful to draw a second line, slightly above the first marriage line, to differentiate these relationships, as illustrated with Henry VIII's affairs and his last wife's three other marriages.

Creating a genogram always requires choices about which details to include, since you can only show so much information at a time. This will mean deciding which facts, relationships, or patterns are most important to depict. Because we were focused on the chronology of Henry VIII, we chose to emphasize the order of his relationships. In a situation where we want to emphasize the couple who are parents of a particular child, we would (as mentioned already) probably choose to put the key couple in the center and other relationships and children on each side.

While it is generally preferable to show children from different marriages in their correct birth order (oldest on the left to youngest on the right), this becomes difficult when there are many partners. In the following illustration of Henry Fonda's family (**Figure 7.5: Fonda Family with Children Shown in Birth Order**) we can show the children in birth order only by omitting the other relationships of Henry's wife, Frances Seymour, and showing Fonda's later wives further to the right. If one of his wives had other children in other relationships, we would be forced to choose whether to show them in birth order or in the order of his relationships.

The youngest daughter, Amy, the daughter of Fonda and Susan Blanchard, lived with the family from ages one to five, at which point her parents separated. So how we construct the genogram would depend on the point in time we want to depict, who was living where, and the sibling constellation at the particular moment we want to illustrate. Showing the siblings in birth order facilitates our understanding of their relationship to each other, but we would also want to know the chronology of the years they spent together and who else was living in the household at each point. With complex families, choices always have to be made, and it may be important to construct several genograms to map out different key moments in the family's history. Hopefully computers will soon be able hold and organize data on complex family relationships, and show a family's evolution as they move through time.

When spouses have had partners of both genders, it may also be necessary to draw the relationship lines at different levels to clarify who was connected with whom. Where there have been many partners, it may also be necessary to be selec-

Figure 7.5:   Fonda Family with Children Shown in Birth Order

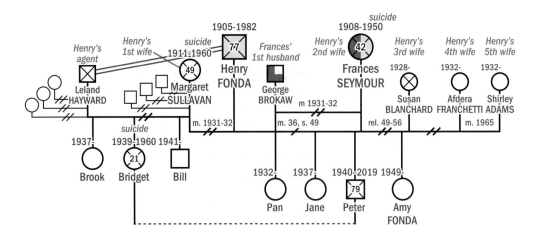

tive, showing only the most significant relationships. If a couple are in a committed relationship, the pairing of a dotted and a solid line indicates the relationship commitment, even if the couple are not formally married, as shown on **Figure 7.6: The Family of Jodie Foster**.

This genogram illustrates the committed relationship of Jodie's mother Brandy and her partner Aunt Jo. Not shown is that Jody's father, Lucius, who left the family at the time of his wife's pregnancy with Jodie, fathered children with four additional partners. Brandy's marriage to Lucius is indicated by "m. '54", her separation by "s. '59", and their divorce by "d. '62."

Recording the specific chronology of couple relationships can be important for tracking family patterns, a process which will, again, become much easier when computer genogram programs can track the entire couple chronology. But only so much information can be depicted at any one moment. Jodie, for example, was conceived and born three years after the parents separated, shortly before their divorce came through. It seems she was the product of the father's financial, emotional, and physical abuse of the mother. Jody was conceived under the father's pressure for sex, before he would provide the child support money that was due.

Figure 7.6:   The Family of Jodie Foster

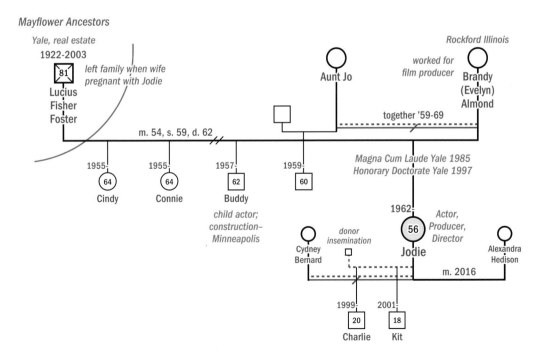

Jodie's mother was in a committed couple relationship with Aunt Jo from 1959 to 1969. The couple began living together in 1962 ("LT '62"). Jo's prominence in the family is indicated by depicting the couple line for Brandy and Jo just above that of the biological father. "Aunt Jo" became a haven of stability for the children, providing financial, physical, and emotional support to them for many years. Jo's husband is shown smaller and higher, along with the woman he spent the rest of his life with. He never divorced Jo and she was thus not free to marry again; his other relationship is indicated with a dotted line. The genogram also shows Jodie's couple relationship with her partner Cydney, with whom she had two children by donor insemination, and then her marriage to Alexandra Hedson.

Exploring Couples in the Context of Culture, Time, and Place

It is vital not only to consider a family's cultural identity, but also the broader sociopolitical context and historical forces that have shaped each partner's experiences. A compelling example of this can be observed in the case of famed painters Frida Kahlo and her husband Diego Rivera. **Figure 7.7: Kahlo Rivera Cultural Genogram** shows their genogram, which is typical of many families in its complex mixture of cultural heritages. It would be impossible to understand Frida Kahlo without considering the historical and cultural context from which her family came. Kahlo was a revolutionary artist born in Coyoacán, Mexico, amidst political chaos. She so identified with her political era that she used to say she had been born in 1910, the year of the Mexican Revolution, although in reality she was born three years earlier! She was fully caught up in the sociopolitical struggles of her culture and times, which are reflected in her work.

Kahlo grappled with the multiple aspects of her identity all her life, including her gender, ethnicity, and national identity, often depicting these themes in her art, with one foot located in the cultural ruins of ancient Mexico, and one foot in the industrial imperialistic U.S. (**Picture 7.1: Kahlo in Two Continents**). She was a complex mixture of conflicting forces. On the one hand she was a young Mexican girl, and on the other a sophisticated woman of the world. Her works are a testament both to pre-Columbian and colonial cultural influences. Kahlo's life and work embodied a clash of cultures that was a reflection of both her historical context and of the unique dynamics in her family's cultural legacy.

Her father was a German/Hungarian Jew who immigrated to Mexico, where he deeply embraced the local culture.

Figure 7.7: Kahlo Rivera Cultural Genogram

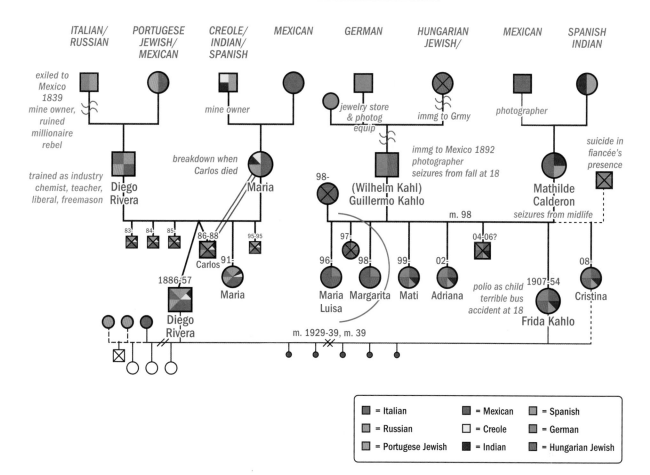

Her mother was the daughter of a native Michoacán woman (a descendant of an empire that rivaled the Aztec Empire) and a Spanish General, and thus the literal embodiment of Mexican culture—namely, a culture forged through the clash between the conquering Spaniards and the conquered indigenous peoples of ancient Mexico. Kahlo identified intensely with her roots on both sides of her family system, finding ways to hold the tension between these contrasting forces.

We often say that she created the first genogram—a diagram of her family with portraits of each, as shown in **Picture 7.2: Kahlo Family Portrait**. The picture shows the complex cultural and racial roots of both her parents as well as some of the complex legacies of the children. It was inspired by the fact that

Picture 7.1: Kahlo in Two Continents

Picture 7.2 Kahlo Family Portrait

genealogical charts were one method the Nazis used to prove or disprove "racial purity," and by 1936 Nazi-oriented manuals on how to conduct genealogical research were distributed in the German School of Mexico City, where many of the teachers joined the Nazi Party and encouraged their students to chart their family trees.

Disgusted by this, Kahlo adapted this Nazi device to emphasize her interracial origins, making her painting a subversive statement—a reflection of her identification with her Jewish and multi-racial roots. Beyond this, her art reflects both her passion for and attunement to the duality of Mexican culture, with its ancient Meso-American and European Spanish roots. Her paintings routinely included religious symbols that were Jewish, Catholic, and Indigenous, further depicting the impact of her family's mixed heritage on her life and her work.

Her father grew up in Germany where he hoped for a university education, but at 18 he suffered a serious accident, which left him with brain damage and seizures. This changed the course of his life and dashed his hopes of university study. His accident and his mother's death the following year, compounded by his father's quick remarriage to a woman with whom Wilhelm didn't get along, influenced his resolve to emigrate to Mexico.

In Mexico he changed his name from Wilhelm Kahl to Guillermo Kahlo. He became a noted photographer, although he suffered ongoing sequelae from his accident. In Mexico, Kahlo married a first wife and had three daughters, one of whom died very early, and then his wife died tragically in childbirth with the third daughter. (See **Figure: 7.8: Kahlo–Rivera Genogram**.)

Kahlo apparently met his future wife, Mathilda Calderon, the very night of his first wife's death. He married her very soon thereafter. She, however, conveyed that she did not want to have to raise the two surviving daughters from his first marriage, so those girls were sent to a convent and he and Mathilda "started over."

Over the next few years, Mathilda and Guillermo had two daughters, a son who died, and then two more daughters. Frida was the first daughter born after the lost son. If we look at the photograph of Frida in her teens (**Picture 7.3**, leaning on father), she does indeed look like a son, perhaps demonstrating again her ability to incorporate many different cultural possibilities.

If we look again at Kahlo's "genogram" portrait of her family (**Picture 7.2**), she appears to have had a strong awareness of not only her cultural heritage but also of the hidden history of her family, including those family members who had died or been cut off. Frida's "genogram" portrait appears to show in birth order her two older sisters, then a baby (the brother who died?), and then herself and her sister Christina. But then on the right are two faceless people and below a boy

Figure: 7.8:   Kahlo–Rivera Genogram

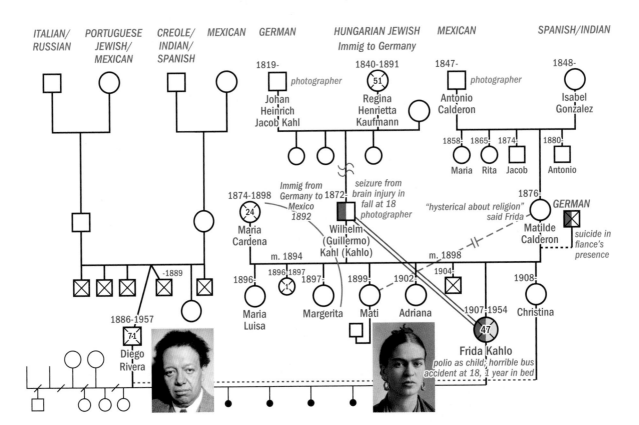

crossed out. Could the two faceless people be her two sisters who were extruded from the family? Kahlo had an amazing ability to convey the concept that those who are lost are never fully gone. As she saw it, the trauma of what has come before never ceases to affect us. Could she be trying to give the message that the two extruded sisters were still part of the family and that her brother was still part of it as well?

She made another "genogram" portrait, **Picture 7.4**, which similarly shows the grandparents on both sides again. Then there is a baby in the mother's stomach. And Frida herself is shown as a small child below the parents in the family's home yard. Is that her brother in the mother's stomach? Is she saying that she is living the life for the lost brother as well as her own life? She does seem to have been, in many ways, a replacement for her lost brother.

The complexity of diverse relationships was something that was deeply embedded in the Kahlo family system. Kahlo's life was always about connecting disparate parts, reflecting the complexity of her heritage.

Picture 7.3

Both Frida's parents experienced severe traumas early in life. Her mother, Mathilda Calderon, was a brilliant and attractive woman of Spanish and Indigenous background. She had been in love with another German, who committed suicide in front of her. All her life she kept a book of his letters, and though she married Kahlo and had four daughters and a son with him, she never seemed to live up to her potential. Mathilda encouraged her husband to go into business as a photographer with her father. Unfortunately, he seems never to have escaped the after-effects of his own earlier traumas. Over the years he became bitter and withdrawn, in spite of his obvious abilities and early efforts to reinvent himself. It was his favorite daughter, Frida, who demonstrated a remarkable ability to transform traumatic experience into hope and beautiful art, through transcendent strength and creative energy, even in spite of much more severe disabilities. She

Picture 7.4

first became ill at age six with polio, which left her right leg weaker and smaller. At 18 she experienced a traumatic bus accident, in which she was impaled on a metal pipe, which went completely through her pelvis and fractured her spine. The accident left her with chronic pain for the rest of her life, in spite of numerous operations. She became her father's favorite child, and the only one given a German name, Frida. Early on she developed an interest in art, his profession, which became her outlet following her accident, as it had for him. Like her father, Frida had dreamed of becoming a scholar and physician. Instead, she became an artist, like her father and her maternal grandfather before that.

Three years after her accident, Frida married Diego Rivera, 21 years her senior, who was already a successful artist. Rivera himself was from a very diverse background: Russian, Italian, Portuguese, Spanish, Creole, and Mexican, including ancestors who had been forced to convert from Judaism to Catholicism. Like Kahlo, his family had experienced many traumas. His parents had lost three baby

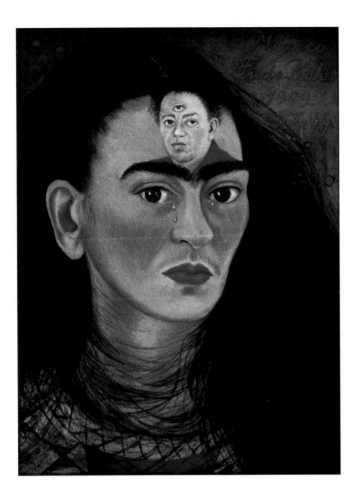

Picture 7.5   Kahlo with Rivera in Her Head

boys before he and his twin brother were born. Rivera's twin brother died at two, as did the youngest son. A younger sister was the only sibling to survive. Rivera himself lived away from his family with a nursemaid in the mountains for two years in early childhood because of illnesses including rickets. By the time Kahlo fell in love with him, he had already been married several times and had several children. She too had already had various other relationships. Kahlo had four miscarriages during the marriage, which must have been extremely difficult and painful for her, compounded by her serious disability from her accident.

Kahlo sometimes portrayed Rivera as being inside her head, as if it was impossible to have an identity that he did not in some way own (see **Picture 7.5: Kahlo with Rivera in Her Head**). Rivera appears to have been the love of her life, but he was never faithful, having multiple affairs, including with her sister Christina. The couple divorced and remarried, and Frida herself had lovers, both male and female, including the famous Russian revolutionary Leon Trotsky. The couple eventually lived in separate but connected homes in Mexico City. Both were extraordinary artists. In spite of her physical and psychological suffering throughout her life, Frida Kahlo was one of the most remarkably inventive, colorful, and creative artists of the 20th century.

Her work radiated with her fierce independence as well as her phenomenal ability to portray multiple perspectives on human identity, as when she conveyed Rivera inside her head. Sometimes she depicted herself from diverse cultural and life cycle perspectives, as in **Picture 7.6: Kahlo with Three Life Cycle Outfits,** where she simultaneously conveys a young girl, a traditional cultural woman, and

Picture 7.6:   Kahlo with Three Life Cycle Outfits

a sophisticated woman. Hopeful and despairing, she vacillated between periods of extreme isolation and wild bursts of exuberance and merrymaking.

Kahlo and Rivera convey the importance of attending to the cohort in time and place to which spouses belong, the cultural groups their families have belonged to, and the creative power of their individual and family struggles and resilience.

Common Couple Triangles to Look For

Common couple triangles include not only those related to children, which we discussed in Chapter 5, and those related to sibling patterns, which we discussed in Chapter 6, but also triangles with parents, in-laws, friends, and others, including, of course, the family dog, as well as other objects or institutions: money, the internet, work, TV, and therapists.

In-Law Issues

Perhaps the most common couple triangle is the in-law triangle. Classically, this involves a favorite son, his mother, and his wife. The in-law triangle may play itself out in a variety of ways. The spouses may divert their own conflicts by focusing on what is wrong with the husband's mother. Or the wife may blame her mother-in-law for her husband's inadequacies, while the mother-in-law blames the daughter-in-law for keeping her "darling boy" away. The husband may enjoy letting his mother and his wife do battle, allowing him to stay out of the fray and perhaps avoid dealing with both of them. It is often a case of "Let's you and her fight." Of course, in-law triangles can occur between two spouses and any of their parents, but the wife often takes a more central and involved emotional role and thus is more likely to become the focus of stress in this situation. Also, in certain cultures, such as Asian, where wives were traditionally brought into the husband's family at marriage and were subject to the control of their mothers-in-law, such triangles might be greatly intensified.

Affairs

Another common couple triangle involves an affair. Clearly, an extramarital relationship has implications for a marriage and can become a major area of concern, even if the marriage survives. The affair may relieve some of the tension of a conflictual relationship by giving one of the partners an outlet, or it may divert the couple from underlying problems.

Wilhelm Reich, one of Freud's followers, spent his life focused on sexuality as the core dynamic of human development. His genogram **(Figure 7.9: Reich Family Triangles)** illustrates the triangles of an affair which led to family tragedy. Wilhelm was the oldest son and had grown up in an extremely close, even sexualized relationship with his mother, and in a negative relationship with his brutal, jealous, and abusive father. But when he discovered his mother was having an affair with his tutor, he felt both curious, resentful, and perhaps jealous of her secret relationship. Later, when the mother revealed to the father that she had found in Wilhelm's pocket a small cigarette rolling device he had taken from the father, Wilhelm felt betrayed and told the father about the mother's affair. The father apparently beat her mercilessly, until she took poison and died a dreadful death. Wilhelm never got over this; it traumatized him at the deepest level. The father seems to have had deep regret himself, and he fell into depression. He took out a life insurance policy and then exposed himself to the elements, so that he became ill and died four years later at the age of only 47, leaving his sons orphans at ages 17 and 14.

Reich's later professional promotion of guilt-free sexuality in all its forms seems to have been an effort to make up for the disastrous results of his part in that family triangle. Sadly, in the next generation, Reich's son, Peter, experienced a similar trauma at the same age. After Reich was convicted of violating a court injunction against selling his unscientific purported cure for cancer with "cosmic orgone therapy," the FBI came to find him, and his son was forced to say where he

Figure 7.9:   Reich Family Triangles

1908	1909	1910	1956-1957

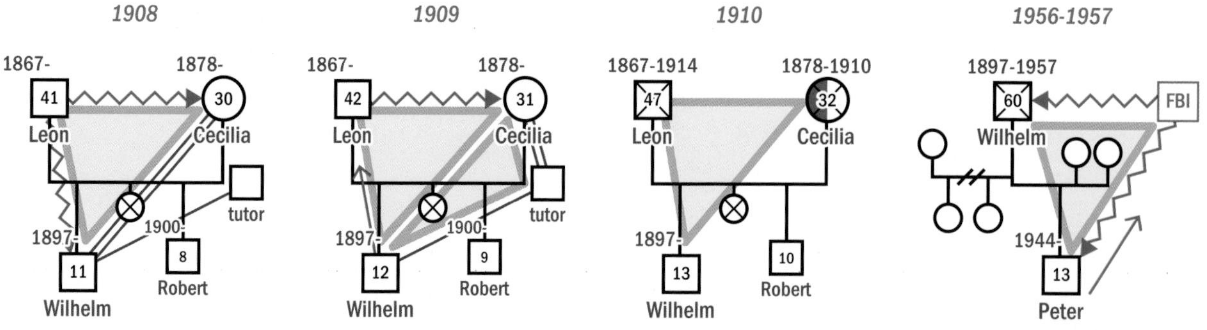

Wilhelm close to mother, terrorized by father

Wilhelm discovers mother's affair with his tutor, and angry at her revealing a misdead of his, he tells his father of mother's affair

Father brutalizes wife who finally kills herself. Father depressed and dies himself. Wilhelm regretted telling about mother

When Peter same age as father was he is forced to tell FBI where father (Wilhelm) is, Wilhelm imprisoned and soon dies. Peter later feared he had given father away

was. Reich was taken to prison, where he died six months later. For years, Peter felt guilt that he had betrayed his father.

Divorced and Remarried Families Have A Whole Extra Layer of History and Potential Triangles

Divorce and remarriage add a whole extra layer of history to the relationship equation of any family. We always have to consider the common triangles that may develop, including those involving the new wife and the old wife, the new children and the old children, and the new family versus the old family. Relationship problems may develop for both spouses, all the children, and the extended family on all sides—aunts, uncles, cousins, and grandparents.

While children can easily get into a triangle with once-married parents, as we have discussed in Chapter 5, when one or both parents remarry, there are additional triangles to explore (McGoldrick & Carter, 2016). Perhaps one of the reasons such triangles are so easy to identify on the genograms of remarried families is that the structure of the family, as much as or more than the personalities of the participants, defines the situation. This makes these triangles rather predictable. Children are basically never prepared to lose a parent, whether by death or divorce. Biological parents are not really replaceable. No parent ever ceases to be important to a child, no matter how many years ago he or she died or disappeared. Thus, the insider-outsider structural pattern in remarried families is endemic to the situation and tends to create triangles. How children respond to new stepparents will depend on many factors, including their gender and life cycle stage at the time of the divorce (McGoldrick & Carter, 2016), but certain triangles are highly predictable. For example, Henry Fonda's remarriage to Susan Blanchard after his previous wife's suicide (**Figure 7.10: Divorce & Remarriage Triangles: Fonda Example**) seems to have elicited a very different reaction from Peter, who was 10, than from Jane, who was 13. Peter still very much needed a mother. Jane was beginning adolescence and breaking away was more predictable for her. When Fonda redivorced four years later, Peter was 15 and Jane 18 and going off to college. Peter was heartbroken at the possibility of losing his second mother, but his father argued that it would be insensitive to him and his new bride, Afdera Franchetti, for Peter to continue to see his stepmother. Peter, as we might expect from a mid-adolescent, retorted that *he* hadn't divorced Susan and would see her whenever he wanted (Fonda, 1998, p. 84). We can easily see the patterns of interlocking triangles that get set in motion by the changing structures of such remarried families.

The following schematic genograms demonstrate some of the predictable tri-

Figure 7.10:   Divorce & Remarriage Triangles: Fonda Example

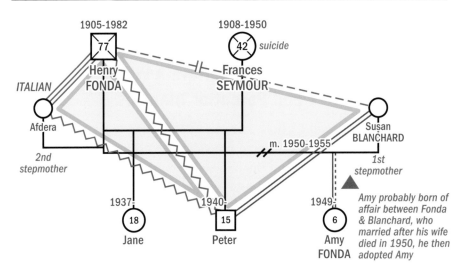

angles in remarried families. One common triangle involves the children in a family with a biological father and a stepmother with whom they do not get along. This pattern is very common, since a stepmother can never replace the biological mother, and children's alliance will usually be with the biological parent rather than the stepparent. Peter Fonda was an exception because he had already lost his biological mother when he was still a child, desperately needing a connection. For the custodial father in a remarriage, the new wife generally offers hope for regained marital love after a loss. For the child the stepparent is a threat, the fear being that she will take the remaining parent away.

Several different types of triangle are most common in divorce and remarriage situations (**Figure 7.11**: **Divorce & Remarriage Triangles & De-Triangling**). One involves the children, the biological father, and the stepmother (**Children, Father, & Stepmother**) with hostility between the children and the new wife (unfortunately too often thought of as the "wicked" stepmother). Western literature is rife with wicked stepmothers (Nabokov's *Lolita* has one of the rare negative portrayals of a stepfather, in Humbert Humbert). The stepmother often feels threatened that her husband gives more attention to his children than he does to her. The husband is usually caught in a loyalty conflict between his new wife and his children; this situation creates an unstable triangle for him, because it is hard to stay connected to two others who are at war. The structure here shows clearly how the father is likely to flounder. But the structure also indicates the solution: The parent must position him or herself to strengthen his connection first to his children, since the new marriage follows a prior commitment to them, and then to

Figure 7.11:   Divorce & Remarriage Triangles & De-Triangling

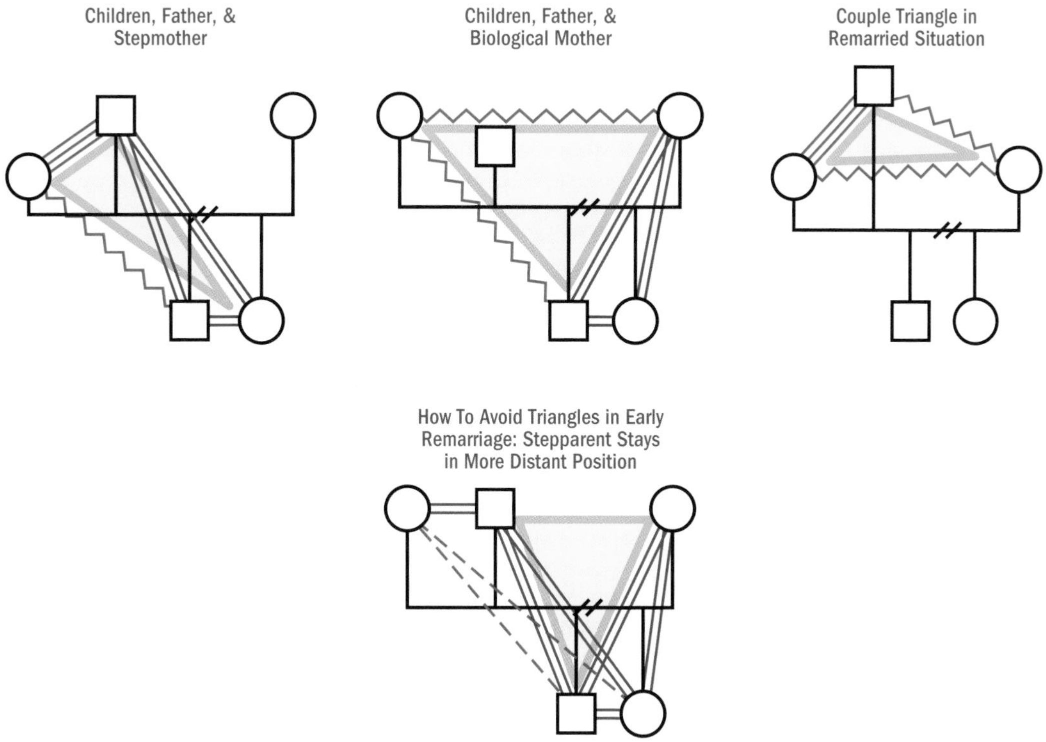

Children, Father, &
Stepmother

Children, Father, &
Biological Mother

Couple Triangle in
Remarried Situation

How To Avoid Triangles in Early
Remarriage: Stepparent Stays
in More Distant Position

the new partner. The parent must work hard to avoid being drawn into triangles by the new partner or the children. The children need first and foremost to feel sure of the parent's love for and commitment to them. The new relationship needs to fit into the context of the previous commitments of the parent-child relationships.

The second triangle, usually interlocking with the first, involves the children, the stepmother, and the biological mother (**Children, The Stepmother, & the Biological Mother**). The children may resent the stepmother's efforts to replace their biological mother. The new wife feels unaccepted in her own home and the biological mother is likely to feel threatened by the new wife. It is common for overt conflict to occur between the biological mother and stepmother in this triangle. Interlocking triangles involving the husband, his ex-wife, and his new wife are very common. There is tension between the new couple and the ex-wife, with the ex-wife obviously being on the outside. Two types of triangles are likely here. The new couple may band together against the ex-spouse, seeing her as the cause of all their problems. Or the new and old wife may have overt conflicts, with the husband perhaps even encouraging his new wife to fight the old battles for him as shown in **Couple Triangle in a Remarried Situation**.

Triangles also occur with a biological mother, her children, and a stepfather. However, because our culture places greater expectations on motherhood than on fatherhood, stepmothers generally have the more difficult experience.

The structure, again, implies the solution (**How To Avoid Triangles in Early Remarriage: Stepparent Stays in More Distant Position**). The key is for the stepparent not to get into a central position in the children's lives that would escalate the loyalty conflict for them in relation to their own parent, fostering instead their connection to their original mother and father (McGoldrick & Carter, 2016).

The other guideline for keeping this set of relationships in balance is for the divorced parents to maintain a working partnership that allows children to stay loyal to both of them, obviously not an easy task for many families. If they cannot at least develop a working partnership, the next best alternative is a structured relationship, so the children have a life that is at least somewhat predictable.

The potentially negative aftermath of such triangles in remarried families can be seen on the genogram of Eugene O'Neill following his third marriage (**Figure 7.12: O'Neill Fusion and Cutoff in Third Remarriage**) (McGoldrick, 2011). After his divorces O'Neill virtually cutoff his relationships with all three of his children. He separated from his second wife, Agnes, when their youngest child, Oona O'Neill, was only three. In bitter disillusionment, he cut off not only his ex-wife, but his children as well, refusing even to mention their names. He resented the "exorbitant" alimony payments he was expected to pay, and his ex-wife, Agnes, was extremely jealous of his new wife, Carlotta. When Oona grew up and married

Figure 7.12:   O'Neill Fusion and Cutoff in Third Remarriage

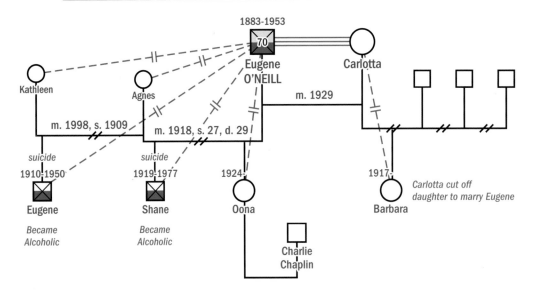

Charlie Chaplin, O'Neill refused to have any involvement with her ever again. This may have been compounded by other interlocking triangles. It seems that Agnes herself may have had an earlier relationship with Chaplin, who had also been a very good friend of Carlotta (Gelb and Gelb, 1987). Triangles can multiply quickly in remarried families.

In-Law and Grandparent Relationships in Remarried Families

Finally, in-laws are usually not neutral in remarriage situations. There may be a great deal of tension between the husband's mother and his new wife, or the wife's family and their daughter's ex-husband. The grandparent generation often gets involved in remarriage triangles, intensifying the process by joining with their adult child, especially against the ex-spouse, whom they may blame for the divorce. They also have a vested interest in their grandchildren and may take sides and "butt in" when they feel their grandchildren's well-being and happiness are at stake. Grandparents sharing their opinions and unsolicited advice with their adult children can make matters worse.

Putting Couples in Perspective

Doing a couple's genogram is the quickest and most effective way to get the "lay of the land" in a family. Even a moderately detailed genogram reveals much about the couple's important relationships, their level of functioning, and their coping styles. The genogram often shows multigenerational patterns that are creating or threatening to create difficulties when the family is stressed. The therapist can use this information to work more effectively with families in crisis. In calmer times, the therapist can coach couples on ways to improve their communication and interactions, to help them better deal with or avert future predicaments.

8

Exploring Families through Time and Space with Genograms: The Family Life Cycle

T racking a family's history over the life cycle is a pivotal way to understand any genogram. Clinically, it is particularly useful for students and clients to do genograms in order to understand family legacies in chronological perspective and to incorporate family narratives from a resilience-based perspective (Walsh, 2016).

When interpreting a genogram, you will also want to look at where individuals and the family as a whole are in the life cycle. Families progress through different phases and transitions, including leaving the home of origin, marriage, births, child-rearing, retirement, illness, and death. Upon reaching each milestone, the family must reorganize itself to move on successfully to the next phase. If patterns rigidify at transition points, they are likely to have trouble adapting to later phases (McGoldrick, Garcia Preto, & Carter, 2016).

The clinician should note what life cycle transitions, if any, the family is adapting to, and how they have adapted to life cycle shifts in the past. When ages and dates do not add up in terms of how the family progressed through various stages, possible difficulties in managing that phase of the life cycle can be explored. For example, if adult children have not left home, one would want to explore any difficulties around beginning a new phase of the life cycle. Or, if a marriage occurred quickly after a loss, this may be a clue about issues of unresolved grief.

Genograms map out a family's past, uncovering the pain as well as the wonder of its history. While the patterns can provide a roadmap and inspiration for the future, they can also be full of secrets, which may be painful and frightening. People's anxiety about the "dicey bits" is an important consideration in any genogram exploration.

It is also important, of course, to recognize that those who do not fit into the typical life cycle patterns at the typical timing in life are often made to feel abnormal, while they may actually be creative or independent thinkers or following other viable life patterns. It is always important to look for the strengths and resilience, as well as the vulnerabilities, of any particular life pattern.

We usually find it convenient to begin discussion with the young adulthood of grown children, who must now establish their lives more independently of their families of origin and generally form couples. This point in the life cycle is often the first time in many years that the family is transformed by having to adjust to the integration of new members. Parents may struggle to accommodate their young adult childrens' partners and in-laws into a new and expanded family constellation.

Example of Sigmund Freud and His Family

We will use the genogram of our psychological ancestor Sigmund Freud and his family to track typical genogram patterns through the life cycle. Because of his tremendous impact on the field of psychology, his genogram is particularly relevant for us in understanding our own assumptions in historical perspective. His legacies may shed important light on our own family heritage.

Freud had a lifelong aversion to biography. Like many other people who are embarrassed or pained by aspects of their background, he downplayed and hid much of his family history. It has taken some digging to uncover what we do know of his family patterns. In his view, there is nothing people want to protect themselves from more than their personal and family histories (Phillips, 2014). His theories appear to have been shaped by his personal family history (as much as he wanted to ignore or forget aspects of it, and as much as he wanted others to ignore or forget it). On at least three separate occasions, he destroyed many of his personal and family papers. He wrote to his wife Minna in 1886 that he had just destroyed many of his papers, because:

> I couldn't have matured or died without worrying about who would get hold of those old papers. Everything that lies beyond the great turning point in my life, beyond our love and my choice of profession, died long ago and must not be deprived of a worthy funeral. As for the biographers, let them worry! I have no desire to make it too easy for them. Each one of them will be right in his opinion of "The Development of the Hero" and I am already looking forward to seeing them go astray. (Freud, 1975, p. 141)

Freud was only 30 at the time he wrote this. He had barely begun his career, yet he was already sure he would have biographers and was hoping to lead them astray. In later years, he twice more destroyed personal and family records, embarrassed, apparently, as so many are, by the mental illness, criminal acts, and other secrets of various family members.

Freud's negative attitudes toward biography have probably shaped our psychological thinking more than anyone else's. He focused almost exclusively on the importance of childhood fantasies about parents, virtually ignoring the realities of one's history—one's own actual life and that of one's parents, as well as the role of siblings and the extended family. He tried to draw our attention away from our family history altogether.

Not surprisingly, many of Freud's biographers, as well as other psychologists, followed their leader and cultivated major blind spots about family history. For example, we would have assumed that Freud's biographers would be interested in his mother, given his theory about the pivotal role mothers play in child development. At the age of 77, Freud wrote, still with great intensity, about the mother's role in childhood resentments about the birth of a sibling:

"What the child grudges the unwanted intruder and rival is not only the suckling, but all other signs of maternal care. He feels that he has been dethroned, despoiled, prejudiced in his rights; he casts a jealous hatred upon the new baby and develops a grievance against the faithless mother" (Philips, 2014, p. 47)

We would expect such an attitude to lead Freud's biographers to want to know more about his mother. Freud's mother lived to be ninety-five years old and always lived in his vicinity. But they gave almost no attention to her life or her role in their family. We know nothing of her relationships with her parents, her siblings, or her early life. It is puzzling why neither Freud nor his many biographers ever asked her about her own life or family. Of course, many of us might ask ourselves the same question: Why did we not ask our own mothers (or fathers or grandparents) about their lives when we had the chance?

Freud wrote about mothers' relationships with sons:

A mother is only brought unlimited satisfaction by her relation to a son; this is altogether the most perfect, the most free from ambivalence of all human relationships. A mother can transfer to her son the ambition which she had been obliged to suppress in herself, and she can expect from him the satisfaction of all that has been left over in her of her masculinity complex. (Krüll, 1986, p. 117)

Freud's mother generally referred to Sigmund as "My golden Sigi." But, as Krüll has pointed out, Freud's reference to the mother-son relationship as the most free of ambivalence must only have referred to her feelings toward him, not to his feelings toward her. He apparently had regular attacks of indigestion before visits with her. Indeed, Freud's mother was described by her grandchildren in later life as a tornado: impulsive, strident, and not warm (Krüll, 1986).

We must also consider the cultural context in which the Freuds lived. They were from Eastern European Jewish families, who had been persecuted and forced to migrate repeatedly for hundreds of years. They had always lived in relatively small marginalized communities within hostile societies, to which they could never belong. So Freud's desire to protect himself from exposure was also a reflection of his cultural heritage, coming from a cultural group who had lived for so long under persecution (Phillips, 2014; Krüll, 1986).

We may then approach Freud's genogram as we do all genograms—with a series of questions. What was Freud's avoidance of history about? Why did he want to deny its relevance? Are there particular facts he wanted to avoid, and, if so, why? Were there secrets in the Freud family that he dared not talk about? Recent research suggests that there were.

Exploring the genogram patterns of the Freud family can perhaps help us to see the things Freud did not want us to notice. Let us begin with the ages of family members as they moved through the life cycle. As can be seen in **Figure 8.1: Freud Family in 1855**, Sigmund Freud's parents Jacob Freud and Amalia Nathansohn were a generation apart in age. Jacob was 40 and his wife 20 when they married. Jacob was already a grandfather, with two grown sons much closer in age to his wife than to him. We see that Jacob had been married before and his first wife had died three years before he married Amalia.

Jacob had been in business with his maternal grandfather, Zisi Hoffman, and had also done business for 10 years with Amalia's father, Jacob Nathansohn, before both men had serious business problems. Jacob had arranged to have his son Emanuel take over his involvement in the business in 1853. Amalia's father was apparently disgraced by his business failure in 1854. We might wonder if this failure influenced Amalia to marry a much older man, who had worked with her father since she was 10. We know that such large age differences were not the norm at that time and place (Krüll, 1986), although substantial age differences were not uncommon with widowers' second wives. Perhaps Amalia's father's recent disgrace and the loss of his fortune explain her decision, as the only daughter, to "settle" for an older man (Swales, 1986).

We know nothing about Jacob's first wife, Jacob and Amalia's decision to

Figure 8.1:   Freud Family in 1855

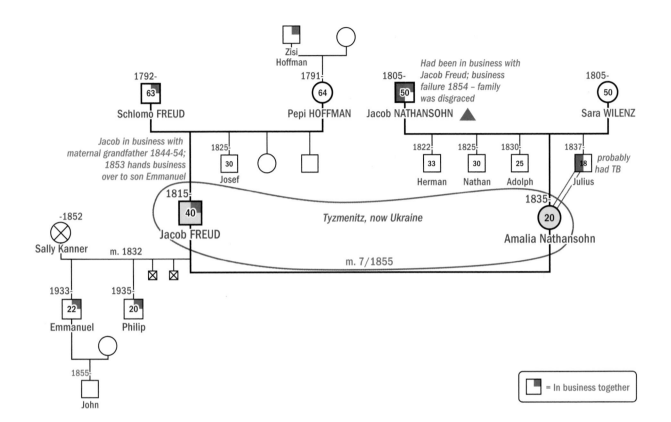

marry, or how anyone in the family reacted to all these changes. Why did no one in the family consider these events or relationships important enough to discuss and record, even later on? We don't know if Amalia knew Jacob's first wife, Sally Kanner, whom he married when he was only 17, suggesting, perhaps, the possibility of an unexpected pregnancy (Anzieu, 1986).

Amalia would surely have known of Sally's existence, as they all lived in the same town, and Jacob had worked for so long with her father. If anyone ever did mention Sally to Freud, there is no record of his discussing her with anyone. Was there something about her of which the family was ashamed?

We also don't know any details of Amalia's relationships with Emmanuel and Philip. We do know from comments Freud made in his adult life that in his fantasy, his mother and Philip were lovers. We know also that within three years of his remarriage, Jacob helped to arrange for his sons to emigrate to England, which may have been partly to put them at a safe distance from his second wife.

What might the legacy have been from Jacob's 20-year first marriage? What thoughts or anxieties might Amalia have had about following in Sally's footsteps? In any case, Jacob began his new family with Amalia in the shadow of both his earlier marriage and the loss of two of his first four children.

Amalia was a vivacious young woman, and the only daughter of her parents. Jacob, for his part, seems to have done fairly well in his thirties as a traveling salesman with his father, his maternal grandfather, and with Amalia's father. But his career seemingly came to a standstill at midlife. One might predict, upon seeing such a couple on a genogram, that marriage would be a problematic life cycle transition for many reasons. Unresolved issues in earlier life phases tend to lead to more difficult transitions and complexities later in life. We can only guess that it was a difficult transition, given Jacob's previous marriage, his mysterious past, the age difference between him and his wife, their financial precariousness, Amalia's father's financial disgrace, and her brother's illness and death around the time of the marriage.

These are all questions we would want to explore for such a genogram. Hypothesizing about possible family patterns and stressors is a crucial part of working with genograms. Exploring patterns helps us develop hypotheses about a family and think of questions that will facilitate our learning more about what happened to understand wherever they are at the moment.

Genograms also often suggest issues in previous relationships, such as fusion or distance from a parent or a sibling that may affect the marital bond. Unfortunately, the only thing we know of the in-law relationships in this generation of the Freud family is that Jacob and his father Schlomo worked for years with Amalia's father, whose business ended badly. But we don't know the details of how that affected their relationships.

The Transition to Parenthood: The Freud Family in 1856

Sigmund was born in Freiberg, Moravia in 1856, the year after the couple married. (**Figure 8.2: Freud Family in 1856**). Often the birth of the first child, more than the marriage itself, most clearly marks the transition to a new family. For the new spouse, the child tends to signify greater legitimation and increases the power of the current family in relation to the family of origin.

Jacob's father Schlomo died at age 63, just three months before Sigmund was born, and Sigmund was named for him. (We have indicated the events around the time of Freud's birth in red on the genogram to highlight the connections:

Figure 8.2:   Freud Family in 1856

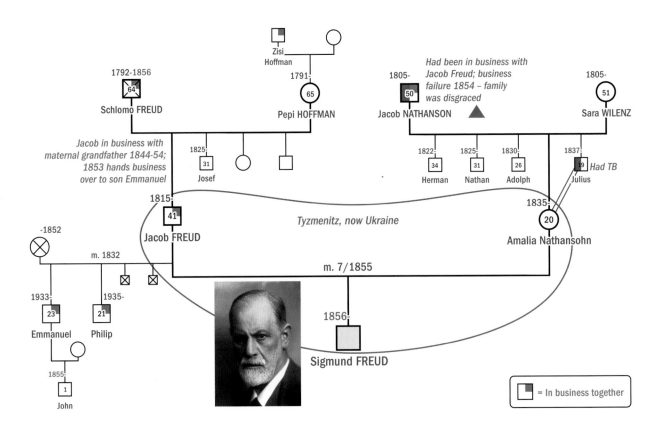

Freud's paternal grandfather's death and the birth of his half-nephew John, who was born just the year before). This grandfather had been rabbi-like, and Freud may have thought that, perhaps, he was born to follow in this grandfather's footsteps, becoming a kind of rabbi: a teacher and an intellectual leader. Freud seems to have had a special place in his mother's heart from the beginning. His role was obviously also influenced by his position as the oldest in the new family and by his being born at the highest point in the family's hopes.

The Early Parenthood Years

The genogram may reveal the particular circumstances surrounding the birth of a child and how those circumstances may have contributed to a child's special position in that family. It can also suggest the typical parent-child triangles that may develop. If we look at a genogram for the three years just after Sigmund Freud was born (**Figure 8.3: Freud Family, 1857-60**), we see an extraordinary series of stresses on the family including migration, birth, loss, and other threats to the system. (Again, we have indicated the key events on the genogram in red to highlight their connection to Freud's earliest childhood.)

Freud's mother became pregnant again eight months after his birth and gave birth to her second son Julius in October 1857. But sadly, Julius died of enteritis at six months of age on April 15, 1858, just one month after Amalia's younger brother Julius died of TB.

The death of a child tends to intensify parental feelings about the surviving children. The child nearest in age, especially a child of the same sex, often becomes a replacement for the lost child. Thus, Sigmund may have become even

Figure 8.3:   Freud Family, 1857-60

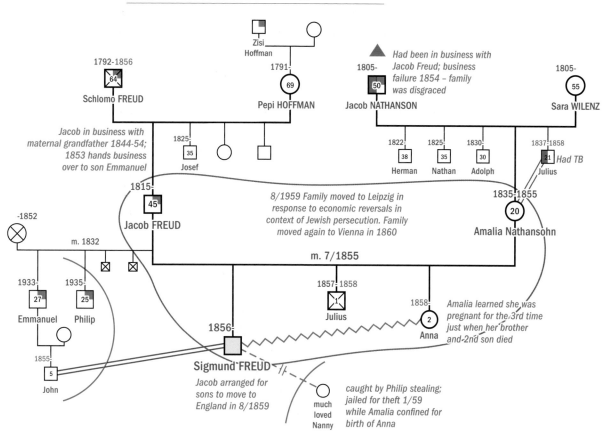

more important to his mother after the death of her second son. That loss was itself intensified by the death of her youngest brother (Krüll, 1986). Amalia must have known that her brother was dying when she named her second son for him six months earlier. The naming is especially interesting, since it goes against the Jewish custom of naming a baby in honor only of someone who has already died. Could it be that the emotional imperative became more powerful than the cultural custom, which had been followed for Sigmund and was a strong tradition in Amalia's culture? In later life, Sigmund said that he had welcomed this brother with "ill wishes and real infantile jealousy, and his death left the germ of guilt in me" (Masson, 1985, p. 268: Letter to Wilhelm Fleiss, Oct 3,1897).

By the time both brother and son Julius died, Amalia was already pregnant with her third child, Anna, born Dec 31, 1858, so this must have been a very stressful time for the family. The month after Anna was born, January 1859, Freud's nanny, who seems to have been his closest caretaker for his first three years of life, was jailed for having stolen from the family. She was challenged by Freud's brother Philip and dismissed for stealing during Amalia's confinement for the birth of Anna. At the same time, Freud's father arranged for his two oldest sons to emigrate to Manchester, England. This meant the loss of Freud's earliest peer relationship with Emanuel's oldest son John, who was just seven months older than Freud. Freud later said that all his friends later in his life were re-incarnations of this earliest relationship, commenting to his biographer, Ernest Jones:

> "Until the end of my third year we had been inseparable; we had loved each other and fought each other and . . . This childish relationship has determined all my later feelings in intercourse with persons my own age" (Jones, Vol. 1, 1953, p. 8).

Freud later wrote:

> My emotional life has always insisted I should have an intimate friend and a hated enemy. I have always been able to provide myself with both, and it has not infrequently happened that the ideal situation of childhood has been so completely reproduced that friend and enemy have come together in a single individual—though not, of course, both at once or with constant oscillations, as may have been the case in my early childhood (with John). (Krüll, 1986, p. 130)

As mentioned earlier, the anxiety about Amalia and Philip developing a relationship might have contributed to Jacob's wanting to move his sons abroad to separate them from his wife. In any case, at this time Jacob moved his family first to Leipzig and then to Vienna, probably because of economic reversals and possibly because of some hidden financial dealings in counterfeit money (Swales, 1986). We have to assume that the Freud family left Freiberg for Leipzig for financial reasons, but neither he nor any other member of the family ever discussed the migration, which was followed the next year by a move to Vienna, which was more welcoming to Jews at that moment.

Within a period of only three years, Sigmund experienced a multitude of losses: the death of his brother, the dismissal of the nursemaid, the emigration of his nephew/"brother" John and his half brothers Emmanuel and Philip, the birth of his sister Anna (which seemed to take his mother away again), and finally the double geographic uprooting of his whole family. The Freuds were never to be as financially stable again. Sigmund's younger sisters, particularly Anna and Dolfi, may have borne the brunt of these negative changes on the family.

Sigmund never got along with his sister Anna. From a very early age, he may have seen her as an intrusion, and she may have resented his special position and privileges in the family. Sigmund was the only one of eventually seven siblings who always had his own room, even when the family was in very strapped circumstances. The oldest often resents the later born, feeling threatened or displaced by the new arrivals, but his distance from Anna continued and they were alienated as adults.

The Middle Childrearing Years

The childrearing years of any family are typically characterized by a task overload for parents as they try to manage their children and support their family. Parents often have extra tasks as their own parents and other older relatives begin to need extra support. The middle parenting years were probably quite difficult for the Freud family, as their finances were not very stable and there were eight children born in the 10 year period between 1856 and 1866. The genogram for 1873 (**Figure 8.4: Freud Family in 1873**) shows the family for the year Sigmund finished gymnasium and began medical school. (On this genogram we have shown in red the many births that occurred from 1859-1866, the father's brother going to prison during this time, and questions about how Jacob was supporting the family.)

Figure 8.4:   Freud Family in 1873

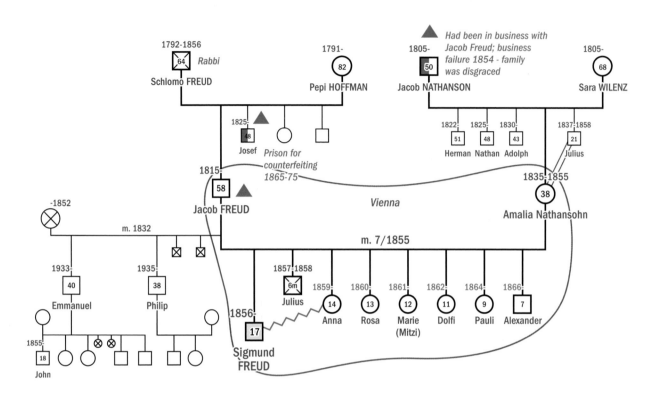

By all accounts Sigmund was the center of the household. There is a well-known family story that when his sister Anna wanted to play the piano, their mother bought one, but got rid of it immediately when Sigmund complained that the noise bothered him. His sister received no further piano lessons. Sigmund's special position is further indicated by the fact that the family gave him the privilege of naming his younger brother, Alexander, born when Sigmund was ten.

As children reach adolescence and become less dependent on their parents, two common patterns of triangles are likely to develop. The first involves (a) the adolescent, his/her peers, and the parents; (b) the second, the adolescent close to one parent but not the other; and (c); the third, the adolescent, the parents, and a grandparent or grandparents. As adolescents are seeking their identity and emerging into their sexual and creative potential, parents are often struggling with the realization of their own limitations in both their work and relationships, which may add to the intensity of intergenerational conflicts.

We have little specific information about the family during the years of Freud's adolescence, but the genogram for this period suggests they were a family with many child-rearing burdens, since there were seven children all still in the home. The age discrepancy between Jacob and Amalia may have felt even greater at this life cycle stage. Jacob, in his fifties, may have been feeling his age. Sigmund later described him as having been rather grouchy and disappointed in his older sons Emmanuel and Philip.

In contrast, Amalia, 20 years younger, was still energetic, attractive, and youthful. Given her devotion to Sigmund and the demands of a large household, it is likely that her energies were more focused on her children than on her husband. Sigmund said also that he felt as though he had to make up for his father's emotional absence. Jacob's brother Josef was sent to prison for counterfeiting for 10 years the same year that the youngest son, Alexander, was born. Freud later said the pain and humiliation of his uncle's imprisonment turned his father's hair gray. Jacob was probably implicated in the scheme—as were his sons Emanuel and Philip, which, as mentioned earlier, may have accounted for their move to England (Krüll, 1986; Swales, 1986).

During adolescence children build interests outside the family, both in school and with friends. Sigmund was at the top of his gymnasium class for six of his eight years there. His success with his peers was less clear. He was apparently shy, intense, serious and focused more on his studies than on socializing.

Our genograms should indicate, especially for adolescents, important peer relationships, to help us see how well family boundaries can expand to embrace outsiders. We know of Sigmund having only one close friend at school, Eduard Silberstein, with whom he corresponded and formed a "secret society." At 16, he had a crush on a friend's sister, Gisela Fluss, but never expressed his feelings to her. Perhaps he was responding to a mandate from his family to excel in school and to succeed in life, to justify his special position in his family and make up for their other disappointments—in the older half brothers and in Jacob, who never really seems to have made a living in Vienna.

The Freud Family at Midlife: Adolescence, Launching, Young Adulthood, Joining as New Couples, and Moving On

Once children reach adolescence, the task is to prepare the family for a qualitative change in the relationships between generations, as growing children become less dependent on their parents and begin to forge their own way in the world. The launching phase (when children leave home to be on their own) usually blended into marriage until our current generation, since children often did not leave home until they married. In Freud's time, late adolescence, launching, young adulthood, and coupling generally occurred in a relatively condensed period.

Freud did take a trip to England to visit his half brothers in 1875 during his medical studies. This trip apparently led him to rethink his views of his parents and his own goals, as is common for late adolescents. Such experiences with others outside the immediate family commonly lead emerging adults to reassess their families. Unfortunately, we do not know the details of Freud's rethinking nor how his parents responded to his changing thoughts, if he even conveyed them, which adolescents and young adults typically do not.

Increasingly in the 21st century, especially in the U.S., this period of the life cycle is often prolonged, and we are talking of a whole extra phase, sometimes referred to as "adultolescence." Some young adults don't finish their education or become self supporting until they are in their 30s.

In Freud's case, this phase was more prolonged than was typical for that generation. The joint genograms of the Freud and Bernays families for 1885 (**Figure 8.5: Freud-Bernays Families, 1885**) shows the third year of his engagement to Martha Bernays. At age 29, 10 years after beginning medical school, he was first embarking on his career but still living with his parents, and his fiancé Martha was still with her family of origin. We see the completed family as Freud's generation was emerging, and the Bernays family that both Sigmund and his sister Anna were marrying into, since they both married Bernays siblings, Eli and Martha.

The launching phase is the cornerstone of the modern family life cycle. It is crucial for all the other phases that are to follow. The short-circuiting of this phase, or its prolongation, may affect all future life cycle transitions.

In the Freud family, as is generally the case in large families, many life cycle phases were occurring at once. The Freuds were "launching" Sigmund at the same time that their youngest children were not even in adolescence. And in the larger extended family, Freud's brothers Emmanuel and Philip were having and raising their families, just as Freud was emerging from adolescence.

We might ask how the Freud family dealt with the changing boundaries as their children became adolescents and began to move on into their own lives. Did the mother hold on to her daughters as she was losing her "Golden Sigi"? Did Freud's father become depressed, having less vigor, fewer financial resources, and less connection to his wife as he aged? Did Freud's closeness to his mother or his father's poor functioning make it harder for him to leave home? Did Freud feel responsible as the oldest son and did his mother try to hold him?

How much did Freud's financial difficulties in planning for marriage influence his escalating conflicts with his sister Anna and brother-in-law, Eli? They

Figure 8.5: Freud-Bernays Families, 1885

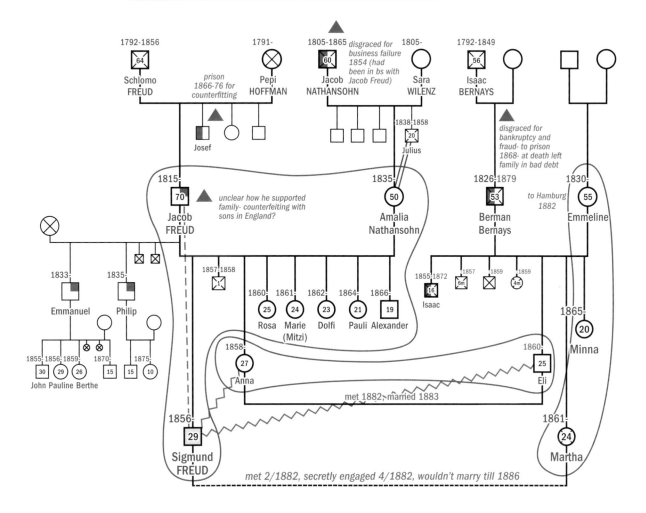

met the same year, 1882, but Eli and Anna had more financial resources and married the next year, 1883, while Sigmund and Martha had to wait three more years to marry.

How may gender constraints have influenced Freud's relationship with his fiancé, Martha, who was sent by her brother, Eli, along with her sister, Minna, to live with and care for their bereaved mother in Hamburg, disrupting Freud's relationship with Martha? Would a son have been sent away to care for a grieving mother? It seems doubtful. Another of the many gender constraints customary at the time was that one of Freud's five sisters, Dolfi, remained unmarried and became the mother's caretaker. Sigmund's daughter, Anna, would do the same for Freud and his wife in the next generation.

Freud's medical studies lasted eight years, until 1881, but it was several more years before he became self-supporting. This was unusual at that time, particularly for students who were not independently wealthy. Perhaps he felt that his mother needed him to stay with her. In any case, he apparently did not think seriously about supporting himself until he wanted to marry Martha. When there is a delay in moving on to the next life cycle phase, as in this situation, the clinician should explore the impediments to moving on. In Freud's case, the obstacles appear to have been both financial and emotional, as well as the anti-Semitism of the era, which put constraints on his career possibilities. Freud continued to live at home until eventually a small inheritance from Martha's aunt was freed up, which allowed the couple to marry and move into an apartment.

The genogram of the time of courtship and marriage can also provide valuable clues to the issues involved in the joining together of two family traditions into a new family. If one spouse or family feels competitive with the other family (as happened with Freud) or if parents do not approve of their child's marital choice, which does not seem to have been the case here, in-law triangles are likely to develop.

Sibling conflicts and triangles may also emerge at this life cycle stage. Such triangling was clear in this family. From early on Freud felt threatened by Martha's relationship to her family of origin; he was demanding, possessive, and overtly jealous of her loyalty to Eli. We might guess also that Eli resented Freud's career and taking away his sister, Martha. During their long courtship, Sigmund wrote to Martha, threatening that his egotism would rise up against her family:

> I will make such a din that everyone will hear, and you understand, no matter how your filial feelings may rebel against it. From now on you are but a guest in your family, like a jewel that I have pawned and that I am going to redeem as soon as I am rich. For has it not been laid down since time immemorial that the woman shall leave father and mother and follow the man she had chosen? (letter to Martha, 8/14/1882, Freud, 1960, p. 23).

Sigmund even threatened to break off their engagement if Martha did not give up her loyalty to her brother, writing her:

> You have only an Either-Or. If you can't be fond enough of me to renounce your family for my sake, then you must lose me, wreck your life and not get much yourself out of your family. (Cited in Appignanesi & Forrester, 1992, p. 31)

The unusual double connection between the Freuds and Bernays in Sigmund's generation suggests complicated relationships between the two families, as well as possible triangles. The oldest son in each family married the oldest daughter of the other family. Sigmund and his sister Anna never got along and their marrying siblings undoubtedly made matters worse. Perhaps Sigmund felt the ordinary sibling rivalry between an oldest child and a younger sister. Or perhaps he associated Anna's birth with the many losses that occurred around that time: his mother who was having another baby, his nanny who was sent to prison, his family's move for financial reasons, and his half-brothers' move to England.

Sigmund clearly resented the fact that his brother-in-law Eli had the money to marry Anna when his own marriage was being put off because he couldn't afford it. Freud was also upset that Eli had begun giving his younger brother, Alexander, money for some project, and felt that Eli was usurping control over his brother as well as his fiancé.

Martha had come from a family with secrets of its own. Her father had also been disgraced, and was imprisoned for fraud when Martha was still a child. He died in serious debt just a couple of years before she met Sigmund. Meanwhile, Sigmund had already been friendly with her brother Eli, who then paired up with his sister Anna. At the same time, Eli pressed Martha to move to Hamburg with her mother and sister because of the debts and embarrassment caused by their father.

Sigmund became resentful of Eli and Anna, and he did not even attend their wedding! In fact, he did not even mention the event in his letters to Martha, although he was writing to her almost daily at the time. Shortly after the wedding, he discussed the possibility of attending the wedding of one of her cousins, certainly a much less important family event. Freud also resented that Eli had invested a small legacy Martha had received from an aunt, which he felt again prevented him from marrying sooner (Young-Bruehl, 1988).

If we compare the genograms of Martha Bernays and Sigmund, we see certain striking parallels. The Bernays family, like the Freuds, had to deal with the death of young children. The oldest surviving son, Eli, very much like Sigmund, was the older brother of younger sisters, born shortly after three older babies had died. The oldest son, Isaac, died at age 17 in 1872, apparently already a seriously troubled youth, though we do not know the details, as so much about the family was wrapped in secrecy.

In 1867, when the children were not even teenagers, the father was arrested and jailed briefly for fraud, bringing disgrace to the family, very similar to the shame Sigmund and his family experienced when their uncle and perhaps their father and half-brothers were involved in counterfeiting. Another parallel in the previous generation would be with Freud's maternal grandfather, whose business failed, leaving the family with a sense of ruin and disgrace when Amalia was 18.

Martha Bernays' father also died when she was 18, leaving the family in great debt. Like the Freud family, with Jacob's apparent unemployment in his later years, it is not clear how the Bernays family survived. Eli, who took over the running of the family, eventually fled Vienna to avoid bankruptcy and the payment of debts owed to friends. Martha's mother moved with her daughters to Hamburg, which, as mentioned, infuriated Sigmund, who had become secretly engaged to Martha the previous year.

We might speculate that the similarities of disgrace and secrets in the background of Sigmund and Martha may have been part of their attraction to one another. Freud's father had serious business problems. It was in the years before his marriage that Freud began destroying family papers, the first time a few months after meeting and becoming secretly engaged to Martha, and again three years later, the year before their marriage. Martha eventually managed to get the small legacy from her aunt that her brother had controlled, and the couple were finally able to marry.

Sigmund's negative feelings toward Anna and Eli only intensified later when the couple moved to New York and the less educated Eli became very wealthy, while the highly educated Sigmund had to struggle to support his family. Triangles seem to have involved conflict over Eli and Anna's family having money, but being materialistic and having "bad" values, while Freud and his side of the family eschewed money but thought of themselves as intellectually superior.

Some conflicts stayed under the rug but remained between the couple throughout their whole marriage. For example, Martha did maintain contact with other members of her family and remained true to her faith, Orthodox Judaism, despite her husband's rejection of religion. After many years of marriage, she said that Sigmund's refusal to let her light the Sabbath candles the first Friday night after their marriage was one of the most upsetting experiences of her life (Appignanesi & Forrester, 1992). As soon as Sigmund died, Martha, then 68 years old, began again to light the candles every Friday night.

The Next Generation

For a family with young children, the early years are always eventful, though often difficult for marriages, with so much of the spouses' energy necessarily taken up with work and children. While Martha handled virtually all parenting responsibilities, Sigmund struggled to enlarge his medical practice and began some of his most creative intellectual work. When a family is in this phase, the clinician should be alert to child-rearing pressures and normative strains on the marriage. Sigmund and Martha, just like their parents on both sides, had six children within eight years (**Figure 8.6: Freud Family, 1896**).

Figure 8.6:   Freud Family, 1896

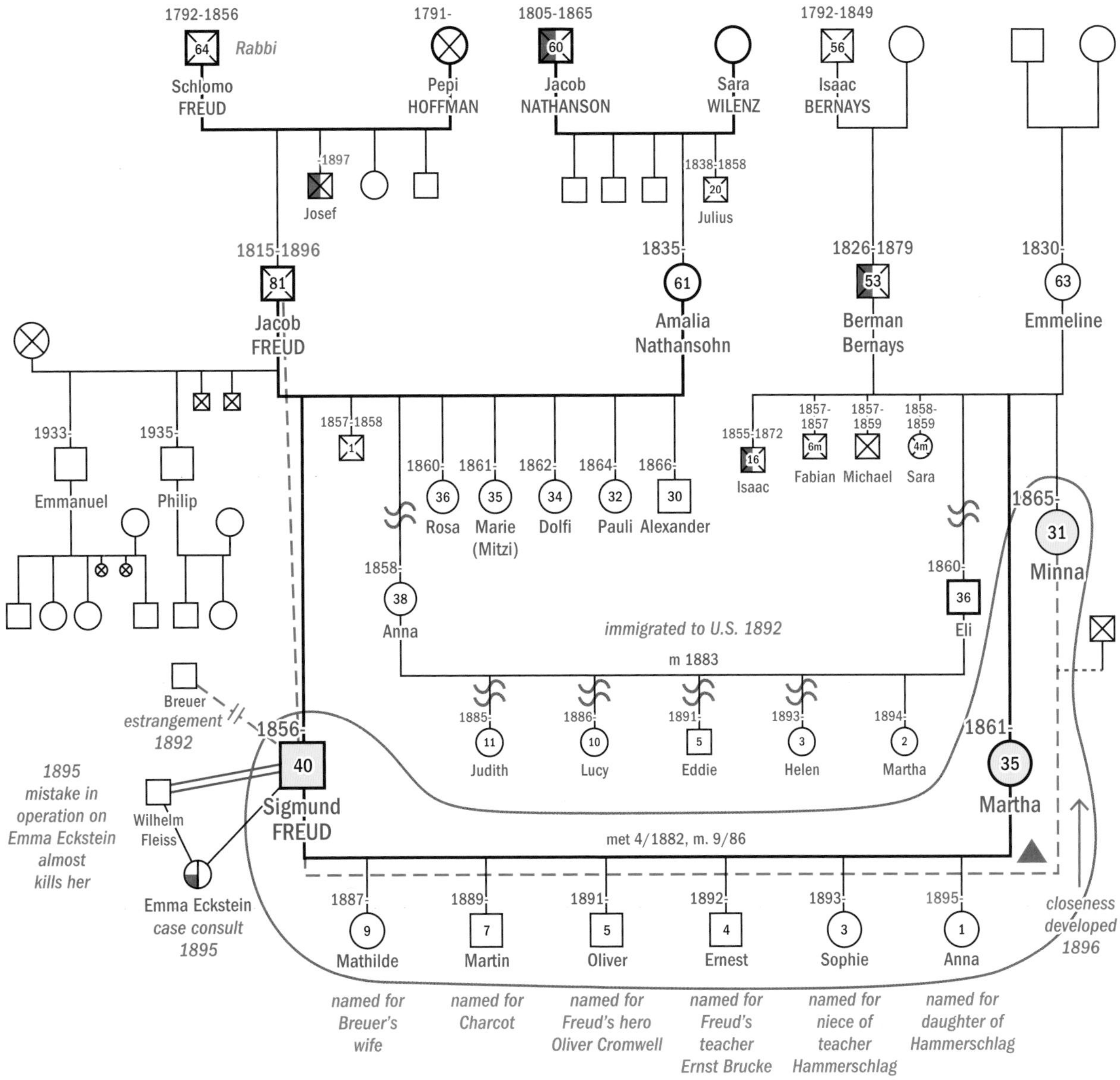

The birth of the last child may be an important turning point in family life. This was true of Anna, born December 31, 1895. She was not named for Freud's sister but for the daughter of his beloved teacher and friend, Samuel Hammerschlag (Krüll, 1986). It seems that after this last child Sigmund and Martha decided not to have another. Sex between the couple apparently diminished considerably from this point (Anzieu, 1986; Roazen, 1993).

In spite of Anna Freud's devotion to her father, she seems not to have felt she was his preferred child. She spent an enormous amount of effort all her life trying to win his approval. She, rather than his wife, took care of him when he was ill. He became her analyst, beginning in 1918, when she was 23, which leaves an odd image of Freud sitting behind her, analyzing her free associations. She even went in his stead to his own mother's funeral! She alone among his children never married, devoting herself to him, and choosing to carry on his work.

It seems that Martha had become very preoccupied with raising her children, while Sigmund, who was not very involved with the children, moved closer intellectually and emotionally to his sister-in-law, Minna, whom he had described to his friend Fliess in 1894 as "otherwise my closest confidante" (Masson, 1985, p. 73). Minna moved into the Freud household the very same month that his last child, Anna, was born. Fourteen years earlier, Minna had been engaged to his close friend, Ignaz Schonberg, who had broken off the relationship shortly before his death from tuberculosis. After Ignaz died, Minna had never married.

By all accounts Sigmund and Minna had an extremely close relationship. Sigmund thought he and Minna were alike: both wild, passionate people, who wanted their own way, whereas Ignaz and Martha were good-natured and adaptable (Jones, 1955). Sigmund and Minna took at least 17 vacations alone together (Swales, 1986), purportedly because they both enjoyed traveling, whereas Martha did not, at least not at Sigmund's pace (Freeman & Strean, 1981). Minna was seemingly much more interested in discussing Sigmund's ideas than Martha was. Indeed, Martha said of psychoanalysis: "If I didn't realize how seriously my husband takes his treatments, I should think of psychoanalysis as a form of pornography" (Appignanesi & Forrester, 1992, p. 45).

Minna's bedroom in the Freud household could be entered only through the master bedroom (Eissler, 1978). Recent research supports Jung's report that Minna told him that she and Sigmund had an affair. In 1898 they signed in to a vacation hotel in Switzerland as Dr. and Mrs. Freud, but he wrote to his wife giving no mention of Minna being with him. There is evidence that Minna became pregnant and had an abortion in 1901 (Swales, 1986). We know nothing about Martha's attitude toward her husband's relationship with her sister.

Freud experienced a major crisis during this phase of the life cycle, repeating his own father's changes at midlife. In addition to the birth of his last child, his changing relationship with his wife and his sister-in-law, Minna, and the death of his father, Freud had just turned 40. He was having career problems and personal symptoms and was struggling to support a large family.

Similar to his father Jacob's midlife changes, which were marked by a new love relationship with Amalia at age 40 as well as an occupational shift and migration, Sigmund's crisis seemed to involve changing intimate relationships and career upheaval. He was able to resolve it more positively than his father with the consolidation of his career, his appointment as a professor, and his growing recognition as the founder of a new theory. Interestingly, in the next generation, Sigmund's oldest son, Martin, repeated this apparent pattern and had an extramarital relationship with his wife's sister (Freud, S., 1988).

Freud's crisis led to some of his greatest intellectual discoveries, including his major formulation of the seduction theory, coming to the conclusion that the early sexual abuse so many women spoke of in therapy was not fantasy but reality. The following year, however, Freud retreated from this assertion back to the idea that it was all women's imagination that they had been sexually abused (Masson, 1992). During these years Freud showed symptoms of depression and anxiety, including "pseudo" cardiac problems and complained of lethargy, migraines, and various other somatic and emotional concerns. It was clearly a period of great turmoil, during which he adopted his friend Wilhelm Fliess as a father figure in his self-analysis, which seems to have been a response to his mid-life crisis. He also constructed the edifice of a new theory, which led to the publication of his most famous work, *The Interpretation of Dreams*.

Chronology 8.1: The Freud Family 1895–1897 shows key events for this point in Freud's life. His daughter, Anna, was conceived around the same time of one of Freud's most explosive professional consultations. He referred his patient Emma Eckstein to his friend and father figure Fleiss, who believed, for some reason, in operating on people's noses to cure them of sexual problems, which he thought resulted from masturbation; it is unclear how nose surgery was supposed to be therapeutic. Fleiss made a mistake during the operation and left gauze in the wound, which caused an infection that almost killed the patient. Freud, whose relations with Fleiss had been extremely intense, experienced a profound sense of disillusionment and distress over this situation.

In 1896, less than a year after Anna was born, Sigmund's father died, a loss Sigmund said was the most significant and upsetting event in a man's life. At the time, Martha was away visiting her mother, and Minna was the only one there to console him, which may have contributed to the close bond they developed. He wrote shortly after his father's death:

> By one of those obscure paths behind official consciousness, the death of the old man has affected me profoundly. . . . His life had been over a long time before he died, but his death seems to have aroused in me memories of all the early days. I now feel quite uprooted. (Masson, 1985; letter from November 2, 1886)

In addition to the loss, a parent's death is a painful reminder of one's own mortality and of the passing of the mantle of responsibility to the next generation. Now Freud had his mother to support as well. In addition, his disgraced uncle Josef and an uncle of Martha's had died that year.

CHRONOLOGY 8.1: THE FREUD FAMILY 1895–1897

1895 (February) Freud has his friend Fleiss operate on his patient Emma Eckstein and Fleiss makes a mistake, leaving gauze in the wound, which almost kills her.

1895 (March) Anna is conceived.

1895 Freud is depressed, having cardiac symptoms, and treats himself with cocaine. He starts smoking again after having given it up for over a year. He decides to begin self-analysis. Fleiss performs a nasal operation on him.

1895 (December) Anna, the sixth and last child, is born, named for Freud's teacher Samuel Hammerschlag's daughter, a young widow and patient of Freud's (Anzieu, 1986). Freud connects the expansion of his practice with Anna's birth.

1895 (December) Minna, Freud's sister-in-law, moves into the Freud family home—her bedroom is located behind the master bedroom with no exit except through their room.

1896 Freud develops extremely negative feelings about his friend and colleague, Breuer.

1896 (April) Freud writes of migraines, nasal secretions, fears of dying.

1896   (May) Freud writes clearest account of seduction theory: his belief that women's anxieties are based on actual childhood sexual abuse. His presentation scandalizes his audience.

1896   Medical community isolates Freud for his ideas.

1896   Freud calls Emma Eckstein's hemorrhages "hysterical."

1896   (October 23) Jacob Freud dies. (Freud is 40, the same age his father was when his own father died and Freud was born.) Jacob had been very ill for a month or so. Because Martha is away visiting her mother, only Minna is there to console Freud over the loss of his father.

1897   (January) Freud is passed over for a university promotion.

1897   (February) Freud learns he will finally be proposed for the title of professor.

1897   (March) Freud's disgraced Uncle Joseph dies.

1897   (March) Daughter Mathilde has a very bad case of diptheria.

1897   (May) Freud is again passed over for promotion and becomes anxious.

1897   (May) Freud has incestuous dream about daughter Mathilde.

1897   (July) Freud takes the first of at least 17 vacations with Minna.

1897   (September) Freud renounces belief in "seduction theory" (he had thought that his father had an inappropriate sexual relationship with his sister Anna). Despondent, he feels need for self-analysis; outlines "Oedipal theory."

1897   (October 15) Freud develops ideas of the Oedipus complex.

1899   Freud writes *Interpretation of Dreams*.

1900   Freud ends his self-analysis.

1900   Trip with Fleiss ends in a falling out that turns out to be permanent.

1900   Trip with Minna in Italy. Did Minna become pregnant by Freud and have an abortion at a clinic? They traveled together extensively from September 12, 1900 through mid February 1901 (Swales, 1982). Jones said she was treated for TB, but there is no other mention of her having that illness.

The Freud Family in Later Life

As members age, families must come to terms with the mortality of the older generation. As each generation moves up a level in the developmental hierarchy, all relationships must be reordered (Shields, King, & Wynne, 1995; Walsh, 2016). There are special problems for women, who are more often the caretakers (Dolfi and Anna) and tend to outlive their spouses (Freud's mother and wife). When the last parent dies, the relationships between siblings become independent for the first time. Often the genogram will reveal which child was delegated to become the caretaker of the aging parents, as well as common triangles among siblings over the management of these responsibilities. Sibling conflicts and cutoffs at this point usually reflect triangles with parents which have persisted from much earlier life cycle phases, especially with regard to who was the favored sibling in childhood.

After Jacob's death, Amalia was left to be cared for by her children for the next 34 years. Dolfi, the middle sister, remained at home with the mother, while Sigmund and his youngest brother, Alexander, took financial responsibility for her and their sisters.

Sigmund also lived a long time, to the age of 83 (**Figure 8.7: Freud Family in 1939**) and was cared for by his daughter Anna. Anna became her father's main follower and intellectual heir. Although Martha Freud was still alive (she lived until 1951), it was Anna who became his primary caretaker through his 33 operations for jaw cancer, the first of which was in 1923. For Anna, as for Dolfi in the previous generation, this meant that she was never able to leave home. She was 44 at the time of her father's death. He had been unwilling to function without her for many years.

Though she had been briefly in love with her first cousin, Edward Bernays, in 1913, she later said it was good that the relationship had not worked out because, since he was her double cousin, it would have been double incest. She had early dreamt that her father was the king and she the princess and people were trying to separate them by means of political intrigues. She became partners with Dorothy Burlingham, an American mother of four children, who was the youngest of eight daughters of the glass millionaire, Louis Comfort Tiffany. Though Dorothy never officially divorced, she and Anna lived and vacationed together for the rest of their lives. Together they ran a war nursery, a psychoanalytic training institute, and a world famous children's clinic. (Dorothy's husband committed suicide in 1938, having tried in vain to convince her to return to him.) When the Freud family migrated to London in the same year to escape Nazism, Dorothy moved with them. She lived in London with Anna for four more decades until her death in 1979.

Figure 8.7:   Freud Family in 1939

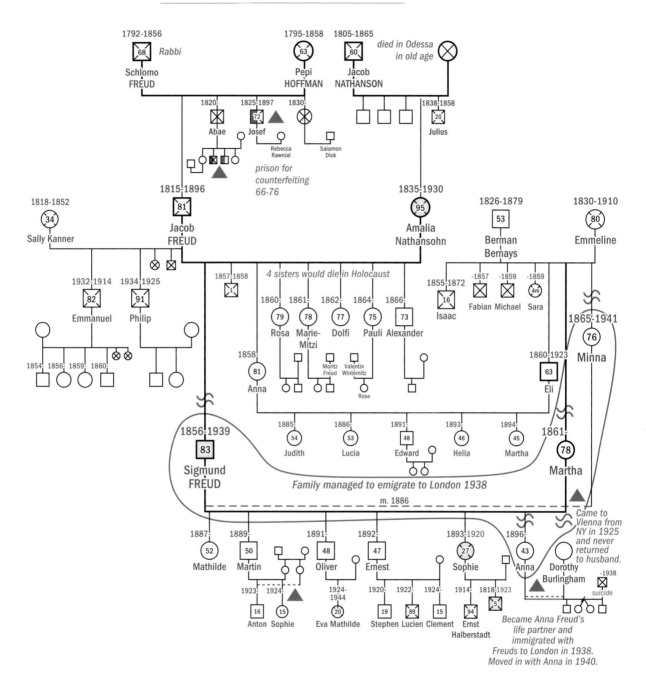

The genogram may be helpful for understanding or predicting the reactions of family members to key events at different points of the cycle. For example, Freud had a very strong reaction to the death of his three-year-old grandson in 1923, shortly after he himself was diagnosed with cancer:

> He was indeed an enchanting little fellow, and I myself was aware of never having loved a human being, certainly never a child, so much. . . . I find this loss very hard to bear. I don't think I have ever experienced such grief, perhaps my own sickness contributes to the shock. I work out of sheer necessity; fundamentally everything has lost its meaning for me. (Freud, 1960, p. 344)

Undoubtedly his own illness did influence his reaction, but there is also the tragedy of child death. A month later he wrote that he was suffering from the first real depression of his life. Three years later he wrote to his son-in-law that since this child's death he had not been able to enjoy life:

> I have spent some of the blackest days of my life in sorrowing about the child. At last I have taken hold of myself and can think of him quietly and talk of him without tears. But the comforts of reason have done nothing to help; the only consolation for me is that at my age I would not have seen much of him. (Jones, 1955, p. 92)

Sigmund's words suggest he was struggling to come to terms with his own mortality. This was particularly difficult, not only because his grandson's death was so untimely, but also because his daughter, Sophie, the child's mother, had died three years earlier, in 1920, at the age of 27.

We can see a great contrast between this loss and Freud's reaction to the death of his own mother seven years later, in 1930:

> On the surface I can detect only two things: an increase in personal freedom, since it was always a terrifying thought that she might come to hear of my death; and secondly the satisfaction that at least she has achieved the deliverance for which she had earned a right after such a long life. No grief otherwise, such as my ten years younger brother is painfully experiencing. I was not at the funeral. Again Anna represented me as at Frankfort. Her value to me can hardly be heightened. This event has affected me in a curious manner . . . . No pain, no grief, which is probably to be explained by the circumstances, the great age, and the end of the pity we had felt at her helplessness.

With that a feeling of liberation, of release, which I think I can understand. I was not allowed to die as long as she was alive, and now I may. Somehow the values of life have notably changed in the deeper layers. (Quoted in Jones, 1955, p. 152)

Sigmund, at 74, was more reconciled through his years of struggling with cancer with his own eventual death. He was relieved that the sequential order of the life cycle would be honored: first, the parents die, and then the children. The untimely or traumatic loss of a family member is typically extremely difficult for families to mourn, and therapists are urged to pay especially careful attention to untimely deaths on a genogram.

The Great Mandala (Wheel) of Life

The life cycle of an individual or family can be conceptualized as a great wheel (mandala in Buddhist teachings) that intersects continuously with the life wheels of prior ancestors and subsequent generations of descendants, as well as with everyone they interact with, in all sorts of interesting ways. The therapist is advised to maintain a scientific reverence and appreciation for being allowed to take part in another's mandala, hopefully to their mutual benefit. In the words of folksingers Peter, Paul, and Mary in their song "The Great Mandala":

"Win or lose now, you must choose now,
And if you lose, you're only losing your life."

Therapists can use awareness of their own mandalas to help others deal better with adversity and sorrow, and make their life passage more resilient and joyful. Sometimes it is a consolation to consider the positive role of disappointment and loss—to provide a contrast that makes the good things in life sweeter and more precious.

9

Clinical Uses of the Genogram

T his chapter offers a few illustrations of the use of genograms in clinical practice. The genogram interview organizes questioning around key family life experiences: birth, marriage, life transitions, illness, and death. For a more comprehensive explication of the clinical use of genograms we refer you to our companion book: *The Genogram Casebook* (McGoldrick, 2016), which lays out in much more detail how to clinically use genograms in ways that reflect systemic theory and practice. Collecting information on these events can often help to open up a rigid family system and assist clients in getting in touch with blocked emotional and interpersonal issues.

Uncovering Family Secrets: The Carusos

The Carusos, an Italian family, were referred for a consultation by their lawyer, who hoped the referral would influence the court case of the oldest of their three sons, John, who had been arrested for selling drugs (**Figure 9.1: Caruso Family**).

Initially the family presented a united front. They were a close, loving family whose son had, they asserted, come under the influence of "bad friends." They denied the seriousness of his crime, offered little factual information, minimized any relationship problems, but said they were willing to do anything they could to help. Few clues were apparent when gathering the basic genogram information until we got to the question of the whereabouts of the maternal uncle. The mother, Carla Caruso, initially said that she did not know where her brother was, but then admitted that he was in jail and had had many previous arrests. This led to questioning about the maternal grandmother's reaction to John's problem, at which point the family's united front began to break down. The parents reluctantly admitted that they had stopped talking to the maternal grandmother since John's arrest because of her "insensitive" response: "Let him rot in jail."

Mr. and Mrs. Caruso had taken a second mortgage on their house to pay their

Figure 9.1   Caruso Family

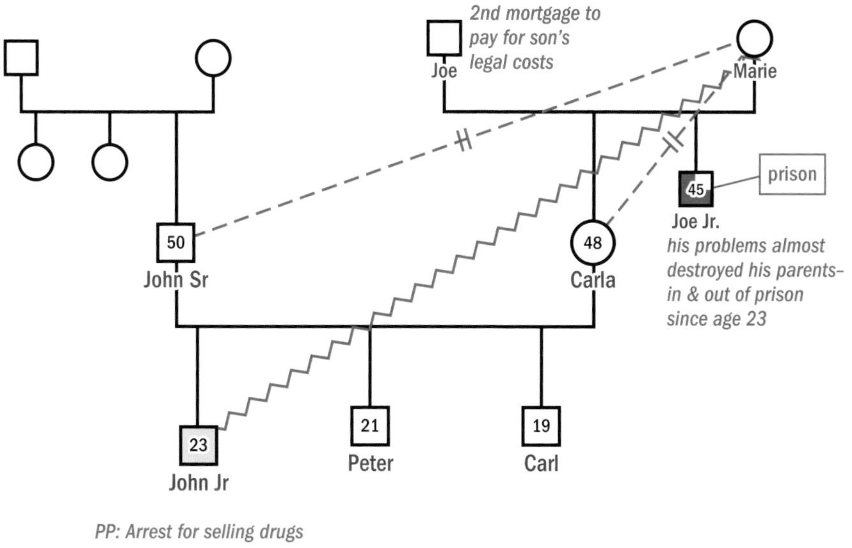

2nd mortgage to pay for son's legal costs

Joe

Marie

prison

45

Joe Jr.
*his problems almost
destroyed his parents-
in & out of prison
since age 23*

50

John Sr

48

Carla

23

John Jr

21

Peter

19

Carl

PP: Arrest for selling drugs

son's bail and legal fees. Carla Caruso said she had always been very close to her mother, but now viewed her as "disloyal." Further detailed questioning about the family history led to the information that Carla's brother had first been arrested at age 23 (John's present age). Because the maternal grandfather had, against the grandmother's wishes, spent all the family savings repeatedly bailing his son out of trouble, the grandmother became very bitter that her son had brought almost total financial ruin on the family. It was only through discussing the details of the uncle's criminal behavior, a family secret that John and his brothers did not know, that the family's "cool" about their present situation was broken.

Carla talked about her pain in watching her own mother's agony over the years, as well as her fury at her brother for the shame he had brought on the family. She was desperately afraid of reliving her parents' experience, but feared that discussing the matter with her mother would confirm that the family was "doomed" to repeat the past. So, she had stopped talking to her mother. As we spoke, John's brothers opened up for the first time in the interview, expressing their resentment of their brother for putting the family in the terrible position of having to decide whether to put their life savings on the line or let him go to jail. The father, who had been the most adamant in denying any family difficulties, talked about his sense of failure and betrayal by his son. It was only through the leverage of the previous family experiences that the family's present conflicts became evident.

In their attempt to avoid dealing with painful past experiences and unresolved emotional issues, families often rigidify their relationships and views of themselves. Calm, nonthreatening, searching questions can often open up these matters, so that family members begin to relate to one another in ways that open up new possibilities for the family. The genogram interview is especially useful for engaging obsessive, unresponsive, or uninvolved family members. Obsessive clients who may otherwise dwell on the endless details often come quickly to emotionally loaded and significant material during a genogram interview. Unresponsive family members may find themselves more engaged as their family story is revealed (McGoldrick, 1981).

Addressing Loss and Trauma

Probably the issue around which families become blocked more often than any other is loss. For a detailed video on clinical issues in addressing loss and trauma, see "Freeing Ourselves From The Ghosts Of Our Families," (available through psychotherapy.net). This video illustrates the life and work of Norman and Betty Paul (1986), who led the way in the use of genograms to unblock the family system by focusing on losses in the multigenerational family. The meaning of clients' symptoms can be expanded by involving them in explorations of deaths or life-threatening experiences in either the immediate or extended family. In the Pauls' view, the distortion and "forgetting" that family members experience around loss are among the most important influences on symptom development. They routinely sent genogram forms to prospective clients to be completed before the first session; this can provide important information about how clients orient themselves to their original family. In the first session the Pauls would carefully track birth and death dates and the causes of death for the past three generations. In their experience, clients usually indicate some degree of mystification about doing their genograms, until they begin to see the hidden connections.

The Pauls' in-depth study of one such couple in *A Marital Puzzle* (1986) illustrated a case in which the husband was asked to bring genogram information to the first therapy session. He left off the fact that both of his parents had died, although he had been specifically asked about them; when questioned, he said he did not remember exactly when they had died. The Pauls' therapeutic model focused attention on the importance of rediscovering such dissociated family experiences. Some years ago, we developed forms that asked for genogram information in multiple ways, including asking for the dates of death of the parents' own parents in three different sections. Respondents frequently left the spaces blank or gave different dates each time, indicating how charged the issue of loss can be.

Clarifying Family Patterns

Clarifying family patterns is at the heart of genogram usage. As we collect information to complete a genogram, we are constantly constructing and revising hypotheses based on our ongoing understanding of a family. We usually discuss our observations with the family and offer these observations as tentative hypotheses that the family may elaborate on or revise as we jointly explore their history.

The Caruso family discussed above illustrates how the genogram can become a guide to understanding patterns for both the family and therapist, clarifying the present dilemma in ways that open up possibilities for alternative behavior in the future. Once we learned the hidden history, we could see a pattern of criminal behavior. After the connection was made between the son's and the uncle's criminal behavior, the family began to look at the son's behavior within the family context and to explore the legacy, conflicts, and secrecy that were perpetuating the behavior. They could also begin to concentrate their efforts on deciding whether and how they might want to change the pattern.

Clarifying genogram patterns serves an important educational function for family members, allowing them to see their lives and behavior as connected to family history. In addition, dysfunctional behavior is often eliminated, once the family patterns that underlie it are clarified and brought into the open.

Reframing and Detoxifying Family Issues

Families develop particular ways of viewing themselves. When there are many problems, family members' perspectives often rigidify and become resistant to change. Genograms are an important tool for reframing behavior and relationships, and for "detoxifying" and normalizing the family's perception of itself. Suggesting alternative interpretations of the family's experience opens up new possibilities for the future.

The genogram interview allows the clinician many opportunities to normalize the family members' understanding of their situation. Simply bringing up an issue or putting it in a more normative perspective can often "detoxify" it. Using information gathered on the genogram, the clinician can also actively reframe the meaning of behavior in the family system, enabling family members to see themselves in a different way.

The family structure suggests normative expectations for behavior and relationships (e.g., "It's not surprising you're so responsible, since oldest children commonly are," or, "Often two youngest who marry tend to be waiting for someone to take care of them. How has it gone with you?"). Similarly, an understanding of life cycle fit can provide a normalizing experience (e.g., "People who marry as late as you did are often pretty set in their ways. Was that true for you?").

Pattern repetition and the coincidence of events show the larger context of problematic behavior (e.g., "Maybe your feelings had something to do with all the stressful events that were occurring at the time."). And relational patterns and family balance help demonstrate the interdependency of family members (e.g., "Most people react that way, when they are the 'odd person out'," or, "Usually, when one person takes on more than her share of responsibility, the other person takes on less.").

Bowen was a master at detoxifying reactive responses with genogram questioning. For example, below is an excerpt of Bowen's interview with a man who felt intimidated by his "domineering, possessive mother":

Bowen: What are the problems of being the only child of an only child mother?

Client: My mother was a very domineering woman who never wanted to let go of anything she possessed, including me.

Bowen: Well, if you're the only one, wouldn't that be sort of predictable? Often in a relationship like that, people can with some accuracy know what the other thinks . . . . In other words, you're describing a sort of an intense relationship, and not too unusual between a mother and an only son, especially a mother who doesn't have a husband. And your mother was an "only." How would you characterize your mother's relationship with her mother?

Here Bowen is using discussion of the family structure to normalize a mother's behavior and the special mother-child bond of a single parent mother with an only child. Bowen Systems Therapy is characterized throughout by such tracking, detoxifying, and reframing of multigenerational family patterns. Such questioning also facilitates the therapist's ability to keep the client the expert on his own family, as he gets to characterize his mother's relationship with her mother.

Using Genograms to Draw Forth Resilience and to Design Interventions

Family therapists with a Bowen systemic approach have been using genograms for many years as the primary tool for assessment and for designing therapeutic interventions. More recently, therapists with different approaches have come to use the genogram for recordkeeping, assessing families, and designing strategic interventions.

Some therapists listen for the descriptors of various family members to get a sense of the family's values that have been passed down from one generation to another. Differences of opinion, of course, become grist for the mill of therapy, and we often urge family members to seek missing genogram information and other opinions between sessions.

Genogram patterns may be used strategically to convey a positive understanding of the present dysfunctional situation, paradoxically challenging the rigidity of the present stabilization. As changes occur, genogram information can again be used to reinforce emerging patterns and to underline the normative evolution of the family.

Genograms can be an important way to counter the invalidation that recent immigrants and families of color experience in most institutional settings. They allow families respectful acknowledgment of their history and help them translate adaptive strategies they used in other contexts to solve current problems. In our "solution focused" society, the history of oppressed groups gets suppressed as a way of keeping the dominant groups in place. Helping families tell their personal and cultural stories in ways that support their resilience is an important part of their liberation from the constraints of oppression.

A major therapeutic task is to empower clients to bear witness to their family's losses and to develop a sense of survivorship, meaning, mastery, and continuity. Families often need help in expanding their view of themselves and seeing their history in context—to see the continuity of their experience with their ancestors, current family, and community, and to realize their connection to those who will come after them. Many forces are at work in our society to deprive people of their sense of continuity. Reversing this puts not just their losses, but their whole lives, in better perspective, strengthening them for their shared future.

We have found that relatively simple interventions aimed at connecting family members to each other and with their past losses can make a considerable difference in their sense of themselves and enhance their resourcefulness for managing their future.

The Chen family brought this home to us in a striking way (**Figure 9.2: Chen Family**). They were referred because Joe, the 14-year-old son, had been involved with drugs and was "acting out" at school. The school had already referred the family to drug treatment facilities several times. They described the parents as noncompliant with therapy and unable to set effective limits on their son, who was seen as a very bad influence on his classmates.

The father, Mr. Chen, a 58-year-old restaurant worker, had been disabled four years previously due to a back injury. He had immigrated to the U. S. from China at the age of 18. He met his wife, an immigrant from Turkey, two years later. The couple had very successfully raised their two older children, who were close in age and much older than Joe. The oldest, Michael, finished college at age 19 and was doing professional research at a nearby university. Their daughter, Rose, was in graduate school in a nearby city. Joe was 10 when the father was injured. Since that

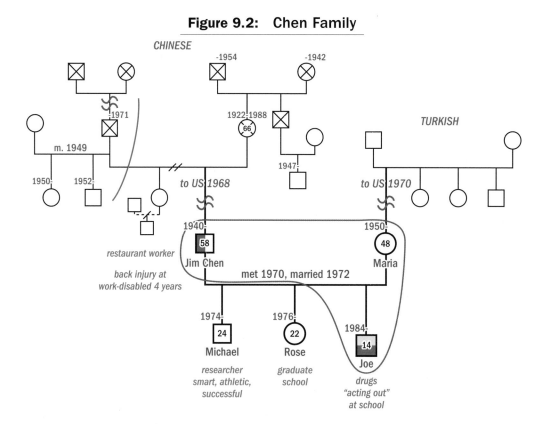

Figure 9.2:   Chen Family

time the father, who had always had a strong sense of responsibility to his family, had felt a terrible sense of inadequacy.

Inquiring about the family's history in relation to the son's drug abuse and acting out, we became convinced that the parents had complied with most actions that had been requested of them. They had not, however, connected to Al-Anon or any other co-dependency-oriented program they were referred to, because they felt the school was blaming them for not "detaching" from their son regarding his drug abuse. They could not make any sense of the concept of "detachment." They had been taking Joe for regular drug screenings, and he had been clean for over a month, but the school was still negative towards him and wanted him removed from the school.

When we began to do the family's genogram, the father became tearful about his father, who had abandoned his wife and children for another woman, moved to the U.S., created another family, and never supported his first family. He had finally died the year before Jim married. We decided to construct a ritual based on the family's genogram history to empower them in the present. We were not sure if the father's pain over his father's death was connected to the present situation, but his obvious emotion about his father made it clear that something was troubling him about it. The father, mother, and Joe were all asked to write letters to the dead grandfather, in the hopes that this could connect relationship patterns from the genogram to the present problem. The following week all three read their letters, excerpted below:

The Father's Letter:

Dear Father:
I think about writing to you all the time. I often think of you in the dim light of evening, which brings me back to my memories of my childhood. Many kids have their golden childhood years. I never enjoyed what I experienced. Instead there was war, hunger and loneliness. I didn't have a chance to attend school. Worst of all, I had no father to guide me. All these memories will remain forever in my heart and mind. They cause me such grief. All I can do is cry. My heart is bound by a rope that chokes it. I feel such heart ache. There are so many questions that I want to ask you. You are a husband and a father. Have you yet fulfilled your duty to your wife and your children? When I was in China we sent you many letters, but never once did we receive word from you. My mother took care of me, when I was a child. She worked hard and made little money, but she did the best she could to raise me. I heard from my uncle that she had a chance to remarry, but, because I was so young, she didn't want me to have a stepfa-

ther. My mother was bound by traditions, which would never allow her to remarry, so you ruined her whole life.

You had a farm in which you took special care of all the seedlings and vegetables and they grew. You took care that all the buds growing in the greenhouse were strong enough, before you took them out to plant them. When you planted them out in the field, you made sure there were no weeds, before you planted your vegetables. You fertilized, watered and cared for your vegetables very, very carefully. You worried that they would not grow.

I also am your seed. How come you didn't take such good care of me? I wanted to go to school—to have a good education, just as you took care of your vegetables, which need fertilizer and water. You make sure that vegetables grow with no weeds to block their growing. I too needed this type of nourishment in the farm of education. Do you agree with me? You never gave me a chance to have a decent education. When I came to the United States, I told you all of this. But your heart was made of iron. You said to me: "You are 18 years old. I have brought you here so you could take care of your mother and your nephew." From such a young age I carried such a heavy burden to take care of my family alone. Do you believe that the way you treated your family is right? Do you feel ashamed of yourself? It's a quiet night. Please think about it. I have very little left to say, so I shall end here. I wish you good health. At last I can tell you that now I am married, with three children of my own. I am a good husband and a good father, not only to provide my family with food and shelter but also to make sure that my children get as much from their education as they can. I love my children and there's nothing I would not do for any one of them.

Your son, Jim Chen

Joe's letter:

Dear grandfather,
How are you? All I can say is that you were pretty "bleeped" up, but I can't really hate you for treating my father like that. I can't really say that I like you either, since I have never met you in my life. But from what I have heard of you, I guess you didn't care about my dad, your son. Well, I have to go.

Peace, your grandson.

The Wife's Letter:

Dear father-in-law:

I didn't meet you because you were dead before I married your son. But I know all about you and how you treated my husband and my mother-in-law. I feel hurt for them, especially for Jimmy. I can imagine how sad he felt through that period of time. Even though he did not have a normal childhood like other kids had, because of you, he always told me that he forgives you. He has always believed in forgiveness, love, and peace. You caused him and the family much pain; he worked to help his mother, her sister, and her nephew, so they could live well. He always told me that he never regretted that. He never saw them as a burden. After we married he still sent his aunt money for her needs as well as for our nephew. How could you as a father treat your son like this? But Jimmy was lucky. He had wonderful uncles and a wonderful grandfather. Jimmy used his grandfather to learn the most from. Today Jimmy is not like you, but like his wonderful grandfather. He always remembers his grandfather with love—he was very firm, but at the same time treated him with affection and love. My husband treats his children just like his grandfather. I am proud of him and I tell my children how lucky they are. They have a wonderful father who is always there for them and any of their needs.

Prior to reading the letters, the son had been bored, turning in his chair, uninterested in the conversation. Following the letters, we were able to mobilize the family to work with us and the school to keep the son engaged, involved at home, and participating in school without further disruption.

In this case, the genogram helped to empower a nuclear family in relation to their history, which had become disrupted and cut off. Rituals that enable family members to come together to share and bear witness to their history, however painful, can be a great source of resilience.

Interventions in Family Medicine

The following examples show how a genogram can be used in medical treatment. The first illustrates the importance of gathering information in the initial interview.

A 29-year-old chemical engineer, Michael Anderson, sought help at a local family practice center for stomach pains on November 22, 2018. Because it was customary for the nurse to take a genogram on new patients prior to the doctor-patient encounter, she created **Figure 9.3: Anderson Intake Genogram**. Working from the genogram, the doctor began her assessment by trying to put the patient's stomach pain in context. She noted that it was a particularly stressful time for him, given his previous wife's death only a year ago, his recent move from California to New Jersey to remarry, and his new wife's pregnancy, all within the past year. She wondered how he was doing with all those stresses. The patient's wife, Rita, was expecting their first child in five months. In addition, Mr. Anderson's sister and her husband had recently separated after two miscarriages, which might be adding anxiety to the family system.

The genogram reflected a number of temporal connections, anniversary reactions, and repetitive patterns that might exacerbate the stress of the upcoming events for Mr. Anderson. His first wife, Betsy, had died in a car accident in August 2017, and thus he could be having an anniversary reaction. There was a repetitive

Figure 9.3:   Anderson Intake Genogram

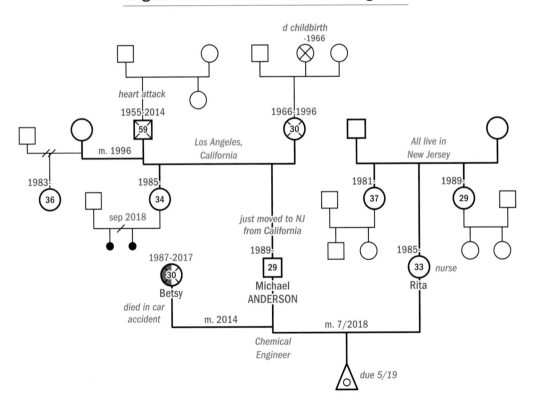

pattern of early female death: His mother and his first wife both died at age 30, and his grandmother died in childbirth with his mother, which might make him acutely sensitive to the physical vulnerability of women. He himself was just turning 30, which could compound his anxiety. His grandmother's death in childbirth might make him specifically more anxious about his wife's pregnancy. It seemed likely that he would be particularly worried about his wife's up-coming childbirth, especially since his sister had had two miscarriages before her recent separation. Might he fear losing the pregnancy or losing Rita, whom he had met the very week after his first wife's funeral? He had then very soon moved across the country to be with her, far from his family and far from where he had ever lived before. Given the short transition period, the physician wondered whether he had dealt with his grief related to Betsy's death, and hypothesized a possible hidden triangle in which Rita might, in some ways, be the outsider to his unresolved relationship with Betsy.

Noticing that Mr. Anderson had no family in the area, while his wife's parents and all her siblings were nearby, the doctor hypothesized that this could leave the couple with an imbalance in emotional resources. During a brief discussion of these family factors, Mr. Anderson acknowledged his fears about the pregnancy, and his continuing thoughts about his first wife, which left him feeling guilty. He accepted a referral for consultation with a family therapist. Physical examination did indicate that he was suffering from gastroesophageal reflux, probably exacerbated by the many stressors of the past couple of years. Medication was prescribed. Mr. Anderson was asked to bring his wife along to his follow-up visit two weeks later. By that time, he had gone for the consultation with the family therapist and his symptoms had disappeared. He and his wife were apparently doing a good deal of talking about his past experiences and he was feeling much better psychologically as well as physically.

The genogram helped the doctor identify a number of potential stressors, and she was able to inquire more about her patient's context and make a referral for a consultation, easing the pressure on Mr. Anderson and his family. It also turned out that he had two college friends who had moved to New Jersey, a close connection with his sister in Texas, and an aunt in California with whom he could also talk openly and who had served as a mother-surrogate after his own mother died. The genogram allowed the physician to practice preventive health care, suggesting not only the family therapy consultation, but urging him to stay in close contact with his friends, sister, and aunt through this stressful time.

Figure 9.4:   Rogoski Family

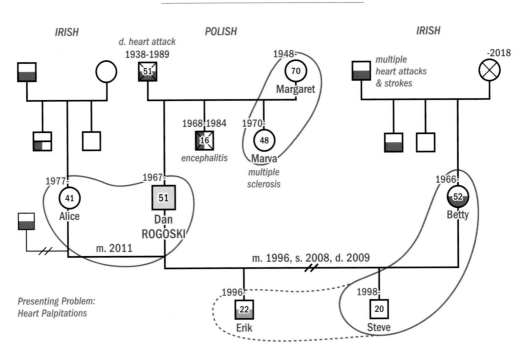

The next example (**Figure 9.4: Rogoski Family**) illustrates a more complex case, in which the response to genogram information was less immediate.

Dan Rogoski, a 49-year-old salesman, went to his physician complaining of heart palpitations. The doctor could find no evidence of any organic dysfunction, so he checked the genogram in his chart. That genogram showed that the patient's father had died of a heart attack and his mother had suffered multiple heart attacks and strokes; she currently lived with his sister, Marva, who had multiple sclerosis and had not been doing well for some time. He had one brother who had died in his early teens of encephalitis. The doctor decided he needed to find out more about Mr. Rogoski's family history, and asked more questions to fill in the genogram.

The physician noted a number of family events that might be affecting the patient. His son, Erik, who had had many behavioral and drug problems before joining the Navy, was due to return home shortly. Perhaps he was worried about this son's problems starting again. His ex-wife, who had a history of alcoholism, had lost her mother recently. He might worry that would lead to an increase in her drinking, which would add to stress on both sons, who would be living with her. Mr. Rogoski's sister, Marva, was also doing poorly. The mother had just turned 78, and might soon be unable to care for her daughter. As the only surviving sibling, he felt responsible for his sister's care. He might also fear his own vulnerability to disease, because of the illnesses of both siblings.

The physician also noticed that Dan was now the same age as his father when he had died of a heart attack, and coincidentally, his older son was 22, the same age he had been when the father died. Perhaps he feared that the heart palpitations were an expression of an impending heart attack and that history would repeat itself.

Finally, there was the pattern of alcoholism in the family. Both of his parents had had drinking problems, as did his son, his first wife, and the families of both of his wives. Based on this history, it was possible that Mr. Rogoski had a drinking problem or that someone in his family thought he did. Or perhaps he was worried that he would develop one.

Using the genogram information, the physician was able to ask him about each of these areas of concern: his son coming home, his ex-wife, his sister's dysfunction, his being the same age as his father when he had died, and his drinking. While the patient admitted to some general concern in each of these areas except drinking, he was sure they had no bearing on his physical state, saying he never let things like that get to him.

As for the drinking, he admitted, when asked, that his wife thought he drank too much, but that was just because her father and her first husband were alcoholics and she was too sensitive. This answer, of course, raised more questions about the extent and nature of his drinking and about his relationship with his wife. Although physical findings and the electrocardiogram were normal, the physician decided, on the basis of the information gathered and the patient's response, to request a follow-up visit with both Mr. and Mrs. Rogoski two weeks later, "just to see how the heart is doing."

At the follow-up meeting, the family stresses were reviewed and Mrs. Rogoski confirmed that she worried about her husband's anxiety and drinking. The doctor mentioned the possibility of their going to AA or Al-Anon or to therapy, but the idea was immediately rejected by both spouses. However, a month later Mrs. Rogoski called back, saying that she felt the tension had not diminished and she would now like the name of a therapist they could consult. The doctor again suggested that she could attend Al-Anon, but she refused, although she did take the name of a local therapist.

At a medical follow-up six months later, Mr. Rogoski proudly announced that he had celebrated his 50th birthday and that he felt very relieved and healthy. He said he and his ex-wife had been trying to deal with their son Erik, who wasn't getting on his feet after leaving the Navy and was drinking too much.

Although neither Mr. Rogoski nor his wife responded immediately to the doctor's observations about the family situation, the genogram did help the doctor to assess the family stresses and relationship factors and eventually became an important resource for the spouses. The groundwork done by the doctor made it easier for them to turn to him again in the future when needed. Having the genogram in the chart will make it easier for anyone on the healthcare team to keep track of ongoing changes, particularly those related to his son Erik, his sister Marva, his conflicts with his ex-wife, and the tension with his present wife over alcohol use.

There are indications that when one member of a family is in distress, others react as well (Huygen, 1982; Widmer, Cadoret, & North, 1980). In this case, by recognizing the multiple stresses Mr. Rogoski was experiencing, the physician became aware of the need to bring in Mrs. Rogoski as well. It was therapeutic to evaluate her response and ability to support her husband, and to at least suggest that other help was available if they should want it. This probably made it easier for Mrs. Rogoski to seek the referral when she did, since her doctor was already familiar with the situation and had directly suggested a source of help to her.

Genogram assessment can show what family patterns are repeating themselves, so that preventive measures can be taken. It identifies the resources a patient has to help cope with a problem; what problems patients may face in complying with suggestions, and what family stresses may be intensifying the difficulty. It gives clues to what further psychosocial intervention might be needed, such as including others in follow-up medical visits or making outside referrals.

Family Patterns, Significant Events, Concurrent Life Stresses, and Cultural Issues

The Montessinos-Nolan Family genogram (**Figure 9.5: Montessinos-Nolan Family**) illustrates a family in which there were extremes of success and failure, health and illness, and serious triangling for several generations. The family sought help because they (especially the mother) had concluded that the behavior of the middle daughter, Barbara, was out of control. Genogram information was

Figure 9.5:   Montessinos-Nolan Family

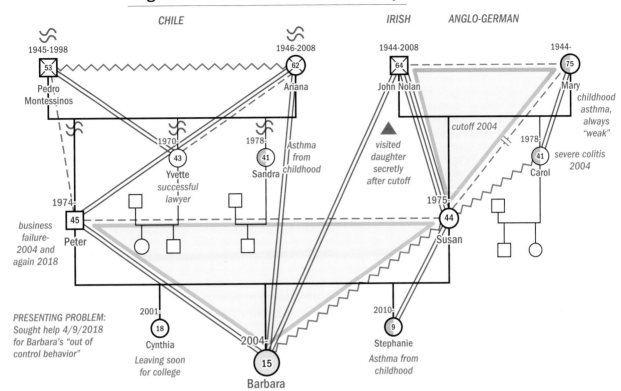

gathered over the first couple of sessions. This provided a quick visual map of many family factors that might be playing a role in the current stress. The following summary outlines the patterns:

Non-Complementary Sibling Position of the Parents:

- Both Peter and Susan were oldest children who appeared to be in a struggle for control (as is typical of marriages between two oldest siblings—see Chapter 6).

Anniversary Reactions:

- Both grandfathers' deaths occurred within a day of Barbara's birthday (the paternal grandfather before she was born and the maternal grandfather when she was four), which also coincided with the time when the family applied for treatment. The maternal grandfather had been very close to Barbara, visiting her on the sly after his wife refused to talk to the family at all.

- Peter's family migrated from Chile when he was 14, the same age that Barbara (the IP) was at the time of treatment.
- Susan's cutoff from her mother and her sister Carol's illness occurred in the same year as Barbara's birth (2004).
- In addition to all these stresses, Peter's business failed the year Barbara was born (2004), and he had again lost his job at the time they sought treatment.

Multi-Generational Triangles:

- In the immediate family, Barbara had a close relationship with her father and a conflictual relationship with her mother. The parents had a distant relationship.
- In her own family of origin, the mother also had a close relationship with her father, cutoff from her mother, and her parents were distant from each other.
- In his family of origin, the father had a close relationship with his mother and a distant relationship with his father; his parents' relationship with each other was hostile.
- The father's middle sister, Yvette, appears in a parallel but converse triangle, close to her father and distant from her mother, which would make it likely that she had conflict with her brother, although so far the siblings on the Chilean side of the family have remained very close.

The Concurrence of Stressful Events:

- Barbara was very close to her paternal grandmother, who had died three months earlier.
- Peter had recently lost his job, and he also had a business fail the year Barbara was born.
- The oldest daughter, Cynthia, was leaving for college in the fall, which would put more stress on the rest of the family.

An Imbalance Between Over-Functioners and Under-Functioners:

- Peter's sister Yvette was a very successful lawyer (a high functioner), and she was their father's favorite. In contrast, Peter experienced multiple business failures and was currently unemployed (an under-functioner).
- Cynthia was a high functioner. There is an apparent imbalance, with Barbara threatening to become the dysfunctional middle sister. The youngest, Stephanie, had chronic asthma.
- Susan, the mother, was always healthy and successful, while her younger sister, Carol was reportedly always viewed as vulnerable and overprotected by the mother, even before she got colitis.

Patterns

- The youngest daughters in the family all had asthma: Peter's youngest sister suffered from asthma since childhood, as did Carol, and Stephanie.
- Susan's younger sister Carol had severe colitis. Her symptoms began in 2004, the same year that Susan and her mother had a falling out and cut-off from each other, after which the father secretly visited the family and remained close.
- The middle daughter, Barbara, had always been identified with her maternal grandfather. She had dreams in which he appeared to her and the family believed she was his reincarnation (they did not speak of this until late in the therapy, though they had acknowledged that they identified her with him).

Finances:

- Peter had recently lost his job and was currently unemployed, and Susan earned a small salary as a substitute teacher. They were worried about having to potentially borrow money to live.
- Cynthia was planning to leave for college that year and it was going to be a major expense for the family.

Cultural Issues—Responsibility to Family

- Peter's family of origin was Chilean. He valued interdependence and taking responsibility for one's extended family, a typical Latino family value.

Susan's family of origin was of British, German, and Irish descent, third and fourth-generation in the United States. Susan valued independence and taking responsibility for one's children only through college, a value consistent with the dominant U.S. culture. These cultural differences were a source of stress in their relationship.

- Peter wanted to spend more time with his sisters' families and he wanted his daughters to be close to their cousins. Susan preferred to spend their free time doing things together as a nuclear family and thought their marriage would be better if Peter spent more time alone with her and their daughters. Susan saw Peter's attachment to his family of origin as a way for him to distance himself from her.

- Susan had been cutoff from her mother since 2004. Peter worried because his mother-in-law was elderly and ill. He wanted Susan to make peace with her mother. Since the death of his own mother, he was even more adamant that they reconcile with Susan's mother. Peter saw Susan's lack of empathy for her mother as "cold." This was another source of stress in their marriage.

The process of collecting information using a genogram is therapeutic in itself. Often the conversation about repeating family patterns, significant events, and concurrent life stresses that occurs while doing the genogram can help families see multiple possibilities and outcomes. When Susan sought treatment for her daughter, Barbara, she was focused on Barbara's "out of control" behavior. Through the telling of their stories, Susan and Peter saw that Barbara's bad behavior was a manifestation of the family stresses related to finances, anxiety about Cynthia's leaving for college, multigenerational triangles, and marital disagreements reflecting cultural differences.

As Susan discovered that she and Peter were repeating the patterns from their families of origin, she began to see the problem in a new way. She wanted to develop a good relationship with her daughter. She did not want a repetition of her relationship with her mother. When Susan and Peter realized they were repeating family patterns in their triangle with Barbara, they were able to work together to change their relationship. As Susan and Peter came together, Barbara's position changed. Because she could no longer depend on her father as an ally in her conflicts with her mother, she and her mother became better at managing their relationship with each other directly.

Although Susan had described her relationship with Peter as distant, they really loved each other and were committed to their marriage. Acknowledging their cultural differences helped them to view their disagreements in a less threatening, more benign way. When Susan saw Peter's attachment to his sisters as a cultural value she realized that he was not avoiding her. At the same time, when Peter came to see Susan's independence as a cultural value, he recognized that she was not "cold." As they began to confer more as parents, and came to agree more on how to raise their children, they grew closer and their marriage improved.

How Genogram Information Can Transform Clients' Perceptions of Themselves

One final case illustrates the power of hidden genogram information to transform a client's experience of himself. Frank Petrucci (**Figure 9.6: Petrucci Family, 2019**) was a successful 50-year-old Italian-Irish businessman, recently married for the third time. He had abandoned his previous children, Sophia and Ophelia, when he left his first two wives. In his third family, he took on the responsibility

Figure 9.6:   Petrucci Family, 2019

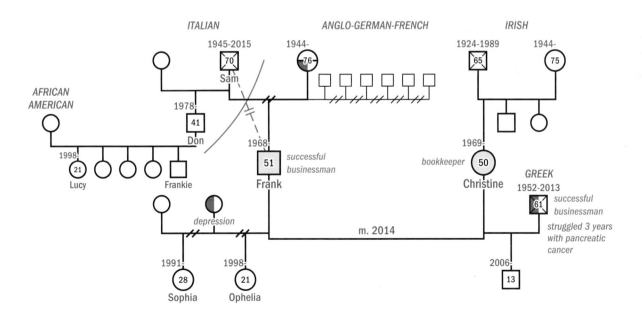

of a stepson who had lost his father, a successful businessman who had immigrated to the U.S. from Greece and had died of cancer.

Christine was trying to continue her first husband's efforts to raise her son to be Greek, a culture she knew little about. But she found herself with a man who seemed to have no sense of culture, and he seemed to withdraw from the very intimacy he said he sought, which left her frustrated and angry. When asked about his family of origin, Frank did not want to talk about it. He admitted that he had grown up in an often-disrupted context, moving frequently as his mother jumped from one relationship to another. His mother had married seven times before he was 24!

He had been cut off from his own father from age seven, when his mother packed him up and moved 1,000 miles away. In the following years he vaguely remembered being "captured" back and forth by each parent, as they fought their bitter battles with each other. His mother was verbally and physically abusive and alcoholic. From an early age Frank had to take care not only of himself, but often also of her. Once, he remembered, his father had tried to reconnect. Frank was about 18 at the time, and they met in a restaurant. When the father tried to show him a picture of his son by his second wife, Frank had become furious and walked out.

Christine used the therapy sessions to work on issues in her own family around the pain of her first husband's long illness, and how it might be contributing to her anger and frustration over her husband's withholding from her. It was a great surprise when, at the end of one couple session in which Frank had said very little, he announced that he had found his father. He said he had hired a detective and had learned that the father had died the previous year. He was pretty sure his father had died in the same apartment in Cleveland where he had lived in his early childhood. He said he had decided to go back to Cleveland and see the house where he was born and visit his father's grave.

When he arrived at the house, he found a young African American woman living there. When Frank introduced himself, she seemed shocked because her name was Lucy Petrucci. It turned out that she was one of five children of Frank's half-brother, Don, who had married an African American woman. Their youngest child and only son was named Frankie Petrucci (an unknowing namesake, as it turns out).

Lucy was the oldest, and she had been the closest to the grandfather, Frank's father, Sam. Sam had lived with the family until he died the previous year. That night the family took Frank out and, as he later described it, he experienced a love and connection he had never even realized he needed. His newly discovered niece,

Lucy, was able to fill him in on much of his father's history that he had never known, since she had been extremely close to him in his last years; she was the last one to speak to him the night he died.

His newly found half-brother shared recollections of their father's longing for Frank over the years, and his pain when Frank had rejected him, the one time he had tried to reconnect. Frank was particularly shocked to feel so close to this Black family, since he had been a strong racist for as long as he could remember. His reconnection made him profoundly aware that he lost a lot more than just his father when the cutoff occurred in his childhood.

And the reconnection affected more than just Frank—his family shared in it, too. It "miraculously," as he thought, facilitated a shift in his relationship with his wife, Christine. As she said, "One reconnection can't change a whole life, but somehow he now seems like a softer, gentler, Frank." He also began to rethink the distance he had kept from his daughters. One regret that he apologized for occurred when he and Christine had gotten married. He had been extremely angry with Ophelia for showing up late and being grumpy at his wedding instead of wanting to celebrate his finally finding happiness. Once he thought about his having left Ophelia alone with her depressed, anxiety ridden mother, and the fact that he rarely visited or even had contact with her, he began to work hard at reconnecting with both his daughters.

Genogram Value as a Therapy Tool

To paraphrase a long-running television advertisement:

> *Therapy without a genogram—valuable.*
> *Genogram-assisted therapy—priceless.*

We hope to inspire readers who are new to the genogram to learn its true value and use it with clients in their training or practices. For those already familiar with the genogram, we hope that reading this will help you use it more effectively in therapy and when working on your own family issues.

10

Genograms in Medical or Psychiatric Practice

Michael Avery Crouch, M.D., M.S.P.H.

Why Do Genograms as a Physician?

To check out patients' bone health, physicians do roentgenogams (X-rays). The genogram is a good way to get quick insight into patients' family health—a roentgenogram without the "roent-." With new patients, it is a time-efficient way to establish initial rapport and gather social and family history data. The genogram facilitates thinking systemically about individuals, in the context of their families and communities. Thinking this way can dramatically improve a physician's effectiveness, biomedically and psychosocially. Some of the many potential patient care benefits of doing genograms are:

- Alleviating patient anxiety
- Fostering a collaborative patient-physician relationship
- Revealing patterns of disease and early death (diabetes, heart disease, cancer)
- Prioritizing preventive interventions (smoking cessation, cancer screening)
- Identifying some commonality or shared patient-doctor interest, which can function as an affiliative bond
- Showing relationship patterns (conflict, distance, abuse, multiple divorces) that may have health implications
- Eliciting familial mental health problems (bipolar, depression, alcohol abuse)
- Disclosing nuclear family social problems (marital conflict, spousal alcoholism, domestic violence)
- Divulging life cycle phase vulnerability (empty nest, retirement, spousal death)
- Exposing family secrets (unplanned pregnancy, scandal, imprisonment)

Why Not Do Genograms as a Busy Physician?

Physicians typically work under considerable time pressure. The genogram may be perceived as an extra task, for which there is no time. But done as an alternative way to get new patients' social and family history, the genogram need take little, if any, extra time. Doing a genogram can actually save substantial time in the long run, and, more importantly, allows the physician to provide better, more timely care.

Another obstacle to doing genograms is an understandable reluctance to "open Pandora's box." This stems, in part, from physicians' desire to do something right away to "fix" problems they uncover; genogram revelations might bring up more time-consuming matters. Physicians with a strong biomedical bent and no counseling training often feel incompetent and/or uninterested in delving into patients' psychosocial issues. The antidote for overcoming this hesitancy is remembering that very few things have to be dealt with immediately. Practical responses to a perturbing genogram disclosure could be something like:

- "Well, that certainly seems relevant. Maybe we can schedule a follow-up appointment to discuss that?"
- "I think that has important implications for your health. If you like, I can refer you to a good counselor to get help with that."

The only way to know how vital the contents of Pandora's box are is to open it and take a quick look. The genogram does this very well. Shutting Pandora's box respectfully, but firmly, when the matter is not one of those truly urgent situations (e.g., high imminent risk for suicide) is an important physician closure skill, which gets easier with practice.

Practical Tips for Doctors Doing Genograms

The genogram is a viable office tool for a busy physician, because doing a "skeletal" genogram is easy and relatively quick (Waters, Watson, & Wetzel, 1994). A skeletal genogram fits on regular paper or the bottom half of a blank genogram form, as shown in Chapter 2. The physician should begin at the bottom with the patient's children or grandchildren and work his or her way up to parents and grandparents.

Using a blank piece of paper in landscape orientation allows room for the lateral mushrooming that occurs each time you go back another generation, and space for new information in subsequent visits. We hope that soon we will be able to add computerized genograms to a medical record and add or show different variables as doctor and patient go along.

Starting to Do Genograms

During an orientation month in my family practice residency in 1977, the behavioral medicine faculty had us do and discuss our own genograms. This included a brief look at our family dynamics. They also shared their own genograms. We then discussed potential personal and professional implications, related to our family dynamics and birth order (Toman, 1976). The focus was on using awareness of our emotional, behavioral, and communication tendencies to relate effectively with coworkers and patients. Through this exercise, I recognized that I had significant unresolved issues with both my mother and father, which could be problematic in patient care and family life. I also realized that I knew very little about past generations of my family.

After completing residency training, I did a two-year fellowship in academic family medicine. I then became a full-time faculty member for two years, during which I completed a part-time family therapy training program. The genogram was the core information-gathering tool of this training in multigenerational family systems (Bowen) theory (Bowen, 1978). It led to clear insights into family emotional life and showed the powerful influence of recurring family patterns on relationships, health habits, illness, and disease. This training allowed me to counsel anxious and depressed patients more effectively. The genogram often pointed the way to preventive steps that might avoid or attenuate harmful family patterns.

Pearls from Doing Routine Genograms Over the Years

During residency, we were encouraged to do genograms with our patients in order to get more proficient and to explore their clinical usefulness. I started doing them routinely with every patient. The first thing I noticed was that the genogram process helped me establish good rapport more quickly than I had done as a senior medical student. I believe this is at least partly because gathering genogram data has the effect of temporarily reversing the usual doctor-patient roles. The patient becomes the expert (on knowledge about his or her family), and the physician becomes the learner.

Gathering genogram information had a calming effect on anxious patients. It allowed them to participate more fully in a collaborative interaction, which was the type of patient-physician relationship that I sought to have as often as possible. The most striking instance involved a young man who was pacing back and forth in the exam room when I entered. He continued to do so after I sat down, even after several minutes of eliciting (with some difficulty) his visit agenda and past medical history. He was extremely tense. Within a few seconds of my explaining that I was going to ask about his family background, so that I could be as helpful to him as possible, he sat down, relaxed somewhat, and became more communicative the rest of the visit.

> *Gathering genogram data has the effect of temporarily reversing the usual doctor-patient roles. The patient becomes the expert (on knowledge about his or her family), and the physician becomes the learner.*

The genogram often quickly revealed things that helped me understand patients and their health risks in ways that I otherwise would have discovered much later, if at all. Surprisingly often, the genogram process elicited a history of childhood or adult abuse (emotional, physical, and/or sexual); this typically came from a woman who had a stepfather or an alcoholic father. After residency, I learned to probe these areas tactfully by asking, "When you were growing up, did anybody *bother* you?" In response, the patient would either look puzzled and say no, or they would tell their sad story, sometimes for only the first or second time.

The main reason I continued to do genograms was to improve the quality of care for my patients. It took a few minutes to do the genogram, but it's necessary to get family medical and psychiatric history anyway, so it usually didn't take that much "extra" visit time. Occasionally something important would crop up during the genogram inquiry that cried for immediate attention, in which case the visit might run somewhat overtime. As I became better at time management and visit closure, I was able to postpone most such discussions to a follow-up visit.

Sometimes a genogram discovery saved me time and frustration in the long run by clarifying something important going on in the background that was muddying the picture diagnostically and/or therapeutically. On such occasions, I realized that I might have run in circles, without ever getting to the heart of the matter, if I had skipped the genogram and limited my inquiry to interview questioning and guesswork testing.

Looking at My Own Family

Family therapy training also stimulated me to learn a lot more about my own family's history (**Figure 10.1: Crouch Genogram**). Since my grandparents were already deceased, I began by connecting better with my parents, siblings, aunts, and uncles. Two years before my emotionally distant father's death from emphysema at age 83, I finally learned how to have a conversation with him. I shared what I was finding out about his ancestors. This was the first stage of a 36-year genealogy exploration.

In expanding my own genogram, I learned that all three of my father's brothers and one younger sister died before age seven, from childhood illnesses and

Figure 10.1:   Crouch Genogram

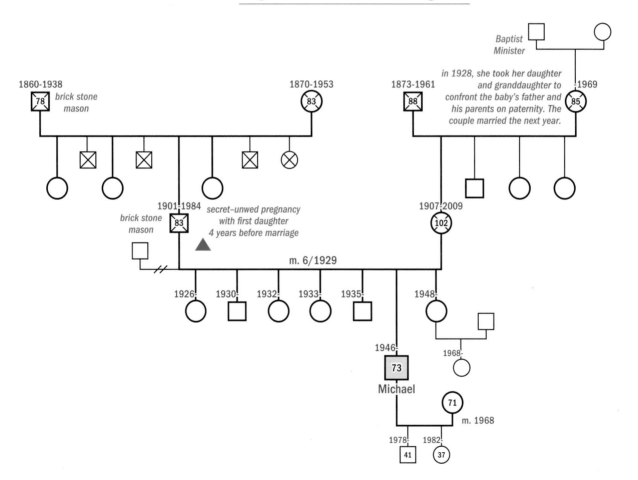

kerosene poisoning. The first two deaths occurred one and three years before my father was born, and the last two were two months apart, eleven years after he was born. I gained respect for him as a survivor of hardship, who worked hard as a bricklayer until age 75. I understood more about why he was so uninvolved with our family, seldom talking to any of us, and not wanting anyone around when he was in his workshop or large organic garden. I came to appreciate how he expressed his love by providing, building, and fixing things for us.

Multiple mourning occasions and family remarks suggest that my paternal grandmother was chronically depressed and a somewhat negligent caretaker for her surviving children. My father received very few verbal or nonverbal signs of love or affection from his parents, and he was unable to express affection until very late in life. He had a fearsome temper, and would occasionally rage and whip me with a belt or razor strop. Communication was so poor in my father's family that he did not know his paternal grandfather's correct name, believing it to be Ezra. (It is actually Enoch Elwood.)

Before my father opened up some, I didn't know what he thought about anything. After I admitted my intense fear of death to him, we talked seriously and joked about death. Shortly before he died, I was able to ask him what he thought about how I'd done in life, and was happy to hear him say that he was proud of me. During this same conversation, he asked if I thought he was ever going to feel any better. (He got very short of breath just getting up out of his chair, even on continuous oxygen supplementation.) I said that his COPD medications were maxed out, and his health was unlikely to improve. He then said, "Well, then I think I'm ready to 'kick the bucket.'" Two weeks later, on my birthday, he died from sudden cardiac arrest. At the graveside after his funeral, I spoke about how hard it was to love and be loved by him, and said that I hoped to continue learning from him. Interestingly, in recent years I have had numerous positive dreams about talking and doing things with my father.

Having a closure conversation with my father de-intensified the negativity in our relationship, and allowed me to talk more comfortably and listen more tolerantly to elderly males in poor health. It also helped me to persist when comforting dying patients and their families, instead of succumbing to the distancing urge that I had learned from my father. I have not resolved my dread of death, but I've mostly accepted its inevitability, and I cope better with my patients' deaths and the prospect of my dying.

During adolescence and early adulthood, my mother's overprotectiveness felt smothering. She often told stories at the dinner table about people being killed in various kinds of accidents and warned me to avoid those situations. When I began dating at age 16, she repeatedly cautioned me, "Do not get some girl pregnant and ruin your life!" I became resentful, and at one point angrily told her to "butt out of my life" (which, of course, made her cry). It wasn't until age 37 that I understood from whence the intensity of this basically sound advice stemmed.

While expanding my genogram during family therapy training, I discovered a 50-year-old family secret—my mother's unwed pregnancy by my father, four years prior to their eventual marriage. She married my father shortly after she divorced another man, whom she had married to give her daughter a father. Now my younger sister understood why, shortly after she got pregnant, then quickly got married, my father was so upset that he got a bleeding peptic ulcer. Ironically, during this episode, an older sister found my mother's divorce decree in a lockbox; she was looking for my father's veteran's papers, when he was in a VA hospital ICU with the ulcer. She told no one, until 14 years later. While filling in details in my genogram, I asked my sister about the discrepancy between my oldest sister's birthdate (1926) and our parents' marriage date (1929), and she told me what she knew. When I asked my mother about it, she was actually relieved to have the secret out in the open.

Mother told me that my father had given her money for a "kitchen abortion," then left their small rural town to find work in the adjacent state. However, she was too far along to have it done. When my grandmother (the daughter of a Baptist preacher) found out about the unwed pregnancy, she insisted on moving to a large Midwest city to avoid the shame. Three years later, my maternal grandmother found an un-mailed love letter from my mother to my father. She took my then-three-year-old sister on the train back to the town they had fled from and confronted my father's parents with "This is your granddaughter!" I am grateful to my grandmother for her courage; without her persistence, I would not be here to write these words.

My relationship with my mother was greatly improved by my working at it steadily for years. Fortunately, she outlived my father by almost 20 years, dying two weeks shy of her 102nd birthday, giving us lots of time to talk. She reminisced a lot about her childhood and her parents, whom I barely knew growing up. I came to appreciate some of their life adversities and how they affected my mother's worldview. Communication was also poor in my mother's family. It was not until after I graduated from medical school and completed a family practice residency that I discovered, through genealogy research, that my maternal great-grandfather had been a country doctor from 1855 until 1910 in the county I grew up in. When I asked her why she never told me about him, she said, "You never asked." Touche! I had been a passive participant in the communication sparsity.

Understanding my family of origin patterns better paved the way for reducing my emotional reactivity in my nuclear family and work systems. After letting go of most of the anger I had felt toward my father and resentment of my mother's over-protectiveness, I felt more differentiated from them and more appreciative of the gifts I got from them. It also allowed me to relate better with patients who reminded me of my mother or father. I got better at encouraging patients who smoked and/or had chronic obstructive pulmonary disease (like my father) to successfully stop smoking. After the smoking-caused deaths of my father and oldest brother (the latter from a massive stroke during coronary bypass surgery, three days after having a heart attack while playing golf with his son and grandson), I often told the stories of their demise to patients who smoked, as cautionary tales.

After doing the family of origin work and becoming a parent myself, I became more empathetic and effective with mothers who were having difficulty with their children's illnesses (e.g., asthma) or behavioral problems (e.g., attention deficit disorder with hyperactivity). I became better at tactfully urging over-protective mothers of teenage children to begin loosening the apron strings and letting them move safely toward independence.

I grew up as the younger brother of two much older sisters who "spoiled" me, and the older brother of a sister two years younger, whom I obnoxiously dominated. Thus, my expectation for females was to be nurtured by them or control them. My oldest brother functioned as a father for my younger sister and me until he left home for the Air Force when I was five years old. So my inner child expects to be ignored, abused, or abandoned by males.

My brother had a seething lifelong conflict with my father. Dad wanted to apologize to him, but he refused to come home when Dad was dying. When Dad died, he drove home from California, instead of flying, so that he would miss the funeral. Sadly, my brother duplicated the conflict with his oldest son. They lived in the same city, but had not spoken in ten years when my brother died. While my brother was in a coma, I said goodbye to him and spoke with that nephew for the first time in 36 years.

My wife is the older sister of a brother seven years younger. She grew up dominating her brother as I did my younger sister. Predictably, we struggled for control and had difficulty making major decisions cooperatively. It took decades of marriage (five, so far) for us to learn to share control and negotiate effectively. I finally got into the habit of going ahead and immediately doing things my wife asks me to do around the house, instead of procrastinating and often forgetting to do them. This may have helped our relationship more than any other change I've made.

I made being emotionally and physically available and demonstrably loving with my son and daughter a high priority. We spent a lot of fun time together when they were young. My only regret is that "my father's temper" surfaced occasionally when I felt frustrated or ganged up on by the rest of my family. They seem to have forgiven me for that. I coached both of them in soccer for ten years, and I am now looking forward to sharing my love for sports with three granddaughters. (Grandchildren are the greatest!)

Given my father's temperament, conflict with males does not surprise me, but a female being angry has been very difficult to deal with. (The latter feels like being emotionally blindsided.) Early in my career, I had more difficulty connecting with male patients, especially angry ones. I tended to over-function with female patients, wanting to rescue them from their problems. My desire to feel needed encouraged over-dependence in some patients, who would delay their care until they could see me. This was sometimes detrimental to their health. I gradually got better at finding a middle ground with clinging patients, instead of getting sucked into their vortex or distancing in a subconscious or conscious attempt to drive them away. I learned to push myself to return phone calls and follow-up just as conscientiously on unfinished aspects of care for patients who felt difficult to me as for those who were easy to like.

Clinicians can gain from doing their own genograms, then analyzing how their own family patterns and issues tend to influence their interactions with patients. Particularly when the doctor-patient relationship seems rocky or unsatisfactory, it is often useful to ask oneself several questions:

1. How might my own family patterns be playing a part in what is going on?
2. How could I change my part of the interaction to avoid repeating my dysfunctional family pattern with this person?
3. What could I do differently in the future, when I realize that a similar situation is threatening to develop into a problem?

When educating patients, it is often more effective to begin by asking systemic questions (e.g., "What do you think you could do to improve your health?"), instead of spoon-feeding information (e.g., "Diabetes puts you at high risk for kidney failure") or delivering admonishments or commands (e.g., "You are morbidly obese. You've got to lose weight!").

Professional training years are an opportune time to begin learning about how one's family background can affect one's effectiveness as a physician (Emerson,

1995; Launer, 2017; Manne, 2009). Family issues can be identified and worked on while learning about oneself and the doctor-patient relationship. Once out in practice, physicians with significant unresolved family issues would benefit from setting aside a regular counseling or psychotherapy appointment with someone they feel comfortable with.

Doing Genograms in the Electronic Medical Record Era

After doing genograms routinely for 20 years, my workplace got its first electronic medical record (Logician, which later became Centricity) in 1997. It did not have genogram capability built in. Despite the human genome project's promise for making family history information much more useful, a genogram or family tree format for recording family history was not added to electronic medical records until 2019 (EPIC). Suddenly, doing genograms, which had been easy and incredibly valuable, became cumbersome. I could still elicit a genogram on paper and have it scanned into the patient's medical record as a stored document. However, viewing it subsequently was a several-step process, and the resolution of the image was relatively poor. New information could be added over the course of time only by printing the scanned genogram, writing on it, then rescanning and storing the new document.

Predictably, despite the best of intentions, I did genograms less and less often. Eventually, I only did them when:

- I was confused about a patient.
- I was having difficulty communicating with a patient.
- Management of a patient's illness or disease was not going well, because I was feeling stuck diagnostically or therapeutically, or we were in conflict over care goals or approaches.
- A patient was more disabled or dysfunctional than the apparent severity of their health problems.
- Serious physical, emotional, or behavioral problems began or worsened in any family member. (Any of these may be a symptom of a family crisis.)
- Each time I did one of these genograms, I was reminded of how useful they are, and once more rued no longer doing them routinely. They are particularly useful for understanding and helping patients with whom the physician is having difficulty by:

—Giving a broader picture of the problems of patients and their families.

—Helping formulate a realistic long-term prognosis.

—Identifying and providing timely counseling for patients at risk for self-destructive behavior, including suicide attempts.

—Allowing for a more realistic assessment of the care goals.

—Decreasing patient and physician frustration, and improving rapport (which may improve adherence with care recommendations).

Looking back at my medical career, several families' genograms and stories are particularly memorable. I would like to share a few of these family genograms and stories from my practice* with the hope that they will inspire the next generation of physicians to appreciate the value of these perspectives.

Greg and Penny

My first week in residency, I was notified that Greg, the 34-year-old father in one of my 25 pre-assigned families, had been hospitalized for an abdominal stab wound. He came to see me for follow-up in the office a few days later. Greg had come home drunk (a frequent occurrence) and gotten into an argument with his wife Penny. At one point, he grabbed a kitchen knife and stabbed himself. At least, that was his story. I still wonder whether his wife might have stabbed him in anger or self-protection instead, and he changed the story to protect her, in a sort of twisted act of chivalry.

I elicited Greg's "skeletal" genogram during that first visit, and gradually fleshed it out in more detail (**Figure 10.2: Greg and Penny**). Right away, it showed a strong pattern of alcoholism and early cardiovascular death. His paternal grandfather died from a heart attack at 52, and his father did the same at age 40. Both of them suffered from alcoholism. At an early age, Greg began locking his bedroom door when his dad was out drinking, to prevent him from beating him up when he got home. He desperately wanted to "not be like my old man," and he was ashamed of how he had repeated the excessive drinking pattern.

Greg's "life script" was "I'm going to die before 40, so I've got lots of life insurance to take care of my wife and child when I'm gone. I'm worth a lot more dead

* Identifying details have been changed.

Figure 10.2: Greg & Penny

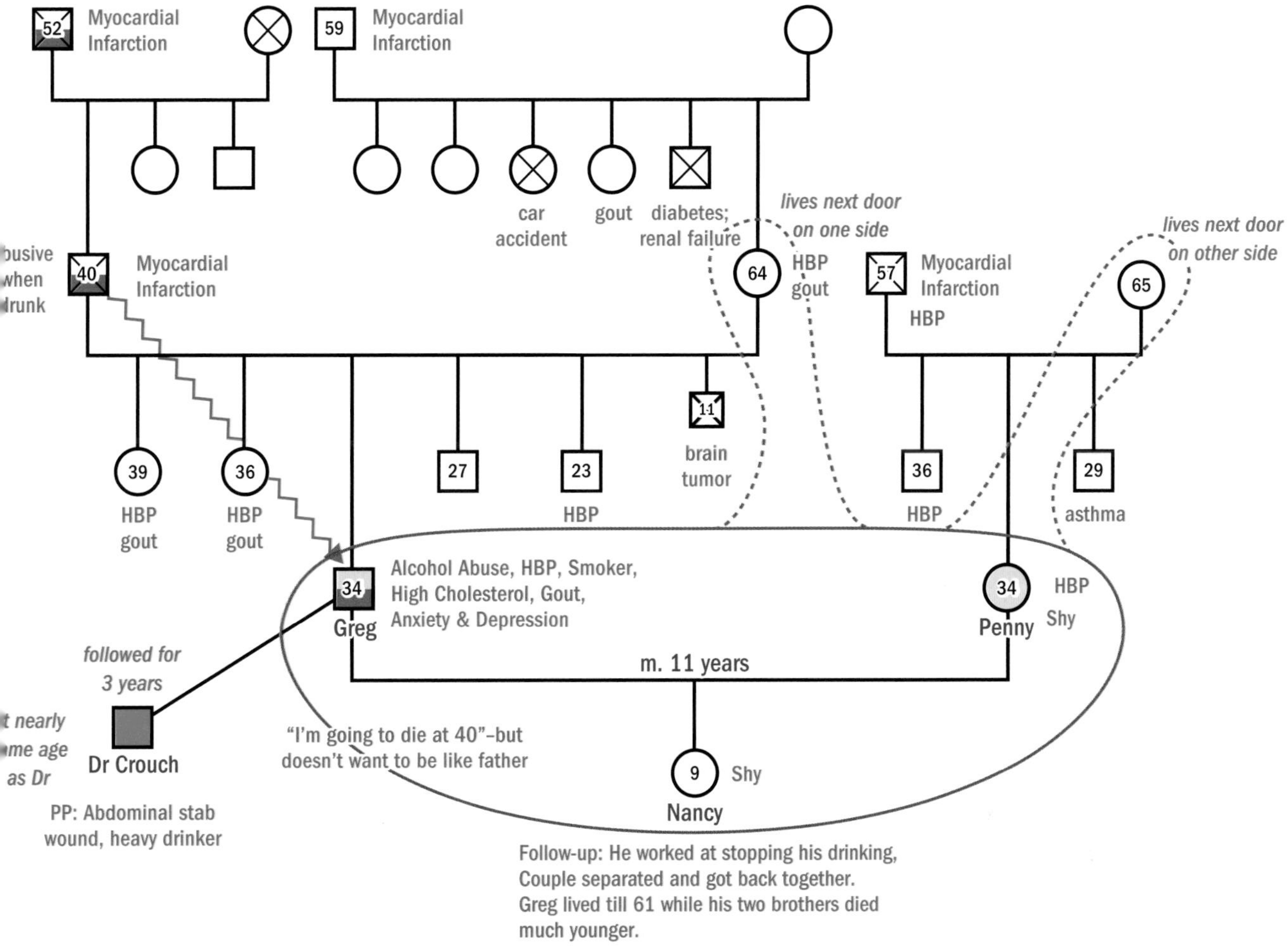

than alive." Penny's father and paternal grandfather also died young from heart disease, so she shared his gloomy prediction. Greg's mother lived adjacent to them on one side, and his mother-in-law lived on the other side. Family therapists call that enmeshment. Greg had lots of chronic health issues, including alcoholism, smoking, diabetes, hypertension, high cholesterol, gout, anxiety, and depression. Many of them, though genetically predisposed, were brought on or exacerbated by his chronic excessive drinking. I saw him often the next three years, and occasionally saw his wife and young daughter. He was only slightly older than I was. I liked him as a person, despite his pervasive pessimism. I regularly urged improving his self-care and health habits, to mitigate his dire outlook and prevent it from becoming a self-fulfilling prophecy.

During the third year, I saw him for a series of supervised counseling visits in our office's family room. He gained a better understanding of his emotional patterns and triggers. At one point, he got sober and stayed that way for six weeks, until his birthday. He decided to celebrate by going by his favorite bar to have one, and only one, drink on the way home. Surprisingly, he did leave after one drink. Unfortunately, as he left, a man mistook him for someone else (who Greg later said he actually did closely resemble), who owed money to him. He and a friend jumped Greg outside the bar and beat him up severely. Greg "couldn't win for losing." When things went badly, he would say, "That's okay. Every dog will have his day."

My group nurse from residency told me some years later that Greg and Penny had split up. However, when I checked again, I learned that they'd gotten back together and stayed married. Hopefully things went better for them, until Greg died at age 61. That was still young, but Greg far surpassed his own forecast. While his two older sisters are still alive, his two younger brothers are not. Greg may have at least partly escaped the shadow of his father's and grandfather's emotional eclipse on his life, surviving longer than any other male in his family in three generations.

Bob and Nell

I met Bob and Nell when the family practice resident physician on the inpatient service asked me to consult on their care while Bob was in the hospital (**Figure 10.3: Bob & Nell, 2015**).

She wanted advice on how to help them cope with their illnesses and the implications for the family. I did their genogram as we talked for two hours. The more I learned, the more worrisome their risk for tragic ensuing developments seemed to me.

Bob and Nell had moved to the area the previous year. They were both 48 years old. Married for 26 years, they had four children (two still at home) and one grandchild (born recently). Bob, a retired Air Force officer, now taught at a military prep school. Nell had returned to work three years earlier, after 22 years of being a homemaker. A year before, she was promoted to head nurse in a nursing home. Their adult children lived far away.

Bob's mother, Vera, was from a working class family, but she had married into a prominent family in a Northeast city. Vera bitterly opposed Nell's marrying her only child, considering her to be unworthy of him and of the family name. Nell's

Figure 10.3: Bob & Nell, 2015

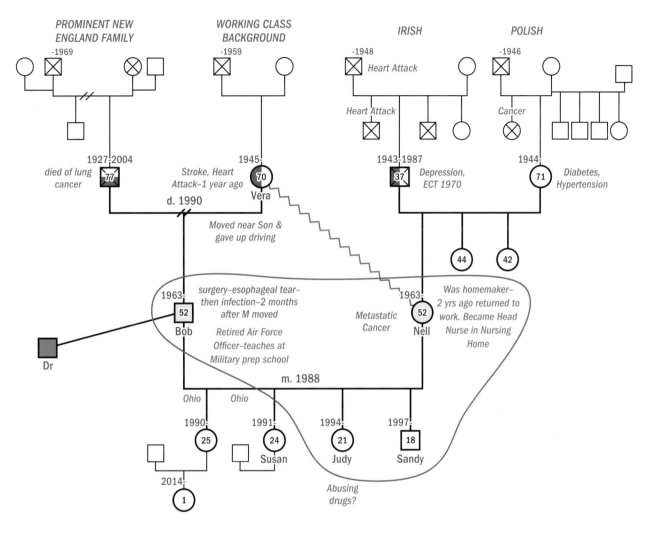

father was a manual laborer whose parents had emigrated from Ireland, and her mother's parents had emigrated from Poland. Vera remained hostile all this time, despite Nell's repeated attempts to build a civil relationship. They half-jokingly referred to her as "The Dragon Lady."

In the preceding year, Vera had a stroke, then a heart attack. She refused to enter a nursing home, and moved instead to an apartment near Bob and Nell. Bob thought it was unsafe for her to drive, so she sold her car and became dependent on them for transportation. Bob lamented the way his mother (an only child herself) had been overinvolved with him, with no siblings to dilute her attention, but he now began repeating the same pattern in reverse, "babying" his mother. Facing an indefinite period of conflictual caretaking, Nell tried to make the best of the situation.

A family pattern of loss through divorce and death complicated matters. Bob's parents divorced the year after the birth of their first grandchild, two years after Bob and Nell's marriage. Bob's father suffered from alcoholism and died from lung cancer when Bob was 39. In the prior generation, Bob's paternal grandparents separated the year after their first grandchild's birth, and divorced the year after the second grandchild was born.

Vera's father died when she was 13. Nell's father was hospitalized and treated for severe depression with electroconvulsive therapy (ECT) when she was seven. He was depressed the rest of his life and died when Nell was 24. Nell's paternal grandfather died when her father was five years old, and her maternal grandfather died when her mother was two years old. Bob's paternal grandfather died when Bob was five.

Given the pattern of instability when adding new family members, the recent grandchild birth and "invasion" by the mother/mother-in-law was predictably stressful for the family. The risk of serious illness or death in the ensuing year would likely be high, especially if the family did not cope better with the changes than past generations had done.

Two months after Vera moved to town, Nell began feeling tired and irritable. One week later, Bob had severe pain after swallowing a bite of meat and began vomiting blood. He quickly underwent surgery for an esophageal tear, but had a postoperative infection that prolonged his first-ever hospital stay. Research has shown that severe family stress is associated with suppressed immune system function (Schmidt, 1983).

A few days after Bob's hospital discharge, Nell was hospitalized for severe anemia and found to have metastatic cancer with unknown primary site; she was treated with chemotherapy. Shortly after Nell came home, Bob was readmitted for an infection around his spleen. At that point, their 21-year-old daughter Judy was refusing to talk with her mother about her cancer, and the resident suspected she was using illicit drugs.

In our interview, Bob and Nell talked openly about the conflict with Vera, but they declined counseling to help deal with the stress. They had always handled problems on their own, and they planned to get any necessary extra support from their church and friends. I felt very uneasy, but as a consultant, I respected their wishes and did not push for an additional family meeting, as I might have done as their primary care provider. When an individual is diagnosed with metastatic cancer, one or more family meetings with their primary care provider and/or a psychotherapist can help the family cope with the treatment difficulties. If treatment is unsuccessful, family meetings can support a dignified dying process, as well as the family's grieving (Worby & Babineau, 1974).

During the next 11 months, Vera had several hospitalizations for vague complaints, and Nell underwent unsuccessful cancer treatment. Bob spent a lot of time away from his children to be with his wife and mother in the hospital. Their primary care physician continued to offer counseling, and they repeatedly declined. Nell died from cancer complications in March 2016. Two family physicians talked with individual family members during the mourning period, but Bob still declined a family meeting and counseling.

Three months after Nell died, Bob killed himself with a gun. His mother lived another two years afterward. My surmise is that Bob could not bear to keep on living without his wife, and with his mother having "re-attached the umbilical cord." Early in Nell's cancer treatment, Vera had urged him to "not wait too long after she's gone, to find a new wife, one better suited for you." I felt badly for their children, especially the two still at home, who had to deal with losing both parents at once. However, I couldn't judge Bob negatively for his decision. I think he made what he thought was the only reasonable choice, in a terrible situation. If I had had a chance to talk with his children afterward, I think that is the main thing I would have said to them.

Doing a genogram may sometimes help physicians understand why people make decisions the physician considers ill-advised, irrational, or even morally wrong. One of our tasks as family doctors is to try not to be judgmental about patients. Promoting acceptance of patients' autonomy to make questionable decisions can be one of the genogram's most useful functions in difficult situations.

Larry and Connie

Larry and Connie first came to my office for a get-acquainted visit with their new doctor. Larry was a 44-year-old Ph.D. who worked in research, and Connie was a 35-year-old homemaker. Initial genogram data included their marriage two years earlier—Larry's second marriage and Connie's third. Larry's first wife, Sarah, had suffered from bipolar disorder, and abused their children verbally and physically. They had separated three years earlier. Sarah committed suicide in the family's lake house six months before Larry and Connie got married. This made the family's ongoing weekend stays there "for relaxation and recreation" feel sort of haunted.

Larry's health was good, except for an adjustment disorder with mixed mood disturbance. Connie suffered from chronic anxiety, recurrent depression, and a mild movement disorder. She was struggling in the often-difficult role of step-mother for Larry's 12-year-old adopted son Bert and 8-year-old biological daughter Briana. Bert was diagnosed with attention deficit disorder at age five, which was improved by taking methylphenidate. Connie's 16-year-old and 14-year-old sons were living in Kansas with her first ex-husband, and things got even more complicated when they came to visit in the summer.

Besides their regular healthcare visits, they came for a series of counseling visits—individual, couple, and whole family—over the next five years. Some of them were preventive and some were crisis-related. The crises were often child-focused, but Connie had periods of despair that prompted individual or couple counseling.

The genogram (**Figure 10.4: Larry & Connie, 1985**) showed a strong pattern of unstable relationships. Larry's parents divorced when he was one year old.

Figure 10.4:   Larry & Connie, 1985

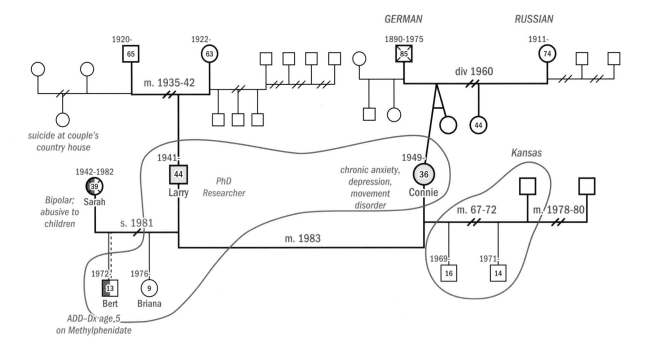

His father remarried twice and had a daughter by the second wife. His mother remarried and divorced four more times; she had three sons by the second husband. Connie's parents divorced when she and her identical twin sister were eleven. Her father had two children by a prior marriage; he was 55 years old when she was born, and died when she was 30. Her mother was 18 years younger than Connie's father. Hometown rumors suggested that her older half siblings' pediatrician was her biological father. Her mother remarried and divorced twice more. Connie got some support from her twin, but not much from her mother or two older half siblings, all of whom lived far away. Because so much had gone on with their parents, the small amount of grandparent information obtained is omitted from their genogram.

Counseling seemed to help Larry and Connie strengthen their marriage partnership while I knew them, but parenting remained a struggle for them both. Larry's children's teen years were rocky. Bert had poor school performance, alcohol abuse, illicit drug use, and several episodes of depression, but eventually did somewhat better. Brianna began suffering from depression episodes at age 10, but she responded better to counseling, got through adolescence and early adulthood okay, and is now a massage therapist and homeopathic practitioner with children of her own.

Although the genogram can identify strong family patterns that counseling can alleviate, some patterns seem inexorable. I recently learned that Larry and Connie eventually divorced and remarried their third and fourth spouses respectively.

Linda, Patrick, and Gino

Linda, a single 23-year-old respiratory therapist, first came to our family practice center having missed two menstrual periods. She was thrilled to learn she was pregnant, but apprehensive about her family's reaction. Her genogram (**Figure 10.5: Linda, Patrick, & Gino, 2000**) showed her living with her Roman Catholic mother and three younger siblings. Her parents had recently divorced. Her mother suffered from depression and had attempted suicide three years earlier. One of her younger sisters was recurrently depressed. Her father's younger brother and father had died from alcohol abuse. Linda had been engaged to her fiancé Patrick for three years (the year of her mother's suicide attempt).

To Linda's relief, her fiancé, mother, and siblings were immediately supportive. Her father initially engaged in laying blame. (His father and brother had both died young from alcohol abuse, and he grew up in an emotionally volatile family.)

Figure 10.5:   Linda, Patrick & Gino, 2000

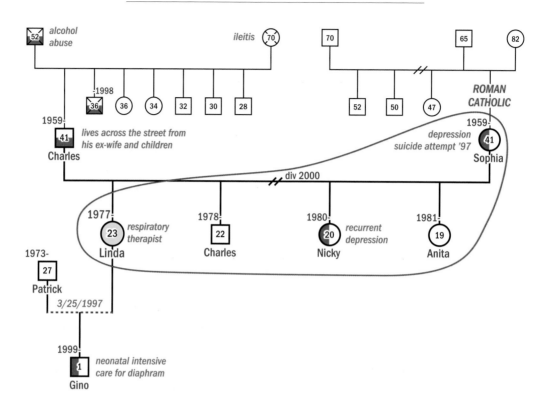

However, he eventually came around to being more positive. After an uneventful pregnancy and labor, Gino was born.

About 10 minutes after birth, Gino's respiratory rate increased markedly, and a neonatologist took over his care in the neonatal intensive care unit. He was diagnosed with diaphragmatic eventration—a condition in which the diaphragm does not tighten and pull downward enough to adequately inflate the lungs. The neonatologist thought that the defect might correct itself.

Less than 24 hours later, Gino was intubated and placed on a ventilator. A review of the medical literature on diaphragm eventration and a phone call to an expert on this rare condition suggested doing immediate surgery to fold the diaphragm over and draw it downward. This would expand the lung volume, allow normal respiratory tree proliferation, and prevent irreversible lung scars (Langer, Filler, Coles, & Edmunds, 1988). The neonatologist, however, was reluctant to approve surgery. The only surgeon in the local community who had ever performed the procedure also recommended watching a bit longer.

On the fourth day of life, Gino was taken off the ventilator. His mother, grandmother, and aunt asked many questions. I withheld my non-expert opinion that he should have surgery as soon as possible to maximize his respiratory potential, not wishing to undermine the neonatologist and surgeon.

For the next four weeks, Gino improved only marginally on supplemental oxygen. I met with the family February 18 and strongly encouraged surgery—the sooner the better. The family was reluctant to proceed with surgery. They still wanted to believe that he might eventually do well with supportive care alone. On February 23, Gino suffered a prolonged hypoxemic episode and went back on ventilator-assisted breathing. I met with the family and again urged surgery soon. I then left town to attend a professional meeting, feeling frustrated, sad, and apprehensive.

At the Family Conference of the Society of Teachers of Family Medicine, I attended a healing ceremony workshop conducted by family physician Howard Silverman. The workshop included an actual ceremony designed to help participants identify reasons they attended the workshop. I had come because of my feelings about Gino's situation.

I decided that a ceremony might be valuable for Gino's family and me. Once back, I drove straight to the hospital. The mother and grandmother were at Gino's crib side. The surgeon had scheduled surgery for three days later. I introduced the ceremony notion, and they said they were very interested. I gathered materials, then went to the family home. I have described some of the details of this ceremony in a recent publication (Crouch, 2016). We focused on letting go of prior hopes and forming new, more realistic expectations for Gino's future.

The ceremony opened the door to a candid conversation regarding everything that had transpired. It decreased our fear, anxiety, and frustration and empowered us to help each other and to cope better with the situation. Participating in the healing ceremony also assuaged some of the guilt we felt. It was the most I ever felt like a healer.

Gino sailed smoothly through two operations a week apart, one for each side of his diaphragm. He went home from the hospital a week later, but he still needed supplemental oxygen for three and a half more months. At each well child visit he had grown well and made slow steady developmental progress.

Over the next ten years, Gino became a normal, active 12-year-old boy. He responded well to his mother's home schooling. At 10, he tested several grades above his grade level in language and math. He was an affectionate, gentle soul, who loved animals, going fishing with his uncle, and riding his bicycle. He far surpassed the hopes expressed in the "realistic" moments of the ceremony, when things looked so grim.

If I hadn't "gotten to know the whole family" through doing a genogram initially with Linda, I might not have had the nerve to ask them about doing a ceremony. The genogram information about the parents' religion, depression, alcoholism, and relationship disruption prompted me to be respectfully careful when discussing marital and life-and-death issues with the family.

Doing unconventional things like ceremonies is outside many physicians' comfort zones. When a clinician is distressed or pained by a patient's predicament, and is unsure about how to respond, he or she is encouraged to seek and arrange appropriate consultation. This is another way to "close Pandora's box" when the genogram reveals toxic issues.

Genogram of Family Medicine/Practice

I once portrayed the putative lineage of the discipline of family medicine and the specialty of family practice in genogram form; despite seeming somewhat sexist, it still appears to have some metaphoric face validity (Crouch, 1989). In this updated version (Figure 10.6: Genogram of Family Practice & Family Medicine), Family Practice and Family Medicine were born in 1969 as fraternal twin offspring of General Practice (the father). It is unclear which liaison was the mother—Social Responsibility, Quality Care, or Political Expediency.

The paternal grandfather, Allopathic Medicine, had two sons (General Practice and General Internal Medicine) and two daughters (Pediatrics and Psychiatry) by the first marriage to Humanism, followed by another son (Medical Specialization) by second wife, the seductive siren High Technology. High Technology had already had a son (Surgery) by previous spouse Barbery. One of Allopathic Medicine's siblings, Osteopathic Medicine, has produced numerous children and grandchildren, who have intermarried with those of Allopathic Medicine. The other sibling, Homeopathic Medicine, has produced relatively few descendants, who have been largely cut off from the rest of the Medicine family.

Family Medicine and Family Practice are 50 years old this year—middle-aged and at risk for mid-life crisis. Family Medicine had a lengthy affair with Biopsychosocial Medicine in the 1970s-90s. Family-Oriented Care and Family-Oriented Research, born in this era, are Family Medicine's under-acknowledged offspring. They seem not fully legitimate, but potentially formidable, like John Snow, in *Game of Thrones*.

With first wife, Managed Care, Family Practice fathered Primary Care Provider (PCP, aka "Gatekeeper"). First Family Medicine, then Family Practice married another seductive siren, Electronic Medical Record, resulting in a division

Figure 10.6:   Genogram of Family Practice & Family Medicine

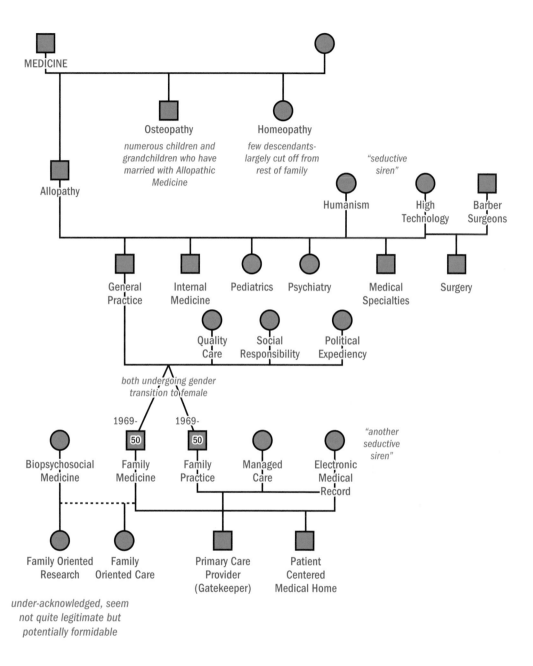

of the physician's attention to the patient and distraction from doctor-patient communication (Crouch, 2004). Family Medicine then fathered Patient-Centered Medical Home. These cousins are trying to work together effectively, in variably harmonious concert with their parents.

Both Family Medicine and Family Practice are undergoing gender transformation, from male to female. The proportion of female family practice residents now exceeds 50%, and many family practice residency program faculties are approaching or exceeding 50% female as well. It will be interesting to see how this shift affects the ethos and organizational decision making of family medicine and family practice in the future. Perhaps, fueled by advances in genomics, family-oriented care and research will blossom once more and bear fruit, stronger and more prevalent than the 1980s surge.

When the Patient-Centered Medical Home was first propounded as the new model of family medicine in 2004 (Green et al., 2004), family systems orientation was omitted from the aims for the 21st century health care system, key characteristics of family medicine, and characteristics of a new model for family medicine practice. The only brief mention of family orientation was in the core values and competencies preamble statement, " . . . health and disease . . . depend in part on the context of patients' lives as members of their family and community." Despite acknowledging the whole person, the individual focus of the operational features of the Patient-Centered Medical Home provides no guidelines, incentives, or rewards for family-oriented care.

As late as 2001, the website of the American Academy of Family Physicians included a page entitled *Facts About Family Practice*, which included this statement:

> "Family practice is the medical specialty which provides continuing and comprehensive care for the individual and families. It is the specialty in breadth which integrates the biological, clinical, and behavioral sciences" (Gutierrez & Scheid, 2019).

Based on the disappearance of that page, and the complete absence of the concept of family from the difficult-to-find "About (Us)" replacement page (*Family Medicine Specialty*), the family practitioners' professional organization appears to have also eliminated family-oriented care and behavioral medicine from its core values and mission.

In contrast, Stange's inspiring 2016 article "Holding On and Letting Go" points the way for future family physicians to honor the discipline's founding values in ways that are adaptive for our rapidly changing society by asking (in part):

> "What if we decide to retain but reinvent, in a new information age, our fundamental understanding that good health care is not just a commodity, but a

relationship based on the tenets of . . . sustaining partnership by deeply know-ing individuals, families, and community?"

My thought is, "May it be so." Or as Westley said to Buttercup in the movie Prin-cess Bride, "As you wish."

The Joy of Doing Genograms

Doing genograms routinely for 20 years made me a better family doctor, diag-nostically and therapeutically. Using genograms greatly enhanced my relation-ship with patients and families. Genograms encourage people to tell their stories. Hearing and being touched by their stories was the most rewarding part of being a primary care provider. Those patient stories are what I treasure the most. My wish for the younger generations of family doctors and other healthcare provid-ers is that they come to see the value of relating to their patients systemically, and experience the value of using genograms to map out their families and enrich their own and their patients' lives.

11

Family Play Genograms

Coauthored with Eliana Gil, Ph.D.

Family play genograms are a natural expansion of the assessment methods and therapeutic benefits of the genogram. Family play genograms were developed by Eliana Gil, with whom we collaborated for many years. They combine the structure of genograms with the playful use of miniature items—people, animals, and objects of all sorts—to allow children and adults to create imaginative genograms that can serve as a revealing assessment and intervention tool with families. This is a powerful technique for making the genogram come to life. For a detailed understanding and illustration of the use of this technique, see our video "Using Family Play Genograms in Psychotherapy" (available at psychotherapy.net). For another interesting artistic expansion of genograms, see also Deborah Schroder's (2015) *Exploring and Developing the Use of Art-Based Genograms in Family of Origin Therapy.*

In the family play genogram exercise, family members choose from an array of miniature people, animals, and objects to represent each family member on a large piece of paper (3' × 4' or so). The exercise brings out interesting information about how family members relate, how they view each other, as well as how they view long-dead family members. The discussion they have about the miniatures each has chosen draws on their creativity, fantasy, and imagination and helps to clarify family history, and expand their view of relationships and conflicts. Sometimes family stories, rumors, or legends influence symbolic representations based on hearsay, rather than on first-hand knowledge. Such views can be explored and expanded with family play genograms, which allow members to create new narratives, building from what each has heard about extended family members.

Family members young and old can use the miniatures as jumping-off points for sharing secret or familiar understandings of family history. As with psychodrama (Moreno, 2019) and family sculpting (Papp, Silverstein & Carter; 1973; Satir, Gomori, Gerber & Banmen, 1991), where participants are asked to visualize and physically demonstrate how relationships could be different in the future if the family were to come to terms with its experiences, family play genogram exercises may include setting up imaginary genograms that take members into a hoped-for future, when their relationships with each other and with their history could be transformed. Introducing the element of metaphor into the discussion of their genogram history often gives family members greater flexibility in imagining possibilities for future change, even while acknowledging that the facts themselves cannot be changed—only their way of dealing with them.

Play genograms also have transformative possibilities for family relationships in therapy. Like other forms of play therapy, they allow family members to express their inner experience within the reality of a miniaturized outer world, expressing their thoughts, feelings, and fantasies about themselves and other members of their family. Miniatures provide graphic but playfully small representations that may indicate how family members are connected and how they are separate or different. Play genograms can be used with an individual, even a small child as young as five, or with an aging great-grandmother of 85. They can be used with multiple family members to understand each person's view of the relationships.

Creating the Genogram Picture

The genogram is typically drawn by the clinician ahead of time or with the person or family on a large sheet of easel paper or poster board. Family members are asked to add not only biological and legally related family members, but anyone who has been important in the family's life, including friends and pets.

The Exercise

Once the drawing is complete, clients are asked to choose an item to represent each person on the genogram, including themselves, from an array of miniatures on a shelf or table. They then place their items on the circles and squares of the genogram that represent the person for whom they have chosen each item. Family members are given as long as they want to make their basic choices, and then asked to share their thoughts about items they have chosen. When working with a young child, the therapist may prompt the child as he or she goes along, to facilitate therapeutic conversation. They are often more comfortable choosing each item separately, and parents may help them place the item near the particular family member. The clinician may give reluctant children examples of concrete and abstract choices to encourage them to explore possibilities.

Some people choose more than one miniature to represent a family member, which may reflect ambivalence or the complexity of a relationship. When working with children in foster care or other family situations in which they have had multiple caretakers, it is helpful to construct a series of genograms on the same sheet of paper. It may also make sense to give a sequence of instructions, to pace the interview and to help process the information before the genogram gets too crowded.

For example, family members may be asked to pick an item for each family member in their current household, including the pets. They may then share information about their choices before moving on to choose items for the extended family. Children in foster care may depict previous family constellations, while other family members may choose items to represent different segments of the extended family. Family members may include friends, therapists, teachers, pets, or other important relationships, both past and present. This can give the clinician a complex, yet easily visible assessment of a family member's relationship world.

Family members then take turns discussing their choices, which facilitates their elaboration of the meaning of the items they have picked for different family members. Therapists can learn a lot about the family's style and patterns of relating and problem solving as they choose and then discuss the items they have chosen. When everyone has made choices, family members are encouraged to look at the family play genogram, and to make comments and ask questions. Rather than asking family members why they chose a particular object, it may help to invite a more open dialogue in which family members volunteer a broad range of information about the items and the relationship between the items and the people in the family. ("Were there any choices that surprised you?" or, "Which items seemed to fit most closely with your own image of that person?")

The first person to speak tends to set the tone for the type of information that will be provided. Thus, it may help if the clinician asks expansive questions to promote a dialogue among the family members, such as, "Tell me a little more about that."

The symbolic nature of the miniatures makes them a fascinating tool for drawing out unrecognized family characteristics and patterns in a creative and fanciful format. Even difficult relationships may be humorously reflected in ways which can reveal the individual's resilience. One client (illustrated on the Family Play Genogram video available at psychotherapy.net), who had experienced many traumatic stresses in her life, chose a rather small male figure for her ex-husband. When discussing her choice, she said that at one time her husband had loomed very large, but these days he played a much smaller role in her life and she thought the silly little cowboy figure reflected this change. This same woman chose an American Indian doll with little babies all over it to represent herself, saying she felt that for many years her life had been focused on raising her children. Her choice of the item was an excellent reflection of the burden and stress she felt, and it allowed her to laugh as she discussed its meaning. Somehow the humor in the play and the smallness of the miniatures allowed her to express her feelings with a humorous appreciation for herself and her situation.

Her teenage daughter chose to represent the mother as "walking teeth"—a wind-up toy with a big mouth that walks on little feet. The daughter had recently been feeling great resentment toward her mother, but somehow the translation into the walking teeth expressed both the daughter's frustration that her mother "talked too much," and the silliness of that aspect of their interaction. Through their choices they learned a great deal about each other's perceptions of themselves and their relationships as well as their perceptions of the extended family. Sharing their perceptions in the context of the family play genogram gave a lightness to their discussion, which had become charged and over-focused on the conflicts they were having with each other. The family play genogram exercise allowed them to see themselves in a much broader context and to find many points of connection.

Once family members have each told their story about the items they have chosen, it is helpful for the therapist to ask permission to take a photograph of the family play genogram. The individual or family may take the photograph home to facilitate additional conversation, and the clinician can keep a copy of the pictures to recreate play genograms at a later time for a continuation of the therapeutic dialogue.

Using Play Genograms to Invite, Engage, and Enliven The Therapeutic Encounter

This technique often bypasses client resistance and can elicit candid disclosures that reveal perceptions people have of themselves and of others. One reason this occurs is because rigid narratives that individuals develop about themselves, their families, and their childhoods often become self-reinforcing. This rigidity can cause new "counter-narrative" information to be discounted or rejected.

Co-creating genograms with families in therapy is an important way to gather and organize information, especially about family composition, structure, cross-generational patterns of achievement and dysfunction, and relational issues between family members (emotional distance, closeness, or cutoffs). Genograms help both the clinician and the family gain a broader understanding of the client's family system and history, while at the same time organizing, reflecting, and bringing new insights about family patterns and significant life experiences.

Play allows for active engagement with fantasy and visualization. In the process of playing, clients often achieve a variety of positive outcomes, including externalizing the problem (which is sometimes more difficult in verbal therapy). Many individuals feel cultural and personal restrictions when speaking about their problems. They may have feelings of disloyalty, discomfort with therapy, fears of exaggerating a problem or making it seem more important by talking about it, or of being seen as vulnerable or weak. Play often allows them a smoother transition into difficult emotional material.

Once symbols are utilized to communicate to oneself and others, different processes become possible. When problems feel overwhelming to a client, "miniaturizing" them may help clients manage them. Play therapy allows clients to infuse objects with emotions or personality traits, which can also create a safer distance from painful issues that can then facilitate acknowledgement, understanding, and working through traumatic issues.

A Play Genogram Session with Jenny

When I (SP) first met Jenny she was 13 (**Figure 11.1: Jenny: Children in Foster Care**) and had already been living in foster care for five years. She was now in her third foster home. She was volatile, depressed, getting into trouble in school, arguing with classmates, and refusing to do her schoolwork. She and her younger half-sister Tammy had been removed from their parents' care five years earlier, because of drug problems. Jenny's father had disappeared from the family soon after Jenny was born. When Jenny was six her mother had a second daughter, Tammy, with a different father, who soon went to prison for drug dealing. Jenny's mother was now also in prison for dealing drugs.

Figure 11.1:   Jenny: Children in Foster Care

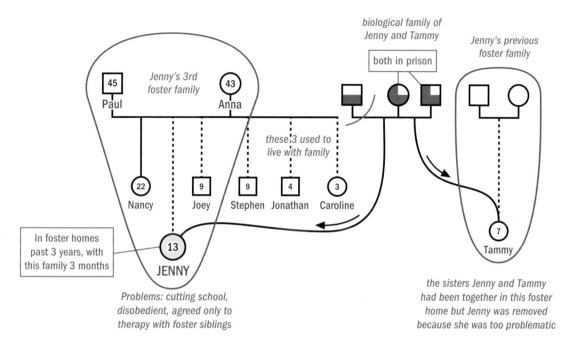

*biological family of
Jenny and Tammy*

both in prison

*Jenny's previous
foster family*

45   Paul   *Jenny's 3rd
foster family*   43   Anna

*these 3 used to
live with family*

In foster homes
past 3 years, with
this family 3 months

22   Nancy   9   Joey   9   Stephen   4   Jonathan   3   Caroline

13   JENNY

7   Tammy

*Problems: cutting school,
disobedient, agreed only to
therapy with foster siblings*

*the sisters Jenny and Tammy
had been together in this foster
home but Jenny was removed
because she was too problematic*

Initially the sisters had been placed together, but Jenny's argumentative behavior had overwhelmed the second foster parents, although they had hoped to keep the sisters together. Tammy, now seven, was much easier to manage, so she stayed, but Jenny was moved to a new foster home, where the parents agreed to keep her long term. But the move meant she was separated from her sister, which was a major loss for her.

Jenny refused to participate in therapy, because, as she said, "talking about things" was useless; it wouldn't change anything. However, she agreed to family therapy with the other foster children in the home. In this session, Jenny and her nine-year-old foster brother, Joey, participated because they were the only foster children then in the home.

Jenny had a strong resistance to exploring family issues, so we created the genogram on a large sheet of paper, beginning with the people who she was living with at the time: Jenny and Joey, the foster parents, and their biological daughter Nancy, who was 22. Then Jenny and Joey were asked to add anyone else they wished to include. They added three other foster children, Steven, Jonathan, and Caroline, who until recently had lived in the home with them. Next they were asked to choose miniatures that reflected their thoughts and feelings about each person in the family, including themselves.

As they made their selections (**Figure 11.2: Jenny: Foster Care Play Genogram**), Jenny and Joey talked about the other foster children who had lived with them and collaborated on items for them. They agreed on a cute baby elephant and a cupcake for Jonathan, and a wizard for Steven because, they agreed, he liked to do magic tricks. They chose a clown for Caroline because she had a cloth clown that she used to take to bed. They wondered if she still slept with it wherever she was now.

When they were finished choosing the miniatures, they were asked to talk about their choices. Jenny said she had chosen a mermaid for herself, because she felt like she was "under water" and that no one understood her.

She went on to say that if the mermaid came out of the water to live on dry land, she would die. This conversation would probably not have been possible if

Figure 11.2:   Jenny: Foster Care Play Genogram

Jenny were speaking directly about her feelings, since she thought talking about things was useless. But through the metaphor of the mermaid, she shared a profound expression of her existential dilemma in a relatively safe play situation.

Joey chose a young warrior figure carrying a weapon, stating that if he had that weapon he would always win. Clearly, having some way to protect himself was important to him. Both children expressed their feelings about their fears, losses, and sense of abandonment. They also spoke about their strengths. Joey had chosen the Cinderella figure to represent Jenny, saying that Cinderella is "pretty and nice." For their foster mother Joey picked a bride and Jenny chose the powerful Star Wars figure, Queen Amidala. Jenny described her foster mother as "a strong lady." For their foster father Joey chose a groom and Jenny chose a funny toy figure, because, as she said, he was funny and easy-going like the figure.

At 13 Jenny was able to use metaphors in her choice of miniatures to represent her feelings for each person. Joey's selections were more concrete, as would be expected of a nine-year-old. The play genogram is a good tool for working with children and families at various developmental levels. In future sessions Jenny and Joey were able to process their feelings further in a non-threatening way by referring to the figures in the play genogram, talking, for example, about how the Little Mermaid could be safe and about Cinderella's strengths. I used the metaphor of the mermaid and being "in the water" to further the discussion about Jenny's sense of alienation from other family members.

We began to focus on what it would be like to be "out" of the water, that is, if she were better understood by others. We noted that if she were out of the water, she would be joining all the other earth creatures in her play genogram. When I asked Jenny what it would be like for her on solid ground instead of in the water, she remarked that she would then have legs and wouldn't be "half-fish" anymore. "If I had legs, I could get places on my own, and maybe there would be places that I would like to visit. I might also like to play or run and maybe I would even learn to drive, if I had legs." She realized that legs gave her a sense of control and that allowed her to feel more mobile and more ready to take action on her own behalf.

We then talked a little about being understood. I asked her to make a list of all the things she would want anyone to understand about her and who she was most eager to be understood by. This led to a very fruitful discussion where she was able to recognize her own holding back more clearly. In future sessions Jenny included her biological family members on her play genogram and spoke about her feelings of anger and loss. She chose a heart with a crack through it for her mother and said she loved her mother and was heartbroken that she was in prison; she chose the Joker for her father, saying she always heard he was sneaky but had a sense of humor. For her sister Tammy she chose a puppy and said she was sweet and loyal, and that she missed her. By recognizing the many ways in which she was connected to the people in her life, Jenny began to process her feelings and express her emotions in a healthier way.

Materials Used for Family Play Genograms

The miniatures used in family play genograms are limited only by the therapist's imagination. At our institute (www.multiculturalfamily.org), we ourselves use small portable kits of miniature items, which can be bought in a dollar-store or craft store, including 2-3 inch play figures, doll house items, vehicles, trees, animals, buttons, and stones. More sophisticated items can be bought from play therapy sites on the internet or in children's or craft stores.

We recommend that therapists attend to the cultural and ethnic background of clients and make sure their collection of items reflects diverse cultures. The skin color of human figures is an obvious issue. It would, of course, be much harder for families of color to relate to a set of figures that have pink skin. Muslim families may resist depicting family members in human form and may prefer more symbolic representation. Another important cultural consideration is to provide items that represent multiple human environments—urban and rural, mountain and desert. We keep clay and paper available and encourage clients to make their own miniatures when they cannot find one among the selections available.

We have also sometimes used stickers and genogram collages to allow children to make family play genograms that they can take home. It is only a matter of time until there is a family play genogram program on the internet, which will allow family members to choose items and place them on their genogram, as they can now do with pictures of individuals in www.genopro.com to create a genogram with family pictures.

Additional Family Play Genogram Exercises

Depending on the clinical situation, the therapist's and family's imagination are the only limits for what can be done using family play genogram items. For specific cases, any of the following might prove useful:

- Doing a genogram of the family at a particular time in the past that was traumatic or difficult, such as a time of loss, adolescent intergenerational conflict, or cutoff.
- Doing a genogram that represents resources and sources of resilience, asking participants to pick items to represent people who have been particularly helpful or meaningful in their lives.
- Contextualizing a serious conflict in the immediate family by exploring specific relationships in the extended family.
- Conducting imaginary conversations among the miniatures chosen. For example, the therapist might ask a family: If the hummingbird and the horse (items representing the beloved grandfather who had just died) could have a conversation about the family, what might they say about Taisha's problem now? If the praying mantis (an 11-year-old boy's choice for his mother, who had lost custody due to accusations of abuse) could speak to the eagle figure (the boy's choice for himself), what do you think she might say? And then what would he say? And what might he say to the chameleon who became an eagle (the sister) or to the little bear cub (his baby brother)?
- Having a discussion about choices the family members made but then discarded.
- Asking family members to move their miniatures—for example, having the adolescent figure turn around to ask a parent a specific question.
- Having the client take the physical posture of his or her chosen miniature and explore how that feels.
- When there is serious conflict or cutoff, having family members choose items to represent themselves and each other at their most positive time in the past, at the worst moment in their relationship, and at a good moment in the future if they can solve the issues.

Play Genograms for Finding Family Resources

The Sansone family (**Figure 11.3: Sansone Family**) illustrates the value of play genograms for finding resources. The couple had been divorced for four years, and the daughters had one after the other begun spending most of their time with their father. The mother, who had struggled with drug and mood problems for some years, had recently lost custody of the 5-year-old son, after someone called the police about her behavior toward him in a shopping mall.

The father was overwhelmed by the parenting task and sought therapy.

Figure 11.3:   Sansone Family

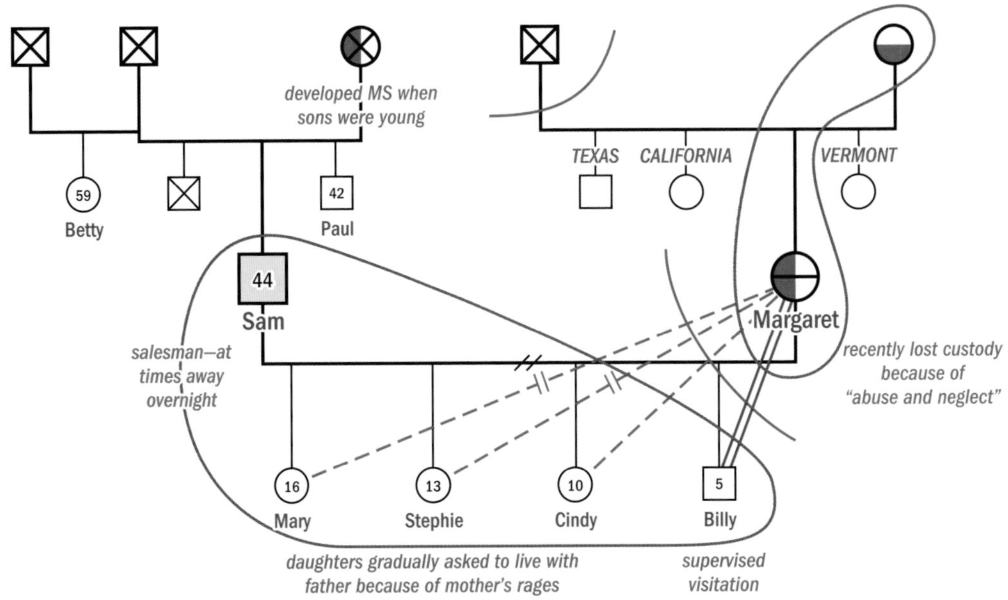

developed MS when
sons were young

TEXAS   CALIFORNIA   VERMONT

59
Betty   42
                                Paul

44
Sam

salesman—at
times away
overnight

Margaret

recently lost custody
because of
"abuse and neglect"

16   13   10   5
Mary   Stephie   Cindy   Billy

daughters gradually asked to live with   supervised
father because of mother's rages   visitation

Figure 11.4:   Sansone Resources Play Genogram

After a few conversations with members of the family, I (MM) decided to do a family play genogram with the children and their father. (**Figure 11.4: Sansone Resources Play Genogram**) I asked them each to choose items for each member of the immediate family and one other person whom they viewed as a resource. For the mother, the children chose: a dragon, a cobra, a man's bust split into dark and light, and a lobster, conveying the difficulties they had trusting and dealing with her. Verbally they had not been able to say much about her, and even now they seemed unwilling to elaborate much on their choices, especially the younger ones.

For the father they chose a business man, a computer, a rock representing "peace," and a clock because he was always hurrying them to be on time. For himself the father chose an eagle with spread wings because, he said, he felt he was always having to hover over his family. The youngest son chose a car to represent himself (young boys often choose cars to represent everyone in the family!), while the daughters represented themselves and each other through sports, fashion, and a pink panther. The father chose a young woman on skates, a guitar, a little dog for each of his three girls and a small boy for his son.

When they finished discussing their immediate family, they described the miniatures they chose for the person who might be able to help them in their current situation. The father, at first, said there was no one he could think of, but then chose a squeaking nun for his half-sister, 15 years his senior, who, he said, had been a mother figure for him and his younger brother when their mother had become ill. The three adolescent daughters all chose family friends—parents of their own friends, to whom they felt attached (represented by a monkey with a baby, a kangaroo, and a wizard), while the youngest son chose his dog, which made the others laugh because they all agreed their dog was their best, most loving resource!

The specifics that came out in creating the family play genogram enabled the family to acknowledge resources they could draw on for help. At the same time, it provided them an opportunity to share stories of good times with these extended "kin," which helped them feel more connected to each other. Over the next several weeks, they had a crisis when the father had to go out of town and couldn't think of anyone to call on for help. I wondered where the "nun" sister was. Initially he said calling her would be impossible; he just could not imagine asking her for help, but pressed to find a solution, he called her, and much to his surprise, she said she'd be more than happy to help. She soon became a much more involved support to her nieces and nephew.

Case of Alexis: Child Sexual Abuse in Remarried Family

Alexis was a 14-year-old Dominican-American girl who was sexually abused by her stepfather over a period of three years, from the time she was 10 years old until she was 13 (**Figure 11.5: Alexis**). The abuse finally stopped when she told her school counselor about it. Her stepfather was arrested, admitted to the sexual abuse, and was incarcerated. Alexis began acting out by staying out late, smoking cigarettes and marijuana, and cutting school. She remained in therapy for six months but refused to discuss the sexual abuse, saying that she had already talked about it, it was in the past, and she did not have any feelings about it anymore.

In therapy I (SP) constructed a genogram with Alexis and asked her to add anyone she wished to include (**Figure 11.6: Alexis Family Play Genogram**). She added her biological father's new family, her best friend, and her boyfriend. We drew a marriage line for her father's second marriage, and added his wife and their children (a girl and a boy) then a circle below for her best friend, Nancy, and a square for her boyfriend, Jimmy. Next Alexis was asked to choose a miniature to show her thoughts and feelings about everyone in the family, including herself.

She placed her biological father looking toward the two young children of his

Figure 11.5:   Alexis

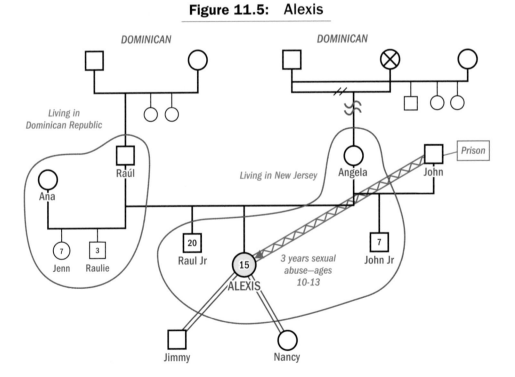

Figure 11.6: Alexis Family Play Genogram

second marriage, and away from Alexis' part of the family. She chose a very small female figure to represent herself, and what she referred to as "the queen" to represent her mother. She chose an ominous figure of an octopus man with weapons for her stepfather. These were all compelling visual representations of her feelings about herself and her parents. Rather than sharing my own observations, I asked her to tell me about her genogram.

She stated, "I chose this figure for my father because he is very handsome." Then she described all of the figures representing the children, stating why she chose each one. She said that she chose the pretty princess figure for her best friend "because she is pretty," and the "light-skinned guy" for her boyfriend because he is handsome and has light skin. She pointed to the small girl and baby miniatures representing her half-siblings and talked about how much fun she had with them when she visited her father in the Dominican Republic. For her older brother, Alexis chose the cartoon figure "Bart" because, as she described it, he is "always in trouble in high school. He can't get away with anything." Interestingly, she did not choose a miniature for her father's second wife. I chose not to comment on this initially, but made a mental note that she was likely avoiding her feelings about her father's new wife who was the reason her father left.

Alexis had not yet talked about the figures she chose for her mother or her stepfather. I asked her to tell me about them. This opened up the conversation and she said, "I chose this ugly guy with weapons for my stepfather because he looks mean and scary." She went on to say she hoped he would stay in jail and she worries that he may get out and come back into their home. She also talked about the figure she had chosen for her mother, stating that her mother had complete power over her. I asked her to tell me more about this. She answered by expressing feelings of fear, anger, and powerlessness. She talked about her biological father's role, saying that if he had been there for her "none of this would have happened." Placing her father's miniature looking away from her family and toward his younger children from his second marriage was a powerful visual representation of her feelings of abandonment.

The play genogram opened up the possibility of Alexis talking about her feelings regarding the sexual abuse, even though she thought she had nothing more to say about it. She also discussed her ambivalence about her mother's power in various ways. Her mother had been powerless when her stepfather was abusing her. Yet her mother gained power as she learned about the abuse and took action to protect Alexis. She had testified against him and then filed for divorce. Alexis said that she felt sometimes that her mother had too much power over her. On the other hand, she said her mother was using her power for good and she was protecting her children.

We took a picture of the play genogram for the file. In later sessions Alexis used this play experience to discuss how the queen became more powerful when she gained knowledge. In the process she recognized that her own figure seemed small and she wondered if her new knowledge increased her power. Working with the metaphors helped Alexis to process her feelings of fear, anger, and powerlessness, and to envision new possibilities for her future.

A few months later I asked Alexis to once again choose items for her play genogram. She chose different items for herself and for her mother, and she added figures for other family members. She chose a larger and more playful miniature for herself and a hen tending her eggs for her mother. She had reconnected with her father and her family living in the Dominican Republic when she visited them during her summer vacation. She began to feel more supported by her family, and this time she added her grandmothers and aunts. Clearly, she was feeling she had more family support by including all these relatives, whose miniatures conveyed quite specific strengths. She was feeling stronger herself, and seemed more connected to her extended family. She was also getting along better with her mother and seeing her as a loving mother hen who would protect her rather than someone who wielded power over her. As can be seen in **Figure 11.7: Alexis Family Play Genogram 2**, she did not yet seem ready to work on her new stepmother.

Figure 11.7:   Alexis Family Play Genogram 2

The Nogucis: A Family of Outsiders

The Noguci family (**Figure 11.8: Noguci Family**) sought help for their 14-year-old son, Brandon, who was refusing to go to school, staying up or out all night, sleeping all day, and destroying furniture when confronted by his parents about his refusal to obey even the most minimal rules. The father, Koji, was a graphic designer who had come to the U.S. from Japan to study art. The mother, Terry, was an art teacher from a working-class Irish background, who had met Koji in college.

Koji and Terry came in feeling that they were not good parents. They thought they were being asked to do something they could not do and were therefore failures. They had been told what to do—namely, to set firmer limits—but they had not been able to do this. They were angry at each other and at the school, as well as at their son. They seemed unable to have any sustained conversation as a couple; their only attempts at conversation were about Brandon.

Although the parents were cooperative in giving genogram information, they did not appear to see their history as relevant, and they were extremely defensive about being asked to participate in therapy. They strongly resisted thinking systemically, perhaps because they were deeply cut off from their families of origin

Figure 11.8:   Noguci Family

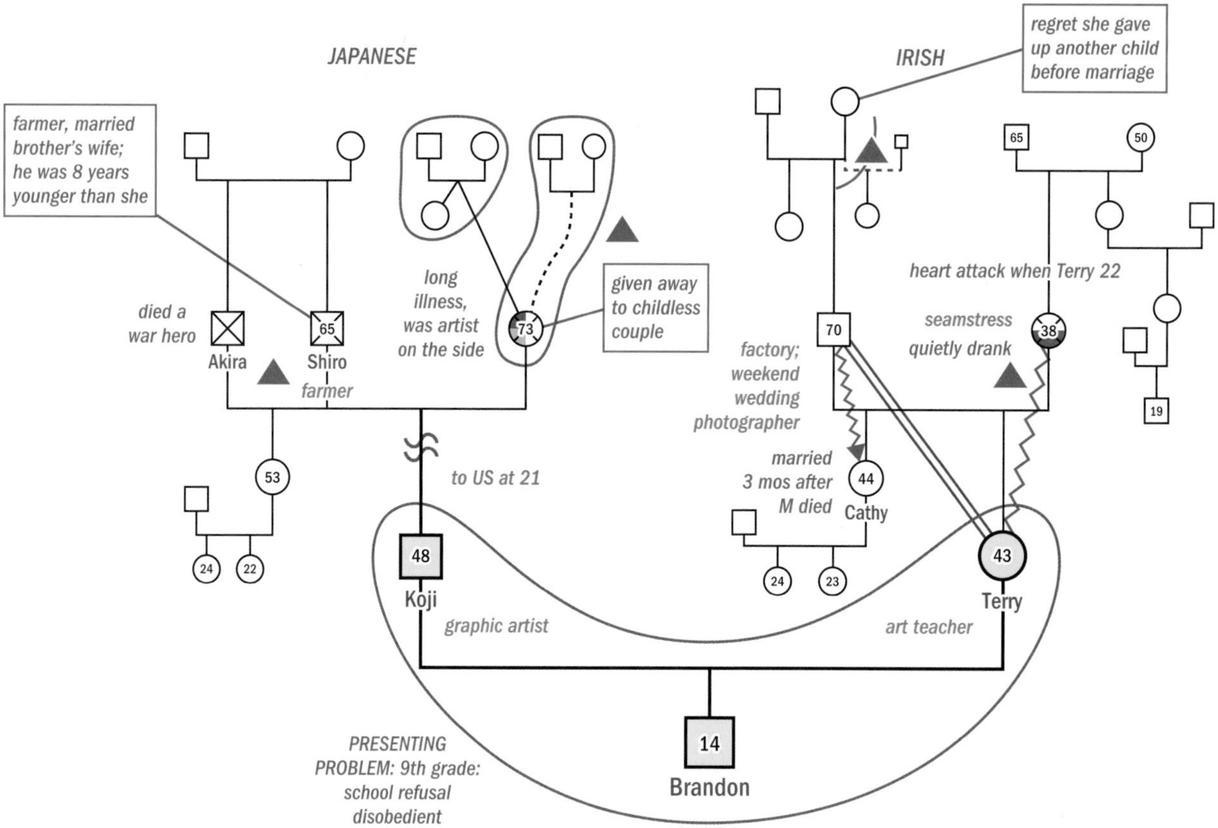

and did not want to identify with them. This seemed to leave them totally lost about how to relate to their son. Brandon was also stuck, unable to move beyond being a child. His parents seemed unable to help him negotiate passage through adolescence toward adulthood.

Because his parents never clarified boundaries, he seemed unclear which generation he belonged to. Whenever the therapist tried to focus on the parents' setting limits or on their relationship with each other, they withdrew or seemed annoyed. Brandon was in general non-responsive in therapy, whether he was with his parents or alone. In an attempt to engage him in a nonverbal medium, the therapist asked him to make a sand tray world using miniatures. In an eloquent expression of his stuckness, Brandon was unable to make even a single choice to include in the sand tray, until his parents joined the session. At that point, encouraged by his father, he reluctantly contributed a few figures.

The following week the therapist decided to do a family play genogram, hoping to help the family in their connectedness to their history and to each other. The family's genogram was drawn on a large piece of paper. Each family member was asked to pick a figure for him or herself and then for the others in the family. (**Figure 11.9: Noguci Family Play Genogram**).

There was, surprisingly, much discussion, inquiry, and laughter about the choices. Brandon insisted on bringing into the family play genogram the items he had included in his sand tray the previous week (a purple monster for himself, a dead chicken for his maternal grandfather, an elephant for his uncle, and the young lion cub for his father). This continuity from the previous exercise was the first indication of continuity or "belonging" since the therapy had begun.

Terry's choices for her parents led to the first open exploration of her struggle to figure out her place in her family of origin. She chose a rolling pin for her mother and went on to talk about how she'd always felt that she belonged to her father and her sister belonged to her mother, whom she described as a "very boring housewife." Her complex feelings for her parents and sister had been compounded by her mother's sudden death from a heart attack when Terry was 22. Her older sister Cathy married and left the state within the next six months, just at the time Terry was graduating from college and was about to leave home herself. She had

Figure 11.9: Noguci Family Play Genogram

felt abandoned by her sister, and at the same time guilty that her father had always favored her over her sister. As she was talking about this, Brandon asked her why she chose a cat for her father and a mouse for her sister. She said, with some intensity, that though she had loved her father, she recognized that he had always been cruel to her sister.

Exploration of Koji's side of the genogram led to an interesting discussion about why he had also distanced from his family. Koji had chosen a soldier to play his uncle, Akira, his mother's first husband, and a dog to represent his father, Shiro, because, he said, he always thought of his father as weak. He had chosen a stretcher bed to represent his mother.

Terry's mystification about these choices led Koji to explain several experiences he had hardly remembered himself until triggered by the play genogram. He had grown up not knowing his family history. At age eight he asked his older sister why their father's picture was kept on the altar with the pictures of all the dead relatives. The sister laughed and told the parents, who were also amused, that he had confused his father Shiro, with his uncle, Akiro, who had died in the war. Koji felt humiliated at being laughed at and took from the experience that he was an "outsider" in his family and could not ask the true history.

It was not until Koji was an adult and leaving for America that his mother, by then quite ill with arthritis and heart disease, told him how grateful she had felt to his father, Shiro, who was eight years younger than she, for agreeing to marry her and take in her little daughter from the first marriage. Otherwise, she told him, she would have had nowhere to go. She told him also that, as a twin in her own family of origin, her parents had given her away to be raised by an older childless couple, while her twin sister was raised by their parents. She had cared for the couple who raised her, but both of them had been frail and died soon after her marriage to Akira.

Koji said he had chosen the stretcher for his mother because she was always ill. At that moment Brandon, who had not chosen an item for this grandmother, whom he had never known, went over to the shelf of miniatures and chose an attractively decorated woman figure, which he placed on the bed to be his grandmother.

Koji said that after what his mother told him, he felt perhaps his father had never been able to replace his older brother Akira, the military hero who died in glory. Being only a farmer, with less education than his older brother, the father took the responsibility for his brother's wife, but could never really take the place of his war hero brother, so he too felt like an outsider—as if he did not belong in his family. He grew up not understanding his history and felt he could not ask about it.

Koji was thus the child of parents who had both seemed to feel that they were outsiders compared to their more desirable siblings. Perhaps when he formed a family with Terry, who herself had an impaired sense of belonging in her family, they complemented each other. Terry seemed to feel she was too central for her father, at the expense of her mistreated sister, and then her family fell apart before she was ready to launch.

Through the creation of the family play genogram, both parents began to tell their stories to each other. Brandon was able to participate, perhaps helping give his family a new-found sense of connectedness in the process. As the three of them shared the meaning of the figures they had chosen to represent themselves, each other, and the extended family, they seemed to join for the first time in being a family who could surmount their difficult history and find a way of belonging with each other. Both parents laughed about the miniatures they had chosen for themselves.

Terry had chosen a "Where's Waldo" figure, which she described as someone who has an idea where he's going, but it's hard for others to find him. Father and son both agreed that this was a very accurate description of her. Interestingly, both father and son's choices for Terry showed her strengths more clearly: Koji chose a paint palate because he said his wife was very creative and Brandon chose a pony, which he saw as appealing and active.

Koji chose a seal for himself, saying he thought at times he was slippery like a seal. But then he added that he had also the chosen seal because of its power and ability to swim fast. Terry had chosen a solid man for her husband, suggesting she saw him differently from how he saw himself.

The miniatures seemed to become an avenue for them to begin talking about the roles they were playing in relation to the roles they wanted to play. Even Brandon's choice for himself, the purple monster with outstretched arms, seemed almost to be making a joke of intimidation. Meanwhile, the parents had chosen symbols of a little duck and a little dog for him, both of which seemed to that suggest someone who needs protection.

In a follow-up discussion with Koji about his role, we wondered if he might not find some position that could be between the powerful, intimidating symbols of the soldier or the dog that he had chosen to represent his uncle and his father, and the symbols he and his wife and son had offered (seal, lion cub, man). Their choices in the family play genogram seemed to indicate that the parents needed to take a stronger, more protective role with their son, and had been hampered by their history in doing this.

Both Brandon and Terry also seemed to be suggesting alternative perspectives to Koji about his mother. Brandon's choice had been a beautiful woman. Terry's choice was a bird, which, interestingly, reminded Koji that his mother had had a beautiful voice and loved to sing when she was young.

There seemed a similar suggestion about Terry's mother. Terry had represented her with a rolling pin, reflecting her constrained role as housewife, while Brandon's choice of the Loch Ness Monster, which at first seemed incongruent, might suggest instead a power that goes beyond death and beyond what can be seen.

This session became a key experience we could refer back to with a kind of shorthand to encourage Terry and Koji to take a stronger position in relation to their son, labeling him as a "play monster" rather than a real monster, who, like a little duck, needed to be taught to swim. Soon after this session both parents were able to follow through on limits for Brandon, to the extent that they insisted he have consequences and go to court to appear before a judge for his truancy. When the judge gave a strong message that it was either school or jail until he was 16, Brandon began going to school.

Combining play, imagination, and creativity with the genogram history often has the effect of opening up families to their history on a deeper level. Perhaps the element of play lowered Koji and Terry's defenses and resistance. Also, perhaps the fact that both parents were artists allowed them to feel more comfortable using the expression of artistic play, helping free them up verbally and emotionally to deal with their issues. The miniatures led Koji in particular to make connections with deep childhood feelings he might not have been able to describe in words. In any case, the family play genogram provided the Nogucis with a structure within which the parents could share stories about their families of origin that they had never really understood themselves, and certainly never shared before. Somehow the metaphors of the miniatures seemed to enable them to convey something about where they were coming from that, in turn, enabled them to begin to transform their roles with each other. Brandon needed clear and definite limit-setting, which the parents, not conscious of how much they had always thought of themselves as outsiders, had been unable to set for him. Through this exercise and the specific items they chose, the family made use of the concrete, symbolic, and non-threatening structure of the play genogram to confront their history and change their present.

Summary

Family play genograms can be used with individuals alone or in couple and family sessions. Symbols and metaphors can help broaden clients' articulation of their family history, relationships, conflicts, alliances, strengths, and vulnerabilities. Toys can also have the effect of lightening up difficult areas by miniaturizing looming dilemmas, and by allowing for management and problem-solving in a distanced way. Family play genograms may in fact reduce resistance to introspection and self-disclosure and ignite playful energy, which is a useful motivator of creative change. They can also help families access sources of resilience and different images of themselves and each other.

Appendix

The Genogram Map

- Symbols and Map Structure- show the family members' legal and biological relationship to each other for generally 3 or more generations. Symbols are used also to show non-biological kinship connections to friends, godparents, pets and other important relationships.
- Relationship Lines showing emotional patterns of family members are the least precise aspect of the genogram, especially because relationships are always changing. But these lines can convey at least a rudimentary sense of family members' relationships including closeness, distance, conflict, cutoff, physical and sexual abuse, and caretaking relationships.
- Other symbols indicate functioning of family members (addiction, mental or physical illness, secrets, migration, and connection to community resources, etc.)
- Family information typically indicated on a genogram includes:
  - Age, Dates of Birth, Marriage, Separation, Divorce, Migration
  - Ethnic Background
  - Religion
  - Current Location
  - Education
  - Occupation
  - Military Service
  - Trouble with the law, emotional or physical problems or disabilities,
  - Social or Community groups members belong to (e.g. AA, Fraternities, political groups

- Therapists and other key professionals involved with family members

Outline for a Brief Genogram Interview

- Start with the Presenting Problem
    - What help are they seeking?
    - When did the problem begin?
    - Who noticed it, how do others view it, and how have family members responded to it?
    - What are family relationships like and have they been changed by the problem?
    - What will happen if the problem continues?
    - What is their greatest hope for change?
- Ask about Household Context
    - Who lives in the household (name, age, gender, occupation, health status)?
    - Where do other family members live?
    - Have they ever had a similar problem in the family before?
    - What solutions have been tried in the past to deal with this or similar problems (therapy, hospitalization, doctor visits, religious helper, family member, medication, etc.?)
    - Have there been any recent changes in the family (people moving in or out, illness)?
    - Ask about Family of Origin:
    - Parents and Grandparents (names, ages, occupation, couple status, health status, dates of birth and death, ethnicity, religion, migration)?
    - Gender roles and rules in the family?
    - Life Events & Stressors: untimely or traumatic deaths, illness, conflicts, cut-offs, resilience, physical or sexual abuse?
    - Relationships: special closeness, over or under-functioning, angels or villains, conflict, cut-off?
- Ask about Family Members' Strengths
    - What are they good at? Talents, Sports, Interpersonal skills, Love of Nature
    - Humor, music, art, work, hobbies?
- What are their Sources of Hope & Resilience

- Spirituality or religion,
- Friends, social and/or community connections,
- Nature, Music, Art, Work, etc.

Patterns to Track on a Genogram

- Relational Patterns and Triangles
  - Power: physical, psychological, financial, career, intellectual, emotional
  - Level of connection or isolation of family members
  - Balance of Over or Underfunctioning, Closeness/Distance, Good Guys/Bad Guys etc.
- Sibling Patterns related to gender, distance apart in age, naming, abilities and disabilities
- Loss
  - Especially untimely, traumatic, ambiguous
  - Concurrence of multiple losses
  - Unresolved Mourning- Ability to recover from an emotionally painful loss, such as a suicide or from the disruptive impact of loss, such as of a primary caretaker or breadwinner.
- Families Through the Life Cycle and Critical Life Events
  - Timing or Off-Timing of Life Cycle Transitions: birth, launching, forming couple relationships, leaving home, educational and career paths, caretaking, death.
  - Cohort for each key family member, that is time & place in history when they grew up. What was the ethos of their era?
  - Moves & Migration
- Missing Information, Discrepancies, & Secrets
  - Encouraging patients' curiosity about secrets and missing information.
  - Encouraging patients' sleuthfulness regarding DNA, genealogical information and interviewing family and family friends to fill in gaps or un-bury secrets.
- Coincidences of Dates
  - Several stressors happening around the same time: may lead to cut-offs, anxiety, illness, marriages following a loss, etc.
  - Stressors happening at the same age or life cycle stage as in previous generations.

References

Adler, A. (1959). *The practice and theory of individual psychology.* Paterson, NJ: Littlefield, Adams.

Ahrons, C. (1998). *The good divorce.* New York, NY: Harper Paperbacks.

Alexander, D., & Clark, S. (1998). Keeping "the family" in focus during patient care. In P. D. Sloane, L. M. Slat, P. Curtis, & M. H. Ebell (Eds.), *Essentials of Family Medicine* (3rd ed., pp. 25–39). Baltimore, MD: Williams & Wilkins.

Altshuler, S. J. (1999). Constructing genograms with children in care: Implications for casework practice. *Child Welfare, 78*(6), 777–790.

American Academy of Family Physicians. (n.d). Retrieved Feb 14, 2019, from https://www.aafp.org/about.html

Andres, F.D., & Lorio, J.P. (1974). Georgetown family symposia: A collection of selected papers (Vol 1). Washington, DC: Family Section, Department of Psychiatry, Georgetown University Medical Center.

Anonymous. (1972). On the differentiation of self. In J. Framo (Ed.). *Family interaction: A dialogue between family researchers and family therapists.* New York: Springer.

Anonymous. Mandala. (2019). Wikipedia article. Accessed March 27, 2019. https://en.wikipedia.org/wiki/Mandala \

Anzieu, D. (1986). *Freud's self-analysis.* Madison, CT: International Universities Press.

Appignanesi, L., & Forrester, J. (1992). *Freud's women.* New York: Basic Books.

Arora, K, & Baima, T. (2016). Friendship across the life cycle. In M. McGoldrick, N. Garcia Preto, & B. Carter, B (Eds.). *The expanding family life cycle: Individual, family and social perspectives,* (5th ed.). New York:New York: Pearson.

Aten, J.D., Madson, M.B., & Johnston Kruse, S. (2008). The supervision genogram: A tool for preparing supervisors-in-training. *Psychotherapy Theory Research & Training, 45*(1), 111–116.

Bair, D. (2003). *Jung: A biography.* New York, NY: Little Brown.

Baird, M.A., & Grant, W.D. (1994). Families and health. In R.B. Taylor, A.K. David, T.A. Johnson, Jr., D.M. Phillips, & J.E. Scherger (Eds.). *Family medicine principles and practice* (4th ed., pp. 10–15). New York: Springer-Verlag.

Baird, M.A., & Grant, W.D. (1998). Families and health. In R.B. Taylor, A. K. David, T. A. Johnson, Jr., D. M. Phillips, & J. E. Scherger (Eds.), *Family medicine principles and practice* (5th ed., pp. 26–31). Baltimore, MD: Williams & Wilkins

Bank, S. P., & Kahn, M.D. (1997). *The sibling bond.* New York: Basic Books.

Banmen, J. (2002). The Satir model: Yesterday and today. Contemporary Family Therapy: An International Journal, *24*(1), 3–22, March.

Bannerman, C. (1986). The genogram and elderly patients. *Journal of Family Practice, 23*(5), 426–427.

Barlow, N. (1958). *The autobiography of Charles Darwin 1809–1882.* New York, NY: W. W. Norton.

Barth, J.C. (1993). *It runs in my family: Overcoming the legacy of family illness.* New York: Brunner/Mazel.

Bateson, G. (1979). Mind and nature. New York: Bantham.

Bateson, M.C. (1984). *With a daughter's eye.* New York: William Morrow & Co.

Beck, R.L. (1987). The genogram as process. *American Journal of Family Therapy, 15*(4), 343–351.

Bepko, C.S. & Krestan. J. (1985). *The responsibility trap: Women and men in alcoholic families.* New York,: Free Press.

Bernikow, L. (1980). *Among women.* New York: Harper & Row.

Bowen, M. (Anonymous) (1972). On the differentiation of self. In Family Interaction: A Dialogue Between Family Researchers and Family Therapists, (Ed. J. Framo)., N.Y. Springer.

Bowen, M. (1978a). *Family therapy in clinical practice.* New York: Jason Aronson.

Bowen, M. (1978b). *Family therapy in clinical practice.* New York: Jason Aronson.

Bowen, M., & Butler, J. (2013). *The origins of family psychotherapy.* New York: Jason Aronson.

Boyd-Franklin, N. (2006). *Black families in therapy: Understanding the African American experience, (2nd ed.).* New York: Guilford.

Bradt. J. (1980). *The family diagram.* Washington. DC: Groome Center.

Bragg, M. (1990). *Richard Burton: A life.* New York: Warner Books.

Brott, P.E. (2001). The storied approach: A postmodern perspective for career counseling. *The Career Development Quarterly, 49*(4), 304–313

Burke, J.L., & Faber, P. (1997). A genogrid for couples. *Journal of Gay and Lesbian Social Services, 7*(1), 13–22.

Butler, J.F. (2008). The family diagram and genogram: Comparisons and contrasts. *American Journal of Family Therapy, 36*(3), 169–180.

Byng-Hall, J. (2004). Loss and family scripts. In F. Walsh & M. McGoldrick (Eds.), *Living beyond loss: Death and the family.* New York: W. W. Norton.

Callas, J. (1989). *Sisters.* New York: St. Martin's.

Campbell, C. (1998). *The real Diana.* New York: St. Martin's.

Campbell, T.L., McDaniel, S.H., Cole-Kelly, K., Hepworth, J., & Lorenz, A. (2002). Family interviewing: A review of the literature in primary care. *Family Medicine, 34*(5), 312–318.

Caplow, T. (1968). *Two against one: Coalitions in triads.* Englewood Cliffs. NJ: Prentice Hall.

Carter, B. (1991). Death in the therapist's own family. In M. McGoldrick, C. Anderson, & F. Walsh (Eds.), *Living beyond loss: Death in the family.* New York: Norton.

Carter, E.A. (1982). Supervisory discussion in the presence of the family. In R. Whiffen & J. Byng-Hall (Eds.), *Family therapy supervision.* London: Academic Press.

Carter, E.A., & McGoldrick, M. (1976). Family therapy with one person and the family therapist's own family. In P. Guerin (Ed.), *Family therapy.* New York: Gardner.

Chrzastowski, S.K. (2011). A narrative perspective on genograms: Revisiting classical family therapy methods. *Clinical Child Psychiatry and Psychiatry, 16*(4), 635–644.

Chappell, N.L. (1991). *Social supports and aging.* Toronto: Butterworths.

Christie-Seely, J. (1986). A diagnostic problem and family assessment. *Journal of Family Practice, 22*(4), 329–339.

Cicirelli, V.G. (1989). Feelings of attachment to siblings and well-being in later life. *Psychology and Aging, 4*(2), 211–216.

Cicirelli, V.G. (1995). *Sibling relationships across the life span.* New York: Plenum.

Clinton, B. (2005). *My life.* New York: Vintage.

Clinton Kelly, V., with Morgan, J. (1994). *My life: Leading with my heart.* New York: Pocket Books.

Cohen, E. & Brown Clark, S. (2010). *John Romano and George Engel: Their lives and work.* Rochester, NY: Meliora Press.

Cohler, B.A., Hosteler, J., & Boxer, A. (1998). Generativity, social context, and lived experience: Narratives of gay men in middle adulthood. In D. McAdams & E. de St. Aubin (Eds.), *Generativity and adult development. Psychosocial perspective on caring and contributing to the next generation.* Washington, DC: American Psychological Association Press.

Colon, F. (1973). In search of one's past: An identity trip. *Family Process, 12*(4), 429–38.

Colon, F. (1978). Family ties and child placement. *Family Process. 17*(3), 189–312.

Colon, F (2019). The discovery of my multicultural identity. In M. McGoldrick. (Ed.). *Revisioning family therapy: Race, culture and gender in clinical practice.* New York: Guilford.

Colon-Lopez, F. (2005). *Finding my face: The memoir of a Puerto Rican American.* Victoria, BC, Canada: Trafford Publishing.

Congress, E.P. (1994). The use of culturagrams to assess and empower culturally diverse families. *Families in Society, 75*(9), 531–540.

Connidis, I.A., & Barnett, A.E. (2018). *Family ties & aging* (3rd ed). New York: Sage.

Crouch, M.A. (1986). Working with one's own family: Another path for professional development. *Family Medicine, 18*(2), 93–98.

Crouch, M.A. (1989). A putative ancestry of family practice and family medicine: Genogram of a discipline. *Family Systems Medicine, 7*(2), 208–212.

Crouch M.A. (2004). A new triangle participant: Commentary on van Walsum, Lawson, and Bramson. *Families, Systems, & Health, 22*(4), 477–480.

Crouch, M.A. (2016). A breath of fresh air: A family ceremony. *Families, Systems, & Health, 34*(1), 64–66.

Crouch, M. & Davis, T. (1987). Using the genogram (family tree) clinically. In M. Crouch & L. Roberts (Eds.), *The family in medical practice: A family systems primer.* New York: Springer–Verlag.

Crouch, M. & Roberts, L. (Eds.). (1987). *The family in medical practice: A family systems primer.* New York: Springer.

Daily Mail Reporter. (2011). Still holding on to his son's legacy: Steve Jobs' biological father clings to his iPhone as he reveals his grief. Retrieved from https://www.dailymail.co.uk/news/article-2047588/

Steve-Jobs-dead-Father-Abdulfattah-John-Jandali -son-met.html

Darkenwald, G.G., & Silvestri, K. (1992). *Analysis and assessment of the Newark Literacy Campaign: A report to the Ford Foundation.* Newark, NJ: Newark Literacy Campaign.

Daughhetee, C. (2001). Using genograms as a tool for insight in college counseling. Journal of College Counseling, 4(1), 73–76.

Davis, O. & Dee, R. (2000). *With Ossie and Ruby: In this life together.* New York: Harper Collins

Dean, P.H. (1989). Paul Robeson. In E. Hill (Ed.), *Black heroes: Seven plays.* New York: Applause Theatre Book Publishers.

Desmond, A. & Moore, J. (1991). *Darwin: The life of a tormented evolutionist.* New York: W.W. Norton.

Dumas, C.A., Katerndahl, D.A., & Burge, S.K. (1995). Familial patterns in patients with infrequent panic attacks. *Archives of Family Medicine, 4*(10), 862–867.

Dunn, A.B., & Dawes, S.J. (1999). Spiritually-focused genograms: Keys to uncovering spiritual resources in African American families. *Journal of Multicultural Counseling & Development, 27*(4), 240–255.

Dunn, A.B. & Levitt, M.M., (2000). July. The genogram: From diagnostics to mutual collaboration. *Family Journal: Counseling and therapy for Couples and Families, 8*(3). 236–244.

Eissler, K.R. (1978). *Sigmund Freud: His life in pictures and words.* New York: Helen & Kurt Wolff Books, Harcourt Brace, Jovanovich.

Elder, G.H., Jr. (1977). Family history and the life course. *Journal of Family History, 2*(4), 279–304.

Elder, G.H. (1986). Military times and turning points in mens' lives. *Developmental Psychology, 22*(2), 233–245.

Elder, G. (1992). Life course. In E. Borgatta & M. Borgatta (Eds.), *Encyclopedia of sociology* (Vol. 3, 1120–1130), New York: Macmillan.

Ellenberger, H.F. (1970). *The discovery of the unconscious: The history and evolution of dynamic psychiatry.* New York: Basic Books.

Emerson S. (1995). A different final exam: using students' own family genograms. *The Family Journal, 3*(1), 57–58.

Engel, G. (1975). The death of a twin: Mourning and anniversary reactions: Fragments of 10 years of self-analysis. *International Journal of Psychoanalysis, 56* (l), 23–40.

Erikson Bloland, S. (2005). *In the shadow of fame: A memoir by the daughter of Erik H. Erikson.* New York: Viking.

Erlanger, M. A. (1990). Using the genogram with the older client. Journal of Mental Health Counseling 12(3): 321–331.

Estrada, A.U., & Haney, P. (1998). Genograms in a multicultural perspective. *Journal of Family Psychotherapy, 9*(2), 55–62.

Falicov, C. J. (2012). Immigrant family processes: A multidimensional framework. In F. Walsh (Ed.), *Normal family processes* (4th ed., pp 297–323). New York: Guilford Press.

Falicov. C. J. (2015*). Latino families in therapy: A guide to multicultural practice* (2nd ed.). New York: Guilford Press.

Falicov, C. J. (2016). Migration and the Family life cycle. In M. McGoldrick, N. Garcia Preto, & B. Carter (Eds.), *The expanded family life cycle* (5th ed.). Boston, MA: Pearson.

Fink, A.H., Kramer, L., Weaver, L.L., & Anderson, J. (1993). More on Genograms: Modifications to a model. *Journal of Child and Adolescent Group Therapy, 3*(4), 203–206.

Fishel, E. (1979). *Sisters: Love and rivalry inside the family and beyond.* New York: William Morrow.

Fogarty, T. (1973). *Triangles. The Family.* New Rochelle, NY: Center for Family Learning.

Fonda, P. (1998). *Don't tell dad.* New York: Hyperion.

Foster, M.A., Jurkovic, G. J., Ferdinand, L. G., & Meadows, L. A. (2002). The impact of the genogram on couples: A manualized approach. *The Family Journal. 10*(1), pp. 34–40.

Frame, M.W. (1996). Counseling African Americans: Integrating spirituality in therapy. *Counseling & Values, 41*(1), 16–29.

Frame, M.W. (2000a). Constructing religious/spiritual genograms. In R.E. Watts (Ed.), *Techniques in marriage and family counseling, Vol. 1. The family psychology and counseling series*, pp. 69–74.

Frame, M.W. (2000b). The spiritual genogram in family therapy. *Journal of Marital and Family Therapy, 26*(2), 211–216.

Frame, M.W. (2001). The spiritual genogram in training and supervision. *The Family Journal, 9*(2), 109–115.

Framo, J. (Ed.). (1972). *Family Interaction: A dialogue between family researchers and family therapists.* New York: Springer.

Freeman, L., & Strean, H.S. (1981). *Freud and women.* New York: Frederick Ungar Publishing Company.

Freire, P. (1994). *The pedagogy of hope.* New York: Continuum.

Freud, E.L. (Ed.). 1975. *The letters of Sigmund Freud.* New York: Basic Books.

Freud, S. (1988). *My three mothers and other passions.* New York: New York University Press.

Friedman, E.H. (1971). The birthday party: An experiment in obtaining change in one's own extended family. *Family Process, 10*(2), 345–349.

Friedman, E. H. (1985). *Generation to generation: Family*

process in church and synagogue. New York: Guilford Press.

Friedman, E. H. (1987). The birthday party revisited: Family therapy and the problem of change. In P. Titelman (Ed.), *The therapist's own family.* New York: Jason Aronson.

Friedman, E. H. (2007). *A failure of nerve: Leadership in the age of the quick fix.* New York: Seabury Books.

Friedman, H. L., & Krakauer, S. (1992). Learning to draw and interpret standard and time-line genograms: An experimental comparison. *Journal of Family Psychology, 6*(1), 77–83.

Friedman, H., Rohrbaugh, M., & Krakauer, S. (1988). The timeline genogram: Highlighting temporal aspects of family relationships. *Family Process, 27*(3), 293–304.

Friedman. L. J. (1999). *Identity's architect.* New York: Scribner.

Friesen, P., & Manitt, J. (1991). Nursing the remarried family in a palliative care setting. *Journal of Palliative Care, 6*(4), 32–39.

Garrett, R.E., Klinkman, M. & Post, L. (1987). If you meet Buddha on the road, take a genogram: Zen and the art of family medicine. *Family Medicine,19*(3), 225–226.

Gartner, J. (2008). *In search of Bill Clinton: A psychological biography.* New York: St. Martin's Press.

Gelb, A., & Gelb, B. (1987). *O'Neill.* New York: Harper & Row.

Genetic Geneology, https://thegeneticgenealogist.com. Retrieved 8/17/19.

Gerson, R., Hoffman, S., Sauls, M., & Ulrichi, D. (1993). Family-of-origin frames in couples therapy. *Journal of Marital and Family Therapy, 19*(4), 341–354.

Gewirtzman, R. C. (1988). The genogram as a visual assessment of a family's fugue. *Australian Journal of Sex, Marriage and Family, 9*(1), 37–46.

Gibson, D. (2005). The use of genograms in career counseling with elementary, middle, and high school students. *Career Development Quarterly, 53*(4), 353–362.

Gil, E. (2003). Play genograms. In C.E. Sorit & L.L. Hecker (Eds.), *The therapist's notebook for children and adolescents: Homework, handouts, and activities for use in psychotherapy* (pp. 97–118). New York: Haworth Press.

Gil, E. (2015). Play in family therapy. 2nd edition. New York: Guilford Press. Ch 11.

Gil, E. (1991). The healing power of play: Working with abused children. New York: Guilford Press.

Gladwell, M. (2008). *Outliers: The story of success.* New York: Little Brown & Co.

Glosoff, H.L., & Durham, J.C. (2011). Using supervision to prepare social justice counseling advocates. *Counselor Education and Supervision, 50*(2), 116–129.

Golden, E., & Mohr, R. (2000). Issues and techniques for counseling long-term, later-life couples. *Family Journal: Counseling & Therapy for Couples & Families, 8*(3), 229–235.

Goodman, R.D. (2013). The transgenerational trauma and resilience genogram. *Counseling Psychology Quarterly, 26*(3), 386–405.

Goodyear-Brown, P. (2001). The preschool play genogame. In H.G. Kaduson & C.E. Schaefer (Eds.), *101 more favorite therapy techniques* (pp. 225-228). Northvale, NJ: Jason Aronson.

Gordon H. (1972). The family history and the pedigree chart. *Postgrad Med, 52*(2), 123–125.

Gordon-Reed, A. (2008). *The Hemingses of Monticello: An American family.* New York: W. W. Norton.

Graham, L.O. (2000). *Our kind of people: Inside America's Black upper class.* New York: Harper.

Granello, D.H., Hothersall, D. & Osborne, A.L. (2000). The academic genogram: Teaching for the future by learning from the past. *Counselor Education and Supervision, 39*(3), 177–188.

Green, L.A., Graham, R., Bagley, B., Kilo, C.M., Spann, S.J., Bogdewic, S.P., & Swanson, J. (2004). Task force 1. Report of the task force on patient expectations, core values, reintegration, and the new model of family medicine. *Annals of Family Medicine, 2*(1), S1:S33–S50.

Greenwald, J.L., Grant, W.D., Kamps, C.A., & Haas-Cunningham, S. (1998). The genogram scale as a predictor of high utilization in a family practice. *Family, Systems & Health, 16*(4), 375–391.

Guerin, P.J. (Ed.). (1976). *Family therapy.* New York: Gardner.

Guerin P.J., & Pendagast E.G. (1976). Evaluation of family system and genogram. In P.J. Guerin (Ed.), *Family Therapy: Theory and Practice* (pp. 450–64). NY: Gardner Press.

Guerin, P., & Fogarty, T. (1972). The family therapist's own family. *International Journal of Psychiatry, 10*(1). 6–22.

Guerin, P., Fogarty, T.F., Fay, L.F., & Kautto, J.G. (1996). *Working with relationship triangles.* New York: Guilford.

Gutierrez, C., & Scheid P. (2019). The history of family medicine and its impact on U.S. health care delivery. Retrieved from https://www.aafpfoundation.org/content/dam/foundation/documents/who-we-are/cfhm/FMImpactGutierrezScheid.pdf

Gwyther, L. (1986). Family therapy with older adults. *Generations, 10*(3), 42–45.

Hall, C. M. (1987). Efforts to differentiate a self in my

family of origin. In P. Titelman (Ed.), *The therapist's own family*. New York: Jason Aronson.

Hardy, K.V. (2018). Family therapy with poor families. In M. McGoldrick & K.V. Hardy (Eds.), *Revisioning family therapy* (3rd ed.). New York: Guilford.

Hardy, K.V., & Laszloffy, T.A. (1995). The cultural genogram: Key to training culturally competent family therapists. *Journal of Marital and Family Therapy, 21*(3), 227–237.

Harmon, A. (2006, June 11). Who's your Great-Great-Great-Great-Granddaddy? *New York Times*, retrieved from https://www.nytimes.com/2006/06/11/weekinreview/11harmon.html

Hartman, A. (1978). Diagramatic assessment of family relationships. *Social Casework, 59*(8), 465–476.

Hartman, A. (1995). Diagramatic assessment of family relationships. *Families in society, 76*(2), 111–122.

Haskins, J. (1978). *Scott Joplin: The man who made Ragtime*. Briarcliff Manor, NY: Scarborough.

Havel, V. (1991). Speech at Lehigh University, Oct 26, 1991.

Hays, E.R. (1967). *Those extraordinary Blackwells*. New York: Harcourt Brace.

Hockley, J. (2000). Psychosocial aspects in palliative care: Communicating with the patient and family. *Acta Oncologica, 39*(8), 905–910.

Hodge, D.R. (2000). Spiritual ecomaps: A new diagrammatic tool for assessing marital and family spirituality. *Journal of Marital and Family Therapy, 26*(2), April, 217–228.

Hodge, D.R. (2001a). Spiritual genograms: A generational approach to assessing spirituality. *Families in Society, 82*(1), 35–48.

Hodge, D.R. (2001b). Spiritual assessment: A review of major qualitative methods and a new framework for assessing spirituality. *Social Work, 46*(3), 203–214.

Hodge, D.R, (2004a). Social work practice with Muslims in the United States. In A.T.Morales & B.W. Sheafor (Eds.), *Social work: A profession of many faces* (10thed., pp. 443–469). Boston, MA: Allyn & Bacon.

Hodge, D.R. (2004b). Spirituality and people with mental illness: Developing spiritualcompetency in assessment and intervention. Families in Society, *85*(1), 36–44.

Hodge, D.R. (2004c). Working with Hindu clients in a spiritually sensitive manner.*Social Work, 49*(1), 27–38.

Hodge, D.R. (2005a). Spiritual life maps: A client-centered pictorial instrument forspiritual assessment, planning, and intervention. *Social Work, 50*(1), 77–87.

Hodge, D.R. (2005b). Spiritual ecograms: A new assessment instrument for identifying clients' spiritual strengths in space and across time. *Families in Society, 86*(2), 287–296.

Hodge, D.R. (2005c). Spiritual assessment in marital and family therapy: A methodological framework for selecting from among six qualitative assessment tools. *Journal of Marital and Family Therapy, 32*(4), 341–356.

Hodge, D.R. (2005d). Developing a spiritual assessment toolbox: A discussion of the strengths and limitations of five different assessment methods. *Health and Social Work, 30*(4), 314–323.

Hodge, D.R., & Williams, T.R. (2002). Assessing African American spirituality withspiritual eco-maps. *Families in Society, 83*(5-6), 585–595.

Hof, L., & Berman, E. (1986). The sexual genogram. *Journal of Marital and Family Therapy, 12*(1), 39–47.

Hoffman, E. (1994). *The drive for self: Alfred Adler and the founding of individual psychology*. New York: Addison-Wesley.

Holmes, T.H., & Masuda, M. (1974). Life change and illness susceptibility. ln B. S. Dohrenwend & B. Dohrenwend (Eds.), *Stressful life events: Their nature and effects*. New York: Wiley.

Holmes, T.H., & Rahe, T.H. (1967). The social adjustment rating scale. *Journal of Psychosomatic Research, 11*(2), 213–218.

Horn, M. (1983). Sisters worthy of respect: Family dynamics and women's roles in the Blackwell family. *Journal of Family History, 8*(4), 367–382.

Huygen, F.J.A. (1982). *Family medicine: The medical life history of families*. New York: Brunner/Mazel.

Imber-Black, E. (1999). *The secret life of families*. New York: Bantam Books.

Imber-Black, E. (Ed.). (1993). *Secrets in families and family therapy*. New York: W.W. Norton.

Ingersoll-Dayton, B., & Arndt, B. (1990). Uses of the genogram with the elderly and their families. *Journal of Gerontological Social Work, 15*(1–2), 105–120.

Isaacson, W. (2011). *Steve Jobs*. New York: Simon & Schuster.

Jacobs, A.J. (2017). *It's all relative: Adventures up and down the world's family tree*. New York: Simon & Schuster.

Johnson, P. (2005). *George Washington: Founding father*. New York: Harper Collins.

Johnson, S. (2018). *Farsighted: How we make the decisions that matter the most*. New York: Random House.

Jolly, W.M., Froom, J., & Rosen, M.G. (1980). The genogram. *Journal of Family Practice, 10*(2), 251–255.

Jones, E. (1953, 1954, 1955). *The life and work of Sigmund Freud*. 3 volumes. New York: Basic Books.

Jordan, K. (2004). The color-coded timeline trauma genogram. *Brief Treatment and Crisis Intervention, 4*(1), 57–70.

Jordan, K. (2006). The scripto-trauma genogram: An innovative technique for working with trauma survivors' intrusive memories. *Brief Treatment and Crisis Intervention, 6*(1), 36–51.

Kağnıcı, D.Y. (2011). Teaching multicultural counseling: An example from a Turkish counseling under-graduate program. *Eğitim Araştırmaları [Eurasian Journal of Education-al Research]*, *44*, 118–128.

Kağnıcı, D.Y. (2014). Reflections of a Multicultural Counseling Course: A qualitative study with counseling students and counselors. *Educational Sciences: Theory & Practice*, *14*(1), 53–62.

Keiley, M.K., Dolbin, M., Hill, J., Karuppaswamy, N., Liu, T., Natrajan, R., Poulsen, S., Robins, N, & Robinson, P. (2002). The cultural genogram: Experiences from within a marriage and family therapy training program. *Journal of Marital and Family Therapy*, *28*(2), 165–178.

Kelly, G.D. (1990). The cultural family of origin: A description of a training strategy. *Counselor Education and Supervision*, *30*(1), 77–84.

Kerr, M.E. (2019). Bowen Theory's Secrets. New York: W.W. Norton.

Kerr, M.E., & Bowen, M. (1988). *Family evaluation*. New York: W.W. Norton.

Kluger, J. (2011). *The sibling effect*. New York: Riverhead Books.

Krüll, M. (1986). *Freud and his father*. New York: W.W. Norton.

Kuehl, B.P. (1995). The solution-oriented genogram: A collaborative approach. *Journal of Marital and Family Therapy*, *21*(3): 239–250.

Kuhn, J. (1981). Realignment of emotional forces following loss. *The Family*, *5*(1), 19–24.

Laird, J. (1996a). Family-centered practice with lesbian and gay families. *Families in Society: Journal of Contemporary Human Services*, *7* (9), 559–572.

Laird, J. (1996b). Invisible ties: Lesbians and their families of origin. In J. Laird & R.J. Green (Eds.), *Lesbians and gays in couples and families*. San Francisco: Jossey-Bass.

Langer, J.C., Filler, R.M., Coles, J., & Edmonds, J.F. (1988). Plication of the diaphragm for infants and young children with phrenic nerve palsy. *Journal of Pediatric Surgery*, 23(8), 749–751.

LaSala, M. (2002). *Triangles, Angels, Villains, and Victims*. Presentation at Multicultural Family Institute, April

Launer, J. (2017). *Why doctors should draw genograms–including their own. Postgraduate Medical Journal*, *93*(1103), 575–576.

Leman, K. (2009). *The birth order book*. Grand Rapids, MI: Baker Publishing Group

Lerner, H. (1984). The cosmic countermove: *Family Therapy Networker*, Sept–Oct.

Lerner, H. (1990). *The dance of intimacy*. New York: Harper Collins. Ch1

Lerner, H. (1994). *The dance of deception*. New York: Harper Collins. Ch1

Lerner, H. (1997). *The dance of anger*. New York: Harper Collins. Ch1

Lerner, H. (2002). *The dance of connection*. New York: Harper Collins.

Lerner, H. (2005). *The dance of fear*. New York: Harper Collins.

Lerner, H. (2012). *Marriage rules*. New York: Avery.

Lewis, K. G. (1989). The use of color-coded genograms in family therapy. *Journal of Marital and Family Therapy*, *I*(2), 169–176.

Libbon, R., Triana, J., Heru, A., & Berman, E. (2019). Family skills for the resident toolbox: The 10-min genogram, ecomap, and prescribing homework. *Academic Psychiatry*, *43*(4), 435–439.

Like, R.C., Rogers, J., & McGoldrick, M. (1988). Reading and interpreting genograms: A systematic approach. *Journal of Family Practice*, *26*(4), 407–412.

Lipset, D. (1980). *Gregory Bateson: The legacy of a scientist*. Englewood Cliffs, NJ: Prentice.

Luepnitz, D.A. (1989). Virginia Satir. *Journal of Feminist Family Therapy*, *1*(3), 73–83.

Maccoby, E.E. (1990). Gender and relationships: A developmental account. *American Psychologist*, *45*(4), 513–520.

Magnuson, S. (2000). The professional genogram: Enhancing professional identity and clarity. *Family Journal: Counseling & Therapy for Couples & Families*, *8*(4), 299–401.

Magnuson, S., & Shaw, H.E. (2003). Adaptations of the multifaceted genogram in counseling, training and supervision. *Family Journal: Counseling & Therapy for Couples & Families*, *2*(1), 45–54.

Magnuson, S., Norem, K., & Skinner, C.H. (1995). Constructing genograms with lesbian clients. *The Family Journal: Counseling and Therapy for Couples and Families*, *3*(2) 110–115.

Malott, K. M., & & Magnuson, S. (2004). Using genograms to facilitate undergraduate students' career development: A group model. The Career Development Quarterly, *53*(4), pp. 178–186.

Mandala. (n.d.). Retrieved March 27, 2019, from https://en.wikipedia.org/wiki/Mandala

Manne J. (2009). Family constellations: A practical guide to uncovering the origins of family conflict. Berkeley, CA: North Atlantic Books.

Maraniss, D. (1995). *First in his class: The biography of Bill Clinton*. New York: Touchstone.

Masson, J. (Ed.). (1985). *The complete letters of Sigmund Freud to Wilhelm Fliess: 1887-1904*. Cambridge, MA: Belnap Press.

Mathias, B. (1992). *Between sisters: Secret rivals, intimate friends*. New York: Delacorte Press.

McDaniel, S. H., Hepworth, J. H., & Doherty, W. J. (1993). A new prescription for family health care. *The Family Therapy Networker*, 17, 18-29-62-63.

McDaniel, S. Hepworth, J. & Doherty (2003). *The shared experience of illness*. New York: Basic Books.

McCullough-Chavis, A. & Waites, C. (2004). Genograms with African American families. Considering cultural context. *Journal of Family Social Work, 8*(2), 1–17.

McGill, D.M. (1992). The cultural story in multicultural family therapy. *Families in Society: Journal of Contemporary Human Services, 73*(6), 339–349.

McGoldrick, M. (1981). Problems with family genograms. *American Journal of Family Therapy, 7,* 74–76.

McGoldrick, M. (1982). Through the looking glass: Supervision of a trainee's trigger family. In J. Byng-Hall & R. Whiffen (Eds.), *Family therapy supervision.* London: Academic Press.

McGoldrick, M. (1989). Sisters. In M. McGoldrick, C. Anderson, & F. Walsh (Eds.), *Women in families.* New York: W.W. Norton.

McGoldrick, M. (1995). *You can go home again: Reconnecting with your family.* New York: W.W. Norton.

McGoldrick, M. (2004a). Echoes from the past: Helping families mourn their losses. In F. Walsh & M. McGoldrick, (Eds.), *Living beyond loss* (2nd ed., pp. 50–78). New York: W.W. Norton.

McGoldrick, M. (2004b). The legacy of loss. In F. Walsh & M. McGoldrick (Eds.), *Living beyond loss* (2nd ed., pp. 104–129). New York: W.W. Norton.

McGoldrick, M. (2011). *The genogram journey: Reconnecting with your family.* New York: W.W. Norton.

McGoldrick, M. (2016a). Becoming a couple. In M. McGoldrick, N. Garcia Preto & B. Carter (Eds.), *The expanding family life cycle: Individual, family and social perspectives* (5th ed.). New York: Pearson.

McGoldrick, M. (2016b). *The genogram casebook: A clinical companion to Genograms: Assessment and Intervention.* New York: W.W. Norton.

McGoldrick, M. (2019). Homelessness and the spiritual meaning of home. In M. McGoldrick (Ed.), *Revisioning family therapy: Addressing diversity in clinical practice and training* (3rd ed.). New York: Guilford.

McGoldrick, M., & Carter, B. (2001). Advances in coaching: Family therapy with one person. *Journal of Marital and Family Therapy, 27*(3), 281–300.

McGoldrick, M., & Carter, B. (2016). The remarriage cycle: Divorced, multinuclear and recoupled families. In M. McGoldrick, N.Garcia Preto, & B. Carter, (Eds.). *The expanding family life cycle: Individual, family and social perspectives* (5th ed.). New York: Pearson.

McGoldrick, M., & Garcia-Preto, N. (2005). Cultural assessment. In M. McGoldrick, J. Giordano, & N. Garcia-Preto, (Eds.), *Ethnicity and family therapy* (3rd ed.). New York: Guilford.

McGoldrick, M., Carter, B., & Garcia Preto, N. (2016a). Overview: The life cycle in its changing context: Individual, family and social perspectives. In M. McGoldrick, N. Garcia Preto, & B. Carter (Eds.). *The expanding family life cycle: Individual,* *family and social perspectives* (5th ed.). New York: Pearson.

McGoldrick, M., Garcia Preto, N., & Carter, B. (Eds.). (2016b). *The expanding family life cycle: Individual, family and social perspectives* (5th ed.). Boston: Pearson.

McGoldrick, M., Giordano, J., & Garcia-Preto, N. (Eds.). (2005). *Ethnicity and family therapy* (3rd ed.). New York: Guilford.

McGoldrick, M., & Hardy, K.V. (Eds.). (2019). *Revisioning family therapy: Addressing diversity in clinical practice & training* (3rd ed.). New York: Guilford.

McGoldrick, M., Loonan, R., & Wohlsifer, D. (2006). Sexuality and culture. In S. Leiblum (Ed.) *Principles and practice of sex therapy* (4th ed.). New York: Guilford.

McGoldrick, M., & Ross, M., (2016). Violence and the family life cycle. In M. McGoldrick, N. Garcia Preto, & B. Carter (Eds.), *The expanding family life cycle: Individual, family and social perspectives* (5th ed.). Boston: Pearson.

McGoldrick, M. & Walsh, F. (2016). Death and the family life cycle. In M. McGoldrick, N. Garcia Preto, & B. Carter (Eds.). *The expanding family life cycle: Individual, family and social perspectives* (5th ed.). New York: Pearson.

McGoldrick, M., & Walsh, F. (2004). A time to mourn: Death and the family life cycle. In F. Walsh & M. McGoldrick (Eds.). *Living beyond loss: Death and the family* (2nd ed.). New York: W.W. Norton.

McGoldrick, M., & Watson, M. (2016). Siblings through the life cycle. In B. Carter & M. McGoldrick (Eds.), *The expanded family life cycle: Individual, family and social perspectives* (5th ed.). Boston: Pearson.

McMillen, J.C., & Groze, V. (1994). Using placement genograms in child welfare practice. *Child Welfare, 73*(4): 307–318.

McNaron, T. A. H. (Ed.). (1985). *The sister bond: A feminist view of a timeless connection.* New York: Pergamon Press.

Medalie JH. (1978). Family history, data base, family tree, & family diagnosis. In J.H. Medalie (Ed.), *Family Medicine: Principles and Applications* (pp. 329–36). Baltimore: Williams & Wilkins, 1978.

McIlvain, H., Crabtree, B., Medder, J., Strange, K. C., & Miller, E. L. (1998). Using practice genograms to understand and describe practice configurations. *Family Medicine, 30*(7), 490–496.

Milewski-Hertlein, K. A. (2001). The use of a socially constructed genogram in clinical practice. *American Journal of Family Therapy, 29*(1), 23–38.

Miller, J. (2019). *The ethos and ethics of global family therapy.* International Family Therapy Association Annual Conference, Aberdeen, Scotland.

Moon, S.M., Coleman, V.D., McCollum, E.E., Nelson,

T.S., & Jensen-Scott, R.L. (1993). Using the genogram to facilitate career decisions: A case study. *Journal of Family Psychology*, *4*(1), 45–56.

Moreno, J. L. (2019). The essential Moreno: Writings on Psychodrama, Group Method, and Spontaneity. New Paltz, New York: Tusitala Publishing.

Mullins, M.C., & Christie-Seely, J. (1984). Collecting and recording family data: The genogram. In J. Christie-Seely (Ed.), *Working with the family in primary care*. New York: Praeger.

Nabokov, V. (1959). *The real life of Sebastian Knight*. Norfolk, CT: New Directions. C

Nagel, P.C. (1987). *The Adams women*. New York: Oxford University Press.

Nealy, E. (2017). *Transgender children and youth: Cultivating pride and joy with families in transition*. New York: W. W. Norton.

Nealy, E. (2019). Identity transitions and transformations across the life cycle. In M. McGoldrick & K.V. Hardy (Eds.). Revisioning family therapy: Addressing diversity in clinical practice and training (3rd ed.). New York: Guilford.

Nerin, W.F. (1986). *Family reconstruction: Long day's journey into light*. New York: W. W. Norton.

Nerin, W.F. (1993). *You can't grow up till you go back home: A safe journey to see your parents as human*. New York: Crossroads Publishing.

Norris, J.E., & Tindale, J.A. (1994). *Among generations: The cycle of adult relationships*. New York: W.H. Freeman.

Oestreich, J.R. (2006, February 19). The asterisks tell the story: What tangled webs operas can weave. That's where a five page diagram comes in. *New York Times*. Retrieved from https://www.nytimes.com/2006/02/19/arts/music/the-asterisks-tell-the-story.html

Okiishi, R. W. (1987). The genogram as a tool in career counseling. *Journal of Counseling and Development*. *66* (3), 139–143.

Olsen, S., Dudley-Brown, S., & McMullen, P. (2004). Case for blending pedigrees, genograms and ecomaps: Nursing's contribution to the big picture. *Nursing & Health Sciences*, *6*(4), 295–308.

Papadopoulos, L., Bor, R., & Stanion, P. (1997). Genograms in counseling practice (Part 1). *Counselling Psychology Quarterly*, *10*(1) 17–28.

Papp, P., Silverstein, O., & Carter, E. A. (1973). Family sculpting in preventive work with well families. *Family Process*, 12(25), 197–212.

Paul, N. (1988). Personal Communication.

Paul, N., & Paul B.B. (1986). *A marital puzzle*. New York: W.W. Norton.

Peluso, P. (2003). The ethical genogram: A tool for helping therapists understand their ethical decision-making roles. *The Family Journal*, *11*(3), 286–291.

Pendagast, E.G., & Sherman, C.O. (1975). A guide to the genogram. *The Family*, *5*(1), 3–14.

Petry, S.S., & McGoldrick, M. (2005). Genograms in assessment and therapy. In G.P. Koocher, J.C. Norcross & S.S. Hill (Eds.). *The psychologists' desk reference* (2nd ed.). New York: Oxford University Press.

Phelps, E., Furstenberg, F.F., & Colby, A. (Eds.). (2002). *Looking at lives*. New York: Russell Sage.

Phillips, A. (2014). *Becoming Freud: The making of a psychoanalyst*. New Haven: Yale University Press.

Pinderhughes, E. (2019). Black genealogy revisited: Restorying anAfrican American family. In M. McGoldrick (Ed.), *Re-visioning family therapy: Race, culture, and gender in clinical practice*. New York: Guilford.

Pinderhughes, E., Jackson, V., & Romney, P. (2017). Understanding power: An imperative for human services. NASW Press.

Rainsford, G.L., & Schuman, S.H. (1981). The family in crisis: A case study of overwhelming illness and stress. *Journal of the American Medical Association*, *246*(1), 60–63.

Rakel, R.E. (1977). *Principles of family medicine*. Philadelphia: W.B. Saunders.

Rembel, G.R., Neufeld, A., Kushner, K.E. (2007). Interactive use of genograms and ecomaps in family caregiving research. *Journal of Family Nursing*, *13*(4), 403–419.

Richardson, R.W. (1987). *Family ties that bind: A self-help guide to change through family of origin therapy* (2nd ed.). Bellingham, WA: Self-Counsel Press.

Richardson, R.W. & Richardson L.A. (2000) *Birth order and you* (2nd ed.). Bellingham, WA: Self-Counsel Press Reference Series.

Rigazio-DiGilio S.A., Ivey, A.E., Kunkler-Peck, K.P. & Grady, L.T. (2005). *Community genograms: Using individual, family, and cultural narratives with clients*. New York: Teachers College Press.

Roazen, P. (1993). *Meeting Freud's family*. Amherst, MA: University of Massachusetts Press.

Robeson, Paul. (1988). *Here I stand*. Boston: Beacon Press.

Robinson, J. (1972). *I never had it made*. New York: Putnam.

Robinson, S. (1996). *Stealing home*. New York: Harper Collins.

Rogers, J.C. (1994a). Can physicians use family genogram information to identify patients at risk of anxiety or depression? *Archives of Family Medicine*, *3*(12), 1093–1098.

Rogers, J. C. (1994b). Impact of a screening family genogram on first encounters in primary care. Journal of Family Practice, *4*, 291–301.

Rogers, J. C. (1990). Completion and reliability of the self-administered genogram SAGE). Family Practice, 7, 149–151.

Rogers, J.C., & Cohn, P. (1987). Impact of a screening family genogram on first encounters in primary care. *Journal of Family Practice*. *4*(4), 291–301.

Rogers, J.C., & Durkin, M. (1984). The semi-structured genogram interview: l. Protocol, ll. Evaluation. *Family Systems Medicine*, *2(25)*, 176–187.

Rogers, J.C., Durkin, M., & Kelly, K. (1985). The family genogram: An underutilized clinical tool. *New Jersey Medicine*, *82*(11), 887–892.

Rogers, J.C., & Holloway, R. (1990). Completion rate and reliability of the self-administered genogram (SAGE). *Family Practice*, *7*(2), 149–51.

Rogers, J.C., Rohrbaugh, M., & McGoldrick, M. (1992). Can experts predict health risk from family genograms? *Family Medicine*, *24*(3), 209–215.

Rogers, J., C., & Rohrbaugh, M. (1991). The SAGE-PAGE trial: Do family genograms make a difference? *Journal of the American Board of Family Practice*, *4*(5), 319–326.

Rohrbaugh, M., Rogers, J.C., & McGoldrick, M. (1992). How do experts read family genograms? *Family Systems Medicine*, *10*(1), 79–89.

Rolland, J. (1994). *Families, illness, and disability*. New York: Basic Books

Rolland, J.S. (2018). Helping couples and families navigate illness and disability: An integrated approach. New York: Guilford Press.

Rutherford, A. (2017). *A brief history of everyone who ever lived: The stories in our genes*. London: Weidenfield and Nicolson.

Salmon, C., & Schumann, K. (2012). *The secret power of middle children: How middleborns can harness their unexpected and remarkable abilities*. New York: Plume.

Satir, V. (1968). *Conjoint family therapy*. Palo Alto: Science & Behavior Books

Satir, V. (1988). *New peoplemaking*. Palo Alto: Science & Behavior Books.

Satir, V., Gomori, M., Gerber, J., & Banmen, J. (1991). Satir Model: Family Therapy and beyond. Palo Alto: Sciencwe and Beyavior Books.

Satir, V., & Baldwin, M. (1983). Satir step by step: A guide to creating change in families. Palo Alto: Science & Behavior Books.

Scharwiess, S.O. (1994). Step-sisters and half-brothers: A family therapist's view of German unification and other transitional processes. *Contemporary Family Therapy*, *16*(3), 183–197.

Schoeninger, Douglas, (2010). Personal Communication.

Scherger, J.E. (2005). The biopsychosocial model is shrink wrapped, on the shelf, ready to be used, but waiting for a new process of care. *Families, Systems, & Health*, *23*(4), 444–447.

Schmidt, D.D. (1983). Family determinants of disease: depressed lymphocyte function following the loss of a spouse. *Family Systems Medicine 1*(1), 33–39.

Schroder, D. (2015). *Exploring and developing the use of art-based genograms in family of origin therapy*. Springfield, Illinois: Charles C. Thomas, Publishers.

Schutzenberger, A.A. (1998). The ancestor syndrome: Transgenerational psychotherapy and the hidden links in the family tree. New York: Routledge.

Scrivner, R., & Eldridge, N.S. (1995). Lesbian and gay family psychology. In R.H. Mikesell, D. Lusterman, & S. McDaniel (Eds.), *Integrating family therapy: Handbook of family psychology and systems therapy* (pp. 327–345). Washington, DC: American Psychological Association.

Shakespeare, W. *Julius Caesar* (I, ii, 140–141).

Shapiro, D. (2019). *Inheritance: A memoir of genealogy, paternity and love*. New York: Knopf.

Shaw, B.M., Bayne, H., & Lorelle, S. (2012). A constructivist perspective for integrating spirituality into counselor training. *Counselor Education & Supervision*, *51*(4), 270–280.

Shellenberger, S., Dent, M.M., Davis-Smith, M., Seale, J.P., Weintraut, R., Wright, T. (2007). A cultural genogram: A tool for teaching and practice. *Families, Systems & Health*, *25*(4), 367–381.

Shellenberger, S., & Hoffman, S. (1998). The changing family-work system. In R.H. Mikesell, D. Lusterman, & S. McDaniel (Eds.). *Integrating family therapy: Handbook of family psychology and systems therapy* (pp. 461–479). Washington, DC: American Psychological Association.

Shellenberger, S., Shurden, K.W., & Treadwell, T.W. (1988). Faculty training seminars in family systems. *Family Medicine*, *20*(3), 226–227.

Shellenberger, S., Watkins-Couch, K. & Drake, M.A. (1989). Elderly family members and their caregivers: Characteristics and development of the relationship. *Family Systems Medicine*, *7*(3), 317–322.

Sherman, M.H. (1990). Family narratives: Internal representations of family relationships and affective themes. *Infant Mental Health Journal*, *11*(3), 253–258.

Sherman, R. (2000). The intimacy genogram. In R.E. Watts (Ed.). *Techniques in marriage and family counseling Vol. 1. The family psychology and counseling series*, pp. 81–84.

Shernoff, M.J. (1984). Family therapy for lesbian and gay clients. *Social Work*, *29*(4), 393–396.

Shields, C.G., King, D.A., & Wynne, L.C. (1995). Interventions with later life families. In R.H. Mikesell, D. Lusterman, & S. McDaniel (Eds.), *Integrating family therapy: Handbook of family psychology and systems therapy* (pp. 141–158). Washington, DC: American Psychological Association.

Siegel, D.J. (2016). *Mind: A journey to the heart of being human*. New York: W. W. Norton.

Siegel, D. J. (2015). *The developing mind: How relation-*

ships and the brain interact to shape who we are (2nd ed.). New York: W. W. Norton.

Slater, S. (1995). *The lesbian family life cycle.* New York: Free Press.

Sloan, P.D., Slatt, L.M., Curtis, P., & Ebell, M. (Eds.). (1998). *Essentials of family medicine* (2nd ed.). Baltimore, MD: Williams & Wilkins.

Soh-Leong, L. (2008). Transformative aspects of genogram work: Perceptions and experiences of graduate students in a counseling training program. *The Family Journal, 16*(1), 35–42G.

Sproul, M.S., & Galagher, R.M. (1982). The genogram as an aid to crisis intervention. *Journal of Family Practice, 14*(55), 959–960.

Stange K.C. (2016). Holding on and letting go: A perspective from the Keystone IV Conference. *Journal of the American Board of Family Medicine, 29*(Supplement 1), S2–S39.

Stanion, P., Papadopoulos, L., & Bor, R. (1997). Genograms in counselling practice. Counselling practice. *Counselling Psychology Quarterly, 10* (2), 139–148.

Stanton, M.D. (1992). The time line and the "why now?" question: A technique and rationale for therapy, training, organizational consultation and research. *Journal of Marital and Family Therapy. 18*(4), 331–343.

Steinglass, P., Bennett, L., Wolin, S., & Reiss, D. (1987). *The alcoholic family.* New York: Basic Books.

Sternbergh, A. (2018, October 4). The extinction of the middle child: They're becoming an American rarity, just when America could use them most. *New York Times*, Retrieved from https://www.thecut.com/2018/07/the-middle-child-is-going-extinct.html.

Stoneman, Z., Brody, H., & MacKinnon, C. (1986). Same-sex and cross-sex siblings: Activity choices, roles, behavior and gender stereotypes, *Sex Roles 15*(9–10), 495–511.

Sulloway, F.J. (1996). *Born to rebel: Sibling relationships, family dynamics and creative lives.* New York: Pantheon.

Swales, P. (1982). Freud, Minna Bernays, and the conquest of Rome: New light on the origins of psychoanalysis. *The New American Review*, 1, 2(3), 1–23.

Swales, P. (1986). Freud, his origins and family history. UMDNJ- Robert Wood Johnson Medical School.

Taylor, R.B., David, A.K., Johnson, T.A., Jr., Phillips, D.M. & Scherger, J.E. (Eds.). (1998). *Family Medicine Principles and Practice* (5th ed.). Baltimore, MD: Williams & Wilkins.

Thomas, A.J. (1998). Understanding culture and worldview in family systems: Use of the multicultural genogram. *The Family Journal: Counseling and Therapy for Couples and Families,* 6(1). 24–31.

Titelman, P. (1998). *Clinical applications of Bowen family systems theory.* New York: Haworth.

Titelman, P. (Ed.). (2003). *Bowen family systems theory perspectives.* New York: Haworth.

Titelman, P. (2007). *Triangles: Bowen family systems theory perspectives.* New York, Haworth.

Titelman, P. (2015). *Differentiation of self: Bowen family systems theory perspectives.* New York: Routledge.

Toman, W. (1976). *Family constellation* (3rd ed.). New York: Springer.

Troncale, J.A. (1983). The genogram as an aid to diagnosis of distal renal tubular acidosis. *Journal of Family Practice, 17*(4), 707–708.

Turabian, J.L. (2017). Family genogram in general medicine: A soft technology that can be strong. An update. *Research in Medical and Engineering Sciences, 3*(1).

Valliant, G. (1977). *Adaptation to life.* Boston: Little, Brown.

Vaillant, G. E. (2012). *Triumphs of Experience.* Cambridge, Mass: Belnap Press of Harvard University

Wachtel, E.F. (2016).*The heart of couple therapy: Knowing what to do and how to do it.* New York: Guilford Press.

Walsh, F. (1983). The timing of symptoms and critical events in the family life cycle. ln H. Liddle (Ed.), *Clinical implications of the family life cycle.* Rockville, MD: Aspen.

Walsh, F. (Ed.). (2009). *Spiritual resources in family therapy.* New York: Guilford.

Walsh, F. (Ed.). (2015). *Normal family processes: Growing diversity and complexity,* (4th ed). New York: Guilford.

Walsh, F. (2016a). *Strengthening family resilience* (3rd ed.). New York: Guilford Press.

Walsh, F. (2016b). Families in later life: Challenges, opportunities and resilience. In M. McGoldrick, N. Garcia Preto, & B. Carter (Eds.). *The expanding family life cycle: Individual, family and social perspectives* (5th ed.). Boston: Pearson.

Walsh, F. & McGoldrick, M. (2004). *Living beyond loss: Death and the family* (2nd ed.). New York: W. W. Norton.

Waters I., Watson W., & Wetzel W. (1994). Genograms: Practical tools for family physicians. *Canadian Family Physician*; 40, 282–286.

Wattendorf, D.J., & Hadley, M.S. (2005). Family history: The three generation pedigree. *American Family Physician, 72*(3), 441–448.

Watts Jones, D. (1998). Towards an African-American genogram. *Family Process, 36*(4), 373–383.

Weiss, E.L., Coll, J.E., Gerbauer, J., Smiley, K., & Carillo, E. (2010). The military genogram: A solution-focused approach for resilience building in service members and their families. *The Family Journal, 18*(4), 395–406.

White, M. (1995). Family therapy workshop. Family Institute of New Jersey.

White, M. (2006) (personal communication).

White, M.B. & Tyson-Rawson, K.J. (1995). Assessing the dynamics of gender in couples and families: The Gendergram. *Family Relations, 44*(3), 253–260.

Wikipedia, (2019). Thomas Wedgewood (photographer). Retrieved 8/19/19: https://en.wikipedia.org/wiki/Thomas_Wedgwood_(photographer)

Willow, R.A., Tobin, D.J., & Toner, S. (2011). Assessment of the use of spiritual genograms in counselor education, *Counseling and Values, 53*(3), 162-236.

Widmer R.B., Cadoret, R.J. & North, C.S. (1980). Depression in family practice. Some effects on spouses and children. *Journal of Family Practice, 10*(1), 45-51.

Wimbush, F.B., & Peters, R.M. (2000). Identification of cardiovascular risk: Use of a cardiovascular-specific genogram. *Public Health Nursing, 17*(3), 148–154.

Worby, C.M., & Babineau, R. (1974). The family interview: Helping patient and family cope with metastatic disease. *Geriatrics, 29*(6), 83–94.

Wright, L. (1995, August 7). Double mystery: The nature of twins . *The New Yorker.*

Wright, L.M., & Leahey, M. (2013). *Nurses and families: A guide to family assessment and intervention* (6th ed.). Philadelphia: F.A. Davis.

Wright, L.M., & Leahey, M. (1999). Maximizing time, minimizing suffering: The 15-minute (or less) family interview. *Journal of Family Nursing, 5*(3), 259–274.

Yarrow P, Stookey P, Travers M. The Great Mandala (song). (1967). http://lyrics.wikia.com/wiki/Peter,_Paul_%26_Mary:The_Great_Mandala_(The_Wheel_Of_Life) https://www.youtube.com/watch?v=xpIh68Kh_-s Accessed March 27, 2019.

Young-Bruel, Elizabeth. (1988). *Anna Freud: A biography.* New York: Summit Books.

Yznaga, S. (2008). Using the genogram to facilitate the intercultural competence of Mexican immigrants. *The Family Journal: Counseling and Therapy for Couples and Families, 16*(2), 159–165.

Zide, M.R. & Gray, S.W. (2000). The solutioning process: Merging the genogram and the solution-focused model of practice. *Journal of Family Social Work, 4*(1), 3–19.

Zill, N. (2015). More than 60% of U.S. kids live with two parents. Institute for Family Studies. Retrieved from: https://ifstudies.org/blog/more-than-60-of-u-s-kids-live-with-two-biological-parents.

Videos on Genograms

McGoldrick, M. (1996). The legacy of unresolved loss: A family systems approach. Video available from www.psychotherapy.net.

McGoldrick, M. (2016). Genogram creation in four minutes. Retrieved from https://www.youtube.com/watch?v=qUbfMufq2uo&t=2s

McGoldrick, M. (2016). Harnessing the power of genograms. Video available from www.psychotherapy.net

McGoldrick, M. (2017). Triangles and family therapy: Strategies and solutions. Video available from www.psychotherapy.net

McGoldrick, M. (2018). Couples therapy: A systemic approach. Video available from www.psychotherapy.net

McGoldrick, M. (2018). Assessment and engagement in family therapy. Video available from www.psychotherapy.net

McGoldrick, M. (2018). Using family play genograms in psychotherapy. Video available from www.psychotherapy.net

McGoldrick, M. (2019). Facing Ourselves from the Ghosts of our Families. Available from the Multicultural Family Institute in Highland Park New Jersey (www.multiculturalfamily.org).

McGoldrick, M. (2019). Racism, Family Secrets and the African American Experience. Available from the Multicultural Family Institute in Highland Park New Jersey

McGoldrick, M., (2019) Creating a genogram. Video available from www.multiculturalfamily.org

Websites

https://thegeneticgenealogist.com
https://www.genopro.com/genogram/examples/
https://www.multiculturalfamily.org
- a source of various genogram videos in the process of development.

Biographical References

Adams Family

Levin, P.L. (1987). *Abigail Adams*. New York: St. Martin's Press.

Musto, D. (1981). The Adams Family. *Proceedings of Massachusetts Historical Society*, 93, 40–58.

Nagel, P.C. (1983). *Descent from glory: Four generations of the John Adams family*. New York: Oxford University Press.

Nagel, P.C. (1987). *The Adams women*. New York: Oxford University Press.

Shepherd, J. (1975). *The Adams chronicles: Four generations of greatness*. Boston: Little, Brown.

Alfred Adler Sources

Adler, Alexandra. (March, 1984, August 1984). Personal interviews.

Adler, Kurt. (Alfred's son). (August, 1984). Personal interview.

Adler, Kurt. (Sigmund's son). (August, 1984). Personal communication.

Ansbacher, H. (1984). Personal communication.

Ansbacher, H.L. (1970). Alfred Adler: A historical perspective. *American Journal of Psychiatry, 127*(6), 777–782.

Ellenberger, H.F. (1970). *The discovery of the unconscious: The history and evolution of dynamic psychiatry*. New York: Basic Books.

Furtmuller, C. (1979). Alfred Adler: A biographical essay. In H.L. Ansbacher & R.R. Ansbacher (Eds.), *Superiority and social interest: A collection of later writings*. New York: Norton.

Hoffman, E. (1994). *The drive for self: Alfred Adler and the founding of individual psychology*. New York: Addison-Wesley.

Nicholl, W.G., & Hawes, E.C. (1985). Family lifestyle assessment: The role of family myths and values in the client's presenting issues. *Individual Psychology: Journal of Adlerian Theory, Research & Practice. 41*(2) 147–160.

Rattner, J. (1983). *Alfred Adler*. New York: Frederick Ungar.

Sherman, R. (1993). Marital issues of intimacy and techniques for change: An Adlerian systems perspective. *Journal of Adlerian Therapy, Research and Practice, 49*(3–4), 318–329.

Sperber, M. (1974). *Masks of loneliness: Alfred Adler in perspective*. New York: Macmillan.

Stepansky, P.E. (1983). *In Freud's shadow: Adler in context*. Hillsdale, NJ: The Analytic Press.

Louis Armstrong Sources

Armstrong, L. (1954). *Satchmo: My life in New Orleans*. New York: Perseus Books.

Bergreen, L. (1997). *Louis Armstrong: An extravagant life*. New York: Broadway Books.

Brothers, T. (Ed.). (1999). *Louis Armstrong in his own words*. New York: Oxford University Press.

Collier, J.L. (1983). *Louis Armstrong: An American genius*. New York: Oxford University Press.

Giddins, G. (1988). *Satchmo: The genius of Louis Armstrong*. New York: Perseus Books.

Terkel, S. (1975). *Giants of jazz*. New York: The New Press.

Bateson/Mead Sources

Bateson, M.C. (1984). *With a daughter's eye.* New York: William Morrow & Co.

Bateson, M.C. (1988). Peripheral visions. New York: Morrow.

Bateson, M.C. (1990). *Composing a life.* New York: Atlantic Monthly Press.

Cassidy, R. (1982). *Margaret Mead: A voice for the century.* New York: Universe Books.

Grosskurth, P. (1988). *Margaret Mead: A life of controversy.* London Penguin Books.

Howard, J. (1984). *Margaret Mead: A life.* New York: Ballantine Books.

Lipset, D. (1980). *Gregory Bateson: The legacy of a scientist.* Englewood Cliffs, NJ: Prentice.

Mead, M. (1972). *Blackberry winter, my earlier years.* New York: Simon & Schuster.

Rice, E. (1979). *Margaret Mead: A portrait.* New York: Harper & Row.

Alexander Graham Bell Sources

Bruce, R.V. (1973). *Bell: Alexander Graham Bell and the conquest of solitude.* Boston: Little, Brown.

Eber, D.H. (1982). *Genius at work: Images of Alexander Graham Bell.* New York: Viking.

Gray, C. (2006). *Reluctant genius: Alexander Graham Bell and the passion for invention.* New York: Abcade Press.

Grosvenor, E.S., & Wesson, M. (1997). *Alexander Graham Bell.* New York: Abrams.

Mackay, J. (1997). *Alexander Graham Bell: A life.* New York: Wiley.

Blackwell/Stone/Brown Sources

Cazden, E. (1983). *Antoinette Brown Blackwell: A biography.* Old Westbury, New York: The Feminist Press.

Hays, E. R. (1967). *Those extraordinary Blackwells.* New York: Harcourt Brace.

Horn, M. (1980). Family ties: The Blackwells, a study of the dynamics of family life in nineteenth century America. Ph.D. Dissertation. Tufts University.

Horn, M. (1983). Sisters worthy of respect: Family dynamics and women's roles in the Blackwell family. *Journal of Family History, 8*(4), 367–382.

Wheeler, Leslie (Ed.). (1981). *Loving warriers: Selected letters of Lucy Stone and Henry B. Blackwell, 1853 to 1893.* New York: Dial Press.

British Royal Family

Bradford, S. (1996). *Elizabeth.* New York: Riverhead Books.

Campbell, C. (1998). *The real Diana.* New York: St. Martin's Press.

Davies, N. (1998). *Queen Elizabeth II: A woman who is not amused.* New York: Carol Publishing Group.

Delderfield, E.R. (1998). *Kings and queens of England and Great Britain* (3rd ed.). Devon, England: David & Charles.

Fearon, P. (1996). *Behind the palace walls: The rise and fall of Britain's royal family.* Secaucus, NJ: Carol Publishing Group.

Kelley, K. (1997). *The royals.* New York: Warner.

Morton, A. (1997). *Diana: Her true story.* New York: Simon & Schuster.

Brontë Sources

Bentley, Phyllis. (1969). *The Brontës and their world.* New York: Viking.

Cannon, John. (1980). *The road to Haworth: The story of the Brontës' Irish Ancestry.* London: Weidenfeld and Nicolson.

Chadwick, E.H. (1914). *In the footsteps of the Brontës.* London: Sir Isaac Pitman & Sons, Ltd.

Chitham, Edward. (1986). *The Brontës' Irish background.* New York: St. Martin's Press.

Chitham, Edward. (1988). *A life of Emily Brontë.* New York: Basil Blackwell.

Chitham, Edward, & Winnifrith, T. (1983). *Brontë facts and Brontë problems.* London: Macmillan.

du Maurier, Daphne. (1961). *The infernal world of Branwell Brontë.* Garden City, NY: Doubleday.

Frazer, Rebecca. (1988). *The Brontës: Charlotte Brontë and her family.* New York: Crown.

Gaskell, Elizabeth. (1975). *The life of Charlotte Brontë.* London: Penguin.

Gerin, Winifred. (1961). *Branwell Brontë*. London: Thomas Nelson & Sons.

Gerin, Winifred. (1971). *Emily Brontë: A biography*. London: Oxford University Press.

Hannah, Barbara. (1988). *Striving toward wholeness*. Boston: Signpress.

Hanson, L., & Hanson, E. (1967). *The four Brontës*. New York: Archon Press.

Hardwick, E. (1975). The Brontës. In *Seduction and Betrayal: Women and Literature*. New York: Vintage.

Hinkley, L.L. (1945). *The Brontës: Charlotte and Emily*. New York: Hastings House.

Hopkins, A.B. (1958). *The father of the Brontës*. Baltimore: Johns Hopkins Press.

Lane, Margaret. (1969). *The Brontë story*. London: Fontana.

Lock, J. & Dixon, W.T. (1965). *A man of sorrow: The life, letters, and times of Reverend Patrick Brontë*. Westport, CT: Meckler Books.

Mackay, A.M. (1897). *The Brontës: Fact and fiction*. New York: Dodd, Mead.

Maurat, C. (1970). *The Brontës' secret*. Translated by M. Meldrum. New York: Barnes & Noble.

Moglen, H. (1984). *Charlotte Brontë: The self conceived*. Madison: University of Wisconsin Press.

Morrison, N.B. (1969). *Haworth Harvest: The story of the Brontës*. New York: Vanguard.

Peters, M. (1974) *An enigma of Brontës*. New York: St. Martins Press.

Peters, M. (1975). *Unquiet soul: A biography of Charlotte Brontë*. New York: Atheneum.

Ratchford, F.W. (1964). *The Brontës' web of childhood*. New York: Russell & Russell.

Raymond, E. (1948). *In the steps of the Brontës*. Rich & Cowan.

Spark, M., & Stanford, D. (1960). *Emily Brontë: Her life and work*. London: Arrow Books.

Stuart, J.A. Erskine, (1888). *The Bronte Country: Its topography, antiquities, and history*. London: Longman, Green & Co.

White, W.B. (1939). *The miracle of Haworth: A Brontë story*. New York: E.P. Dutton.

Wilks, B. (1986). *The Brontës: An illustrated Biography*. New York: Peter Bedrick Books.

Wilks, Brian. (1986). *The illustrated Brontës of Haworth*. New York: Facts on File Publications.

Winnifith, T.Z. (1977). *The Brontës and their background: Romance and reality*. New York: Collier.

Wright, William. (1893). *The Brontës in Ireland*. New York: D. Appleton & Company.

Bush Family

Kelley, K. (2004). *The family: The real story of the Bush dynasty*. New York: Doubleday.

Minutaglio, B. (2001). *First son: George W. Bush and the Bush family dynasty*. New York: Three Rivers Press.

Phillips, K. (2004). *American dynasty: Aristocracy, fortune, and the politics of deceit in the house of Bush*. New York: Viking.

Burton/Taylor Sources

Bragg, M. (1990). *Richard Burton: A life*. New York: Warner Books.

Ferris, P. (1981). *Richard Burton*. New York: Coward, McCann & Geoghegan.

Kelley, K. (1981). *Elisabeth Taylor: The last star*. New York: Simon & Schuster.

Morley, S. (1988). *Elizabeth Taylor*. New York: Applause Books.

Maria Callas Family

Allegri, R., & Allegri, R. (1997). *Callas by Callas*. New York: Universe.

Callas, J. (1989). *Sisters*. New York: St. Martin's.

Huffington, A. (2002). *Maria Callas: The woman behind the legend*. New York: Cooper Square Press.

Moutsatos, K.F. (1998). *The Onassis women*. New York: Putnam.

Stassinopoulos, A. (1981). *Maria Callas: The woman behind the legend*. New York: Simon & Schuster.

Bill Clinton Family

Brock, D. (1996). *The seduction of Hillary Rodham*. New York: The Free Press.

Clinton Kelly, V., with J. Morgan (1994). *My life: Leading with my heart*. New York: Pocket Books.

Clinton, R. (1995). *Growing up Clinton*. Arlington, TX: Summit Publishing Group.

Clinton, B. (2005). *My life*. New York: Vintage.

Gartner, J. (2008). *In Search of Bill Clinton: A Psychological Biography*. New York: St. Martin's Press.

King, N. (1996). *The woman in the White House*. New York: Carol Publishing.

Maraniss, D. (1988). *The Clinton enigma*. New York: Simon & Schuster.

Maraniss, D. (1995). *First in his class: The biography of Bill Clinton*. New York: Touchstone.

Morris, R. (1996). *Partners in power*. New York: Henry Holt.

Warner, J. (1993). *Hillary Clinton: The inside story*. New York: Signer.

Darwin Family

Darwin, C. (1958). *The autobiography of Charles Darwin 1809–1882*. Ed. Nora Barlow. New York: W. W. Norton.

Desmond, A. & Moore, J. (1991). *Darwin: The life of a tormented evolutionist*. New York: W. W. Norton.

Heiligman, D. (2011). *Charles and Emma: The Darwin's leap of faith*. Square Fish.

Keynes, R. (2001). *Darwin, his daughter and human evolution*. New York: Riverhead.

Quammen, D. (2006). *The reluctant Mr. Darwin*. New York: W.W. Norton.

Stott, Rebecca (2012). *Darwin's Ghosts*. New York: Random House.

Steffof, A. (1996). *Charles Darwin: And the evolution revolution*. New York: Oxford.

Engel, George

Cohen, E. & Brown Clark, S. (2010). John Romano & George Engel: Their lives and work. Meliora Press.

Engel, G. (1975). The death of a twin: Mourning and anniversary reactions: Fragments of 10 years of self-analysis. *International Journal of Psychoanalysis*. *56*(l), 23–40.

Erikson Family

Erikson Bloland, S. (1999, November). Fame: The power and cost of a fantasy. *Atlantic Monthly*. 51–62.

Erikson Bloland, S. (2005). In the shadow of fame: A memoir by the daughter of Erik H. Erikson. New York: Viking.

Friedman. L. J. (1999). *Identity's architect*. New York: Scribner.

Fonda Family Sources

Collier, P. (1992). *The Fondas*. New York: Putnam.

Fonda, A. (1986). *Never before dawn: An autobiography*. New York: Weindenfeld & Nicolson.

Fonda, P. (1998). *Don't tell dad*. New York: Hyperion.

Fonda, J. (2006). *My Life So Far*. New York: Random House.

Guiles, F.L. (1981). *Jane Fonda: The actress in her time*. New York: Pinnacle.

Hayward, B. (1977). *Haywire*. New York: Alfred Knopf.

Kiernan, T. (1973). *Jane: An intimate biography of Jane Fonda*. New York: Putnam.

Sheed, W. (1982). *Clare Booth Luce*. New York: E.P. Dutton.

Springer, J. (1970). *The Fondas*. Seacaucus: Citadel.

Teichman, H. (1981). *Fonda: My life*. New York: New American Library.

Foster Family

Foster, B., & Wagener, L. (1998). *Foster child*. New York: Signer.

Chunovic, L. (1995). *Jodie: A biography*. New York: Contemporary Books.

Freud Sources

Anzieu, Didier. (1986). *Freud's self-analysis*. Madison, CT: International Universities Press.

Appignanesi, L., & Forrester, J. (1992). *Freud's women*. New York: Basic Books.

Bernays, A.F. (Nov. 1940). *My brother Sigmund Freud*. The American Mercury, 336–340.

Bernays, Edward. Personal interview.

Bernays, Hella. Personal interview.

Carotenuto, Also. (1982). *A secret symmetry: Sabina Spielrein between Jung and Freud*. New York: Pantheon.

Clark, Ronald.W. (1980). *Freud: The man and the cause*. New York: Random House.

Cooper-White, P. & Kelcourse, F.B. (2019) Sabina Spielrein and the beginnings of psychoanalysis. New York: Routledge.

Eissler, K.R. (1978). *Sigmund Freud: His life in pictures and words*. New York: Helen & Kurt Wolff Books, Harcourt Brace, Jovanovich.

Freeman, L., & Strean, H.S. (1981). *Freud and women*. New York: Frederick Ungar Publishing Company.

Freud, E.L. (1975). The letters of Sigmund Freud. New York: Basic Books.

Freud, M. (1982). *Sigmund Freud: Man and father*. New York: Jason Aronson.

Freud, S. (1988). *My three mothers and other passions*. New York: New York University Press.

Gay, Peter. (1988). *Freud: A life for our time*. New York: Norton.

Gay, Peter. (1990). *Reading Freud*. New Haven: Yale University Press.

Glicklhorn, R. (1979) The Freiberg period of the Freud family. *Journal of the History of Medicine*. *24*(1), 37–43.

Jones, E. (1953, 1954, 1955). *The life and work of Sigmund Freud*. 3 volumes. New York: Basic Books.

Krüll, M. (1986). *Freud and his father*. New York: Norton.

Mannoni, O. (1974). *Freud*. New York: Vintage.

Margolis, D.P. (1996). *Freud and his mother*. Northvale, NJ: Jason Aronson.

Masson, J. (Ed.) (1985). *The complete letters of Sigmund Freud to Wilhelm Fliess: 1887–1904*. Cambridge, MA: Belnap Press.

Masson, J. (1992). *The assault on truth*. New York: Harper Collins

McGoldrick, M., & Gerson, R. (1985). *Genograms in family assessment*. New York: Norton.

McGoldrick, M., & Gerson, R. (1988). "Genograms and the family life cycle". In Betty Carter & Monica McGoldrick, (Eds.). *The changing family life cycle*. Boston, MA: Allyn & Bacon.

McGoldrick, M., & Gerson, R. (1998). History, genograms, and the family life cycle: Freud in context. In B. Carter & M. McGoldrick (Eds.), *The expanded family life cycle: Individual, family, and social perspectives* (3rd ed.). Boston: Allyn & Bacon.

Nelken, Michael. (In press). "Freud's heroic struggle with his mother". Manuscript in preparation.

Peters, U.H. (1985). *Anna Freud: A life dedicated to children*. New York: Shocken.

Phillips, A. (2014). Becoming Freud: The making of a psychoanalyst. New Haven: Yale University Press.

Roazen, P. (1993). *Meeting Freud's family*. Amherst, MA: University of Massachusetts Press.

Ruitenbeek, H.M. (1973). *Freud as we knew him*. Detroit: Wayne State University.

Schur, Max. (1972). *Freud: Living and dying*. New York: International Universities Press.

Sullaway, Frank (1992). Freud: Biologist of the mind. Cambridge: Harvard University Press.

Swales, P. (1982). Freud, Minna Bernays, and the conquest of Rome: New light on the origins of psychoanalysis. *The New American Review*, 1, 2/3: 1–23.

Swales, P. (1986). Freud, his origins and family history. UMDNJ-Robert Wood Johnson Medical School. November 15.

Swales, P. (1987). What Freud didn't say. UMDNJ-Robert Wood Johnson Medical School. May 15.

Young-Bruel, Elizabeth. (1988). *Anna Freud: A biography*. New York: Summit Books.

Gandhi-Nehru, Indira

Ali, T. (1985). *An Indian dynasty*. New York: Putnam.

Frank, K. (2002). *Indira: The life of Indira Nehru Gandhi*. New York: Houghton-Mifflin.

Tharoor, S. (2005). *Nehru: The invention of India*. New York: Arcade Publishing.

Wolpert, S. (1996). *Nehru*. New York: Oxford University Press.

Henry VIII

Fraser, A. (1994). *The wives of Henry VIII*. New York: Vintage.

Lindsey, K. (1995). *Divorced, beheaded, survived: A feminist reinterpretation of the wives of Henry VIII*. New York: Addison-Wesley.

Jefferson Family

Binger, C. (1970). *Thomas Jefferson: A well-tempered mind*. New York: Norton.

Brodie, F. M. (1974). *Thomas Jefferson: An intimate history*. New York: Norton.

Fleming, T. J. (1969). *The man from Monticello*. New York: Morrow.

Gordon-Reed, A. (1997). *Thomas Jefferson and Sally Hemings*. Charlottesville, VA: University of Virginia Press.

Gordon-Reed, A. (2008). *The Hemingses of Monticello: An American family*. New York: W. W. Norton.

Halliday, E. M. (2001). *Understanding Thomas Jefferson*. New York: Harper Collins.

Lanier, S., & Feldman, J. (2000). *Jefferson's children*. New York: Random House.

Smith, D. (1998, November 7). The enigma of Jefferson: Mind and body in conflict. *New York Times*, B 7–8.

Wills, G. (2003). *Negro president*. Boston: Houghton Miflin.

Woodson, B.W. (2001) *A President in the family: Thomas Jefferson, Sally Hemings and Thomas Woodson*. Westport, CT: Praeger.

Steve Jobs

Gladwell, M. (2008). *Outliers: The story of success*. New York: Little, Brown & Co.

Isaacson, W. (2011). *Steve Jobs*. New York: Simon & Schuster.

Brennan-Jobs, L. (2018). *Small fry: A memoir*. New York: Grove Press.

Simpson, M. (1992). *The lost father*. New York: Vintage Books.

Joplin Family

Berlin, E.A. (1994). *King of Ragtime: Scott Joplin and his era*. New York: Oxford University Press.

Gammond, P. (1975). *Scott Joplin and the ragtime era*. New York: St. Martin's Press.

Haskins, J. (1978). *Scott Joplin: The man who made Ragtime*. Briarcliff Manor, NY: Scarborough.

Preston, K. (1988). *Scott Joplin: Composer*. New York: Chelsea House.

Curtis, S. (2004). *Dancing to a black man's tune: The life of Scott Joplin*. Columbia, MO: University of Missouri Press.

Jung Family

Bair, D. (2003) *Jung: A biography*. New York: Little Brown.

Broome, V. (1981). *Jung: Man and myth*. New York: Atheneum.

Cooper-White, P. & Kelcourse, F.B. (2019). Sabina Spielrein and the beginnings of psychoanalysis. New York: Routledge.

Dunne, C. (2015). Carl Jung: Wounded healer of the soul. London, England: Watkins Media Limited.

Hannah, B. (1981). *Jung: His life and work: A biographical memoir*. New York: Perigee, Putnam Books.

Jung, C.G. (1961). *Memories, dreams, reflections*. (Recorded and edited by Aniela Jaffe, translated by R. Winston & C. Winstons). New York: Vintage.

Stern, P.J. (1976). *C.G. Jung: The haunted prophet*. New York: Delta, Deli.

Kahlo/Rivera Families

Alcantara, I., & Egnolff, S. (1999). *Frida Kahlo and Diego Rivera*. New York: Prestel Verlag.

Drucker, M. (1991). *Frida Kahlo*. Albuquerque: University of New Mexico Press.

Grimberg, S. (2002). *Frida Kahlo*. North Digton, MA: World Publications Group, Inc.

Herrera, H. (1983). *Frida: A biography of Frida Kahlo*. New York: Harper & Row.

Herrera, H. (1984). *Frida*. New York: Harper Collins.

Herrera, H. (1991). *Frida Kahlo: The paintings*. New York: Harper Collins.

Kettenmann, A. (2002). *Frida Kahlo, 1907–1954: Pain and passion*. New York: Barnes & Noble Books.

Kahlo, F. (2001). *The diary of Frida Kahlo: An intimate self-portrait*. Toledo, Spain: Abradale Press.

Kahlo, F. (1995). *The letters of Frida Kahlo: Cartas apasionadas*. San Francisco: Chronicle Books.

Kahlo, F. (2010). *Frida Kahlo: Sus fotos*. Mexico City: Museo Frida Kahlo. Editorial RM.

Marnham, P. (1998). *Dreaming with his eyes open: A life of Diego Rivera*. New York: Knopf.

Rivera, D. (1991). *My art, my life*. New York: Dover.

Rivera, J.C., Pilego, R., Zavala, M., Rivera, D. (2008). Diego Rivera: Illustrious words 1886–1921, Volume 1. Colonia Cuauhtemoc, Mexico: Editorial RM, SA, de C.V.

Tibol, R. (1983). *Frida Kahlo: An open life*. Albuquerque: University of New Mexico Press.

Kennedy Family Sources

Andrews, J.D. (1998). *Young Kennedys: The new generation*. New York: Avon.

Collier, P., & Horowitz, D. (1984). *The Kennedys*: New York: Summit Books.

Davis, J. (1969). *The Bouviers: Portrait of an American family*. New York: Farrar, Straus, Giroux.

Davis, J. (1984). *The Kennedys: Dynasty & disaster*. New York: McGraw-Hill.

Davis, J. (1993). *The Bouviers: From Waterloo to the Kennedys and beyond*. Washington, DC: National Press Books.

DuBois, D. (1995). *In her sister's shadow: The bitter legacy of Lee Radziwell*. New York: St. Martin's.

Gibson, B., & Schwarz, T. (1993). *The Kennedys: The third generation*. New York: Thunder Mouth's Press.

Hamilton, N. (1992). *JFK reckless youth*. New York: Random House.

Heymann, C. David. (1989). *A woman named Jackie*. New York: New American Library.

James, Ann. (1991). *The Kennedy scandals and tragedies*. Lincolnwood, IL: Publications Internations Limited.

Kashner, S. & Schoenberger, N. (2018). *The fabulous Bouvier sisters*. New York: Harper.

Kearns Goodwin, Doris. (1987). *The Fitzgeralds and The Kennedys*. New York: Simon & Schuster.

Kelley, K. (1978). *Jackie Oh!* Secaucus, NJ: Lyle Stuart.

Kennedy, R. (1974). *Times to Remember:* New York: Bantam Books.

Klein, E. (1998). *Just Jackie: Her private years*. New York: Ballantine.

Klein, E. (2003). *The Kennedy curse*. New York: St. Martin's Press.

Latham, C., & Sakol, J. (1989). *Kennedy Encyclopedia*. New York: New American Library.

Leamer, L. (2001). *The Kennedy men: 1901–1963*. New York: Harper Collins.

Maier, T. (2003). *The Kennedys: America's Emerald Kings*. New York: Basic Books.

McTaggart, Lynne. (1983) *Kathleen Kennedy: Her life and times*. New York: Dial Press

Moutsatos, K.F. (1998). *The Onassis women*. New York: Putnam's.

Rachlin, Harvey. (1986). *The Kennedys: A chronological history 1823–present*. New York World Almanac.

Rainie, H., & Quinn, J. (1983) *Growing up Kennedy: The third wave comes of age*. New York: G.P. Putnam's Sons.

Saunders, F. (1982). *Torn lace curtain: Life with the Kennedys*. New York: Pinnade Books.

Taraborrelli, J. R. (2018). *Jackie, Janet & Lee*, New York: St. Martin's Press.

Wills, Garry. (1981). *The Kennedy imprisonment: A mediation on power*. New York: Little, Brown.

King Family

Carson, C. (Ed.). (2001). *The autobiography of Martin Luther King*. New York: Warner Books.

Franklin, V.P., (1998). *Martin Luther King, Jr. Biography*. New York: Park Lane Press.

King, M.L., Sr., with C. Riely (1980). *Daddy King, An autobiography*. New York: Morrow.

Lewis, D.L. (1978). *King: A biography* (2nd ed.). Chicago: University of Illinois Press.

Oates, S.B. ((1982). *Let the trumpet sound: The life of Martin Luther King, Jr*. New York: New American Library.

O'Neill Sources

Black, S. (1999). *Eugene O'Neill: Beyond mourning and tragedy*. New Haven: Yale University Press.

Bowen, C. (1959). *The curse of the misbegotten*. New York: McGraw-Hill.

Gelb, A., & Gelb, B. (1987). *O'Neill*. New York: Harper & Row.

Scovell, J. (1999). *Oona: Living in the shadows*. New York: Time/Warner.

Sheaffer, L. (1968). *O'Neill: Son and playwright.* Boston: Little, Brown.

Sheaffer, L. (1973). *O'Neill: Son and artist.* Boston: Little, Brown.

Reich Family

Mann, W.E. & Hoffman, E. (1980). *The man who dreamed of tomorrow: The life and thought of Wilhelm Reich.* Los Angeles: Tarcher.

Corrington, R.S. (2003). *Wilhelm Reich: Psychoanalyst and radical naturalist.* New York: Farrar, Straus & Giroux.

Reich, L.O. (1969). *Wilhelm Reich: A personal biography.* New York: Avon.

Sharaf, J. (1983). *Fury on earth: A biography of Wilhelm Reich.* New York: St. Martins

Wilson, C. (1981). *The quest for Wilhelm Reich: A critical biography.* Garden City, NY: Anchor Press/Doubleday.

Robeson Family Sources

Dean, P.H. (1989). Paul Robeson. In E. Hill (Ed.). *Black heroes: Seven plays.* New York: Applause Theatre Book Publishers.

Duberman, M.B. (1988). *Paul Robeson.* New York: Alfred Knopf.

Ehrlich, S. (1988). *Paul Robeson: Singer and actor.* New York: Chelsea House Publishers.

Larsen, R. (1989). *Paul Robeson: Hero before his time.* New York: Franklin Watts.

Ramdin, R. (1987). *Paul Robeson: The man and his mission.* London: Peter Owen.

Robeson, P. (1988). *Here I stand.* Boston: Beacon Press.

Robinson Family

Falkner, D. (1995). *Great time coming: The life of Jackie Robinson from baseball to Birmingham.* New York: Simon & Schuster.

Rampersad, A. (1997). *Jackie Robinson: A biography.* New York: Knopf.

Robinson, J. (1972). *I never had it made.* New York: Putnam.

Robinson, R. (1996). *Jackie Robinson: An intimate portrait.* New York: Abrams.

Robinson, S. (1996). *Stealing home.* New York: Harper Collins.

Tygiel, J. (1997). *Baseball's great experiement: Jackie Robinson and his legacy.* New York: Oxford University Press.

Roosevelt Sources

Asbell, B. (Ed.). (1982). *Mother and daughter: The letters of Eleanor and Anna Roosevelt.* New York: Coward McCann & Geoghegan.

Bishop, J. B. (Ed.). (1919). *Theodore Roosevelt's letters to his children.* New York: Charles Scribner's Sons.

Brough, James. (1975). *Princess Alice: A biography of Alice Roosevelt Longworth.* Boston: Little, Brown & Co.

Collier, P., with D. Horowitz (1994). *The Roosevelts.* New York: Simon & Schuster.

Cook, B. W. (1992). *Eleanor Roosevelt 1884–1933: A life: Mysteries of the heart* (Vol. 1). New York: Viking Penguin.

Dallek, R. (2017). *Franklin D. Roosevelt: A political life.* New York: Viking.

Donn, L. (2001). *The Roosevelt cousins.* New York: Alfred A Knopf.

Felsenthal, C. (1988). *Alice Roosevelt Longworth.* New York: G.P. Putnam's Sons.

Fleming, C. (2005). *Our Eleanor.* New York: Simon & Schuster.

Fritz, J. (1991). *Bully for you, Teddy Roosevelt.* New York: G.P. Putnam's Sons.

Hagedorn, H. (1954). *The Roosevelt family of Sagamore Hill.* New York: Macmillan.

Kearns Goodwin, D. (1994). *No ordinary time. Franklin and Eleanor Roosevelt: The home front in World War II.* New York: Simon & Schuster.

Lash, J. P. (1971). *Eleanor and Franklin.* New York: Norton.

McCullough, D. (1981). *Mornings on horseback.* New York: Simon & Schuster.

Miller, N. (1979). *The Roosevelt chronicles.* Garden City, NY: Doubleday.

Miller, N. (1983). *FDR: An intimate biography.* Garden City, NY: Doubleday.

Miller, N. (1992). *Theodore Roosevelt: A life*. New York: Morrow.

Morgan, T. (1985). *FDR: A biography*. New York: Simon & Schuster.

Morris, E. (1979). *The rise of Theodore Roosevelt*. New York: Ballantine.

Pringle, H. F. (1931). *Theodore Roosevelt*. New York: Harcourt, Brace, Jovanovich.

Roosevelt, E. (1984). *The autobiography of Eleanor Roosevelt*. Boston: G.K. Hall.

Roosevelt, E., & Brough, J. (1973). *The Roosevelts of Hyde Park: An untold story*. New York: Putnam.

Roosevelt, E., & Brough, J. (1975). *A rendezvous with destiny: The Roosevelts of the White House*. New York: Dell.

Roosevelt, J. (1976). *My parents: A differing view*. Chicago: The Playboy Press.

Roosevelt, T. (1925). *An autobiography*. New York: Charles Scribner's Sons.

Youngs, W.T. (1985). *Eleanor Roosevelt: A personal and public life*. Boston: Little, Brown.

Queen Victoria References

Auchincloss. L. (1979). *Persons of consequence: Queen Victoria and her circle*. New York: Random House.

Benson, E.F. (1987). *Queen Victoria*. London: Chatto & Windus.

Hibbert, Christopher, (1984). *Queen Victoria in her letters and journals*. London: Penguin.

James, R.R. (1984). *Prince Albert*. New York: Alfred A. Knopf.

Strachey, L. (1921). *Queen Victoria*. New York: Harcourt, Brace, Jovanovich.

Weintraub, S. (1987). *Victoria*. New York: E.P. Dutton.

Wilson, E. (1990). *Emminent Victorians*. New York: Norton.

Woodham-Smith, C. (1972). *Queen Victoria*. New York: Donald Fine, Inc.

George Washington Sources

Bourne, M.A. (1982). *First family: George Washington and his intimate relations*. New York: W.W. Norton.

Ellis, J.J. (2004). *His excellency: George Washington*. New York: Knopf.

Furstenberg, F. (2006). *In the name of the father: Washington's legacy, slavery and the making of a nation*. New York: The Penguin Press.

Johnson, P. (2005). *George Washington: The founding father*. New York: Harper Collins.

McCullough, D. (2005). *1776*. New York: Simon & Schuster.

Mitchell, S.W. (1904). *The youth of Washington*. New York: The Century Company.

Moore, C. (1926). *The family life of George Washington*. Boston: Houghton Mifflin Company.

Randall, W.S. (1997). *George Washington: A life*. New York: Henry Holt.

Wiencek, H. (2003). *An imperfect god: George Washington, his slaves and the creation of America*. New York: Farrar, Strauss & Giroux.

Yarrow, P., Stookey, P., & Travers, M. (1967). The Great Mandala (song). Retrieved March 27, 2019 from http://lyrics.wikia.com/wiki/ Peter,_Paul_%26_Mary:The_Great_Mandala_ (The_Wheel_Of_Life) https://www.youtube.com/ watch?v=xpIh68Kh_-s

Image Credits

Chapter 4

Erik Erikson © Jon Erikson
  Science Source

Her Majesty Queen Elizabeth II Head of State of the United Kingdom and Commonwealth and National Memorial Arboretum Staffordshire

Mike Twigg, fotocapricorn / Alamy Stock Photo

Maria Callas, publicity photo for "Maria by Callas: In Her Own Words" circa (1957)
  PictureLux / The Hollywood Archive / Alamy Stock Photo

Chapter 5

Bill Clinton
  Bob McNeely / The White House

Charles Darwin, a portrait of 31-year-old Charles Darwin by George Richmond in 1840
  The Picture Art Collection / Alamy Stock Photo

Thomas Jefferson by Gilbert Stuart, 1821
  National Gallery of Art

Steve Jobs shows off the white iPhone 4 at the 2010 Worldwide Developers Conference, June 8, 2010
  PictureLux / The Hollywood Archive / Alamy Stock Photo

Chapter 6

Portrait of Alfred Adler (1870–1937). Museum: PRIVATE COLLECTION
  Album / Alamy Stock Photo

Princess Diana following her press availability at the American Red Cross in Washington on June 17, 1997
  MediaPunch Inc / Alamy Stock Photo

Jackie Robinson, April 18, 1948
  AP Photo / file

Sigmund Freud, Stanley Hall, Carl Gustav Jung, Abraham A. Brill, Ernest Jones, Sandor Ferenczi in front of Clark University. Museum: PRIVATE COLLECTION.
  Album / Alamy Stock Photo

George Washington by Gilbert Stuart, 1803

  National Gallery of Art

Rev. Martin Luther King, head-and-shoulders portrait, seated, facing front, hands extended upward, during a press conference
  Library of Congress

Paul Robeson
  Shutterstock

Jawaharial Nehru, India's Prime Minister, 1959
  Everett Collection Historical / Alamy Stock Photo

Indira Ganhdi, Prime Minister of India
  Tim Graham / Alamy Stock Photo

First Lady Jacqueline Kennedy Accepts Silver Pitcher Robert Knudsen. White House Photographs. John F. Kennedy Presidential Library and Museum, Boston

John Adams by Gilbert Stuart, 1800/1815
  National Gallery of Art

Eleanor Roosevelt
  Library of Congress (LC-USZ62-107008)

Franklin D. Roosevelt
  Library of Congress, Prints & Photographs Division, LC-USW33-042784-ZC

Theodore Roosevelt
  Public domain

Richard Burton – Welsh actor (1925-84)

Pictorial Press Ltd / Alamy Stock Photo

Elizabeth Taylor / Elephant Walk 1954 directed by William Dieterie
  ScreenProd / Photononstop / Alamy Stock Photo

Margaret Mead and Gregory Bateson. Image No. 0114672.
  The Granger Collection

Portrait of Henry VIII of England by Hans Holbein the Younger
  Classicpaintings / Alamy Stock Photo

Chapter 7

Picture 7.1: Frida Kahlo Self-portrait along the border line between Mexico and the United States 1932
  Archivart / Alamy Stock Photo

Picture 7.2: My Family, Unfinished by Frida Kahlo 2019 Banco de M.xico Diego Rivera Frida Kahlo Museum Trust, Mexico, D.F. /

Artists Rights Society (ARS), New York
DIEGO RIVERA 1939: CSU Archives / Everett Collection
  Everett Collection Historical / Alamy Stock Photo

Mexican painter Frida Kahlo, October 16, 1932, photo by Guillermo Kahlo File
  PictureLux / The Hollywood Archive / Alamy Stock Photo

Picture 7.3: The Kahlo Family with Frida Dressed in Her Father's Suit, 1926
  Vicente Wolf Collection

Picture 7.4: My Grandparents, My Parents, and I, Family Tree, Frida Kahlo, 1936
  Peter Barritt / Alamy Stock Photo

Picture 7.5: FRIDA KAHLO (1907-1954). Image No. 0037854.
  The Granger Collection

Picture 7.6: Frida Kahlo Self-portrait, Memory aka the Heart, 1937
  Archivart / Alamy Stock Photo

Chapter 8

Sigmund Freud
  GL Archive / Alamy Stock Photo

Index

In this index, *f* denotes figure.